Praise for

THEY FOUGHT ALONE

"This remarkable story of guerrilla fighting in the Philippines during World War II is a serious military book that is also an acutely perceptive study of human nature under almost unbearable stress. Taken at either level, it is absorbing reading. . . . More remarkable still, though it contains death, torture, and desolation, it bubbles with humor."

—*The New York Times Book Review*

"A true and admirably researched account of an American hero who refused to accept defeat. His courage was incredible and his resourcefulness equally so. . . . I have read scores of books in this genre, and Keats' is one of the best."

—*Chicago Tribune*

"An engrossing account about one of the most unusual heroes of World War II . . . reads like a novel but is based on fact . . . a remarkable addition to the nation's history of World War II, as well as being a tribute well deserved by a man."

—*San Francisco Sunday Chronicle*

"An inspiring story—one which proves, among other things, that Americans can, when necessary, fight a successful guerrilla war."

—*New York World-Telegram and Sun*

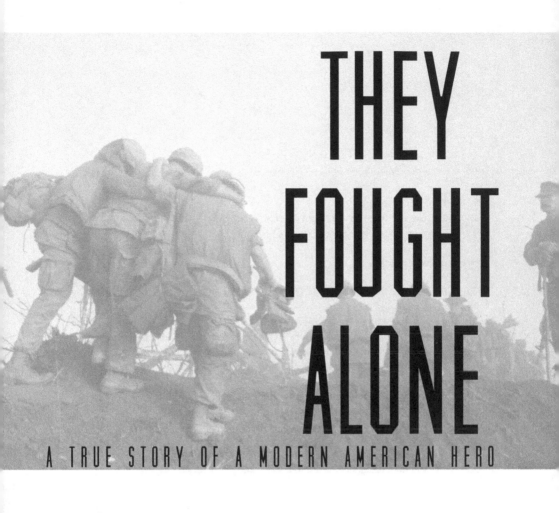

THEY FOUGHT ALONE

A TRUE STORY OF A MODERN AMERICAN HERO

JOHN KEATS

TURNER

Turner Publishing Company
424 Church Street • Suite 2240 • Nashville, TN 37219
445 Park Avenue • 9th Floor • New York, NY 10022

www.turnerpublishing.com

THEY FOUGHT ALONE: A TRUE STORY OF A MODERN AMERICAN HERO

J. B. Lippincott edition published August 1963

Cover Design: Taylor Reiman
Book Design: Glen Edelstein

Library of Congress Cataloging-in-Publication Data

Keats, John, 1920-2000.
  They fought alone / by John Keats.
    pages cm
  Originally published: 1963.
  ISBN 978-1-63026-076-7
  1. World War, 1939-1945--Underground movements--Philippines--Mindanao Island. 2. Fertig, Wendell W. 3. Guerrillas--Philippines--Biography. 4. Guerrillas--United States--Biography. 5. Soldiers--United States--Biography. 6. United States. Army--Biography. 7. Guerrilla warfare--Philippines--Mindanao Island--History--20th century. 8. Mindanao Island (Philippines)--History, Military. I. Title.
  D802.P5K4 2015
  940.53'5997--dc23
                                    2014040759
  ISBN: 978-1-63026-076-7 (paperback), 978-1-63026-751-3

Printed in the United States of America
15 16 17 18 0 9 8 7 6 5 4 3 2 1

PREFACE

THIS BOOK DESCRIBES a group of Americans and Filipinos who refused to surrender when ordered to do so. Nothing herein is intended to reflect on the courage of those who, obeying orders, surrendered to the Japanese.

The persons, places, and events described are by no means fictitious. Some characters bear fictitious names, but the events in which they take part occurred on the island of Mindanao during the Second World War. The only wholly imaginary scene is that which takes place in Japanese headquarters on Mindanao. It is fictional only in the sense that it was imagined on the basis of probability. Therefore, this is not a work of fiction, although it is cast in the form of fiction. This book is a synthesis; an attempt to re-create, out of reality, not the letter but the truth of that reality. It is an attempt, with literary license, to recapture the essential spirit and meaning of an actual adventure.

From beginning to end, this is essentially the story and the work of Colonel Wendell W. Fertig. Not only did Colonel Fertig live the experience, but he provided diaries, memoirs, an official military history of the Mindanao guerrilla, and a 600-page rough draft of a manuscript of his own. He also escorted the author to the Philippine Islands and spent hundreds of hours in conversation with him. Further, Colonel Fertig wrote much of the dialogue, particularly in the scenes involving himself and William Morgan. He was at all times helpful and, above all, patient. Parts of the book are based on the diaries and manuscripts of several Americans who served in the guerrilla, and on conversations with Filipino guerrilleros on Mindanao.

The author wishes to thank the Defense Department for providing him with military transportation to the Philippine Republic for the purpose of writing this book, which the Defense Department has in no way censored. He is also much indebted to the courtesy of Carlos P. Romulo, Ambassador of the Philippine Republic, and to the considerable—indeed, essential—support of the John Simon Guggenheim Memorial Foundation.

JOHN KEATS

CONTENTS

A NOTE ON FOOTNOTES

Translations of unfamiliar words appear at the foot of the page on which the words first occur. Thus, if a Filipino said, "Kaibegan, where are you going?," the following would appear as a footnote:

kaibegan = friend

The Southwest Pacific Area / 1942

SCALE AT EQUATOR

0   500   700   1,000

BOOK ONE

Surrender

HERE, ON THE ISLAND OF MINDANAO, *we find Celdron Bonsukan phlegmatically preparing his rice paddy, because tending rice is all that he has done since he could walk. The war will have no meaning for him until it comes into his field. Therefore, he walks behind his carabao, turning muck with a wooden plow that is simply a sharp stick. Two miles away, the Japanese burn a barrio.*

In between Celdron and the Japanese, the former populace of the barrio is trying in a tangled way to step aside and let the war go past. Three miles away, there is another Japanese patrol. Elsewhere, and in between, and all around, there may even be business as usual: the women washing in the river, the fishermen coming back to the beaches with their dying catch feebly stirring in the bilges of the carved vintas, the Chinese merchant raising the price of his needles, lovers making furtive arrangements for the evening despite the vigilance of the girl's mother. While the military situation is still fluid, the armies have only to run from and chase each other while everyone else goes about his business.

Only after the defeat will Celdron learn just what the war has to do with him and his rice. It is then that the refugees learn there is no place to hide, that everyone understands that not even the business of love can continue as usual. Until the defeat, however, any man who so desires may try to ignore the war, or run away from it, or through it or around it. He is even free to imagine that conquerors are men like himself. Later, after the defeat, he learns something of the nature of conquerors.

1

IN EARLY MAY 1942, when few Americans remained alive and free in the Philippines, two men stood alone in a deserted grass building in a mountain village of Mindanao. Private Robert Ball stared out the open window with a rifle in his hands. He saw the trail the Japanese would use.

"Remember, soldier," the officer told him, "all we want to do is get back to the States alive."

Ball turned, his boy's face haggard with disbelief. He had been hearing surrender talk for weeks, but not from any officer.

"Maybe that's all you want to do!" he said, his voice threatening to crack. "I wouldn't know about you, but I joined this man's army to *fight!*"

The word *fight* came out in falsetto, to Private Ball's intense embarrassment.

"You're going to surrender tomorrow," the officer said flatly.

His only thought had been to comfort a youngster, and it enraged him to find that he could not do even this. The officer drew himself into a towering attention.

"That's an order, soldier," he said.

"Yeah," Private Ball said. "Sure."

He tried to say it tough, like Jimmy Cagney, and he failed.

"What's that, soldier?" the officer demanded. "Stand at attention! Say *sir* when you speak to an officer!"

But Private Ball turned back to the window in disgust, not daring to trust his changing voice again. The officer muttered weakly, "You better watch yourself, soldier," and after a while left the room.

No doubt Private Ball's ignorance of military science and courtesy could be attributed to the fact that he was only nineteen years old and lacked a West Point education. He had a few ideas firmly fixed in his tough, handsome head, and one of them was that a man was supposed to fight for his country. Private Ball honestly could not see how a man could defend his country if he was shut up in a cage. He also suspected that even if a man could not fight, he would nevertheless be uncomfortable in a prison, particularly if he was a young man who liked to drink and give the girls a good time and who had joined the service to see the world. When it came right down to it, Private Ball did not like people who tried to push him around. That night, he discussed these points of view with his fellow enlisted men.

"Let's get out of here while we can."

He looked anxiously from face to face, and Sergeant Knortz, who was nearly as young as Private Ball, nodded in agreement. But the old soldiers shook their heads.

"Are you crazy?" the old soldiers asked. And then they, who knew a thing or two about the Philippines, told the young men about this island of Mindanao.

There were wild black bees in the forest, bees that can sting a horse to death, they said. There were cobras, naked spearmen who hunted through the hills, Moros who would kill a wandering soldier simply because he was a Christian. The last Moro-pacification campaign, they said, had taken place only four years ago, and they had fought in it. There were leeches, crocodiles in the streams; there was malaria and a thousand other diseases. They told of the python that had caught a five-foot Filipino and had crushed him and stretched him out to seven feet long before beginning to swallow the still-living man . . .

Here were matters that Private Ball had not considered, for he had never heard of the Philippines until he boarded a troopship in San Francisco seven months ago. He glanced at Knortz uncertainly.

"We'll be exchanged," the old soldiers said, pressing in.

"There's the Geneva Convention," the old soldiers said, passing the word to the punk young kids.

"It won't be long before we get an army out here that can whip their ass," the old soldiers said, seeking an excuse for themselves.

"All you gotta do is sweat it out," the old soldiers said, figuring the angles. "It ain't gonna be forever."

"Relax and enjoy it," they said, whistling in the dark.

"You got to obey orders," the old soldiers explained, nailing it down.

Private Ball and Sergeant Knortz, a minority of two, could not find the words to meet the arguments of age. The next day, against all their instincts, they stacked their rifles with the others. Obediently, they shuffled along in a line of prisoners, herded toward the cage the Japanese had prepared for them near Malaybalay. The Japanese were not unkind. They offered them cigarettes.

IN A PRISON CAMP near Davao, the news of Major General William Sharp's surrender was the cause of singular rejoicing. A Japanese patrol entered the camp and set free those whom the Americans had interned as enemy aliens. One was a German named Waldo Neveling.

Herr Neveling was a man of medium height, who therefore stood head high above the Japanese. His blond hair was bleached almost white by the tropical sun, and his cold, light-blue eyes were deep set in a bony skull over which a tanned skin stretched tight. Herr Neveling's lips were wide and thin, and it was sometimes possible for him to smile with real pleasure. He did so now. The Japanese bowed politely and sucked in their breath and smiled toothily back. It was a pleasant meeting of the Axis powers.

Would Herr Neveling please to go into back country and persuade all American civilian in hiding, all miner, all missionary, all schoolteacher, to come to Japan Army headquarter for beneficial concentration?, the Japanese captain wanted to know. Would he please tell all American if he do not make happy choice, Japan Army will send soldier to kill <u>him</u>?

Herr Neveling said nothing could please him more. He pocketed the special pass the Japanese gave him and, waving a cheery good-bye, set off upon his mission.

IN THE HILLS of Lanao province, near the border of Bukidnon province, news of General Sharp's surrender reached a worried traveler who walked alone, save for two Filipinos who staggered along behind him with a wooden crate slung between two bamboo poles and for another Filipino who marched ahead, half buried beneath a billowing mattress. The crate and the mattress were the property of the traveler, Samuel J. Wilson, owner of the Wilson Building in Manila.

Hearing that the fighting was now definitely and finally over, Sam Wilson involuntarily thrust his hand into his pocket and his fingers clenched about the Boy Scout knife he carried there.

Wilson had no fear for himself. He had already been so badly frightened so many times in Manila and on Corregidor and here on Mindanao that nothing would ever frighten him again. But he was afraid for Susie and the boys. The Japanese had them now in the prison they had made of Santo Tomas University in Manila. He felt the knife in his pocket.

Just before Manila fell, the Navy made Sam a lieutenant and assigned him a secret mission. He could say good-bye to his wife, but nothing more. He had driven from Navy headquarters through the blacked-out streets to his palatial home, driving nervously through the stinging smoke that billowed from fires along the waterfront, seeing gangs of looters running fitfully through the darkness, seeing the Pasig River winding through the city with thousands of gallons of oil burning on its surface. He hurried to his darkened house and clung to Susie for that last time, talking softly so as not to wake the children, telling her it would be all right even though he knew quite well it was all more wrong than anything could possibly be. He told her he was going on a little trip and that, when the Japanese came, to do whatever they told her and that she and the boys would be all right.

But the younger boy, wakened by the low, hurried tones of his parents, came sleepily into the living room with his Boy Scout knife in his hand.

"Here, Dad," the boy said. "You can borrow my knife. If you lose your gun, you can kill them with this."

Sam looked dubiously into the hills about him. His solitary, secret Navy task was done. There would be no more orders for him. He was no fighting man but a middle-aged speculator in mining stocks and real estate who had come out to the Islands years ago as a poor young printer from Philadelphia. For him, the Islands had been Manila. He knew nothing about survival in the hills, nor did he know the local dialects. A millionaire, he had plenty of money, and with this he thought he might buy a hiding place. But Sam also knew that gossip was the chief diversion of the Islands, ranking ahead even of politics and love-making. Who could resist talking about the hiding place of one of the richest and most prominent Americans in the Islands?

And, if word reached the Japanese that he was alive . . .

They would take Susie and his sons out of Santo Tomas to the torture dungeons of Fort Santiago. They would never be able to understand that Susie had no idea where he was. They would work away on her, deaf to her screams, misunderstanding her denials for bravery.

He clenched the knife in his pocket.

How can I ever face the boy if I give up?

The knife did not tell him what he should do.

Undecided, Sam Wilson followed his mattress, and behind him the heavy crate swayed on the creaking poles.

AT THIS SAME TIME, high on the slope of a mountain overlooking the Mirayon Valley, which was itself a mile-high pass leading into the central hills of Mindanao, three men paused to rest. It was still possible, in the early morning, to sit in the shade of the trees and not sweat. But the morning was already beginning to gather into itself the stupefying heat that would surely come within the next half-hour, a heat that would grow until it was merely unbearable and then, by midafternoon, become unbelievable. In short, it was a morning like any other on Mindanao, but Wendell Fertig wondered how many more such mornings there would be for him.

Fertig was a tall, athletic man of forty-one who had the oddly boyish face so many American men of middle years are apt to have. He wore the uniform of a lieutenant colonel of United States Army Engineers. His command that morning consisted of a stolid, thick-bodied chief petty officer of the United States Navy who had neither ship nor shipmates, and a small, slender, and irritable army captain who was in charge of a motor pool that quite probably no longer existed. The three men sat silently on the hillside in the shade of the trees, Chief Elwood Offret draining a cup of black native coffee, Captain Charles Hedges angrily relighting an almost fireproof cigarillo, and Fertig absently picking his teeth. They were all, Fertig included, waiting for Fertig to make up his mind.

"Goddamn thing," Hedges muttered, throwing the cigarillo away. He pushed his straw sombrero back and peered at Fertig.

"I swear, Wendell," he said, "sometimes I think you're the most bullheaded man I know. *Now* do you believe Sharp's quit?"

"We'll know when we get there," Fertig said.

"Oh, don't be a damned fool," Hedges said. "If the boys were still fighting, we wouldn't be able to hear ourselves think. Tell me one thing: you hear anybody shooting at anybody?"

There was only the sound of a light wind stirring among the flat, shiny leaves of bushy young coffee trees.

"Let's move out," Fertig said.

Hedges slammed his straw hat down over his eyes. He glared venomously out from under the sombrero, to which he had pinned his captain's bars, and rose to lead the way. Offret followed, stuffing the heavy white china cup into his pack, and Fertig brought up the rear, rubbing his lips with coconut oil, which he carried in a small vial. Despite his five years of running mining camps in the Islands, Fertig still suffered from the tropical sun. His lips were badly chapped.

The three Americans moved with bold caution through a country-side that, except for its coffee trees, the occasional banana groves in the bottom lands, jackfruit trees, and the iguanas running, terrified, over the rounded boulders of the trail, seemed like Maryland in July. They looked carefully into every grove, every bush, because a Filipino countryside is almost exactly like one of those pictures in which you are challenged to find the hidden faces. At first, all you see is a banana grove, with the harsh white sunlight; the dark, tattered green leaves; the trashy brown stalks; and the black, black shadows. You stare into this dapple a bit longer, and things begin to emerge—such as a bamboo house nearly invisible among the leaves. Then you notice a grunting, swayback sow and her farrow, perhaps a couple of slinking brown and white dogs, then a man asleep on a porch bench, a woman nursing a baby at a window, a carabao buried to the horns in a wallow, half a dozen naked children playing with a leaf, a few assorted chickens and ducks. Shift your point of vision a degree or so, and another scene as infinitely varied opens before you in that same banana grove.

They looked carefully as they walked, for at any moment the hidden faces in the picture could be Japanese. They had been cut off from General Sharp's army and were seeking to rejoin it, trying to work around and ahead of a Japanese column they believed to be in the valley below the trail they were following. On they went, three men in dirty clothes, blankets rolled into a horseshoe pack over one shoulder, bandolier of rifle ammu-nition slung across the other, a pistol riding in a low-worn holster at the right thigh, canteen riding high on the left hip, rifles sometimes carried, sometimes slung. They might have been a detachment of Pancho Villa's infantry. They walked automatically, neither fresh nor tired, not striding or scuffling, but simply one step after another. They had been marching thus for nearly a week, through deserted villages, past the occasional burned-out omnibus, past the untended fields. They walked along in the wake of war, and it might have seemed that they were the last men alive in a sud-denly emptied and untidy world through which they were now damned to move forever. Day after day, they had hung on the heels of the Japanese column, waiting for a chance to try to work around it, never knowing that the column they followed was not on its way to war. The Japanese were simply hurrying as fast as they could toward the mountain village of Al-anib, to take charge of the Americans who had surrendered.

All along the way, the three Americans met gaggles of former Filipino soldiers coming through the countryside with tiny Japanese flags in their hands. The Filipinos stepped into the gutters of the trails as the white men marched past, some pulling off their hats in the old token of respect the Spanish had taught them, but none saluting as soldiers would. "The war is over, sair," the Filipinos would say, and Fertig would reply, "For you only," and walk on.

In one village, the three Americans discovered the front wall missing from every house. The Japanese had made cooking fires of the flimsy walls, and the bamboo houses stood there on their stilts looking like doll houses, displaying the mud stove, the lithograph of the Virgin, the woven sleeping mats, the crooked stick that had served some child as a toy. Flowers still grew around the deserted houses, and, except for the missing front walls, nothing had been destroyed in a physical sense, yet the destruction was utterly complete. The things of life lay there naked, but life had gone. The lightly touched, empty village was desolate of human will. A completely ruined village, Fertig thought, might have implied defiance.

Once, they paused to fill their canteens at a schoolyard pump, and, through the windows of the empty schoolhouse, they saw that a Japanese had written on the blackboard, "Filipino soldier—coward soldier." When they reached Pantalan, the town was burning, and burning with it was a vast army supply dump. There were no signs that anyone had tried to defend the town: no bodies, no shell holes, no bullet hole in any wall. Who had set the dump afire? The retreating army? The pursuing Japanese? In the buildings the fire had not yet reached, there were still enough stores to have equipped an infantry company for a year, but there was no one to carry them away. Moodily, the three Americans helped themselves to new blankets, rifles, shoes, uniforms, ammunition, and canned goods. They took all that they could carry.

Except for the exploding ammunition in burning Pantalan, there was no sound of war, and now, working deeper into the mountains where Major General Sharp was to have made his last stand, the silence was definitive. Yet Fertig drove them on.

"All we know is what quitters have told us," Fertig said. "You sure can't take a quitter's word for anything."

Eventually, they reached a place from which they could look down toward Alanib. The village had been a part of General Sharp's headquarters area, and Fertig had the curious feeling that he had lived this moment before, had known what he would see before he set the field glasses to his eyes.

In the little round picture that appeared in the binoculars, he saw a ragged line of Filipinos working along a steep trail, each carrying one of the miniature Rising Sun flags.

Fertig found Hedges tugging at his sleeve.

"Let's find a place to hole up," Hedges said.

But Fertig kept staring at the tiny figures toiling up the trail. Finally, he put the field glasses back into their leather case.

"Charley," he said at last, "nothing is worse than surrender."

"What the hell," Hedges said.

"It's one thing to take a beating," Fertig said. "Every man has to take his beating. But, damn it, no man has to surrender. It's the same thing as castration."

"The only thing I'd like to know," Hedges said without comment, "is, what are *we* going to do?"

"Any damn thing but surrender," Fertig said.

2

THE FIRST REFUGE WAS a deserted grass house at the edge of a farm on a hillside overlooking the Mirayon Valley road, and, each day, curious farmers would come down from their hiding places even higher in the hills to stare at the strange Americanos who would neither go to Malaybalay for concentration nor run away. Plainly, such Americanos were a mystery, and the farmers did not like mysteries. Finally, the country people appointed a delegation to see whether the mystery could be solved or, better, persuaded to go away.

The delegation stood in the bare dirt yard before the grass bahi and took off its hats and shuffled its bare feet hopefully. Eventually, it nudged a spokesman forward.

"Oh, sair," the spokesman said at last, "you must go. The Hapons will learn you are here, and they will punish *us.* "

This was not what he had intended to say, but it was what he had meant.

"We will go even now," Fertig told him, much to the farmer's surprise. "But the way is very far, and we must carry many vianda."[1]

The farmer nodded. Fertig had not said where he intended to go, but the point was that the Americanos would leave, and, wherever they went, they would surely have to move across the back country, for the Japanese held the fat lowlands, the roads, and watercourses. But, while the back country was relatively free of Japanese, the farmers knew that it would be necessary for Fertig's party to keep moving simply to find enough food. The interior was a land of kaingineros,[2] who grew on their tiny clearings barely enough to feed themselves.

---

1. vianda = food
2. kaingineros = nomadic gardeners

Fertig looked at the Filipinos and thought of the Swiss pastry shop in Manila. A year ago at this time, he would have been taking coffee at the shop, doing business over the coffee cups in the leisurely fashion of the Islands. A year ago, he would have begun his day with hot coffee, eggs, toast, bacon, and fresh mangoes. Then he would have kissed Mary and the two girls good-bye and climbed into the rear seat of his new black Dodge, and the chauffeur would have driven him from the pleasant little house in Paranaque down Taft Boulevard, around the Luneta, over Jones Bridge, and to the Escolta; to the office that said Wendell W. Fertig, Mining Consultant. As recently as six months ago, he still had his house, his servants, and his Dodge, although Mary and the children had left with the last of the Army wives to be evacuated before the war. It was very lucky for her that he had been called into the service; the Government had refused to evacuate the American civilian families for fear of destroying the morale of the Filipinos. He wondered who was living in his house now. The Dodge was at the bottom of Manila Bay.

Fertig shrugged, remembering the splash the Dodge had made.

"We have many baggages," he heard Hedges saying. "We have flenty potatoes, flenty coffees. We have our banigs[3] and our clothings, huh? You will bring a carabao, yes?"

"Oh, yes," the spokesman said, smiling brightly. Now there would be no need to try to kill the Americanos, which could be very dangerous since the Americanos had guns. "I be happy to bring my carabao and go with you."

He assumed a stricken look, the look of a man who has just remembered something.

"But it cannot be," he said sadly. "My grandmother is sickly and old, and she has only me. Besides, my wife is fregnant and will deliver soon. Oh, sair, I wish to go, but it is not to be."

The spokesman waved to include his fellows.

"My companions are all sickly and malarial," he explained. "Very sad, but, yes, they cannot go either. Besides, there is one carabao only, and too bad, but it is sickly also."

The spokesman half-raised his arms, to let them fall, tragically. He turned and spoke rapidly in Visayan to his companions, who immediately looked as sickly and malarial as possible. Then, saying salaamit[4] many times, the delegation left as rapidly as their illness allowed.

---

3. banigs = woven sleeping mats
4. salaamit = thank you

"What was that all about?" Offret wanted to know.

Hedges watched the peasants working their way across the upland pasture to the trail that led to the hills.

"They want us to get out, but they don't want to help," he said.

For the next several days, the three Americans sought to find a carabao, as rumors filtered through the countryside. One said Brigadier General Fort had defied the order to surrender and was still holding out with his Moros in the Kapai Hills of Lanao province. As long as there was an army, Fertig knew that he belonged to it. But the way to Fort was long, and, without a pack animal, it could be impossible. Everywhere the Americans asked for help among the mountain farmers, however, the answer was the same.

"What the hell's got into these people?" Hedges said one night. "They sure don't know what to think. You saw those people on the trail, Wendell? They'd look at us in a dirty way that said, 'Are they so big, these Americanos?' In all the years I've been here, I never saw them act this way before. You ever seen anything like it, Wendell?"

Hedges looked narrowly at his friend. Fertig was wrapped in another of the black silences that had been growing on him since they came to the hills Sharp had surrendered. Fertig grunted and rose to wash his messkit in the pot of water simmering over the woodfire Offret had built on the mud bench that served their grass house as a stove. It was possible to indulge in the luxury of fires at night and in hot water, because of the great fear among the taos.[5] If the Hapons should come to the hills, the taos would run to tell the Americanos to begone at once, lest the Hapons punish the people for having helped Americanos.

"Now, I never seen anything like it," Hedges went on, talking to Offret. "Why, Christ A-mighty, Ducklegs, I'll tell you so that even an ignorant sailor like you can understand. Six months ago, three months, if I'd said shit to those people, they'd have squat and thanked me for telling them . . ."

"Not a soul took time to tell them anything, not even lies," Fertig interrupted harshly. The red stubble on his jaw caught in the firelight like bright copper wires. "I've heard our officers call them gooks and black bastards," Fertig said thickly. "Do you think they didn't know what those officers thought of them? How the hell are you going to call a man a gook and then expect him to fight for you? By God, they might be ignorant, but they're not stupid."

He stared at Hedges and Offret in a wild fury.

"We quit!" he shouted.

---

5. taos = farmers

He looked at them crazily, living again the debacle on Luzon Island, the one the newspapers had called the brilliant retreat into Bataan Peninsula.

"Goddamn it, we just up and *quit!*" Fertig shouted. "Then we expect *them* to fight!"

"I can hear you," Hedges muttered. "Can you hear him, Chief?"

The light left Fertig's eyes, and he seemed to remember that he held his messkit in his hand. He looked at it carefully.

"All right," he said at last. He crossed the circle of firelight to replace his messkit in his pack that leaned against the wall.

Offret idly turned his coffee cup around and around.

"You'd think they'd have fought for their own country," he said, thinking of the Filipinos straggling home with the flags of defeat.

"I saw *white* troops run on Luzon," Fertig said.

"Look, Ducklegs," Hedges said kindly, "the Old Man's right. I don't know what else we could expect. We told the Filipinos they're our little brown brothers, huh? OK. For forty years, we treat 'em like kids. But then big brother gets his teeth knocked out and his face stomped in the dirt. If that happens to big brother, what the hell is little brother supposed to do?"

"But it's their country," Offret insisted. To him, the matter was clear.

"One of the troubles," Fertig said, "is that it is not their country. They never did have one."

Offret looked puzzled.

"The poor devils never had a chance," Fertig said. "Not against the Spanish, and not against us. They don't even have a common language."

"I thought they spoke that what-you-call-it, that Tagalog," Offret said.

"Now *that's* the goddamned trouble with being a sailor," Hedges said. He reached for a cigarillo, lit it, and leaned back luxuriously.

"First," Hedges said, "to be a sailor, you have to be stupid, because everybody else in the world knows that all a sailor ever sees is the goddamned ocean, and you just *got* to be stupid to want to look at that. Next, when sailors come to port, they go straight to a bar, and it doesn't take any more than sign language to get a drink anywhere in the world. And with sailors, after one drink, they can't even speak their own goddamned language."

Offret grinned good-naturedly.

"Isn't that right, Wendell?" Hedges asked.

"Here, they speak Visayan," Fertig said softly. "These people are just a lot of Malay tribes that speak a hundred dialects."

He looked up from depths of his own, and slowly, with a certain condemnation, said:

"All a Filipino really has is his family. His family, his parientes who are his cousins to the third degree, and his town mates. He will fight to protect his family if they cannot all run away together."

No one spoke. Fertig sighed.

"The Filipino will fight for his barrio if it is surrounded," Fertig said. "But he has no larger loyalty, so why fight for his country when he is drafted and shoved in the army and told, 'Oh, now you are a great patriot'? The army is run by white men. The country is run by white men. To the Filipino, his barrio is the only country he knows. He may live all his life within five miles of the place he was born. So why fight for someone else's barrio? 'They are not my cousins, they are not my town mates,' he thinks. 'Let them do their own fighting.'"

Offret removed an unlighted cigarette from his lips, looked at it, and put it back in his pocket.

"Sir, about this surrender . . . ?"

"What about it?"

"Sir, I mean if General Sharp *has* ordered everybody to surrender, are we under his orders? I mean, for instance, I'm in the Navy . . ."

He let the question hang in the firelight.

Hedges snorted.

"I can't help feeling sorry for Sharp," Fertig said. "You know, he told me once that he hadn't ever wanted to be a general in the first place. He said he was happy in a staff job, but he sure didn't want command. Then, all of a sudden, the chips were down, and Sharp's staff was makeshift. His intelligence ranged from poor to none. His units were untrained and his officers untried. Many of his officers were so new to the country that they had been here only a few days before the war started. Yet poor old Sharp was committed to fight the Sixteenth Imperial Guards, the conquerors of Singapore and the pride of the Japanese Army. His units broke and ran, his demolitions failed, and he was cornered. To end your career in surrender, when you never really wanted to be a commander, is ironic as hell."

He looked at Offret as though he had just heard the question.

"Chief Offret," Fertig said with the distant tones of immutable authority, "until you are returned to United States Navy control, you are on detached service with this command. As senior United States officer present, I assign you to this command, and you will act only under my orders."

"Oh, horseshit, Wendell," Hedges interrupted. "Why don't you just tell Ducklegs that we'll look out for him?"

"Captain Hedges concurs," Fertig said stiffly. "Chief Offret, Captain Hedges is chief of the war plans staff of this detachment. For your information, this command does not envision either the need or the possibility of surrender."

There was the faintest suggestion of a grim smile in Fertig's eyes. Offret flushed, and, as he did, Fertig and Hedges laughed.

"Don't let that old rascal snow you, Ducklegs," Hedges said. "When you've been around the Old Man as long as I have, you'll find out what a damn fool you are.

"Hell," he continued, "don't let that soldier talk or these costumes fool you, either. Neither Wendell nor I is a soldier boy, which is most likely why we're still alive. Now, Wendell here is really just a two-bit miner, and I'm a two-dollar, cigar-smoking lumberman, but I'll tell you one thing, Chief: There isn't a Jap that knows this island a damn bit better than I do, and there isn't anybody that knows the Filipinos any better than Wendell.

"You know," Hedges went on gently, "the trouble is that these soldiers and sailor boys don't know how to *do* anything, Wendell. Now, you take the Chief here. There isn't a thing in the world the Chief doesn't know about engines. How about that, Ducklegs?"

Offret guessed amiably that that was so.

"But now, when we crossed that river, the Chief almost drowned, if you'll remember. Twelve years in the Navy and he never learned how to swim. I catch us a chicken, and it turns out the Chief doesn't know how to clean it. Never cleaned a chicken in his life. You'd think they didn't have chickens in Utah. Doesn't know how to make a carabao go, either, when any fool knows you just kick it in the ass. He takes an ax to split wood and damn near cuts his leg off. What's wrong with the Navy, Chief? I thought sailors could turn their hand to anything?"

"You give me an engine, and I'll fix it," Offret promised.

"Now, *that's* just the goddamned trouble," Hedges said, tapping the ashes from his cigarillo. "What the hell can you do when you don't have an engine? You're just a damn specialist, and all a specialist knows is what's in his stupid book, and, if he comes to something that isn't in the book, he's as helpless as a new-laid egg. Specialists are the curse of this world; here we need men, and they give us specialists.

"Now, you take that time Fort wanted to bring the torpedo boat up from the coast to Lake Lanao," Hedges went on, settling back to tell his story. "Fort wanted it to help defend the lake. I was sitting in on the staff conference as transportation officer. The goddamned Navy said it couldn't be done. 'Oh,' the Navy said, 'you'd need a special crane to lift her out of the water, and a special trailer to transport her, and the closest crane was in Pearl Harbor, and there wasn't any special-built trailer.' I sat there listening to that crap until I couldn't stand it any more, so I finally said, 'Oh, horseshit. I'll move your damned canoe.'"

Fertig grinned expectantly. He and Hedges spoke the same language.

"Well," Hedges said blissfully, "everybody looked at me like I was something that had crawled out of the woodwork and fallen into their soup. Here was a lousy captain, not even a regular captain at that, telling off all that brass. Old Fort went 'humpf,' and somebody told me to watch myself, but I just walked out on 'em. I went down to the beach with a six-by-six truck and a logging trailer. Hell, nobody needed any damned crane. I just ran the logging trailer down to the beach and sank her in shallow water. Then I had my Filipinos move the torpedo boat over the trailer, and I waited. Well, what the hell. The tide went out, and the boat came down on the trailer, and my boys tied her fast, and I told the truck driver, 'Take her away!' and out she came, slick as that. So then I told the Navy, 'There, you damned fools, if you'd had any brains you could have done it yourself.'

"I swear to God, Wendell, you'd have thought the Navy might at least have known the tide comes in and out."

"It was the same thing on Bataan with the Army," Fertig said. "The one standard field problem was the defense of Bataan. The Army worked on it for years, practicing it until you'd think they could do it in their sleep. They stocked the place with guns and ammunition and gasoline months before the Japs attacked.

"But there was just one thing they forgot," Fertig said. "Food. Here they were in mountains and forests that didn't have enough farmland to raise breakfast for a platoon, but none of those soldiers thought to stock the food dumps. So we had no food, and no quinine. No quinine in a place full of cerebral malaria. God knows we had plenty of ammunition. I helped blow up a hundred thousand tons of it before we pulled out to Corregidor. We would still be on Bataan if we'd had food and medicine, because the front was so narrow nobody could run away."

Hedges shook his head.

"The whole tribe of them are stupid," he said of the military in general.

The three men talked together of mistakes, disasters, and evil chance, but, despite all they said in disparagement of the fighting services, they came, inevitably, to The Aid.

The Aid was a myth. But it was a myth in which they believed because to believe in it was to believe in their nation, and, if they could not believe in their nation, they could not really believe in their own survival.

The Aid consisted of fleets of warships, divisions of tough fighting men, mountains of supplies, columns of tanks, and sky-darkening swarms of warplanes.

Even General MacArthur believed in The Aid. He had no reason to believe otherwise. No one had told him that Washington had already written off the Philippines and had no intention of recovering the Islands during the course of the war with Japan. General MacArthur believed that The Aid was actually crossing the ocean, and it was not until he reached Australia that he was told, to his infinite horror, that there was no Navy, and that The Aid did not exist, except on the official United States radio broadcast. Meanwhile, the survivors of the Japanese holocaust in the Philippines listened to the radio and clung to their belief in The Aid, and Fertig guessed that it was, at most, six months away. He believed, as did Hedges, that they would be alive to welcome it ashore.

"It's bound to come," Fertig said. "It's going to *have* to come, because we can't do anything *but* live up to our promises to the Filipinos if we are going to have any face left in the Far East."

"And God help the Jap," Hedges said, "when it gets here."

Something in Hedges' voice made Fertig look up.

Hedges was shining with sweat. Rain seethed on the million surfaces of the thick leaves that grew about the house and fell, spattering, into the muddy lake of the yard outside, and the lean wind that drove the sheets of rain across the darkened hills was cold, and Hedges was sweating.

He was weak and staring and shivering, and the sweat poured down his blanched thin face. Fertig rummaged in his pack for the 200-tablet bottle of quinine. There were few tablets left; the doses would have to be rationed. Just enough at a time, Fertig decided, to get Charley over the worst of it, each time it came. Each time it came, until the tablets were gone.

Hedges took the canteen cup with a shaking claw; drank, dribbling water down his unshaved chin, as his teeth clicked against the metal cup.

"Ssson owva bitttch," Hedges muttered.

"Take it easy," Fertig said.

Offret and Fertig bundled Hedges in all the blankets they had, holding them down while Hedges' thin body jittered with the first chills.

"The Filipinos say," Fertig said, "that you never get malaria unless you're hungry. You have it all the time, but it doesn't hit you until you miss a couple of meals and get run-down.

"We all have it," he said. "I have it, you have it, Charley has it. Charley's had it for years. Malaria is endemic here. The quinine just suppresses it. But it doesn't cure it. You noticed that bulge Charley has in his belly? That's an enlarged spleen. Malaria does that."

The two men watched through the night, watching by the light of their road torch. The flame burned dull red, and the grass house smelled of pig dung, rain, wet clothing, coffee, sweat, and the stink of a burning rag wick and kerosene. The first chills gave way to fever. Hedges' skin flushed deep red in the glare of the kinkie[6] lamp. His skin was dry, terribly dry, and hot. With the fever came delirium and thrashing. Then, as it seemed that Hedges' flesh would almost sear any touching hand, the sweat came and the flesh paled, and, with the sweat, the next chills.

Hedges' eyes rolled whitely up into his head, and his hard, sinewy body shook convulsively beneath their restraining hands.

"My God, is he going to die?" Offret whispered.

"I don't think you could kill him with a meat ax," Fertig muttered. "Charley's the meanest man that ever got out of Oregon. Nothing can kill a man as mean as he is.

"But," Fertig said, "I never saw malaria hit a man so hard before."

He looked anxiously at Hedges' ghastly face, and all the comfort of the evening became a mockery. With Hedges beside him, Fertig felt he had an army. Without Hedges, Fertig knew that he was merely a hopeful man.

"Don't let him die," Fertig breathed.

Hedges' body stopped shaking, and he passed into a hoarse, exhausted sleep. The first attack was over. Fertig did not let himself think of those to come. He and Offret stayed beside Hedges until it was nearly dawn. It was still raining. It rained all that next day.

---

6. kinkie = a kerosene or coconut-oil road torch

3

WHEN THE RAINS COME to Mindanao, they lower over the island, slowly descending from the mountaintops, gradually falling to the lower slopes and finally reaching the plains in June. It is possible in the middle of May to stand on the plains of the Bukidnon in the aching hot sunshine and see the rains sweeping over the mountains of Lanao province. It is possible then to walk from the plains up and into the rainy season, but, ordinarily, no one who lives on the plains would think of going into the mountains for any purpose at any season. Likewise, it does not normally occur to those who live in the mountains of Lanao to venture into the country below. The people of the mountains despise the lowlanders as cowards, and the lowlanders hold themselves to be superior in every way to the ignorant barbarians of the hills, and, with the exception of traders who speak both the dialects of the plains and the dialects of the hills, there is little intercourse among the peoples. For centuries before the Japanese war, cultural exchanges most often assumed the form of raids.

One reason for the raids was quite trivial. It was that the mountaineers believed that the greatest ecstasy a lowland woman could know was to be entered by a mountaineer. Lowland men, however, were openly skeptical of this opinion, and unfortunate altercations between the peoples were a sad but somehow inevitable result of the disagreement in sexual points of view. During the period of American rule in the Islands, the number of lowland women carried off to Lanao's mountains was more or less minimal, but the sudden intrusion of the Japanese resulted in a kind of legal vacuum, which was immediately filled by ancient custom, and the paying-off of old scores.

If hill folk and lowlanders were separated by differences of opinion, language, habits, residence, and religion, so were the mountaineers themselves separated from one another. Here, the Moros, or Moslem Filipinos, despised the Manobos, a race of forest dwellers who had come earlier to the Islands from Malaya. Believing that Allah the Compassionate was deeply interested in the extirpation of infidels, the Moros religiously fell upon Manobo villages with the same enthusiasm they brought to their visits to the lowland Christian communities, retiring to their homes with newly created pagan widows for their harems, and with Manobo orphans for their slave pens. The Moro penchant for such excursions was a source of annoyance to the Manobos, who expressed their resentment by showering the Moros with spears whenever the opportunity presented itself.

In addition to these inimical populations, the Lanao Hills were (and, for that matter, still are) also inhabited, or infested, by Magahats and Negritos. While the Magahats are Malays, like nearly all Filipino peoples, and thrive on banditry, the Negritos are of entirely different stock and follow other customs. Negritos are black, nomadic aborigines of near-pygmy proportions who have no houses but who hunt through the forests and sleep in nests of leaves. Ordinarily, they stand well clear of their taller and more powerful Malay neighbors, but the Negritos are not helpless. They are perfectly familiar with the uses of the snare, the bow, and potassium cyanide.

The diverse populations of Lanao province are not, however, brave or warlike in the Western senses of these words. None of them relish a stand-up, face-to-face fight, and none could be expected to hold a line like British regulars of foot. Their raids, ill planned and silly for the most part, could scarcely be likened to the thoroughness of a responsible Western war, and the fact of the matter is that none of these people are brave in our sense of the word, because none of them fear death. A Moro, for instance, brought to bay and convinced that his time has come, will fall somewhat joyously upon his foe, shouting and shrieking, insensible of his wounds, splitting the air with his wavy kris, utterly possessed by thoughts of mayhem. He is even more formidable when juramentado.[7] Then, clad in white, his privates and belly bound tight with bajuco vine, the light of Paradise in his eyes, he considers himself already lost to this world in which he lingers only to send infidels ahead of him into Heaven to be his slaves. A juramentado will kill until he is killed. If you capture him and put him in hospital to recover from his wounds, he will begin to kill the nurses and patients about him as soon as his strength begins to return. It

7. juramentado = religiously amok

was because the United States Army's .38-caliber projectiles were found inadequate to stop the juramentado charge that the .45-caliber Colt automatic pistol was adopted.

Fighting from a corner, or charging in hopeless counterattack is, however, as unpopular with the island folk as defense in any form. Mindanao's altercations are most usually short, one-sided affairs conducted from stealthy ambuscade. Silent approaches from the rear have enjoyed a 700-year-old vogue among the Moros, and these are particularly inevitable whenever six Moros find it possible thus to approach one lone, unsuspecting stranger.

Stratagems, too, are favored—such stratagems as that of a host who offers a guest a tidbit from the pot while a servant standing behind the guest raises a two-handed kampilong for a decapitatory stroke. Such little ruses de guerre are not unknown elsewhere, but they often inspire the more unimaginative Westerner with disgust. He is apt to agree with Charley Hedges that the Moros are a bunch of worthless, shiftless, sneaky sons of bitches.

The indigenous view is more charitable, but the inhabitants of Mindanao's Lanao province nonetheless take certain precautions against the possible exuberance of their neighbors. Even today, an army vehicle groaning with troops will precede the automobile of the stranger who wishes to drive up the stone road from Iligan to Dansalan, and the back-country trails are still apt to be sown with suyoks.[8] A properly planted suyok can penetrate a tennis shoe to transfix the foot. They are often smeared with carabao and pig dung in the fervent hope that tetanus will thus be induced.

In addition to the suyoks, a considerable number of simple, effective man-traps, such as pits and snares, may line the trails between suspicious villages, and, what with one thing and another, it is not advisable for a stranger to move across the mountains of Lanao without local guides.

During the third week of May 1942, three tired, dirty, wet Americans and eleven half-naked Manobo children, who carried packs that very nearly equaled their body weights, pushed through these jungled hills in a steady rain. They enjoyed the services of a full-grown guide. He walked ahead of the single file of men and boys with a lasso of bajuco vine tight around his neck. Behind him, holding the other end of the lasso, was Wendell Fertig.

It was the third day of real jungle, and according to Hedges' calculations, they should have struck the headwaters of the Iligan River the day

---

8. suyoks = sharpened bamboo splinters, concealed in mud

before. Since the guide no longer made any pretense of knowing where he was going, and, since, from the start, he had shown a curious tendency to disappear into the brush, he was now on a leash, serving a useful purpose. If there were suyoks or traps on the trail, he would be the first to discover them.

It was the seventh day, or perhaps the sixth, or ninth, since the three Americans had left the Mirayon Valley. They had left as soon as Hedges' malaria tentatively withdrew, leaving him strong enough to totter. Splashing now along the jungle trail, Fertig decided they had had more luck than they had any right to expect, even though he believed very strongly in his personal luck. He, Hedges, and Offret had worked their way north, toward Macajalar Bay, keeping to the hills but finding enough to eat. They had the good fortune to find villagers willing to sell them sacks of rice and to rent them carabaos to carry the rice as far as the Lanao border. When they reached the Kapai foothills, they had been able to hire this accumulation of Manobo children to act as cargadores.[9] The carabaos were sent back; the loads set upon the children's heads. The plan was to work west into the mountains, skirting the worst of the Moro country, then turn south and inland toward the rumored position of General Fort and the last unsurrendered American force in the Philippines. But all was not now going according to plan, and it had not been going to plan from the moment they and their children had climbed well into the rain forest.

It is more accurate to say they fell into the forest. They fell, slid, staggered, and splashed their way into it, at once beset by leeches, surrounded by biting insects, slashed by briar vines, their army shoes filling with thin, liquid mud. This was not the relatively well-traveled, clearly marked forest of the lowland hills; this was, as Offret put it, an uphill swamp in a hothouse.

For the three Americans, each step was a wrench and pull, for their shoes sank into the suck and squelch of the trail; the foot ahead, sinking, could find little purchase from which to pull up the foot that followed; meanwhile, the warm rain beat down through the billion leaves of the forest and ran down their collars and, mingling with their sweat, collected inside their waists at their belts and soaked through the canvas packs. They worked through the wet and the muck in a stifling heat, swinging bolos to clear the new vines that had looped across the trail since the last travelers had come that way, and by noon on their first day they were tired beyond caring.

They had also reached that point of fatigue where no man will admit to another that he is tired, each subconsciously thinking *if he can make it,*

---

9. cargadores = porters

so can I, and the sight of the spindly barefoot children was a constant re-proof that drove them (and, of course, the children) for yet another hour through the mold-smelling wet tangle of the jungle web.

Each of the three Americans was a proud, powerful man. Fertig was tall, deep-chested, with the long, flat muscles of the trained athlete that he still was in his early forties; Hedges, outwardly a wisp of a man, was yet compounded of sinews bound together by anger; Offret was a stocky engine built for brutal wear. Yet this jungle through which Fertig could not stride, which Offret could not smash, which Hedges could not sear or lay waste—this thing of ooze and give and grip; this steaminess and wet slap of leaves; this all-surrounding, dark, unending one-foot-at-a-time wrench and skid—brought all thought to nothing and spent their strength on nothing.

When they stopped at last on that first day, Fertig stood numbly search-ing for breath in the fetid air, his thigh muscles uncontrollably twitching. Hedges' life was in his bitter eyes; Offret's thick chest was heaving. The Manobo children slid the packs heavily from their thin shoulders and chat-tered happily together until the guide sent them scurrying into the brush. They returned with branches they fashioned into a trellis; on this, they laid the huge leaves of the anahaw, or palmabrava—leaves which look for all the world like gigantic palm-leaf fans. They split open the trunks of sap-lings to find drier wood. The guide unstopped a length of bamboo and produced a smoldering coal, which he blew into flame. In the smoke in the palm-leaf shelter, they ate a lunch of boiled camotes and brine-soaked, sun-dried jerky made from a wild bull that Hedges had shot days before. While they rested, the children played and skylarked; the guide prepared his betel nut with leaf and lime, chewed, and spit scarlet.

"You know Mr. Lluch, huh?" Hedges asked the Manobo. "You know Mr. Lluch, his 'vacuation place?"

The guide's face brightened. The bright-red–stained lips parted to show the sharp-filed blackened teeth in the red-stained gums. Like the black-tooth Moros, the Manobo had stained his teeth with acid. It was quite a smile. He scratched inside his trousers.

"Oho," he said doubtfully. "Meestair Lluch."

"Oh, shit," Hedges said.

Salvador Lluch was a trader, a politician, the biggest man in Lanao; none but the most stupid could fail to know him. It was Hedges' hope to reach the evacuation place of this man to hear the news; since leaving Mirayon, they had met no one who knew any informations, as the Filipinos say, but, if anyone would know anything, it would be Salvador Lluch. The evacuation camp was, according to rumor, somewhere on the Iligan River. Hedges tried again.

"You know Iligan dailan?" he asked. "Iligan, big place, flenty houses, huh?"

"Dailan? Yis, oh, my yis."

"God," Fertig said. "He knows the word for *trail*. That's something. But Iligan? I doubt it."

"We go Iligan, huh?" Hedges said, pinning the guide down.

"Oh, yis," the Manobo said doubtfully. "Iligan."

Hedges tried him in Visayan, which produced another of those wonderful smiles. Apparently, the guide's inability to understand Visayan was equal to his ability to misunderstand English, and Hedges gave it up.

"Oh, hell," he said. "We'll just keep going till we cut across a stream. We can always follow it down to the sea. Or to the Japs."

"You are The One," Fertig said, putting into the accents of Filipino-English the habits of a lifetime spent in the organization of mining camps. Years ago, Fertig had learned to make the basic decision and then to choose the man best suited to carry it out and to let that man do the job. Hedges had spent his years cruising timber and living on the trail, and he knew more of Mindanao in general, and of Lanao province in particular, than Fertig. As far as Fertig was concerned, Hedges was the trail boss.

It was a vague trail they followed, hardly different from the game trails of wild pigs and deer. They followed it until the gray forest light began to fail. At dusk, they rolled into wet blankets on the hot ashes of their campfire on the high slope of a mountainside. As the ashes chilled, the raw, wet night air came into their clothes to spend the night with them.

They began the second day's march in reasonably good spirits, thinking to arrive upon the Iligan River in the afternoon, but, when the afternoon came, it was obvious that the guide was lying when he kept saying, "Bery near." They were near nothing but each other. Sometimes the ground underfoot slanted sharply up; sometimes it dropped precipitously before them, and they had to reach out for brush and roots and vines to pull themselves up and to lower their skidding weight down the slopes, but, all around them, the trees grew thick, and there was no sun, and it rained. Each yard, each mile, was exactly like the last, and like the next. By that second afternoon, they no longer marveled at the Manobo boys who carried the bulky packs.

"What the hell, they're used to it. They don't know anything else," Hedges said.

By now, the three Americans were also so used to the endless monotony of wet and damp and skid and tangle and insect-song that it seemed to them that life was nothing else. This *was;* other worlds were not. Close at hand was the lowland world, where women washed in the bright light that fell upon the white stones of their stream; and the world where American prisoners ate scraps in a cage; and the world where men stubbornly fought because they could do nothing else, and these worlds, too, were as far from each other as they were from the world of Hedges, Offret, and Fertig. All the coincident worlds were as self-contained and as separate as any worlds that were, or might ever be.

Fertig's world was step and wet and suck of mud, damp warm air whistling through the open mouth, and sweat stinging the eyes. It was a world where mold grew green on leather overnight; the gunslings were green; their muddy shoes were green beneath the mud; the brass fittings on the gunslings and pack and belt buckles turned green; dark green dots of spores appeared on their wet and rapidly rotting khakis, and the smell of mold and fungus entered their clothing and their leather and permeated the paper of Fertig's diary.

In this green, wet, mildewed snarl of a world, the little wounds the leeches make do not heal. Scratches do not heal. There is no way to keep the wounds dry; there is no sun to help the healing. The little wounds therefore grow larger, and rotten. They become tropical ulcers, and the flesh in time rots away to expose the shiny-white bone, which quickly yellows with lymph and blood and ooze. It is easy to die in the world of the jungle, although death is apt to come slowly, beginning with the first fevers of any of a considerable number of infections or diseases. The most usual path to death is the one that is most convenient: to become lost. Here is a world where visibility is limited to yards. In the rainy season, when there is no sun, it is difficult to maintain a sense of direction. A man comes to an impassable tangle and decides to work around it. By the time he has done so, he may be setting out, now, on a path that leads to a different mountain than the one he thought he was climbing. Or he may keep working around one tangle and then another and finally perish of fatigue, starvation, and disease within a few hundred yards of the place where he entered the forest. Therefore, it is imperative in such a world to keep to the trails. But there are many trails. Some of the trails in the world through which Fertig's party moved led to places it would be unwise to visit. Any of the trails might be used by travelers whom it would be no pleasure to meet. Except for the primitive, nomadic Negritos, no one lives in this world, but, during the dry season, many pass through it.

When the rains come, the number of travelers dwindles, and the trails become quickly overgrown, and, as the tangle thickens, it is important to guess correctly among the vestiges of trails. Which leads in what direction? It is sometimes difficult to say. Meanwhile, there is always the close, endless monotony of this wet world in which effort so quickly produces that exhaustion that makes further effort seem as ridiculous as it is frighteningly necessary. By the time of the second day, the jungle—by doing nothing but simply existing—had brought Fertig, Hedges, and Offret to such a point of exhaustion that they did not bother to try to cook a supper. Like Filipinos, they simply chewed a few soggy balls of cold boiled rice and rolled into their wet blankets and slept. Fertig was so tired that he did not reflect that it was probable that they were lost. It was enough to know that nothing more could be done that day.

Late on the third day, the land began to slope steeply and steadily, and Hedges guessed they were descending to the headwaters of the Malindang River. They came to a stream abruptly. The leaves parted, and there it was, at their feet: a white torrent running in a deep bed, dashing against huge, rounded granite boulders covered with green slime and moss. For the first time since entering the jungle, they could see more than yards ahead. From the steep bank, they could look through the misty air to see the water fall into a valley half a mile downstream. It was, however, a narrow valley of green rushes, a swamp in a saddle of the hills. The jungle closed in around it at once. There was simply the stream, the swamp, and the jungle.

The guide was delighted. He gazed upon this realm as a justified Columbus stared when the first dim island swam up out of the sea.

"Oho," the guide said. *"Bery* near."

"What name, huh?" Hedges asked. "Malindang River?"

"No Malindang," the guide said happily. "Bery near."

"Iligan River, huh?" Hedges persisted.

"Oh, sair, bery, bery near," the guide said again. "One day, two day maybe. Yis, bery near!"

"Very near what place?" Fertig interrupted.

"Yis, bery near," the guide replied, gesturing downstream with pointing chin and lifting shoulders.

"For Christ's sake," Hedges grumbled, "this damned stupe has just discovered the other side of the mountain.

"C'mon, Ducklegs," he said. "We're going back to sea. Let's get wet. We might as well try wading down the river. It should be a hell of a lot easier than hacking our way through this goddamned jungle. God, how I hate the jungle."

They lowered themselves over the steep bank, and the cold water that filled their shoes and swirled around their legs was a caressing shock, a glad contrast to the incessant thin, warm rain that took their strength. The boulders, however, were far larger than they had seemed from above, and so slick were they with the green scum of algae that it was nearly impossible to climb them or to walk across them. Even the prehensile toes of the Manobos could find scant purchase on the boulders, and the army boots of the Americans were no help at all. Worse, three days on the mountain trail had caused Fertig's boots to fall apart—the soles peeling from the uppers—and, although he had bound the shoes together with thin vines, the compromise was, like all compromises, impossible. Whole shoes, or no shoes, would have been better, but Fertig had never been able to go barefoot successfully, even as a boy.

In many places where great boulders choked the stream, it was necessary to embrace the slimy stones to crawl atop them in order to slither down the farther side, and here the Manobo children formed a chain and handed the packs over the stones. It was two hours before they gained the swampy valley, and everyone was beaten, drenched, and smeared with rotting algae. Below the valley, the stream poured down another race of stones.

Hedges admitted his error and suggested they return to the routine difficulties of the jungle, but no trail led from the swamp. Only game tracks wound into the trees.

"We'll stay parallel with the stream," Hedges said, but, when they entered the forest, the stream promptly vanished behind a curtain of vines and leaves.

For hours, they worried on, trying to maintain a sense of direction. They stopped to listen for the sound of the stream on their right, but no sounds carry in a rain forest. A rifle fired fifty yards away might be unheard. Any sound is close and is heard only once; there is no echo. The three men stopped, trying to listen to the stream, and monkeys cursed them from the trees above their heads. Then they moved again, with the guide now idiotically insisting that a village was very near, and looking about uneasily. The Manobo children caught their elder's mood, moving apprehensively. The Manobos were far outside their territory, farther from home than they had ever expected to be. They moved with shy fear, working downhill, sometimes hearing the sound of the water, and, all at once, the jungle opened. A house appeared before them; a platform on stilts with no walls.

A woman squatted on the platform. She was an antique, wrinkled, black-tooth Mora, whose breasts were as thin and fallen as a hound's ears. She wore a loose dress of brown abaca.[10] She had been left alone because no one would desire her and she owned nothing worth stealing. She was cooking rice and eggs. She looked contemptuously at the Manobos and offered to share her dinner with the Americans. They must stay the night, she said, for the evacuation place of Salvador Lluch was a morning's march down the trail that opened, clearly, below her house.

"Let me make a pot of coffee," Offret said, and the Americans added rice and vianda (as the Filipinos call anything that can be eaten, other than rice) to the blackened clay cooking pots of the aged Mora.

The rain pounded on the roof and slanted across the clearing, and the Americans had hot rice and steaming coffee on the wooden platform while the Manobos ate on the ground below, and all the world they lived in now was good.

"Charley," Fertig said, "I don't know about you, but, by God, I feel fine."

"We should all feel good," Hedges said, peering through the cracks in the rough floor at the Manobos gorging happily on the plenteous rice Fertig had allotted them, "but I don't know who guided who.

"You and that Manobo on a leash, God, you were a picture! 'Brave American Conquers Wilderness.'"

"Listen," Fertig said. "We're over the mountains, and no Moros, so let's have none of your damned wit."

"We were so far lost that nobody, not even you or Chief, knew where we were," Hedges said, his harsh smile slashing his thin face. "But you, Old Lucky, you came through smelling like a dirty green rose. Fact is, you stink, if you really want to know. But I can't smell you because I'm so used to it.

"Hey, Chief!" Hedges said. "Don't the Old Man stink?" Offret looked up with a brief grin, then concentrated on his work. He was holding a cigarette close to his ankle, far enough away not to burn the skin but close enough to burn the leech. The ugly, bloated growth writhed and fell. Offret rubbed it into a dark smear of blood on the bamboo floor with his shoe.

"Forty-three," he said. "Since I've been keeping count."

"Since we *started?*" Hedges asked incredulously.

"Since this morning," Offret explained.

"We're damned lucky we didn't get any in our eyes," Hedges said. "They get in your eyes, they suck the fluid right out of your eyeballs."

---

10. abaca = a hemp fibre

Fertig stretched luxuriously. Charley had stood the trip better than he had hoped. He had come through so far, and—so far—no Moros.

It was perhaps just as well that the Americans did not then know that the Moros in the country they had crossed were then engaged in the pursuit of far bigger game. Unknowing, they rested deeply on the bare floor under a roof in the rain, Hedges and Offret smoking and drinking black coffee; Fertig writing on a school child's pad of cheap paper with widely separated lines, telling his diary something he would never have told anyone else.

The future is still so bleak, that to think ahead is to encourage despair.

He paused to look at his friends. He wrote:

Never have I rested better and felt more a sense of achievement than after crossing these mountains.

The Mora crone squatted at a corner of her platform with her thin arms folded across her knees. Her filmed black old woman's eyes watched Fertig write. She studied him for a long moment, and then she looked as long and as steadily at the sprawled forms of Hedges and Offret, who were sliding down into sleep. She turned her head and spat a long jet of scarlet betel onto the ground below. She watched that, too.

She saw the betel juice fall onto and briefly stain the soft mud. Almost all the red disappeared at once. Then the hissing rain, bit by bit by bit, quickly washed the rest of the red away.

4

PRIVATE ROBERT BALL unwound himself from his cot and bowed. The Japanese were not unkind, in their fashion. They slapped Americans who did not bow to the guards, but on the other hand, they slapped their own men for equally trivial misdemeanors.

"Radio?" the Japanese shouted, as though a flood of sound could break through the language barrier. "You radio, yiss?"

"Yeah," Private Ball said. He was not worried, merely puzzled. The time for the beatings, tortures, beheadings, and deliberate starvation was still in the future. Meanwhile, the Japanese allowed their captives to go shopping in a little town within the area of the concentration camp; they held judo matches for themselves and their prisoners, and there was a certain amount of fraternization. Yet the Japanese were something of a dangerous mystery, and Private Ball walked out of the barracks ahead of his guard, guessing what he might have done wrong.

But the Japanese merely wanted Private Ball's help as an Air Corps radio technician. There was something wrong with the Japanese captain's radio. Ball was about to say that he knew nothing about how a radio worked, when a sudden light flooded his mind.

"I'll see what I can do," he promised.

Wherefore, Private Ball climbed the roof of the commandant's office and shinnied up the aerial mast. Sitting on the crosstrees, Private Ball could see where the guards paced. He timed their movements. He got into his head the location of the stream, the trees, the barracks, the fences, the town, and the surrounding jungle. When he came down from the roof, Private Ball knew more about the geography and conduct of the prison camp than the Japanese.

He fooled briefly with the receiving set. But Private Ball, in making a small repair, also carefully adjusted the set so that it would receive only one station: the one in San Francisco that, in addition to American jazz, also broadcast the news from the Allied point of view, sending messages of hope in English and Tagalog, and spoke about The Aid.

"Look," Private Ball told Sergeant William Knortz that night. "I don't like this place, and I don't like Japs. I'm going to walk right out of this dump. Are you coming with me?"

"When do we go?"

Ball had chosen his friend with care. The Japanese themselves held Knortz in great respect, for he was a Black Belt. The Black Belt is the highest honor in judo, and it is won by removing it from a man who holds it. At the judo matches, the Japanese would quickly defeat the Americans who tried to wrestle against them, and then Knortz would step into the ring and throw the Japanese experts out of it, and the Japanese paid honor to the blond American warrior.

It was Knortz' idea to tell their barracks mates about the pending escape, fixing a date.

"We don't want to go then," Knortz said. "We want to pass the word around so that even the Japs get to hear about it, and then we *don't* go. Get it?"

Ball caught on. The word was passed, and the camp waited. As Knortz supposed, the rumors came to the ears of the Japanese, and the guards were doubly vigilant. When the day of the escape came and went, the old soldiers jeered.

"Hey, kid!" the old soldiers shouted, "What's the matter? Ain't you escaped yet?"

"You get to thinking about them Moros, hey?" the old soldiers called.

It got to be a joke. Even the Japanese guards were laughing about it. And then Ball and Knortz slipped away.

They went to the town to shop, under guard, and once among the rickety, tangled houses, mingling with the tattered crowd, they eluded the guard and ran, head down, following a route that the view from the roof had etched forever into Ball's mind, and they did not stop running until they were deep in the forest.

IN THE HILLS OF SURIGAO, Herr Waldo Neveling stepped briskly along the trails, a tolerant, amused man.

"What dumbheads are those Japanese!" he thought. The Americans had been just as stupid. Both the Americans and the Japanese had thought, *once a German, always a German,* but Herr Neveling had not remembered that he was a German until the Americans had reminded him of it by putting him in prison. He had not seen Germany since 1914.

When the First World War ended, Herr Neveling had been in Turkey, part of a technical crew working on the Berlin-Baghdad railway. His experience had been pleasant, and he had acquired a taste for travel. What would there be to do in a defeated Germany? Nothing would there be, he told himself, and so Herr Neveling had become a soldier of fortune, hiring himself out to tribal chieftains in Arabia. Thence, by various stages, Herr Neveling had fought his way across Central Asia to the camps of petty Chinese warlords, improving his skill with a variety of weapons and sharpening his instinct for infantry tactics. To him, fighting was fun. His lean, hard body bore numerous white scars of all the fun he'd had. For the past few years, he had been master mechanic for mining companies in the Philippines, for there was nothing he did not know about diesel engines, rule-of-thumb engineering, or, indeed, anything mechanical. But coming to the Islands had been a mistake, because life had been so dull. Now, he reflected, the prospects were brightening.

He sought out unsurrendered American civilians in hiding, as he had promised the Japanese he would.

"I tell you," Neveling said, "I have seen the Japs in China. I tell you, this is a war between the white race und the yellow men. That is what the Japs say it is, und that is exactly what they mean. I think maybe the white race must stick together already. If we stick together, maybe we can do a little something to make it more interesting for the Japs?"

But none of the Americans shared Herr Neveling's enthusiasm. Some were suspicious of the German; others were afraid.

A missionary's wife said, "It is soldiers like you on one side, and soldiers like you on the other, who bring these horrible, horrible wars upon us all. What do you think you will accomplish by resistance, except to bring more suffering to innocent people?"

"You just wait," Herr Neveling told her. "You will very soon see how the innocent people suffer whether they fight or don't. You will see what I tell you is absolutely correct. If you do not believe me, you will very soon find out for yourself. The Japanese are no joke, I assure you."

But the American schoolteachers and technicians had questions. How long would the war last? they wondered. Nearly everyone believed in an eventual American victory, but when would it take place? Six months? Could they not do what the Japanese said, and endure internment for six months? Would they not be exchanged before that time anyway? There would at least be doctors in a Japanese internment camp, they argued. What, they asked, would they do if little Billy got another earache? Where could they find a doctor in the jungle? Wouldn't it be better just to go into internment?

"If you take my advice," Herr Neveling said, "you will stay as far away from those liddle bastards as you can."

Not at all disheartened by constant refusals, Herr Neveling moved on through Surigao, confident that sooner or later he would find someone who would like to join him in having a little fun.

HIGH ON A MOUNTAINTOP, from which he could look north toward the distant blue of Macajalar Bay and southwest toward the Kapai Hills, where the war was still believed to be flickering, Sam Wilson made an interesting discovery: there was very little for a millionaire to eat in the hill country. Within a measurable time, there would be nothing to eat at all. Starvation in solitude was apparently the price of security, although, in fact, real security could not be purchased at any price, nor, for that matter, could true solitude.

From time to time, taos would appear on the trail below Wilson's grass house, sometimes bringing food. Perhaps the Filipinos came out of pity, but perhaps they were moved by simple curiosity, for the location of Sam's house marked it as that of a naïve man. Filipinos know better than to build on the crest of a hill, and they had built Sam's house reluctantly, although the pay had been good. The trouble was, as all knew, that the winds carry bad spirits who reach forth their skinny hands to clutch at the projecting stones and trees of hilltops as the wind flows over the land; thus does evil come to man. Therefore, perhaps the taos came to see what might have happened to Meestair Weel-son. In any event, when the taos came, they came with gossip. Days ago, when Fertig and his party worked their way through the valley below, en route to the Kapai Hills, a tao came to Sam with the news.

"They are not to know I am here," Sam said.

"Yes, sair," the tao said. "They do not know. But the Colonel Fer-teeg say you are welcome to join him and his companions. They have much rice."

"Who said I was here?" Sam demanded. "He does not know me. I do not know Colonel Fertig. I am not here, you understand? You have seen no one."

The tao shrugged.

"Yes, sair," he said. "Not one knows. I tell Colonel Fer-teeg it is not to be."

Sam tried to tell the tao again what the message should be, but he knew very well how futile it was. He wondered how Fertig had come to Mindanao, wondered where Fertig had been going. He would have liked very much to see Fertig again, for he knew him well and had not seen him since the days before the war in Manila. The last time had been at a party at the Polo Club. They had watched the Elizalde brothers and Chick Parsons playing polo, and afterwards they had had stout and tonic on the patio, and then Wendell had suggested they move the party to his house for supper.

It had been a fantastic, fairy-tale life in Manila before the war, and one of the amazing features had been the parties. You could call your houseboy from the Club and say, "Ambrosio, there will be 20 for supper," and Ambrosio would say "Yes, sair," and, by the time you left the Club and arrived home, there would be the table set for 20 and—although you had not said who was coming—you would find that your guests' servants had joined your servant staff to help out, and to have a party of their own in the kitchen, and that they had brought with them any additional china or silver that would be necessary to set such a table. No one knew how the servants always knew, but nothing was as efficient as the bamboo telegraph. The thought of the bamboo telegraph wrenched Sam back to reality, and he looked down from his mountaintop with hunger, longing and fear for his imprisoned family. He had fought his war. Now he would not admit his existence, even to old friends. He was a man cloaked in hopeless silence; admitting nothing; denying nothing—a rumor on a hilltop.

5

FERTIG WAKENED in a rose-gold light. The morning sun, falling through a break in the clouds, suffused the mist rising from the forest, and, although the smooth green tops of the betel palms at the edge of the clearing could not yet be seen, the slender trunks were touched with gold, and gold lay upon the glistening mud beneath the house where the Manobos were stirring. Offret sat at the edge of the platform with a rifle across his lap while the ancient Mora blew upon the charcoal of her earthen stove. A foot nudged Fertig's side, and he looked to see Hedges standing above him.

"Piss call," Hedges announced.

A kalao bird creaked suddenly in the luan trees nearby; then Fertig could hear the forest noises of small lives in the morning. He followed Hedges and Offret to the clear stream that ran behind the clearing, and the three Americans lavishly soaped away the accumulated filth and rot of the trail. Fertig looked into a distorted face, soaped it, and shaved away its red bristles. The Army's steel mirror, he reflected, left something to be desired. Or did he really look like that now?

His shaving done, he carefully removed the double-edged blade from his safety razor. Holding the blade between thumb and forefinger, he twirled it round and round inside a thick water tumbler. He could not remember who had told him how thus to strop razor blades, who had advised him to carry a heavy drinking glass in his pack. Was it Hedges? No matter. But, Fertig thought, it is amazing how much we know that we did not think we knew. The jerky, for instance. Although neither he nor Offret nor Hedges had ever made jerky before, they somehow knew how to soak the strips of meat in brine to keep insects from it and to dry it in the sun. Was this something they had read and remembered, or something they had heard someone describe during their Western boyhoods, or was it simply one of those accurate makeshifts that practical men always seem to devise at need?

They returned to the house to see the Manobos wolfing down handfuls of hot white rice. Hedges had ordered a whole pot of it for them—enough for 20 men. The undersized children, to whom white lowland rice was a delicacy, were busily devouring all of it, including the crust left in the pot, which they called the heel.

The extra uniforms that had been found in Pantalan were still clean, and still somewhat pressed, and even somewhat dry in the middle of their packs. The Americans changed into them, and Fertig retied his decaying army boots with new lengths of vine as a messenger from another world stepped into the gathering sunlight.

He wore neither fez nor turban; he wore no loincloth; there was no sacred kris in a horizontal scabbard at his belt. He was a barefoot man in shirt and trousers. He smiled.

"Good morning, sairs," he said to them in general, and then, fixing on Fertig's silver oak leaf, he said: "Don Salvador Lluch says that tonight you will be his guest. You will stay until . . ."

He shrugged slightly to mean "bahalana."[11]

"We will be most happy," Fertig said, marveling at the accuracy of the bamboo telegraph. The fact that he had seen no one on the trails did not mean that no one had seen him. But perhaps the Mora had sent word in the night.

"You are to guide us to don Salvador now?" Fertig asked.

"I will be The One," the Filipino said.

The Americans made a gift to the Mora who had sheltered them. She put a hand before her face and smiled in embarrassment, nodding her head many times to mean that there was no need, and shyly took one can of salmon. She kept looking after the Americans as they left, holding the can tight in her hard, thin hands.

The trail widened steadily below the clearing and fell gently into the lowlands of rapidly thinning forest. Families were moving along the trail; others were converging upon it from adjacent clearings. Everyone wore clean clothes, the women carrying woven sleeping mats folded on their heads. The whole countryside was moving, and it was obviously moving to a fiesta.

"Today is the fiesta grande of don Salvador," the Filipino said proudly.

11. bahalana = who knows? or who cares?

"The padre from Iligan will be there to hear confessions, and the misa cantada will be said. Also, there is a wedding."

He smiled with anticipation.

"The padre has not been here since the war began," he said. "In these troublesome times, he cannot come often, but today he will be there. There will be a wedding! Also, you will be there! Don Salvador is having the fiesta grande! My, oh, my!"

"How did don Salvador know we were coming today?" Fertig asked.

"Ah, sair," the Filipino smiled, as though that was a foolish question, "you Americans and the padre will be his guests."

The Filipinos they met on the trail offered to serve as cargadores and thus relieve the spindly Manobos, but the little mountain people and their elder would not give up the burdens. The children fairly skipped and jumped along the easy trail, laughing and chattering in their dialect. For the first time in their lives, they had crossed the mountains, and they had no intention of returning without seeing how civilized Filipinos lived.

"What's the scoop on this don Cuspidor?" Offret wanted to know.

"Oh, sair," Hedges told him, "He ees beeg wheel. He ees beeg politico. He charges feefty percent interest, only."

And he told Offret the story of Salvador Lluch. He was the mestizo[12] son of a Basque sea captain who married a mestiza and settled near Iligan. Salvador Lluch grew up to be a businessman and politician and had for years controlled the province of Lanao or, rather, that portion of the Lanao seacoast to which pioneering Christians clung. But Salvador Lluch could also go places that no other Christian dared enter. He could even go to Lake Lanao, for he was the principal banker to the Moro population. By that, Hedges explained, he meant that Lluch was a pawnbroker, accepting the Moros' treasures of brass jars and gold-hilted daggers as securities against loans. The Moros had no bankers, and they had killed such Chinese moneylenders as had been foolish enough to visit them. It was to Lluch that the Moros turned, because no other broker offered such low interest.

"You borrow one sack of palay,[13] huh?" Hedges told Offret. "Come the next harvest, you owe two sacks. If you can't pay then, by the next year, you pay four sacks or eight the year after that. If you no pay *then*, you lose your rice paddy. It's rough, for you can get stuck for 800 percent interest in three years, and, the next, you lose your farm, and all for one sack of unhulled rice.

---

12. mestizo = mixed blood
13. palay = unhulled rice

"But now take Lluch. He charges a flat fee of only *fifty* percent each year. In this country, that makes him a good guy. No blood; just fifty percent."

Lluch's monopoly had made him rich, Hedges said, and, as his influence grew and American power in the Moro country was curtailed after the Filipinization Act of 1936, Lluch was elected governor of Lanao province. His business and his casa were in Uigan, but now that the Japanese had come, he was living at his farm upriver from the town, a farm which he had planted years ago with corn, rice, cowpeas, and ramie.[14]

Armed guards, still dressed in Philippine Army uniforms, saluted the Americans as they approached the lands of don Salvador, and the Christian guide explained that they had been soldiers, but now, since the Japanese had come and all law had gone, the former soldiers were hired by the Christian community as guards against the Moros. There seemed to be some question as to whether Salvador Lluch had hired these men or whether the soldiers had offered a Chicago version of protection to don Salvador, but the guide did not elaborate.

"Do the Japs know about the soldiers?" Fertig asked.

"For why, sair?" The guide smiled.

That's it, Fertig thought. Ask a question and get a question. That was the Philippines: always a question and never an answer.

The principal house of the farm had been enlarged since the war; nipa[15] outbuildings had been added as dormitories; all stood within a fenced compound, and the compound was decorated with new palm branches and fronds woven into hearts, stars, and crucifixes. New fronds and bright crepe paper fluttered about an outdoor altar.

"You watch and do what they do," Fertig muttered hastily to Offret, and, as they passed before the altar, the Americans clumsily imitated the practiced genuflections of the Catholic Filipinos.

In the bright light falling on the compound, two pigs reddened, smoked, and spattered hot grease onto the beds of coals above which they slowly turned. At smaller fires, boys labored with that patience that expects reward, turning chickens that had been split in half, stuffed with slices of yams, and skewered together again. The sun fell on piles of fresh corn prepared for roasting and on piles of varicolored fruits and melons. The three Americans walked dazedly through this new world of light and food, and on the steps of the house, don Salvador Lluch greeted them not with brazos fuertes[16] but with a firm handshake.

---

14. ramie = a fibrous plant from which a light, strong cloth is made
15. nipa = a swamp palm, used for thatching
16. brazos fuertes = embrace

Lluch looked to be a Basque: gray-eyed, with only slightly darker-than-Spanish skin. He was short, stocky, with the torso of a heavyweight wrestler, and he had an air of quiet competence. His unaccented English was excellent, if rococo; his Spanish was better, and his Visayan and his Maranao—the local Moro dialect—were perfect. He laughed politely when Hedges said, "Hi, Salvador, you old thief."

Mrs. Lluch appeared, a pretty, buxom woman in her forties whose dark hair was touched with brown. Her skin was the color of light caramel and without blemish. She seemed at once delighted to welcome her guests and, at the same time, remote and serene.

Graciously, the Lluches asked forgiveness. "You will please remain a moment, por favor," Mrs. Lluch said. "The girls will prepare the sala[17] for you."

The sala was the largest, central room of the casa, and, when the Americans entered it, they found it absolutely bare, except for three chairs arranged together at the farther end. Fertig found himself pressed to the middle chair with Hedges on his right and Offret at his left. They were to sit there enthroned as the principal guests. Slowly, the room filled with men, and, one by one, the heads of Filipino families came to be presented to the seated Americans. News of Talakag and Cagayan was politely exchanged for that of Iligan, and Fertig listened closely to each man's name as he was introduced. He pronounced each name carefully. Later, he would astonish everyone by remembering all the names. It was not a party trick. Fertig simply found the social practice useful. He was well aware of his vast and unusual memory, but sometimes it played him tricks. He was worried because he could not remember how he knew about the razor blade and the water glass.

"Ubaldo Laya," Fertig found himself saying to a sallow man whose light brown eyes were in startling contrast to his thick jet brows and pale, thin face. "You are the provincial treasurer of Misamis Oriental?"

"Why, yes," Laya said.

"I have heard of you," Fertig assured him.

"Laya, the Colonel heard that you ran off with all the moneys of goberment," Hedges said, grinning to show he did not mean it.

"No, no," Laya said hastily. "That is not truthful."

"May I present Chief Petty Officer Elwood Offret?" Fertig interrupted, to the treasurer's profound relief.

Thus the afternoon passed with three fugitives holding court among brown faces in a huge bare room under a nipa thatch, and, as Offret

---

17. sala = parlor

fidgeted and Hedges sprawled at ease, waving to Mindanaoans he knew well, Fertig played the part he felt his colonelcy compelled him to play. He held himself straight and spoke deliberately, acting—as he later told his diary—"in a military manner." It was not until the fiesta began that Hedges found an opportunity to bring Fertig back to earth.

The wedding had been held at the outdoor altar in the compound while the shapes of children leaped around a bonfire, and the southern stars leaned over the trees, and after the wedding, everyone feasted at benches and tables set about a floor of hard-packed earth; the bonfire at one end and the head table at the other; the women in their transparent mestiza dresses at the tables on one side, and the men, brave in their barong tagalogs,[18] facing them across the way. At the head table, Fertig was lost in a trance of deep content and self-importance. He talked idly with don Salvador and listened to the music and the young men singing. He twirled a long-stemmed glass of Fundador in his fingers, and then Hedges' voice ate into his ear.

"Goddamn it, Stupid," Hedges muttered, "don't you know you're don Juan around here? Until you ask the Missus to dance, no one else can start!"

Fertig looked up, startled, suddenly conscious that the orchestra of five guitars and a violin had been laboring for some time and that the dalagas[19] were shyly glancing at him from behind their fans and that the men were looking nervously at the head table. Fertig waited a moment, then turned to Mrs. Lluch.

"Missus," he said, using the Filipino honorific, "may I have the pleasure of this dance?"

Mrs. Lluch accepted with a regal smile. As they rose together, the orchestra moved into a waltz, and the tall red-haired colonel in the tied-together broken shoes, and the cameo-faced first lady of Lanao circled a floor of clay. Scarcely had they completed the first circuit when the bolder of the young men rushed across the space to claim the dalagas who waited demurely, opening and closing and fluttering their tiny fans, and the fiesta grande of don Salvador at last exploded into the tropical night.

The dancing would obviously last until the smallest hours, and so, it seemed, would the food. The tables were piled with lechon;[20] with wild pigeon, roast chicken, boned chicken filled with stuffing and sliced; with fish and fresh-water shrimp from mountain streams. There was jackfruit

---

18. barong tagalog = embroidered shirt of filmy cloth, worn outside the trouser
19. dalagas = ladies
20. lechon = roast pig

cooked with coconut milk, the large seeds roasted separately and served as nuts. There was a fresh salad of pineapples, bananas, and pamelos, drenched with a dressing of coconut milk and muscavado sugar. Roasted casava roots served as bread. There was white rice and the rough-cracked corn the Filipinos cook like rice and call corn-rice; there were the soft tips of ferns and camote leaves and ripe avocados the size of coconuts. For those who wished it, there was Scotch whisky, Fundador, Chinese rice wine, native tuba,[21] San Miguel beer, and—most desirable of all to most Filipinos—there were even bottles of warm Coca-Cola.

The three Americans fell upon this feast much as the Manobo children had wolfed down their pot of white rice in the morning. They ate to the point of misery and then tried to deaden their discomfort with Fundador. They ate while dancing couples furtively left the floor to slip into the shadows beyond the fire, returning as inconspicuously half an hour later to feast and dance again. The servants of the hacienda and Fertig's Manobo cargadores slept at the edge of the clearing undisturbed by the noise or by their distended stomachs. The Manobos would leave in the morning to tell tales in their remote villages in the forest of the party at which there was enough food to maintain whole tribes for weeks, to tell of the unbelievable marvels of the outside world.

Brandy, food, light, and laughter coming so suddenly and absurdly after the wet blankets that smelled of mold and damp ashes . . . It was ridiculous, Fertig thought. It was ridiculous but wonderful, and it must end. Heavy with food and exhausted by the tension of delight, Fertig turned to don Salvador and asked if an old man could be excused, to leave the night to the young.

The bed was in the sala. It stood alone in the vast room, a huge, antique Spanish four-poster bed, canopied with mosquito netting and crackling with crisp new sheets. The room was large enough for a dozen beds, and it was obvious that a dozen people had been turned out of it in order that the Colonel might sleep in peace.

Fertig could always sleep. He sank into the bed and tried to sleep. But the bed was too unbelievable for sleep. It was too luxurious for sleep. Fertig had eaten too much and had drunk too much Fundador for sleep. He was too tired. He lay there in discomfort, looking up at the billowing mosquito netting and listening to the unabated noise of the fiesta, wondering why he couldn't simply shut his eyes and go to sleep. And then he found the reason. It was not the bed, nor the food, nor the brandy. In the midst of his unease, he was suddenly aware that there was something lacking in the fiesta.

---

21. tuba = a coconut beer

He thought very carefully, recalling each face he had met and what each face had said, and he considered the whole spectacle of the wedding, the feast, and the dancing, and then it came to him. Don Salvador was not enjoying his own party. The idea of a Filipino not enjoying any party—particularly the idea of a Filipino host not enjoying a party—was so unthinkable that Fertig rose, dressed, and found his way to the table at which Lluch still sat with two older men.

"Don Salvador," Fertig said, drawing the mestizo aside, "I want to thank you from the bottom of my heart for the hospitality of you and your family."

Don Salvador nodded with a ceremony equal to the formal cadences of Fertig's Filipino-English constructions.

"To a homeless man," Fertig continued, "this is a glimpse of the life I knew before December eighth: pretty girls, good food, and happy people. I have not known that since the war came. You have many problems, your family, your lovely wife and beautiful daughters. All this I know, but tonight you are restrained and sad at your own fiesta. There is something that I do not know, that you have not told me?"

Don Salvador looked around before he spoke. Then he said, "You are right. I have told no one. Here, at my own fiesta, my own heart is breaking. Come, we will talk with Captain Hedges, for this is for you both."

They walked into the shadows beneath the trees, and, after looking to be sure that the shadows contained no lovers, don Salvador said, "No one knows, for it is not good to have bad tidings for the sweet at a fiesta.

"General Fort surrendered today.

"I know it is true, for he sent a friendly Moro yesterday with the word that only I would know beforehand that he does this thing. My friend, General Fort . . ."

"I see," Fertig said.

"Outlaw Moros stole his food supplies," don Salvador said. "His ammunition caches were looted. His troops were going home one by one, then by squads and whole platoons.

"This morning, he notified the Japanese Army that he would surrender his forces as ordered by General Wainwright. He did this, not because of the order to surrender, for he did not believe that was right. He had nothing left with which to fight.

"I think," don Salvador said, "this may be our last fiesta until The Aid comes. My children will know much sadness. You see that it is important to be happy tonight. You see why I did not wish to injure your happiness by telling you this news when you have come so far to join your general?"

Hedges watched the fruit bats flickering among the trees. "The Moros, huh?"

"The Moros," don Salvador said.

"I did not wish to say, but you have asked," don Salvador said, holding out his hands. "I tried to hide my sadness, for General Fort was my amigo mio. Better we go back now and smile. We must not bring the sadness to my people tonight. They will have much sadness soon."

"It is a wonderful fiesta, don Salvador," Fertig said. "The memory will last a long, long time."

"Yes," don Salvador said, "you are wise and kind. Let us go back smiling like men who know a little joke. Tomorrow we will talk about these other things."

6

IT WAS DIFFICULT in the morning to recognize the dalagas of the night in the barefoot, plainly dressed women whose shimmering gowns and sequined shoes had been folded into the bundles they carried on their heads. Ficsta was over, and the war—or that strange sense of unknowing fear that the Filipinos then knew as war—had returned. Fertig, Hedges, and Offret took their rifles to walk into the morning to look over don Salvador's hacienda, pausing beside a fish trap built across the river.

"Simple, huh?" Hedges said. "So easy to get in, and then you can't get out."

"I was afraid that Fort had quit before we got here," Fertig said.

"Well, what the hell," Hedges said. "It was only a matter of time, anyway. Maybe it's best. If we'd been with him, we'd have been caught along with the rest of them."

Hedges stared into the fish trap.

"You any bright ideas?" he asked Fertig.

"Listen," Offret said. "You two make up your minds, and I'll tag along."

"Thanks, Chief," Fertig said. "We can sure use you."

"We'll make out," Hedges said, watching the fish.

"We'll *have* to make out until The Aid gets here," Fertig said. "We'll have to find someplace where we can trust the people and where the Japs aren't likely to come."

"What's wrong with right here?" Offret asked.

"Nothing," Hedges said. "Pretty girls, lots to eat. Old Lluch would be glad to have us. He's a good guy. 'Course, he'd probably send us a board bill after the war."

Hedges was about to say something more, but he stopped.

A small boy was pelting toward them, his hands clenched into fists and his arms pumping like a sprinter's.

"Ha-Ha-Hapons!" he gasped. He struggled for breath and brushed his dark hair out of his eyes. "Oh, sirs, the Hapons are here! Don Salvador says maybe it is better you do not be seen!"

"Where are they?" Fertig asked, unslinging his rifle.

"There are two only," the boy said. His small chest was still heaving. With great scorn, he said, "They are civil-yans. They come to talk to the people. But don Salvador thinks they should not know you are here."

"You will return to don Salvador," Fertig said, kindly but firmly. "You are to ask him to return our packs upriver, huh? You say to don Salvador for the Colonel, 'Return our baggages to the house he knows. The house where we were benighted, before the fiesta.' This you will say, now repeat for me."

"Yes, sair, no need, sair," the boy said. "The baggages are there already. But I will tell don Salvador that the Colonel say to do."

"You are not to run," Fertig said.

"Oh, sair, I will run but fast," the boy said earnestly.

"The Hapons will see if you run and they will think, why is the boy running?" Fertig said gently.

"Ah, yiss," the boy said, big-eyed. "I will run slowly." Hedges grinned as the boy flew away, and the three Americans moved into the field of ramie plants, which always reminded Fertig of the tall horseweeds of the Colorado plains. Making their way through the ramie in a roundabout course to the casa, they came near the compound to see two small figures in alpaca business suits talking to a circle of Filipinos. Fertig drew his binoculars and, shading the lenses with one hand, brought the two men up close to him.

"They're sure enough Japs," he said. "And they're sure enough civilians. No soldier who had any kind of training could disguise himself that sloppy."

He passed the glasses to Hedges.

"They're not any local Japs," Hedges muttered. "But I bet they been in Mindanao a hell of a lot longer than the Jap Army."

Hedges handed the glasses to Offret and put his arm through the sling of his rifle, raised the leaf sight, and methodically adjusted the set screws for distance.

"Don't be silly, Charley," Fertig said.

"Don't, for Christ's sake, tell me not to be silly," Hedges muttered, sighting on the Japanese.

"No," Fertig said.

"Wendell, all I'm going to do is kill two Japs."

"No, you're not."

"Wendell, I can do it."

"I *know* you can do it."

Hedges glared at Fertig's taut face.

"Two unarmed civilians," Hedges ground out. "Two damned *civilians* coming here to count the Filipinos. Hell, we *ought* to kill them for that."

"You use your head," Fertig said. "We knock them off, and a patrol comes up here. Our Filipino friends go to prison or get killed, and you and I are not going to eat so good again."

"You're being right doesn't make me feel a damn bit better," Hedges said. "I don't like being chased by a couple of slant-eyed bastards I can kill with a couple of shots, and I'm going to get rid of them right now."

"No," Fertig said.

"I don't mind being chased by an army, but I'm damned if I'm going to be chased by civilians," Hedges said.

"You're not going to shoot anybody today. We're going upriver," Fertig said in a voice Hedges had not heard before.

Hedges disgustedly snapped the leaf sight down. They worked their way back through the tall ramie and then through fields of corn, to strike the trail that led to the house of the ancient Mora. The house was deserted, but their packs were there, beneath the platform, and on them was an unsigned note that said, "Wait."

Toward dusk, the Christian guide came again, and they followed him in the darkness to the hacienda, where Mrs. Lluch would not let them talk until they had eaten. Then, breaking a Filipino convention, she remained at the table while the Americans spoke with don Salvador and Ubaldo Laya, the onetime provincial treasurer of Misamis Oriental.

"The Japanese," don Salvador said, "came to invite us to return to our homes in Iligan. They are so sorry, but if we do not come back, our houses will be given to others who want them. There must be people in Iligan, and the houses will be filled. Besides, the Japanese Army will not protect those who hide in the forest or live on their farms. Only in Iligan can they give protection from bandits and bad Moros who may come and kill."

Don Salvador shifted his weight in his chair.

"The Japanese did not hear that any Americans were here," he said, "but if they come back again, someone will tell them. We do not want to go to Iligan, and yet we are afraid."

"*I* cannot go to Iligan," Laya said, his dark brows drawn deeply down, "for they will tie me up and beat me, for I do not have the money that foolish people say I have. There are many Filipinos who would tie me up and beat me, too, thinking this story about the treasury."

"The Japanese who came," don Salvador said, "have said that we should go to Iligan for a meeting with them. Perhaps if we do not go, they will come here and take us."

"They say we should be their friends," Laya said, "but, if you do not bow to a Japanese soldier, they hold your arms and box you in the face. And then you must bow."

The sallow treasurer made them all a satiric bow.

"I do not like to bow," he said. "Who does?"

"What do you think?" don Salvador asked. "Must I go to Iligan because the Japanese say we must meet with them?" Fertig found the question addressed to him. Mrs. Lluch, don Salvador, and Laya were waiting for his answer. Fertig looked to Hedges for help; these were old friends of Hedges'. Perhaps because they were old friends, Hedges stared at the table and was silent. An excellent way to keep friends is to give them no advice.

From somewhere outside himself Fertig heard himself speaking. It was very curious. He was speaking like a field commander, making decisions in other people's lives, issuing order, not advice. It seemed to him that he had gone through this scene at some time before; these sensations had been occurring since the war began. Did it mean, he wondered as he spoke, that each man lives his life over and over again and that memories of the last prior life come flooding in close at the end of the current one, so that you suddenly know you have heard this and said this before?

Distantly, he heard himself say, "First, I will answer Mr. Laya. Neither you nor your family will go to Iligan. If your family goes, the Japanese will mistreat them until you come in. I would not trust my lovely daughters to the Japs if I were you.

"Remain here or go somewhere that may be safer. But you have nothing to do with Iligan. You are from Misamis Oriental. You have no home, no people in Iligan. Stay away from the Japanese.

"Now, don Salvador," Fertig said. "If you go to Iligan, the Japs will hold you as hostage. You will work for them, for first, they will make your family come to Iligan with you. Then you have no choice. Do you want to work for them? I think not. But you will have no choice if you go to meet with them. Therefore, it is better that you send someone; one of your parientes who could be held hostage without great damage to your family. Someone whom the Japs would eventually see was unimportant and later release. He would then come back to you when they release him, and tell you what the Japs really want.

"There will be a time when you must go to them, but now you must delay. First, you will make excuses: 'There is no food; my house has been looted; my family is sick; my wife cannot be moved; my animals will die if I leave them on the farm and move to town; there are no roads for the carts because the April flood destroyed the road after I came to my farm.'

"When the excusas are 'use up,' you will start over again. Do not go to town until they force you, and then only you go; you did not know they meant 'bring the family—sorry, I did not know.' The Japs will eventually force you to move your family to Iligan, but not all of your family at any time. Leave the hijas here with Laya. Of course, the Japs may lose their temper and kill you. That is the risk you must run, but *I* should never go to Iligan as long as the jungle is open behind me. You know I do not like the jungle."

Fertig paused.

"The jungle is bad and no place for any man," he said, almost to himself, "but it is to be preferred to the Japs."

There was a general silence, and then they talked of valleys in the deep mountains and of hidden valleys near the main road, where men might hide. It was obvious that the Japanese would establish outposts along the roads. Then the Japanese would establish outposts in the river valleys and thus control the farm countries in the valleys as they already controlled the seacoast towns of Iligan, Kolambugan, and Cagayan. The solution for Salvador Lluch, Fertig suggested, would be to find a place to hide that was not too far from the food supply of this hacienda; a place into which he could slip at need.

"Just how far is this place from Iligan?" Offret asked.

"It is four kilometers," don Salvador said.

"Four kilometers?" Fertig said.

"Yes," don Salvador said, "it is not far."

"No," Fertig said drily, "it sure isn't."

He turned to Hedges.

"Captain Hedges," he said, "please make a note. The next time we get drunk at a fiesta, make sure that it is at least four kilometers away from a headquarters of the Imperial Japanese Army."

"The Colonel and I feel," Hedges said to Salvador Lluch, "that we should leave at once. We do not wish to harm you by staying here. If we leave soon, you can tell the Japs that we forced you to feed us, for we came with guns."

"I do not wish you to go so soon, amigo mio," don Salvador told him, "but it is better for all that you go."

He looked directly at Fertig, his gray eyes holding neither accusation nor apology, nor any fear. He was simply a man who dealt with a fact.

"The Japanese will return, and some foolish person will talk about the American colonel," he said. "You know how it is. Someone will say; someone will hear. Nearly everyone knows Captain Hedges. The Japanese will hear about Captain Hedges."

"We have heard something about a Mr. Deischer," Fertig said, plugging into the bamboo telegraph circuit.

"Yes," the stocky haciendero said, "that is a very good idea. It is rumored that Mr. Deischer has a camp about three days from here near Rogungan but closer to Momungan. Three days, four days, it is somewhere, not far. The Manobos say there are many Americans there. They say they are all young, for they do not have beards or shave often. From there, you might go to Momungan or, Captain Hedges, to your old lumber camp behind Kolambugan."

"If everybody's heard of this Mr. Deischer, won't the Japs know about this Mr. Deischer?" Offret asked.

"Yes, that is true," don Salvador said, "but the way to Mr. Deischer is very difficult, and perhaps the Japanese will not wish to go."

"The Japs won't be tackling the back country for a while yet," Hedges suggested. "I'll bet they never get around to it before The Aid comes."

"We all have the same problem," Fertig said. "We must find a secure place to wait for The Aid. If we can stay away from the Japs for five months, six months, then no more worry."

"That is true," don Salvador said with a politeness that could have meant anything. It might have been the politeness of a Spaniard who had seen another conqueror come to stay on Mindanao for forty years.

"Can you furnish guides and cargadores to Mr. Deischer's?" Hedges asked. "We could leave tomorrow if we have cargadores."

"Could we have the cargadores at dawn?" Fertig asked.

"Yes, at dawn," don Salvador said.

"Then we will return to our baggages," Fertig said, rising as though to leave, "and expect the cargadores there."

"No, no," don Salvador said. "Tonight you should be my guest. There are people watching. If anyone comes, someone will see and tell us. Tonight is all right. You should stay."

Fertig sat down, half ashamed for having so bluntly hinted at an invitation to spend another night in civilization, yet badly wanting a last night in that fantastic four-poster bed before committing himself once again to the wet blankets of the trail camp.

"Maria," don Salvador said to his wife, calling her by name for the first time before his guests, "bring the brandy, and we will have a farewell drink with our friends."

Fertig looked up, oddly moved.

"Dona Maria," he said slowly. He looked into the mestiza's serene, round face.

"My wife," Fertig said suddenly, "is also named Mary."

"Perhaps," he asked, looking from dona Maria to don Salvador and back again, "the boys could play some music for our despedida?

"There is a song," he plunged ahead. "'Maria Elena.' 'Maria Elena' always reminds me of my wife, and I may not hear music in the mountains."

"Of course," don Salvador said, bringing a square hand down heavily on the table. "Of course. Maria, have the girls tell the boys to come play for us, and we will sing and drink brandy tonight."

It was a large request, and a small one, Fertig thought, as the men moved from the room to the porch of the casa. It was not polite, he told himself, and yet nothing is so easily assembled as an orchestra in these islands, where it seems that everyone has at least a guitar. Besides, he reassured himself, Filipinos like to sing on any provocation. Still, he thought, what a thing to suggest! What a way for a guest to order something from a host! And what a thing to order! He wondered whether a Regular Army colonel would have done it. The hell with it, he told himself. I want it and I did it.

That night, young men and girls of the hacienda sang in the shadows as men whose world had been lost still clung to the fragments of that world, smoking cigarillos and sipping Fundador, that sweet-dry memory of Spain, listening to the sad, gentle music of the Islands. Lost in nostalgia for two worlds he had loved—the color, profusion and ease of the prewar Islands, and the clean distances of the West where Mary lived—Fertig realized for the first time that all the island songs were sad. They were tales of unrequited love, of abandonment, of disaster, of the loss of loved ones at sea. All were told in that tinkling sad music of the Islands, all told in the soft labials and vowels of the dialect. Last of all, they sang "Maria Elena" for the strange colonel whose wife was Mary.

The brandy was gone.

The Colonel went back to the huge, clean, lonely bed, and, as he stretched on the sheets, he began to take into his mind the awful fact that whatever he did from now into an indefinite future would be entirely up to him. It was a position few men have ever truly known.

As long as there had been an army fighting on Mindanao, he could believe himself part of it and bound up within that army's demands and actions. Even though he had not really expected Sharp or Fort to make much of a fight against the Japanese, Fertig could still imagine himself as being—in the Army's phrase—under military control. As long as there had been some army or even some rumor of an army to walk toward, he had something to do, and something outside himself in which to believe.

What was there to believe in now?

God?

The Aid?

"God," he said aloud to the mosquito netting, "you've helped me this far. Thank you for your help. Ill try to do the best I can, and I hope you'll want to go on helping me.

"God," he told the mosquito netting, "if it is my fate to tell other people what to do, please help me to guess right."

If they've all surrendered now, what does that make me? Fertig wondered. Who am I to tell other people what to do?

You are, he told himself, probably the senior United States officer alive and free on the island, and possibly in all the Philippines. You are the commanding officer of all the Army there is left, namely, Captain Charles Hedges and Chief Petty Officer Ducklegs Offret. On this island, you are the United States Government since this island is United States Territory, and since you are the United States, in a way, that is why you can tell other people what to do.

Well, they asked me, and I told them, Fertig thought. As the United States Government, I told them to go away and hide. That is the official policy of this headquarters, and it will be implemented by all means at the disposal of this command. Gentlemen, we will all get the hell out of here. But first, gentlemen, a little music if you please! Hey, Amado, Jose, Luis, get your goddamn guitars on the double! The Commanding Officer wishes to think about his wife.

Some commander.

And while the Commanding Officer goes away to hide, this is what you will do, gentlemen: You will preserve the security of the main body, gentlemen. You will sacrifice a pawn. You will pick out some poor, damned fool in your family that nobody thinks is worth a damn, and send him to the Japs. They'll slap his face until he's silly, and then they'll ask him questions he can't possibly answer, and when he doesn't answer them, they will take his clothes off and hang him up in a tree by his thumbs with his arms twisted up behind his back, and, by means of a cord tied to his penis,

they will swing him back and forth in that graceful movement which the
Japanese, with their well-known flair for delicate poetry, call the butterfly
swing, meanwhile flailing him with split bamboos. Let him yell his fool
head off; he can't hurt anybody because he won't know anything.

That is what you do when you are a senior United States commanding officer. You tell people, "Don Salvador, you are too valuable to go to
Iligan. Send your wife's cousin's brother's nephew and let the Japs beat him
instead of you. And now, don Salvador, you must excuse me, for I must
go away and hide."

But they asked me, Fertig thought, and I told them. It seemed now
to Fertig that the answer had come so readily because the kind of life he
had been leading since December eighth had prepared him automatically
to think in such terms. If you must lose a man, lose an unimportant man.

It was a great philosophy. All men were now divided into the important and the unimportant. The important men were those who could, one
way or another, help you or harm you. The unimportant were those who
could not.

Fertig lay upon the crisp sheets and stared at the filmy netting. What a
hell of a thing about poor old Fort. Those damned Moros. For years, the
Moros went around saying that Fort was their friend, that Fort understood
them. So, when the chips were down, the Moros stole their friend blind
and let the Japs have him. Our friends, the Moros.

You have a great choice, Fertig told himself. You can stick around
the lowlands, and the Japs will either grab you or beat the hell out of any
Filipinos who help you. Or you can go into the hills to live with our well-
known friends, the Moros. Meanwhile, you as senior officer present tell
everybody what to do.

Your trouble, Mary always said, is that you don't like to play any game
that you can't win.

"Each one is bound to the Wheel," he said aloud to the white netting,
perhaps to God. "And the Wheel turns, and turns again."

The sutras.

It was the brandy.

And then he slept.

7

THEY WORKED DOWN the divide and up the farther slope, keeping the lighter part of the sky on their left, and then they climbed up into the hard rain where the sky held no light. In the late afternoon, they found a house in the dripping forest where a Moro lived with his old wife, his young wife, and a slave. The slave wore the blue denim of the Philippine Army.

The Moro was dark-skinned and harsh-featured, and he wore a dirty maroon fez and a dirtier malong.[22] The hilt of a kris projected from a wooden scabbard at his belt, and his black eyes flickered over Fertig's party without welcome. The women wore rough, plain, shapeless dresses, not the varicolored and often quite beautiful scarves and robes of the lighter-skinned Moras of Lake Lanao or of the more prosperous lowlands. The older woman watched everything with great curiosity and with a certain friendliness, as though delighted with this sudden change in the routine of her days; as though she had, perhaps, uncertain memories of a life beyond the hills. The younger wife was openly contemptuous and hostile. The slave would not lift his head.

"Good day," Fertig said in English, and the Moro in broken Visayan said that he did not speak English.

"Charley, ask this sport how far it is to Rogungan."

Hedges spoke briefly. The Moro grunted.

"He says this *is* Rogungan," Hedges said. "I'm going to tell him we will stay here tonight."

"With him?"

"It's sleep here or out in the rain."

---

22. malong = the Moro all-purpose cloak and sleeping blanket

Hedges turned back to the Moro and told him how fortunate he was to be able to entertain such distinguished guests, and the Moro sullenly said they could sleep on the porch. Then the Moro snapped at the young wife to prepare supper, and when she angrily protested he cuffed her into the house. She in turn snarled at the slave, who followed numbly, never looking at the Americans or their cargadores.

Supper turned out to be a filthy pot of ill-cooked brown mountain rice in which there were little arms and legs and hands. The pot was not graciously extended but was thrust at them by the young wife, who said nothing to Hedges' Visayan. Offret looked upon the ghastly mess and guessed that he was not as hungry as he had thought he was.

"Monkey," Hedges said, gnawing a fingerbone. "Go ahead, Chief; it's no worse than eating babies."

"Just a little gamier," Fertig said. "How about seconds?" Hedges talked with their sullen host, who made no comment until Fertig drew two .30-caliber rifle cartridges from his pouched web belt and handed them to the Moro. At once, the Moro's manner changed from surly to calculating, and the young wife angrily refilled the pot. The instant the wretched meal was over, the Moros went into their house and slammed and barred a wooden door, leaving the Americans alone on the porch in the fast-gathering night. They could hear the bar fall into place.

Fertig tried to talk to the Filipino slave, only to be met with slack-jawed evasion. The Filipino would not look directly at them, but, from his half-answers, the Americans gathered that he was a man from the island of Negros—one of the several hundred who had escaped with their rifles from the scene of General Fort's surrender. He had come through the hills only to be met by the Moro, who offered him sanctuary if he surrendered his rifle. The Filipino handed over the weapon and rapidly degenerated into slavery. In a matter of three days, he had become so cowed that he was incapable of doing anything more than existing. Offret had never seen a man with a broken spirit before, and seeing one now, he could not quite believe that what he saw was true.

"These hill Moros can beat it right out of them," Hedges assured Offret. "You'd kill a white man before you could do a thing like that to him, but the Moros got the Filipinos' number."

"These hill Moros," Hedges went on, "live according to the Koran as interpreted by some illiterate, flea-bitten imam who heard from some crooked hadji what was supposed to be in the Holy Book. What they get out of it boils down to polygamy, slavery, and brutality."

"Do they know and obey the Koran's code of hospitality?" Fertig wanted to know. "'If a man eat thy salt, even though he be an infidel, then thou must protect him from all harm'?"

"What did you do, memorize the damn thing?" Hedges asked. Then, answering Fertig's question, he said, "They'll believe in that hospitality stuff as long as we have this many men."

In the morning, however, they found they had no men. Don Salvador's cargadores had vanished without waiting for pay, wanting no more part of Moro civilization. The choice was now quite plain: The Americans, carrying what they could, could search alone for Mr. Deischer's camp with its alleged collection of American fugitives, or they could try to recruit Moro cargadores from the hills who might well murder them for their rifles. While they considered the prospect, a troop of black monkeys emerged into the gray light to shriek and tear at the Moro's corn patch.

The door behind them flew open, and their host kicked his slave through it and shouted at him to drive the monkeys away. Wordlessly, Hedges picked up his Springfield rifle, threw it to his shoulder and fired all in one motion.

The heavy *blang* of the Springfield was still ringing in Fertig's ears as the last of the monkeys disappeared, leaving one twitching corpse in the cornfield, its head shot off.

The Moro looked at the Americans with different eyes.

"Oho," he said, which, in Visayan, is the polite way of saying, "Yes, sir." On this occasion, it also meant that the Americans could stay in the area as long as they wished without being molested, as least not until their ammunition ran out.

Hedges pursued his advantage to talk with the Moro, learning that the Datu of Rogungan was a powerful Manobo who lived but four hours away. The Datu, it seemed, was the current chief of one of the few Manobo tribes that had been too strong for the thirteenth-century Moro invaders to drive into the deeper hills. He was able not only to hold his own against the present-day Moros but even to exercise some community leadership over them. The Americans were not sure just how welcome they might be at the house of a pagan warrior, but two things were clear: They were not welcome where they were, and, if the Datu of Rogungan controlled the territory through which they must pass to Deischer's camp, they might as well arrange passage with the Datu himself. They loaded themselves with all they could carry and left the rest of the packs on the Moro's porch.

"We will remain our baggages," Hedges told their grudging host, "for the Datu's men to bring to us."

He looked steadily into the Moro's dark face, and the Moro completely understood all that Hedges did not say.

The last the Americans saw of that household was the slave carrying the body of the headless monkey toward the house for the women to cook. He took it by the hand.

The trail followed a riverbank, a broad path beneath great trees with the clear river running in a sand bed, and at midday the trail turned. There, on the sloping beach of a bend in the river, set against betel palms, jackfruit trees, and slender mountain bamboos, was a house that had come straight from the Dyak country of Borneo. It was a house with a fantastically high peaked roof with steep slopes and overhanging eaves, a house that stood on huge piers that had been partially squared and then left rough as though someone had thought the work had been too hard to be really worthwhile. It was a very old house whose nipa roof had been patched many times with round thatches made of betel-nut palm, and the different materials of the roof made it seem the hide of a straight-haired dog afflicted with a mange that had erupted in circular blotches.

As the Americans entered the clearing, the women who had been working beneath the house disappeared. A small boy who wore a bright scarf folded into a kind of turban, a dagger with a gold-embossed hilt, and a clean pair of shorts climbed down the steep ladder that led into the house. He walked with a great dignity toward them.

"You have come," he said in heavily accented English. "I am Jaime. I have four grades in the school of English. My grandfather, the Datu, will talk with you. But he say that earlier, before you talk, you will have food and take siesta."

Proudly, the boy led the Americans across the hard-packed clearing, and as they went into the house, Fertig marveled at the strategic thought that had gone into the placement of the building and its entrance. An enemy would have to cross cleared, rising ground. Then he must climb a steep ladder, thrusting his head up through the floor of the porch, entirely at the mercy of anyone above. Then the narrow porch confined him until he was past the unrailed stairwell, whereupon he would have to turn a right angle to enter the dark interior.

The Datu of Rogungan was standing with quiet pride on the porch. He was a wizened old man with sharp-filed black-stained teeth and the red lips of the betel-chewer, dressed in the simple elegance of skin-tight purple trousers, a yellow shirt, gold-embroidered scarlet vest, and batik turban. His wide-bladed short spear stood against the wall at his side. He spoke neither English nor Visayan but a dialect Hedges and Fertig had never heard, but his meaning was clear before the grandson translated. He was welcoming them as one warrior to another, without comment, and said they would talk later. Then he waved them to a bench that paralleled the porch wall and, taking his spear, went into the darkness beyond the door as a woman appeared with a fragrantly steaming clay cooking pot.

It was a chicken stew, and Fertig, who was familiar with hot Indian curries and who fancied the chilies of Mexico, found himself eating a dish that went far beyond his wildest imaginings of spiced food.

"Hooof!" he said, unscrewing his canteen top. "You could run a factory on the heat of this stuff."

It was a dish that, like the house, had come straight from Malaysia, a dish from the Spice Islands, whose food even Mexicans find somewhat overwhelming. At least a double handful of black peppercorns had gone into the one clay pot of chicken stew.

"It's good, once you get used to it," Offret said, tears in his eyes, but the throats of the three Americans were still smoldering when the grandson summoned them from their siesta to an audience with the old gentleman, as Fertig found himself thinking of the Datu.

They were shown into the main room, the throne room, a room nearly forty feet square and forty or more feet from floor to ridgepole. The plank floor was polished each day by women who skated over it with coconut husks bound to their feet. It was splotched with the thin light that fell through random holes in the tattered roof and through the chinks in the walls made of bamboo pounded flat. The turbaned Datu sat cross-legged at one end of this room on a dais flanked with engraved brass vases. He held a stout tube of bamboo in his lap. He stretched out an imperial claw and motioned for Fertig to come sit beside him as his equal.

"Datu Soong, my grandfather," the boy said, "says that you are first Americano soldiers to come in many years."

Fertig cautiously replied that the American Army was happy to be able to call on an old friend, and, as he spoke, the aged Datu unstoppered the bamboo tube and calmly extracted a roll of yellowing, cracked, and fading papers.

Fertig took one gently in his hands and found himself reading a military letter that commended the Datu of Rogungan for having kept his people neutral during the wild, early days of the first Moro-pacification campaign. It was signed, respectfully, "John J. Pershing, Lieutenant Colonel, United States Army."

"Phwarshan," Datu Soong nodded approvingly. Then he extracted another letter that thanked the Datu for aid in battle.

"Signed," the letter ended, "Arthur MacArthur; delivered by hand by Douglas MacArthur, Captain, United States Army."

"Mwartha," Datu Soong murmured politely to the first American officers he had received since Douglas MacArthur had been a captain.

"Tell him," Fertig told the boy, "that General MacArthur sends his best wishes to his old comrade in arms. To his old companion."

The old Datu inclined his head politely, and Fertig wished he knew what the old man was thinking. He wondered if the Datu knew what the letters really meant or whether the old pagan considered the faded papers in their bamboo tube to be a kind of anting-anting[23] given him by inexplicable strangers. Or did he know perfectly well that the letters were merely the Army's pious hope that the Datu would maintain a kind of tacit armed truce between his people and the Americans?

"Tell him," Fertig said to the grandson but looking at the man who had led a battle line, "that General MacArthur does not forget his friends and will return to kill all the Hapons who have come to Mindanao."

The old man sat up straight-backed and bright-eyed at this, and then he told, in his strong, hard voice, of the man he had been, and had become in war. The boy stood, solemn and proud, translating (in a mixture of fourth-grade English and Filipino words adapted from the Spanish) a story of spears and swords and of how, in the end, the surviving Moros either accepted the Datu of Rogungan's leadership or left the Rogungan Valley. The three Americans sat enthralled, clearly understanding what the old man meant— particularly when he pulled aside his yellow shirt to bare a deep livid scar on his breast. The scar was the mark of a Moro barong, and the grandson told how the Datu had won that fight, skewering his adversary to the jungle floor with a pig spear. Everyone smiled at the reference to the pig spear, for the Moros, like all Moslems, abhor the pig.

"Ask him if he knows Mr. Deischer," Fertig said, and the boy told them that Mr. Deischer had some gold claims in the area, that he was said to have a camp two days deep into the mountains, toward Momungan, and that the old Datu had already prepared an evacuation place for Mr. Deischer should the American be driven out of his present location. The Datu said, the boy told them, that there was no reason for them to go to Mr. Deischer's camp, although he well understood they might wish to be with their own people but that they were welcome to stay in Rogungan as long as they wished. Since there were only three of them, the Datu said, and since he had many people to do his bidding, his people could easily provide food for three more mouths.

---

23. anting-anting = magic charm

While the Datu spoke, two round-faced, flat-nosed, flat-footed, squat, heavily muscled, big-breasted girls silently entered the room and stood against the splintered wall, showing their filed, blackened teeth and twisting their gilt bracelets.

"My grandfather says these are his nieces," the boy said. "They will cook your rice and are for your bed."

"Thank him with all my heart," Fertig said, trying not to look at Hedges' sardonic features nor at the frankly intrigued girls, while yet trying to seem to observe the bold-eyed maidens with proper appreciation and to include the gratitude of his friend Captain Hedges. "Tell him he is very kind."

The old man moved a hand to indicate it was nothing. And then he reached on the dais beside him and brought up a reed nose flute, which he clapped to one nostril and, looking courteously upon Fertig, began to play.

In the afternoons, it seemed, the old man held court in his throne room, played the flute, and drank basi,[24] and thus he enjoyed the afternoon of his powers, the lord of a jungle valley that had belonged to his grandfather's father's father. True, the valley was now threatened, as it had been threatened a thousand times before, but men watched all the trails, and no stranger moved unnoticed into the Datu's domain. If a stranger came, one wooden gong would talk to another along the trails, passing the message quickly to the gong within earshot of the high-roofed house. As long as watch was kept and as long as men believed in their spears and in the Sun, the Big Snake, the Tall Trees, and the Small People of the Ground, no man would take this valley, and it would be the valley of his grandson's son's son.

Sometimes, in the late afternoon, the basi made the old man sleepy, and he would fall asleep on his dais, and the women would carry him to his sleeping cubicle, and sometimes, if he woke when they placed him there, he would want one of the women, and she would remain to lie with him. It was good to be the Datu of Rogungan, and it was well that the long-nosed Americanos came to give him their names. He had heard that the dwarf-people who had come from the sea did not give their names, any more than a Moro did. If the dwarf-people came to the valley, he would give them a spear. All this was explained to the tall one with the red hair and the red beard, who was the Datu of the Americanos.

If life seemed simple and, on the whole, rather decent to the Manobo Datu, Fertig found it impossible. To be sure, he was reasonably safe, both from the Moros and from the Japanese, who would not be likely to con-

24. basi = a wine of sugar cane and herbs

cern themselves with primitive areas until their conquest of the civilized lands was consolidated. Fertig could, as Hedges put it, sit here on his duff until the goddamned war was over. So much was immediately apparent.

But it was also immediately apparent to Fertig that he had not been designed to rusticate in a jungle valley with a tribe of near-naked primitives, to allow one day to blend imperceptibly into the next. When a man has nothing to do, it means that he has nothing in which to believe, and lacking belief, he has no will or need for will, and lacking this, he ceases to be a man.

On the other hand, there was nothing to do outside the jungle, for the Japanese owned the world that lay beyond and had proclaimed that all Americans who failed to surrender would be shot on sight. Resistance to the Japanese seemed out of the question. The only way to remain unshot was to remain unseen. But who could live outside the jungle and remain unseen?

To Fertig, the answer seemed to be to find some healthful place in which to live in peace, doing some kind of work—and this led him to think again of the Americans reported to be in Deischer's camp. It was all very well to believe, intellectually, in the brotherhood of man, and certainly the flat-faced Manobos of the Rogungan Valley were friendly enough, but the ties of tribe and nation were stronger to Fertig than intellectual speculations on brotherhood. All white men on Mindanao would need each other, simply for company if for no other reason. If the young Americans at Deischer's turned out to be armed soldiers, perhaps they could establish a fortified, disciplined camp in the hills and maintain themselves by farming and hunting. At least it would give the Americans something to do, something in which to believe, and prevent them all from simply degenerating into so many bamboo Americans to whom life consisted of a native woman and a brood of naked half-castes playing in the mud but which held neither hope, nor love, nor any point at all.

On the other hand, Rogungan was not a wholly impossible place; there were tended fields by the riverbank and a patch of sky above and a basic security of sorts. Moreover, Fertig was tired of walking about Mindanao searching for armies that evaporated before he reached them, and, while quite willing to move on, he was unwilling to act on rumor alone.

"Charley," he said, "you are The One. It looks as if I'm elected to keep the Datu happy. The Chief is no woodsman and no Filipino, so we can't send him. You'll have to go to Deischer's and figure out the deal. Find out who's there. If it's a better place, we'll move. If not, see if Deischer's boys will come here."

Fertig explained some of his thought to the old Datu, and it was done: Hedges left the valley with four cargadores and the Datu's grandson to act as guide, translator, and guarantee of safe conduct.

The next four days slipped quietly and rather quickly by. Offret and Fertig spent their mornings hunting in the river for fresh-water shrimp, learning that these were best if cooked with coarse salt and sweet-potato leaves. They waded in the deep pools and tried to catch in their hands the small white fish that lived there. They did not bathe together but with one man guarding the rifles and clothes while the other splashed in the river, for poor as the Americans were, the Manobos were poorer still. Despite the protection of the Datu, it was unwise to tempt the Manobos, who could not help looking at the potent beauty of the American rifles.

In the afternoons, Datu Soong sent for his guests in the throne room, and, although there was no one to translate now, the Datu would speak and point and make signs in the air, and the Americans would try to guess his meaning and reply in kind. Then the Datu would offer them bowls of basi and play his nose flute, and the two nieces would lead other girls in clumsy dances that consisted of simple stampings and gestures, dances which apparently told tales in pantomime.

The fifth day came and then the next, and there was still no word from Hedges. Fertig began to worry. Deischer's camp was supposed to lie at the end of a two-day march, and, allowing Hedges time to survey the camp, surely he should have returned by now.

"I don't know what's happened," Fertig told Offret plainly, "but I think the old man's worried, too."

"We ought to go look for them," Offret said.

"It wouldn't do any good," Fertig said. "Charley can look out for himself in this country better than we can."

"Maybe the Moros got him," Offret suggested.

"There's no use worrying about it," Fertig said.

It didn't do any good to worry, but he could not help seeing Hedges' decapitated body rotting in the brush. He could not worry, but he had to think what the Datu's attitude might be if the grandson, so obviously the Datu's pride, did not return. He could not worry, but he could not help wondering, and the tension lay in him and grew. He sewed together a pair of crude shoes fashioned of partially tanned boarhide and wondered about Hedges. He read and reread a biography of Cardinal Richelieu that he had carried in his pack all through his wanderings, and wondered what had happened to Hedges. He told the Datu, in pantomime, that he and Offret should go the way Hedges had gone, but, when the Datu caught his meaning, he objected with such violent gestures that Fertig felt his worst suspicions confirmed. On the ninth day, the grandson and the four cargadores came into the clearing, filthy and exhausted.

In the Datu's throne room, the child told the story first to his grandfather and then to the Americans.

"The way was bery deef-icult," the boy said. "And far. No two days, but three, and deef-icult. No houses, no people."

"What happened to Captain Hedges?" Fertig burst out.

"Very bad," the boy said simply. "At last we are there at Meestair Deischer's, Captain Hedges say, 'You rest one day, then you return back.' Then Captain sick in head.

"He have bad malaria; bery bad. Three days he not know one thing, and Meestair Deischer say, 'You, Jaime, you stay, so Captain Hedges can send his Hello, I am OK.' We stay, we eat, sleep, eat, and then Captain Hedges say, 'Goddamn it, Jaime, you go plenty fast to Colonel. I am OK. You git.' I got fast. Two days, I am here."

"We will go to Mr. Deischer's," Fertig said. "Tell the Datu that we will go to our friend even now."

"The Datu speaks," the boy told Fertig. "'You are my guests and must stay with me. The way is hard. The Kapai River is in flood. My men have gone into the forest to hunt. The danger is most great. Here with me we have food, women, and good conversation.'"

"Tell him that is all true," Fertig said. "But I have given my companion my name, that I would follow him, and I must do so. Tell him I would stay with you, but my duty says I must go."

"If you have given your name, you must go," the Datu agreed. "But we will hold bitchera before you leave. Two days and then one night must pass. Three days before you can go."

He held up three gnarled fingers.

"Thank him but say I will go tomorrow," Fertig said.

The old man smiled.

"You cannot go tomorrow because all men are in the forest and there are not one to carry your baggages," the boy translated. "He say, 'I will send word that we have bitchera, and all will come, thinking to drink basi and dance all night. The morning comes, and I will say, "You make love all night, you can walk all day. This day, you will carry the baggages of my honored guests. If not, you can work in the fields with the women." When I speak, many men will wish to help you.'"

Then the Datu told his grandson, "Jaime, go to your father and uncles, saying, 'The Datu will hold bitchera on the day after the next by two. You will bring a wild boar, monkeys, and many bananas. I will make basi.' Go *now*!"

The boy translated and fled to tell the men to bait the boar traps with young monkeys and to do their father's bidding. The women of the compound began that day to hack down the sugar cane and grind it between crude wooden rollers, pouring the juice into a demijohn partially filled with an evil-smelling mess the Datu prepared, and, as the day of the feast drew near, families filtered in from the jungle, each bringing brown mountain rice, rough-cracked corn, and sacks of camotes. The fish, the birds, and the meat would come on the last day, dressed out that morning, else this food would quickly rot in the damp heat of the jungle. The bitchera was largely a bring-your-own-banquet affair, and Fertig wondered why. The answer was simple: No one area of the jungle produced enough food to support a large population. Each family found it difficult enough to raise its own few crops, and no food could be stored except the tough-hulled rice.

At dawn on the feast day, cargadores arrived from the distant seacoast, carrying nets of fresh coconuts slung beneath bamboo poles, and four five-gallon demijohns of fresh tuba. The cargadores also brought stories of the Japanese.

With the surrender and imprisonment of all Americans, they said, most of the Japanese had left Mindanao to fight in Australia. There were fewer, now, along the coast, and the Filipinos were no longer afraid to talk with them. The people were not the friends of the Japanese, the cargadores said, nor yet their enemies. All waited to see what the Japanese meant to do. If a man bowed to the Japanese soldiers, there was no trouble. Many men, not desiring trouble, had learned to bow.

At dusk, the skies cleared, and a gibbous moon raced among tattered clouds above the jungle. Fertig and Offret sat among the Datus, picking at crayfish fried in brown sugar, watching the young men dance. The men stamped rhythmically in a circle, calling plaintively after the manner of the wood pigeon, shuffling, stamping, and calling out until one girl, bolder than the rest, either joined or was pushed into the circle. Then another girl came, and another, and the men began to chant, and the chant gained in cadence and deepened with a heavy grunt to mark each stamp of hard bare feet. A guitar picked out a lonely sound and then was at once lost in the booming of a hollow log drum and the flat clanging of a stone beating on an overturned iron pot. The pace quickened, and the dancers formed a line that undulated in the fashion of the Great Serpent; the line grew, and Moros, Christians, and Manobos writhed together in honor of their common snake god of lost centuries. The Moros danced at Datu Soong's bitchera in fez or turban, the Christians were bareheaded, and the Manobos draped scarves around their necks.

Offret thought the scarves had a familiar look. He peered closely as a dancer stamped past, and saw that the scarves were towels, bath towels with a blue strip running down the center, and on this strip were white letters. "Manila Hotel," they said.

The dance became erotic, and the girls would posture close to Offret, touching their breasts and indicating with their eyes the hidden promise between their legs, but they did not thrust their loins toward Fertig, for he was a great Datu who would choose as he pleased, when he wished.

The dance went on, the cooking fires died, and the old Datus sitting in the places of honor stirred restlessly. Suddenly one of them, the Moro Datu Hamid, jumped to his feet and shrieked. The dance abruptly stopped. The hollow log drum boomed out once more and was stilled. All eyes turned to the turbaned Moro, who launched into a passionate harangue, glancing contemptuously from time to time at Fertig as he spoke.

"He is telling them," the Datu of Rogungan's grandson said in too loud a voice, "that you are a great warrior but that you now have no soldiers, and so you are not so great. Instead, you must look for help from the Manobo. He says it is well you do not ask for help from the Moros, because the Moro will not help you unless he is paid and you now have no money and cannot pay. He says that you were great but you are great no more and that men should know you are not what you were."

"Why, the son of a bitch," Fertig muttered, preparing to rise in answer, when the Datu of Rogungan got to his feet and drove the haft of his spear into the hard ground. The wide blade glittered in the dying firelight.

"My father," the old Datu said, speaking bitterly into the silence, "was friends with the Americanos when they defeated the Moros and the Moros burned their own cottas[25] to fly to Rogungan. Now I protected the Moros when they came running, and I will protect my honored guests who have eaten salt with me and drunk basi made from my own cane. The Americanos will not be harmed, nor will my people accept pay from them, even if it is offered. They are my guests until they reach Mr. Deischer's camp. After that, Mr. Deischer will protect them, for they are his kind of people."

Then he touched his lips, glaring at the Moro Datu.

"I have said these words," he said, thrusting his hand outwards from his lips and letting it fall to grasp his spear.

---

25. cottas = Moro stone forts

BOOK TWO

Decision

1

LOLING WAS A SLENDER, barefoot girl of seventeen in a white dress, and one sunny day in late June, shortly after the surrender of the American armies on Mindanao, she went to market with her family in a barrio near Cagayan. Why not? Life does not stop because an army surrenders. The stores were open, the corn mills still ground corn, and refineries still produced bajuco bags of muscavado sugar. True, the Japanese had stolen much, but most of what had been on Mindanao before the war was still there, redistributed by its owners or, more generally, by looters. Curtain rods, for instance, had disappeared from the stores but not from the island; drums of gasoline had vanished from the bodegas of the oil companies but not from Mindanao. Trucks, machine tools, and canned food had been hidden in the jungle by farsighted entrepreneurs when the war began. Therefore, Filipinos went to their markets after the surrender to find out where things were hidden, for, other than foodstuffs, there was nothing to be seen.

There were Japanese soldiers in the market that June day, but Loling paid no particular attention to them, for the presence of the Japanese was now taken for granted, although they were still something of a curiosity to Loling, as foreign men are to any woman. Loling's father hoped that it would prove possible to be friends with the Japanese, who spoke of a prosperous Asia for the Asiatics.

Loling and her mother paused to talk with friends beside the stall where small, dried fish were sold. They gossiped about a woman who was believed to have medicines to sell, and of where it was still possible to obtain a permanent wave, and of marriages and births. They told one another of Chinese merchants who could mysteriously produce khaki cloth, needles, soap, tin pans, rat traps, shoes, sunglasses, pop bottles, wicker suitcases, empty kerosene tins, and other luxuries, and of how the Chinese would not accept the new Japanese pesos, which they called Mickey Mouse money, but demanded plata, or silver. The women talked of these and other matters when—at a far end of the market place—there was a sudden shout. There was a shot, and screaming, and everyone was running: it all happened at once.

Loling began to run, too, and then something was thrust between her legs—even as country people catch a chicken—and she sprawled in the dust, soiling her dress. Hard hands twisted her arms behind her back, and with a wrench that nearly dislocated her shoulders, Loling was hauled upright and jumped along past the fruit stalls by men she could not see who held her arms. They brought her to a dump truck. There were already three girls in it, and Loling wildly recognized a schoolmate as she was lifted and dropped over the metal sides.

En route to the schoolhouse where Loling had attended classes in home economics, she and the girls in the truck were each defeated several times on the bright emerald grass of a coconut grove. In Loling's case, because of the struggling, it at first required five men to defeat her: one man to each arm; two to force and hold the slim legs apart, and a fifth to do the work. Then the men changed around so that each had a turn.

Before the truck reached the schoolhouse, a novel idea occurred to the driver. The truck stopped again. By the time she reached the schoolhouse, Loling's white dress was filthy with blood and dirt, and her dark eyes were glazed with shock. She saw, without really seeing, the long line of giggling soldiers waiting for her in the familiar schoolyard.

The next morning, she was dead. Since no autopsy was held, cause of death was never established.

News of Loling's brief career as a Japanese Army comfort girl shot through the facilities of the bamboo telegraph with the speed of light.

The Hapons do not ask; they take, the bamboo telegraph reported in an ecstasy of horrified incredulity. Rape, of course, was not unknown in Mindanao, but, in a land where sexual intercourse was so freely offered, rape was a far more monstrous crime than in the inhibited West. It was a crime binding the girl's family to a blood feud with the perpetrators. But an army had done this thing to Loling and her schoolmates, and how were fathers without guns to conduct a blood feud with an army?

What happened to Loling was all the more hideous for being so exactly contrary to the prior actions of the Japanese in her town. True, the Hapons had been harsh, the people said. Men had been beheaded; men had been crucified; men had died head down over slow fires. But those things had happened during the fighting. Did the Hapons intend that such things would continue?

They most certainly did. What happened in the market place that bright June day was only the beginning. What the people of Mindanao did not know was that the Japanese who had conquered the island were no longer on it. The uniforms were the same, but the men were different. Like all combat veterans, the Japanese first-line troops had done their grisly job with a strange compassion. They conquered without anger, giving the expiatory candy to the orphans in the towns and the comradely cigarettes to the prisoners. Then they left Mindanao to resume the impossible burden of their austere pity in the South Pacific. They left Mindanao to the Kempetai, the unbelievably sadistic Thought Police, and to the occupation troops. The occupation troops, chiefly Koreans and Formosans, were the refuse of the Japanese Army, and it was they who were to bring the real meaning of defeat to Mindanao.

It is not the women only who are unsafe, the bamboo telegraph warned. *Did you hear of the Chinese merchant? When the Hapons found him hiding in a carved chest, they laughed like children playing games. They tied the chest tight with wire. They carried it out of the house and piled brush around it. Many people saw this thing. When the fire began, they could hear the Chinese, although the chest was thick and well made. The Hapons laughed much, but the people who saw this felt it was not good, even though it was only a Chinese.*

Did you hear of the horse? the bamboo telegraph asked. *The Hapons buried a horse in the plaza, raising a monument. The Hapons say the horse is a hero of the war, and all must bow to the dead horse of the Hapons.*

The Hapons are sick men, the bamboo telegraph said, *for who but sick men could think of the things they do?*

They are not only sick but very stupid, the bamboo telegraph reported, *for they are unable to distinguish between an idiot and an intelligent man. They questioned a foolish boy, who naturally did not know that he was being questioned. Hapons held him while others began to strip the flesh from his legs because he would not answer them.*

Still the boy could not answer but kept crying and shrieking because this hurt very much, and of course he did not know why this was happening. But the Hapons, still not understanding the nature of the boy, kept cutting until the boy was dead with the bones sticking out below his knees, and still the Hapons had learned nothing.

In the face of this horror that came to Mindanao in June, as unrelieved as it was capricious, men did what they could. Some raced to embrace the Japanese. Their number was small and almost exclusively restricted to those of wealth, who sought to save what they could for themselves by taking office in the Japanese-created civil government, an instrument that did not govern but confiscated. Others accepted rank in the puppet Bureau of Constabulary—a police militia—and others engaged in business with the Japanese.

Most Filipinos, however, stayed as far as possible from the Japanese, flying from their barrios at the news of a patrol approaching. Many who had come back to the towns in the moment between the surrender and the beginning of the defeat now returned to their former evacuation places.

But in the country, another horror appeared: bandit gangs. These were bands of criminals; of tough guys; of village carabao thieves; of those young men and boys for whom peace has little place but who find purpose in violence and opportunity in chaos. Armed with a variety of weapons ranging from bolos to stolen rifles, they began to raid villages for loot, food, and women. If anything, they were more terrible than the Japanese. Once again, the Moros were also raiding, and at this point, many Filipinos of good will went to the Japanese, begging them to exterminate the bandits and stop the Moros, but the conquerors blandly smiled.

As the meaning of defeat became increasingly clear, there remained nothing to the people but jokes, the last defense of the helpless. They took to calling the Great East Asia Co-Prosperity Sphere "Prosperity Akko." Pleased with what they thought a popular abbreviation, the Japanese took up the phrase. Later, when the Japanese discovered that akko meant "for you only" in the dialect, the Japanese reprisals were gruesome indeed.

Yet, because unmitigated horror cannot be borne, the jokes continued, and one of the best was that of the young boy who had gone to high school.

The boy was coming down the road into Iligan from his barrio, the bamboo telegraph reported, *and he stopped to talk to the Hapon who guards the bridge and who likes young boys.*

"Have you killed many Americanos with your bayonet?" the boy asked, and the guard said he had.

"Show me how you killed them," the boy asked, and the guard roared, stamping his feet, thrusting at the air with his bayonet.

"If I join the Hapon Army, will I be given a bayonet to kill Americanos?" the boy asked, and the guard said yes.

"Show me again," the boy said, and the guard roared and stamped, thrusting into the air, and the boy asked if he could try to do these things with the guard teaching him. So the guard gave the boy his rifle and stood beside him.

"Like this?" the boy asked, roaring in his high voice and stamping, and the guard said, "No, like this," and then gave the rifle back to the boy to see whether he had learned.

"Oh," the boy said, jabbing at the air, but moving a bit away. "Like this?"

The guard said yes, that was better, and the boy roared and thrust, but moving a step farther off as the guard watched. And then, jabbing and roaring, the boy killed many Americanos in the air, always moving a little farther away, and when he was several yards away, the boy shouted, "Charge!" and dashed off to fight more Americanos in the air with the guard watching stupidly.

Then the guard gave a great shout, but the boy was running now, and the guard started running after the boy who had stolen his rifle. But just then three carabaos came across the road between the guard and the boy who was running away. The guard shouted at the man who owned the carabaos, and boxed him in the face many times, but the boy was gone.

And this is what proves the Hapons are stupid, the bamboo telegraph said. *The Hapons did not know that the carabaos belonged to the boy's uncle.*

Thus the bamboo telegraph reported the events of late June 1942 on the island of Mindanao, and, for the several hundred Americans who hid in the hills and jungles, there was a sort of special branch line that carried news of interest to them. When Moros murdered an American family in Lanao province, the news was not long in reaching Americans in Zamboanga to the south and Americans in Surigao in the north. By word passed along from mouth to ear, as the people said, the fugitive Americans learned of one another's presence and general whereabouts, and so, of course, did the Japanese. It was a curious situation, something like a rural party-line telephone circuit, with everyone listening in and sometimes with several people speaking on the line at once. Every scrap of gossip and unsubstantiated rumor that the bamboo telegraph carried ultimately became common property, and all of it was carefully studied in a patch of burned-over jungle near Momungan, where a tall man with a red goatee spent his days scratching with a crude hoe among charred stumps, planting mongo beans.

TURNING THE FIRE-BLACKENED earth and ripping out the complicated root systems of the subsoil with his somewhat delicately boned hands, Wendell Fertig had planted corn and tobacco. Now he was planting the little beans that were a kind of pea about the size and texture of BB shot, the beans the government used to feed the prisoners before the war. Gravely, Fertig considered that people who thought mongo beans were fit only for pigs and prisoners were making a great mistake. Alone of all the islanders, the prisoners' hair had been naturally sleek and oily, their faces fat, and their skin lustrous. Alone of all the islanders, the prisoners ate mongo beans.

Fertig's sun-chapped lips split in a smile. The inference was inescapable. He wished all his problems were as susceptible to orderly conclusions. He thought of mongo beans and of many other things as he scratched the ground of his kaingin. The garden was not primarily important to him for what it might produce, although food was in short supply and, to add to all the other problems of the island, the seven-year locusts had come together with the usual locusts this year. There was also a plague of rats.

Clearing the jungle, then fighting it each day with his hands to prevent it from reclaiming his land, gave Fertig busywork. The work tired him sufficiently to permit him to go to his sleeping mat at once when night came, but it left his mind free. The garden was essentially Fertig's thinking place. Hope was the crop he was really trying to raise from the thin, damp loam. It was characteristic of everything he did that his work in the garden also produced something else. Food was its by-product.

The clearing was barely two miles from the Momungan road, at the edge of land owned by Mrs. MacMichael, an aged Mora who had married a veteran of the Spanish-American war. Fertig had come to it with Hedges and Offret because Deischer's camp had proved to be nothing but a wet hole in the jungle, lacking even the amenities of Datu Soong's village in the Rogungan Valley. The thirty-some American soldiers and sailors at Deischer's were as impossible as the camp's location. They wanted only to be left alone. They resented officers, would not take orders, and would do nothing but sit there, rotting in the jungle, living off the store of army rations that Deischer, an old prospector and boar hunter, had somehow acquired. Fertig wondered what they would do when the food was gone. The young Americans did not seem to know or care.

Wholly apart from the apathy of the fugitives, Deischer's camp was not healthful. The MacMichael farm was exposed, but it was open, light, and as free from malaria as any place on Mindanao could be. Sunlight and fresh food would help keep Hedges' malaria in check. Moreover, the MacMichaels could be trusted, for not only had the woman married an American, but Fred, one of her sons, had once worked for Hedges. Further, the farm had the jungle behind it, into which a man could slip at need, and meanwhile it was attuned to all the channels of the bamboo telegraph, as Deischer's camp was not. Few rumors filtered as far back as Deischer's, but each week, Mrs. MacMichael would walk ten miles to the Japanese-garrisoned town of Dansalan to barter for fish and matches, bringing back all the gossip of the market place.

Fertig went to his garden each day in a freshly laundered uniform glittering with the badges of his rank, taking his rifle with him. He wore his uniform with conscious pride, and the red goatee was as deliberate an addition to his appearance as General MacArthur's gilt-gay hat was to the General's. Fertig had raised his goatee for three reasons: first, to make himself look older in a land that believed age implied wisdom; second, because almost no Filipinos had beards but were in awe of those who did; and third, because his beard was red. Fertig decided that he would be the unsurrendered colonel with the sun helmet and the red goatee. He wanted no mistakes made. He was not hiding. He would not don the wide, conical hat and tattered clothes of the tao to appear at a distance as just another kainginero scratching out a life on the edge of a forest. He wanted everyone to know from afar exactly who he was. He was an American officer, armed and free, standing on United States territory; the living reminder that this was—despite the presence of the Japanese—still United States territory and that The Aid would come.

But, as the Japanese casually robbed, tortured, and raped a defenseless people in a land from which all law and order had vanished, belief in The Aid was rapidly becoming academic. Unwilling to give up belief in a myth, men still spoke of The Aid, but, each day that it did not come, the Americans were increasingly regarded as the proof of broken promises, as derisive examples of the basic emptiness and false pride of the white man. At best, the position of the unsurrendered Americans was ambiguous. Some were robbed and killed. Some Filipinos sought favor with the Japanese by reporting the hiding places of Americans. But other Filipinos died under torture without betraying their American friends. Perhaps most Filipinos were loyal, but no American could be sure that all the Filipinos he met were, in fact, his friends.

Meanwhile, the Japanese terror increased. There was no foreseeable end to it, no escape from it, no apparent way to stop it. To emphasize the latter point, the Japanese announced a celebration: There would be a Fourth of July parade down the National Road from Dansalan to Iligan. Fertig and Hedges were among the hundreds who watched it from hiding.

They lay with their rifles beside them among the anonymous bushes and feathery talahib grasses that grew in the shade of a jackfruit tree. From their nest atop a steep bluff, they could see the road, white and shimmering in the heat, twist down from the southern uplands to pass directly beneath them. Then the road turned to fall beside the swift river that led to the banana groves and the coconut trees of the northern coast.

They lay quietly, sweating lightly in the shade, and at noon, they heard the sound of a truck, bumping and complaining downhill in low gear. Then they could see the truck moving slowly toward them, the dust rising dejectedly behind it.

"Here they come," Hedges said needlessly, his voice as empty as the washed blue of the sky. His hand closed around the polished stock of his rifle. "Who have the bastards got in the truck? It looks like Fort," he said.

It was. It was Brigadier General Fort, leading the parade.

He was sitting alone, bareheaded in the sun. The two men in hiding did not need field glasses to identify the General. They could see well enough the slight, spare frame, the thinning gray hair. The General was sitting as stiffly as he could in the open bed of the truck that jolted over the hand-laid stream boulders of the road, wearing his silver stars.

As he came closer, they could see the familiar, weather-burned but somewhat schoolteacherish features. General Fort was holding tightly to his pride while his troops shambled along in his wake. They could not march well with their hands wired together behind them. The wires ate into their livid wrists, and they were all wired together, so that, when one of them staggered, his companions also staggered.

Like their general, the American soldiers were bareheaded. Many of them had fragments of uniforms; all of them were ragged, dirty, and un-shaved. Those who were barefoot never looked up but hopped and faltered and jerked in their telephone wires as they picked their way over the hot stones of the road in the dust and exhaust fumes of their general's truck. They were gaunt and sick and seemed past care, and they loomed ludicrously tall over the strutting little soldiers who prodded them along the road.

"Son of a bitch," Hedges said, softly. It was not a comment but a prayer.

The little soldiers in the sloppy gray-green uniforms carried rifles with long bayonets. Some had tied handkerchiefs over their faces to keep out the dust. Their dark eyes glittered above the dirty handkerchiefs, and they clomped across the cobblestones in their hobnailed boots, lightly jabbing their bayonets into the buttocks of the trussed Americans to keep them moving briskly down the National Road in the bright light of high noon on the Fourth of July.

The parade passed beneath the bluff, and, as it turned down the curve that led to the north, the watchers saw one of the Americans lurch and fall. He fell slowly, partially supported by the wires. Three of the guards dashed in from the sides of the column and kicked him, poked at him first with the butts, then with the bayonets of their rifles. The watchers could hear their shrill, excited voices. Their voices always worked into a higher pitch when they were worried, or frightened, or drunk, or overjoyed. They shouted at the fallen American and at each other in harsh, staccato eruptions.

The bandy-legged little gray-green soldiers cut the American loose from his companions and half-carried, half-hurled him across the road toward a clump of banana plants. At the side of the road, two of them held the American up by his armpits, his head lolling above them, while a third stopped, set himself, and lunged. The American screamed once as the steel went in. It was a surprisingly loud scream for a man so tired. The guard put his left foot up against the American's belly and kicked the bayonet loose. The two guards released him, and the American fell. Then all three guards stabbed at the twitching figure at their feet.

Then they threw it into the banana grove and, shouting, followed it into the shade of the leaves.

The men on the bluff glanced briefly at each other. They could hear the light rifles cracking among the bananas. They saw the guards come running out of the grove and down the road to resume their positions along the flanks of the military parade that, meanwhile, had continued impersonally to pour down the hill and around the turn.

Later that day, Fertig and Hedges learned what had happened when the parade reached Iligan. There, the Japanese halted the Americans to give them water. They allowed them to drink from the filthy gutters at the edges of the dirt street. Then the Japanese put the half-starved Americans to work as stevedores on the docks, to show the Filipinos that Americans could not themselves do well the kind of work that Americans had always paid Filipinos to do. They set American officers to servants' tasks in a camp of Filipino officer-prisoners. They tried in every way possible to degrade and humiliate the white man before the Asian eyes of the people of Iligan, but the people of that town learned a lesson the Japanese least suspected. They learned there was a brotherhood of human suffering. Never again in Iligan was the position of the fugitive American in the least ambiguous.

Listening to the stories from Iligan, shaken by what he had seen on the road, Fertig found himself hounded to the decision he had long known, somewhere in his mind, that he would one day have to make, the decision for which he had subconsciously been preparing himself. In all the time he had hoed his garden, sorting out the stories, fitting everything into place, he had known that no man can forever sit idle with a gun in his hands and watch his friends be bayoneted. No man can ever hide from any evil or pretend that it will go away of its own accord.

Hiding was no answer; moreover, hiding was impossible. Three times now, the bamboo telegraph had spoken in Fertig's ear. Each time, the message said that the Japanese commander in Momungan wanted Fertig to know that, if he would surrender quietly, no one would be harmed.

Indeed, Captain Yamato in Momungan had even sent Fertig a personal letter.

Do you feel duty to flow your blood while you have no master to serve for? Captain Yamato had written. *You should not be so fooly as to flow your blood standing for America when your comrades accepting Japan heartful advice are surrender. It is necessary to flow your blood in behalf of Philippines now? I believe that God did not teach you to perform such a funny duty. Do you think God help you to perform such a foundless duty.*

I herewith declare solemnly that I will guarantee the safety of your life if you obey my advice instantly and come to Japan Army. You must keep in your mind that I gave strict order to all companies and soldiers, never to threaten your life or even do any injuries to you. Now I want to tell some more latest. I wish you to understand my will, and obey my words instantly, impressing in your mind that there would be no again opportunity to send you my heartful advice, and pray to your God together with you that you will be happier. Respectfully yours, Yamato, commander, Japanese Army in Momungan.

Fertig had ignored the messages, but now, after this grotesque celebration of the Fourth of July, he decided the time had come to surrender himself to the Japanese, but not in the sense that Captain Yamato had in mind.

"Charley," he said, suddenly feeling as weightless as a man who drops a heavy pack at the end of a long trail, "you and I are going to make it as rough as we can on the little bastards."

2

FERTIG CAME DOWN from his kaingin to the MacMichaels' house to find the guerrilleros squatting on their haunches in the farmyard. They were slender, hard-faced riflemen, barefoot, dressed in an uninteresting assortment of straw hats, cloth caps, parts of uniforms, and rags. They rose as Fertig approached, saluting in a variety of ways. Fertig crisply returned their salute and strode through the yard to meet Hedges, who waited for him on the steps.

"Wendell," Hedges said flatly, "Bill Tait's here."

Hedges' dour look held no warmth, no disapproval. As far as Hedges was concerned, he had delivered his warning as a highway curve sign delivers its warning.

"Good," Fertig said.

The sala of the farmhouse seemed to be filled by the tall, muscular figure of a coal-black Negro, dressed in a dirty Moro malong. The Negro slammed himself into an exaggerated attention and held a proud salute until it was returned. Fertig extended his hand, which seemed to surprise his visitor, and waving him to a chair, Fertig said, "You have come far to see me, Lieutenant."

"Yes, sir, Colonel," Tait said, smiling with a flash of white teeth. "It's an idea I hope you'll be interested in."

Like a dog that turns around once before lying down, Tait instinctively glanced about the room before accepting the proffered chair. His black eyes slid over Offret, who was standing in a corner of the room behind the chair, and over Hedges, who stood negligently against the wall in the opposite corner, behind Fertig, from which position Hedges could also see into the yard where the guerrilleros squatted.

Tightly controlling his excitement, Fertig ordered his features into a somewhat stern if not brutal look. Tait came right to the point.

"Colonel, sir," he said earnestly, "Captain Morgan sent me here to ask if you'd take command of our troops."

"Oh, he did, did he?" Fertig asked, searching Tait's handsome face.

"Yes, sir, Colonel, sir," Tait said quickly, nodding vigorously. "Yes, sir. It was Captain's idea, sir."

"Many speak of you and of Captain Morgan," Fertig said non-committally.

"And *I'm* one of them," Hedges interrupted from his corner. "*I* told the Colonel you were a damned thief."

Tait smiled in the way that Orientals smile to cover a momentary embarrassment.

"I just want you to know where we stand," Hedges said.

"Yes, sir," Tait said.

"Before you tell me why Captain Morgan wishes me to take command," Fertig said evenly, "you will tell me about yourself, Lieutenant. Then you will tell me about Captain Morgan and your organization. We have heard much rumor, but now we will hear the truth."

Tait politely inclined his head and readily admitted that what Captain Hedges said was true. There had been some little troubles. But that, he said, was before the war. He then embarked on a story more or less like the stories that Fertig had already heard. The whole of it, not all of which Tait told, was this:

Tait was the mestizo son of an army veterinarian who had served with the old Negro cavalry regiments in the Moro Pacification Campaign and who had married a Mora and settled near Momungan in the homestead community of Spanish War veterans. Physically, Bill Tait seemed as purely Negro as his father but proved to be as wildly harum-scarum as any Moro that might have graced his mother's tribe. As a youth, he was always in and out of mischief and later was involved in endless petty breakings or bendings of the law. When war came, Tait volunteered but was turned down—ostensibly because of lack of training. Although Tait always spoke and thought of himself as an American citizen, he joined the Japanese puppet Bureau of Constabulary immediately after the surrender. The Japanese assigned him to be a translator for Kamimai, a spy who had lived in Mindanao for six years before the war with no visible means of support. After the surrender, Kamimai tramped the trails of Lanao and Misamis Oriental and Occidental provinces, giving a prepared speech in each little municipality.

"All must cooperate with Imperial Japanese Government," Kamimai would shout in broken Visayan.

"Let us kill this fool. He is not armed," Tait would shout in English, aping the utterly serious pomposity of Kamimai, and the young people of the village who knew English would raise a startled cheer.

Then Kamimai would portentously read the famous Japanese Seventeen-Point Proclamation, which stated that violation of any of its clauses would be punished by death. He would conclude: "Civil government will function in normal manner. All men bring families back home, live happy life."

And Tait, towering over this representative of His Imperial Majesty, would solemnly shout in English: "Do not believe this fool. He has no authority. Keep your wives and daughters in the mountains."

At the end of each of Tait's sentences, the villagers would shout their approval, while Kamimai swelled with pride. Returning to Iligan, Kamimai praised Tait so highly that the Japanese made the former carabao thief their police chief of Momungan, whereupon Tait asked for a hundred rifles in order that he might combat raiding Moros. The Japanese sent the rifles at once, whereupon Tait demanded more. Eventually, the Japanese caught on to the fact that the rifles were passing into guerrillero hands, but Tait's sensitive antennae warned him in time to abscond before the punitive patrol arrived. Tait's last official act as police chief was to shoot all the paid informers who had sold their services to the Japanese. He fled to the northern coast and made his way to Baroy, where he had become a lieutenant in Morgan's band.

From the bamboo telegraph, Fertig had already heard much of Luis Morgan, or, as he was sometimes called, William Morgan, or, as he sometimes called himself, fancying a descent from the pirate, Morgan Morgan. An American mestizo, Morgan had been a junior lieutenant of Philippine Constabulary. According to rumor, Morgan had been ordered to take his troops from Kolambugan to Lake Lanao when the Japanese struck. Instead, after wantonly burning the big sawmill at Kolambugan, Morgan marched his company off to the sleepy, out-of-the-way town of Baroy, deep at the end of the southeast coast of Panguil Bay, collecting en route 400 other Filipino soldiers. Promoting himself to captain, Morgan assigned himself the mission of protecting the Christian farmers of Baroy from Moro raiders. A burly, harsh policeman who believed in direct action, Morgan first rounded up the thirty Moro men, women, and children who lived peacefully in Baroy with their Christian neighbors, and had them machine-gunned to death in a warehouse. Such protection had a price. Emerging from the shambles in the warehouse, Morgan demanded a woman for the night. He made it clear to the presidente of Baroy that he would expect a different woman each night, and rice and money for his men. Then he established a perimeter defense against Moro vengeance and sat down in the middle of his new grand duchy to exact tribute while the Americans lost the war. Tait, however, told Fertig that Morgan was a fearless patriot who had escaped the surrender, keeping a well-armed, disciplined force intact.

"But the trouble is, Colonel, sir," Tait told Fertig politely, "that we, Captain Morgan, now have so many men that some Filipino officers who did not fight but 'vacuated only now think to come down and take command and be big *shots*. All have higher rank than Captain Morgan. Soon they will come, for one is already whispering. It is like politics, Colonel, sir."

Tait paused expectantly, but Fertig remained silent. The situation Tait was describing was exactly what Fertig had predicted to himself. Ever since the Fourth of July parade, Hedges had been raging at Fertig to make good his promise and do something. Hedges wanted at least to kill a sentry, to cut telephone lines, to bushwhack a patrol, to do anything to break the endless monotony of the tropical days and give them all some feeling of purpose. But Fertig had insisted that they wait. Over and over again, Fertig had argued that Americans could not start a guerrilla, that nobody would follow the Americans who had lost both the war and their face, that impetus for a guerrilla must come from the Filipino people. We can lead a guerrilla, he told Hedges, but we cannot start one.

Meanwhile, as Hedges fumed, July had become August, and scores of guerrilla bands appeared throughout the island. Arming themselves with homemade weapons, men collected around former Philippine Army sergeants who called themselves lieutenants and around lieutenants who promoted themselves to majors, colonels, and even generals. The guerrilleros called themselves patriots, and each insisted that his movement was the first and only true guerrilla, but few fought against the Japanese. Rather, they fought the bandit gangs in their neighborhoods and against each other, jockeying for obscure political power in their remote principalities. The Japanese paid them little attention, being entirely willing to allow the guerrilleros to kill one another, but Fertig found hope in this chaos.

"We'll sit tight," he told Offret and Hedges, "until some guerrillero gets too big for his britches. The first one that puts together some real following is going to find himself in over his head, and he'll need help. He won't get it from his rivals, and he sure won't get it from the Japs, and that leaves us. He'll come to us or to some other Americans, because, even if the white man's face isn't worth a dime right now, we are still the ones who know what needs to be done and how to make things work. But just remember this: Things will never be the same out here again. No longer do we barge in and tell them what to do. We wait until we're asked. Then we'll help."

Now, apparently, such a moment had come, but Fertig let Tait see nothing of his thoughts.

"So Captain Morgan has this idea," Tait said, disconcerted by Fertig's silence. "Not one, no, sir, not even one person has more rank than a United States Army colonel, sir. If you come and take command, they might murmur, but not one will say anything—not one damn thing, sir. You would be The One, the only real commander. Captain Morgan, because these are our men, would be chief of staff."

"Yes," Fertig said. "I see your point, Lieutenant."

Fertig saw the point very well. Morgan and Tait would use him as their front man, meanwhile carefully retaining control over their banditti. Tait smiled appreciatively at the Colonel's understanding.

"Now, sir," Tait said briskly, "this is what Captain Morgan says. We will start a rumor that an American general has come from General MacArthur in Australia to assume command of all guerrilla forces on Mindanao. Not one will question an American general from Australia, sir, and everybody is feeling good that General MacArthur has remembered and sent us a general."

"And I'd be that general," Fertig said drily.

"Yes, sir, you'd be that general," Tait said seriously.

"And Captain Morgan, as chief of staff, would be a colonel, no?"

"Oh, yes, sir, of course, sir," Tait said. "A general's chief of staff is always a colonel, sir."

"And you would be a major, or maybe a lieutenant colonel?"

Tait chose to regard the question as rhetorical. He maintained a polite silence while Fertig sorted the matter over in his mind. It was a typically indirect, Oriental notion. It was also a brilliant one. The propaganda potential was fantastic. No matter how much face America had lost, General MacArthur had lost little. To the Filipinos, he was a legend, a hero, a father. A general officer from MacArthur's headquarters *could* legitimately claim command not only of Morgan's organization but of all the squabbling guerrilla bands on Mindanao and, indeed, of all the guerrilla bands in the entire archipelago. Such an officer could give the guerrilla the single source of direction it badly needed. A commander from headquarters would also be the *de facto* military governor of the island, if not of all the Philippines,

invested with the delegated authority of both the Philippine Commonwealth and the United States government. Fertig wondered if Tait and
Morgan had seen this far. If they had not, they lost nothing; if they had,
they had much, much more to gain than command over 500 of the kind
of men who squatted impassively on their haunches outside the farmhouse. Fertig wondered if Morgan, the policeman, or Tait, the sometime
village delinquent, saw themselves in the presidential palace in Manila.

The trouble was, Morgan had more of a reputation as an extermina-
tor of Moros than as a killer of Japanese. If he were to take up Morgan's
offer, the first thing he would have to do would be to arrange some kind
of understanding with the Moros.

But that was not the only trouble. Tait had not told everything. It was
Tait's habit of not saying quite everything that had always made Hedges
wary of him before the war. Fertig also sensed there was probably more to
Tait's proposal than met the eye, but what neither he nor Hedges guessed
was this:

It was not Morgan's idea. It was Tait's, and his alone. Tait had risen
thus far with Morgan. But Tait knew that, if Morgan was supplanted by
one of those senior Filipino officers, there would be only crumbs from
the banquet for himself. And Tait knew also that Morgan was too proud
to turn his command over to any such officer without a fight that could
shatter the organization beyond repair.

Therefore, this is what Tait had told Morgan: "General MacArthur
has sent an American general to command the resistance. He came by
submarine to Nasipit. He is now at Momungan. If we get to him first, we
make a deal so that you become commander of all the guerrilla troops,
while he does the office work that generals do and talks with the civil-yan
big shots. The rumor says that he is making inspection only at this time.
Why don't I go bring him to us?"

Morgan, suspecting nothing, agreed at once. Tait was well aware that
Morgan was not the kind of man on whom one can safely perpetrate little
hoaxes, but he had already planned how to divert Morgan's wrath when it
came. He would say that he, Tait, had also been misled by the false rumor
about an American general. But, since they had now asked Fertig to be
their commander, why not use him just as if he had really been a general
sent from Australia; why not bluff it out and insist that he was? Because he
was not what he seemed, Fertig would be all the easier for them to control.

Fertig, unaware of the extent of Tait's deviousness toward both himself and Morgan, sat stroking his goatee, his face an alert, unreadable
mask. Of course he would accept!

Rising suddenly, offering Tait his hand in farewell, Fertig said: "Thank you very much for coming here, and give Captain Morgan my regards."

"You will take command, sir?" Tait asked.

"I shall send Captain Morgan notice of my decision," Fertig said coldly, escorting Tait to the door.

"YOU AREN'T GOING TO THROW your hand in with them, are you, Wendell?" Hedges wanted to know as soon as Tait and his ragtag army were out of sight.

"I think we will," Fertig said. "It sounds like just what we've been waiting for."

"I wouldn't trust that Tait any farther than I can throw an anvil," Hedges said, "and I wouldn't trust that murdering bastard Morgan at all."

"We're not going to trust them," Fertig said. "We're going to command them."

"That's not what they think."

"Maybe they'll change their minds," Fertig said. "You know, a commanding officer is in a peculiar position. If he wants to exercise command, all he has to do is to command."

"What's that supposed to mean?"

"Look at it this way," Fertig said carefully. "We're not going to go down there to Baroy just to sit in a three-card monte game in a hideout with Tait and Morgan. We'll go down there and inspect the troops, and, by God, they'll know there's been an inspection. We'll have an officer's call. We'll meet all the junior officers as individuals, and every one of them— not just Tait and Morgan—will meet the new commanding officer. By the time we're through, every one of them, officers and soldiers, will know that I *am* the general from Australia."

"Who do you think you're going to be kidding?" Hedges demanded. "You think they won't know what the score is?"

"Now look, Charley," Fertig said. "Here it is: Morgan's going to have to play along with us. He's got to be sure that everybody believes this story, or the whole scheme blows up in his face. If that happens, he doesn't have an army any more. Some politico will not only move in on him, but Morgan will have lost so much face that he couldn't even stay in Baroy.

"Once his boys believe that I *am* the commanding general," Fertig continued, "Morgan is no longer the commander. Now they're *my* troops, and not *Morgan's*. It's coming through, huh? They won't be guerrillas, they'll be United States troops. By definition, a commanding general cannot be a subordinate. All a commander has to do to exercise command is to issue orders, knowing that they will be obeyed, because they are issued in a manner that cannot be questioned. You see, he *is* the commanding general.

"It struck me," Fertig concluded, "that maybe those two smart boys hadn't figured this one out."

"That sounds too easy, Wendell. There's got to be something wrong with it."

"Well, we don't know," Fertig said. "Maybe there is. We'll let Tait and Morgan sweat it out for a few days, so it won't look as if we'd been summoned like a couple of houseboys. Then we'll go down and see what's going on. From here, it sounds good, but it might not look so good up close."

"I don't trust those birds," Hedges said.

"Cheer up," Fertig said. "Neither do I."

3

THE WOMEN RAN, howling, their loose breasts flopping under thin dresses. They clutched their skirts up around their bellies in order to run faster, not caring who saw their bare bottoms in the daylight.

"Hapons! Hapons!" they shrieked, spattering down the trail that led through the village. Behind them, gaining on them, came the stubby little Texan Charles Smith, who had been standing guard up the trail. Smith was also shouting as he ran.

Hedges and Jordan Hamner flew down the bahi's bamboo ladder and down the trail to the north, the way the women were running. People burst from every house in the village and scattered in a dozen directions, into the bamboos, down the trail, into the bananas, into the fields, anywhere, with chickens exploding from under the houses and all the dogs of the barrio yapping delightedly and running, too. In this same moment, a file of Japanese broke cover to the south, and Fertig, who had been transferring eggs from skillet to messkit when the shouting began, threw the messkit one way and the skillet another.

He threw all the packs that were on the porch beside him into the tall grasses that grew around the bahi.

Still all in the same moment, he came tumbling down the ladder to grab the panting Smith. They ran heavily around to the back of the house, bending low, and raced through the high grass up a little hill that lay west of the trail. Atop the hill, Smith fumbled with a pair of field glasses. He muttered something about counting the Japanese. Fertig swung him around to the north.

"Look!" Fertig said. "Another bunch! Coming *up* the trail! Goddamn it, we're boxed! My God, Ham and Charley are going to run right into them!"

At this moment, it appeared that Hedges and Hamner realized their mistake. Fertig could see them stop, hesitate, and plunge into a field of man-high cogon. But the Japanese had seen them, too. Fertig could see the puffs of smoke before he heard the light rifles snapping.

Oh, Jesus, Fertig thought, but there was no time for the image of Hedges to more than hurtle through his mind, because he and Smith were running down the hill, across a narrow valley toward a higher rise covered with stunted coconut trees. Halfway up, sheltered in the trees, they looked back. The Japanese were methodically fanning out to encircle the cogon into which Hedges and Hamner had disappeared.

"There isn't anything we can do," Fertig said.

"Not one damn thing," Smith agreed.

They turned and worked to the top of the rise, finding that they could sit beneath the trees, hidden well enough in the grasses that grew there, and watch all approaches.

A light breeze brought them an occasional thin screaming. They wondered whether the Japanese had caught the two men, or the women. The sounds were too distant to tell.

They sat quietly on the hilltop while locusts chirred in the heat. Now and again, they heard the light crack of a Japanese rifle and the random yapping of the barrio dogs. They sat tense, needing to listen to any sound.

So this is the way it is, Fertig thought, listening. You grow up, fall in love, get married, have children, work at your job. What else was life? Then they take your wife and children away, take your job away, give you a gun, and leave you stuck alone on some god-forsaken naked hill. He consciously relaxed, feeling alive. He had never felt less like dying. He saw the sweat glistening among the dark hairs on Smith's bronzed neck. Smith was alive, too.

Offret hadn't come. They had left Offret at the MacMichael farm, twisted with dysentery. Everyone pretended to believe that Offret would follow them to Morgan's headquarters at Baroy as soon as he could walk. Smith and Hamner had come to the farm just as Hedges and Fertig were about to leave to join Morgan. They were mining engineers whom Fertig had known before the war, and they arrived at the MacMichaels' after an odyssey as confused as any fugitive's. They, too, had passed through Deischer's jungle camp, which, they said, had been attacked by Moros. Neither Hamner nor Smith wanted anything to do with the war. They wanted to buy or steal a native boat and sail to Australia.

Australia was the other dream. One dream was The Aid, and the other was Australia. Neither dream had a damned thing to do with reality. In one dream, "they" would bring The Aid to save you. In the other, "they" would protect you in Australia. But the reality was, there was no "they." There was only you. The Japanese in the fields were looking for you.

Japanese had hounded them ever since they left the relative security of the back-country farm. Japanese trucks ceaselessly patrolled the seacoast highway that led to Baroy. Japanese launches stopped every fishing boat offshore, searching for Americans and smuggled rifles. Japanese moved everywhere throughout this fertile coastal plain, and, in addition to the routine patrols, it was clear that a special detachment was hunting Fertig's party. But, always before, there had been plenty of warning. Someone must have told the Japanese during the night, some wretched little barrio traitor trying to save his daughter or his rice or his carabao.

The day hung still. There was no sound, except that of the locusts. Nor could Fertig see any Japanese working in the cogon.

In the late afternoon, a Filipino began to make his way up their hill. He moved in an aimless fashion, like a dog casting for a scent. Our pal, the barrio traitor, Fertig thought, slipping the safety catch of his rifle.

Smith and Fertig peered through the grass, their rifles trained on the solitary Filipino. He was an antique, barefoot man in rags who, seeming to move aimlessly, nonetheless came steadily toward them. As he picked his way along, they heard him saying softly: "Kaibegan[26] . . . salaamit Opo . . . I am friend . . . kaibegan . . ."

They waited for him to find them.

He was a farmer.

He said that the Hapons had had lunch at his house. He and his wife had not run because they were too old to run, and he did not think the Hapons would use his wife, although sometimes they used old women as well as the little girls. He said they had not used her. Most of the Hapons had returned to Kolambugan, he said.

No, he did not know what had happened to their companions, but the Hapons had no prisoners when they came out of the cogon. There had been much shootings in the field, he said.

Not all the Hapons had gone, but he felt sure the last would leave before dark, because the Hapons did not like to move in the back country at night unless the moon was full. The Hapons are very terrible when the moon is full, he said.

But here, he said, and fishing in his rags, he brought out a banana leaf folded into a package.

"You will be hungry," he told them. Unfolding the leaf, he showed them the double handful of cooked rice.

---

26. kaibegan = friend

"Remain here," he said, "until you are benighted. If no one comes, you are to come to my bahi."

With that, he gave them directions and moved down the hill with the same apparent lack of purpose he had assumed on his way up. If the Hapons saw him, they would realize he was an old man in rags who had nothing in particular to do but wait until it was time for him to die.

The rice was gritty, unsalted, undercooked, and cold. It was breakfast and lunch. They ate every chewy grain.

The afternoon dragged on, and once there was a thin clamor of distant dogs and a faint flapping of rifleshots.

Then the silence, and the locusts.

THE TWO AMERICANS stared into the valley.

"There's no way of knowing," Fertig said at last.

"They were two damned good men," Smith said.

Neither spoke of their friends. Friends are an unbearable luxury in a war. In a war, you meet people and live with them a while, and either you go away or they go away or something happens and there are new people to meet and live with for a while.

No Japanese came.

Smith reached into his shirt pocket for a packet of cigarillos that Hedges had given him.

They waited on their hilltop for the tropical night to slam day's door. They felt their way down in the blackness to a creekbed. They stumbled over wet stones to the house of the old Filipino.

The farmer's wife whom the Japanese had not wanted had stewed three whole chickens and a great heap of rice and many vegetables, but thinking of what had happened in the cogon, neither of the two Americans looked upon the feast with much appetite. Yet once they began, their need for food, if not their appetites, returned, and they ate nearly all of it.

"It has been a long day," Fertig told the farmer. "We would like to talk with you and Missus, but we are plenty tired. We will now go to bed, for we must leave this place very early. Can be?"

"Can be," the farmer said. "You sleep now, and bery early, my grandson comes to you."

"It was plenty good chow, Missus," Smith said, and the old woman smiled and said salaamit.

It seemed to Fertig he had not been asleep at all when he heard familiar voices below the window of the farmer's bahi, voices he could not quite place. He sat up and listened to the night sounds. He heard the voices again.

"Charley!" Fertig called softly into the darkness.

Smith stirred, reaching for his rifle.

"What is it?" he asked.

"Shh," Fertig said.

"Charley!" Fertig called again.

"For Christ's sake, where the hell are you?" a voice complained. It was a querulous voice Fertig knew very well.

"Goddamn it, Wendell, is that you?" Hedges wanted to know.

All thought of sleep forgotten, the four strangely reunited Americans trooped into the kitchen, where Hedges and Hamner, dirty and bloody from the cogon, demolished the rest of the reheated chicken stew before setting out with the farmer's sleepy grandson to find the coastal road that led to Baroy and Morgan. They would attempt the road again, despite its dangers, because the country trails led only into the interior and not to Baroy. There was only one way to go, and they had to take it.

"Damn, they finally had us cornered," Hedges said, "but the dogs started barking over some fool thing or other in another part of the field. The Japs—I swear they weren't a yard away from us then—all rushed to where the dogs were barking, and we crawled into an area the Japs had already searched. We just lay there with the goddamned ants eating us until it was dark. We didn't dare move to brush the ants off, I thought I'd go right out of my mind. The Japs left two men watching the cogon, but we crawled around them. We went back to the house and found you gone, but we found the gear you'd thrown away. It was a damn good thing you called, because we didn't know where the hell you were, and I was getting tired of carrying your goddamned pack."

The coral road stretched through endless coconut groves and nipa swamps. They could see the glitter of the sea through the trees, and the road was white gold in the moonlight, blotched with shadows of palm fronds and with shapeless shadows that would suddenly lurch into motion with a snorting and gusty flatulence to become startled carabaos. The carabaos would lumber aside, swinging their heavy horns with angry uncertainty.

Fertig wondered if he was not living a crazy dream. Lightheaded from fatigue and from the emotion of losing Hedges only to find him miraculously alive, Fertig wondered if the hope he pursued was not as elusive as the fireflies that winked in the shadows. Moreover, the fireflies had no chance against the bats. Even if all the fireflies in the world gathered together, Fertig doubted if they could do much about the bats. Fertig felt he watched an image of himself walk in the moonlight down a coral road full of water buffaloes.

Toward what, God only knows, Fertig thought. The odd thought struck him that God *did* know. He really did.

Fertig stumbled, and a pain shot through his hip. The stone road was impossible. His broken shoes, gritty with sand that wore his flesh, flapped as he stepped, and Fertig winced each time his weight came down on an unseen sharp stone. He hobbled along, and his three companions drew ahead. They would draw ahead and wait impatiently for him to come up. So they moved unevenly down the road, with Fertig wincing and hobbling, falling behind and catching up. He soon reached the point where all the world became gray and strange, but he did not know this was because of the coming dawn. All he knew was a single thing that kept running in his head like a broken record. Stumbling in his gray world, Fertig kept thinking, "This is a hell of a way to start a war, a hell of a way to start a war, a hell of a way to start a war."

4

FROM THE PORCH OF a bamboo house on a hillside. Fertig saw naked boys, small as monkeys, ride the necks of carabaos to the river. Downstream from the wallowing carabaos, a group of men urinated into the water, and, a few yards below, women sang as they rhythmically pounded clothing on flat stones in the riverbed. Some women bathed through their shifts. The transparent cloth creased in their honey-brown buttocks and clung to their tight nipples, but the women believed their modesty was preserved if they wore shifts while bathing. Downstream from the carabaos, the urinating farmers, the bathers, and the laundry, girls collected drinking water in bamboo tubes.

Looking on this scene, Fertig reflected that the facts of life of Asia were as public as they were illogical. For two weeks, Fertig had been living quietly in this green island of peace. Everyone in the valley was aware of the rumor that an American had been sent from Australia to command Morgan's guerrillas, and everyone knew that Fertig was The One. But Fertig had not gone to Morgan, whose headquarters were only three miles away over the low hills. He had not even sent Morgan word that he had arrived in the area. To indicate that he was aware of Morgan in any way would have betrayed anxiety, which, to the fatalistic Asiatic, is ludicrous. More important, Fertig wanted all to see Morgan come to him, for commanders can never appear to be errand boys, summoned at request. For his part, Morgan tried with equal patience to pretend that Fertig was not there. He wanted all to see Fertig come to him, to know that the Americans had chosen Morgan as the one to whom to send The Aid. To rush to Fertig would betray weakness; to go to Fertig at all would be to lose face. Everyone, including the girls carrying the drinking water, understood the silent struggle between the American and the Filipino, but everyone pretended that no such struggle existed, even while they breathlessly waited to learn how it would be resolved.

Two weeks thus passed in a stalemate curious only to those to whom Asiatics seem inscrutable. To a narrowly objective Western mind, such footless dawdling in time of war might seem incomprehensible. The West always wants to know the facts and get on with the job. But the West is intolerant of individuals; it is ridden by a witch of Time. To the Asiatic, individual face is of paramount concern, and Time is another of those brutal facts that are too .depressing to think about. Meanwhile, Time passed, as it will, no matter how much anyone wishes to pretend that it does not, and Morgan's position steadily deteriorated. It diminished to the point where Morgan had to lose some measure of face if he wished to retain any face at all. And so, at last, Morgan came to Fertig. He came in sullen state, with Bill Tait grinning whitely to his left and a pace behind him, followed by a squad of smartly uniformed soldiers carrying Browning automatic rifles.

Morgan halted his men. He spoke again, and the soldiers trotted off to take positions around the house, covering the approaches. Then Morgan strode across the yard and up the porch steps without waiting for an invitation. Fertig took one look at the guerrillero and instantly knew why the people once said, *If a man is brave, and has a gun, he joins Morgan.*

There was no question: Morgan was a king. He would have been a leader among any race of men. There was little of the Asiatic's slender roundness about him. Morgan had the firm-jawed, rectangular face of a Western athlete. He moved quickly and surely without conscious hurry. His immaculate khaki uniform was stiff with starch, and his jet hair was neatly parted and sleek with fresh coconut oil. The mestizo's skin was the deeply tanned pelt of a white man who has spent a lifetime in sun and sea-wind; his eyes were that peculiar blue-tawny color found in the eyes of the untrustworthy strain of German shepherds. A few suspected Morgan because of his eyes, but he nevertheless had the eagle look of command and the virile force to back it up. A handsome, hard-drinking, absolutely fearless young fighting man, Morgan compelled the loyalty of men and the passion of women. When he wanted a woman, he had only to ask, and it was only the customary lovers of Morgan's women who complained. Yet Morgan was a king whose power was rapidly and mysteriously disappearing, even as the moment of full tide is the beginning of the ebb. Morgan could not understand this, and things he did not understand made him uneasy and angry. He did not know that power is merely an idea in other people's minds. All he knew was that his power was melting away and that there seemed to be nothing he could do about it. All this, and more, was apparent in the way Morgan moved imperiously up the porch steps and in the way he saluted, saying: "Sir, Captain William Morgan is here to speak with *Gen-er-al* Fer-tig."

The ponderous form of military courtesy that Morgan aped would have required him to say, "requests permission to speak to the Commanding Officer." Fertig returned the salute with an irony as elaborate as Morgan's, understanding the mestizo's need for arrogance. It would be necessary for each to pretend to believe in the other's pretense. Morgan opened the conference that followed by admitting, without apology, that things were growing beyond his control; that former Philippine Army officers, the sons of ilustrado families, were scheming to gain control of his guerrillas.

"Since you are the senior United States officer on this island, I request that you take command," Morgan said.

The words were humble, but the tone was that of an imperial edict. Briefly, Morgan reviewed his problems but in a way that left no doubt of the use he intended to make of Fertig. He looked challengingly at the American, demanding an answer.

But Fertig did not answer at once. He stared contemplatively at his visitor, weighing Morgan's handsome young strength. Here was exactly the kind of Filipino leader the guerrillas demanded, if only he could be controlled.

"Captain Morgan."

The words were very cold. Fertig's mouth was a tight, downturned scar in his bearded face.

"Yes, sir," Morgan said. He had not meant to say sir.

"General Fort ordered you to take your constabulary troops from Kolambugan to the defense of Lake Lanao."

"Yes, sir," Morgan said again.

"Why did you not do so?"

"Because I knew we were going to lose," Morgan said. "So I did not obey the order."

He said this in a way that made clear just what an order meant to him. If he agreed with it, he might obey it. Then, less defiantly, Morgan found himself explaining. He had brought all his troops, with all their weapons and supplies, to Baroy.

Speaking of his troops reminded Morgan of his strength. Who was this fugitive white man to talk to him like a father to a child? Here was no general from Australia; here was simply a lieutenant colonel. He was not even a real lieutenant colonel but a mining engineer who had been given a commission. Morgan had recently learned the truth about Fertig but had agreed with Tait to spread the false rumor and use Fertig as a figurehead.

"Those who obeyed stupid orders surrendered and lost their guns," Morgan said. He, however, was free and armed. His voice hardening, Morgan spoke of his 600 riflemen, 60,000 rounds of ammunition, heavy machine guns, and automatic rifles.

Fertig let it go. He had made his point; Morgan had made his. If Fertig persisted, charging Morgan with desertion in the face of the enemy, this would whisk away the necessary web of pretense. He and Morgan had reached their first point of mutual understanding.

"Just what are your plans?" Fertig asked.

Morgan's bronze fingers drummed on the arm of his chair.

"Sir," the mestizo said, "I am glad you are free. If it is possible to work together, I think we can protect the Christians from the Moros and drive the Japs out of this area."

"Out of *what* area?"

"This—this place," Morgan shrugged. It was a shrug that could have implied the geographical limits of the municipality of Baroy or those of East Asia. What difference did it make? He wanted a simple yes or no to a question. So far, the question had not been answered, but he could not merely give Fertig his orders, for this would destroy Fertig's face and make it impossible for Fertig to pretend to command.

"Show me your table of organization," Fertig pressed in. He glanced at Tait, as though to hold Morgan's lieutenant responsible—and not Morgan—for having failed to bring staff documents to the conference.

"Table of organization?" Morgan asked. "We have no time for tables."

"Most men guard against Moros," he said, beginning to lose his English and his temper. "Organization work is not complete. I have other . . ."

"Captain Morgan," Fertig cut in, "have you brought any staff studies with you? I would like to know your logistical situation. I want to see your order of battle, your lines of march, your operational plans. I want to see the efficiency ratings of your units. You maintain a position around Baroy. Is it a static defense in depth with interlocking fields of fire? If I am to command, I need to see a precise picture of your organization."

"We can work something out," Morgan said, with an angry little gesture meant to wave all pettifogging questions aside. He had never heard of some of the terms Fertig was using, and he did not want to know what they meant, although he had a sinking feeling that perhaps they might be important. All Morgan knew was that Fertig was not leaping at the chance to gain face by accepting nominal leadership of a small army, and he could not understand this at all. He swung around to glare at Tait, who had pushed him into this farce. Tait returned an amiable Negro smile.

"Captain," Fertig's cold voice went on, "if I am willing to assume command, and if you accept my conditions, then we will begin to function as a military organization. Is that clear? We will function as a United States Army unit and not as an organized band of robbers."

Morgan's tawny eyes narrowed.

"I suggest that you return here in three days," Fertig said, sensing that he possessed bargaining power. He rose to put an abrupt end to the interview.

"I suggest that you bring all your senior officers with you," Fertig said, "so that we can discuss matters in detail and so that, if I decide to accept, everyone will understand the basis on which we will work together."

"It has been great pleasure," Morgan murmured as he got to his feet.

With supercilious politeness, Morgan saluted, faced himself about, nodded curtly to Tait, and stalked from the room. He took no notice of Hedges, who had been present throughout the interview and who now followed Morgan to the door, remaining on the porch to make sure that all of Morgan's automatic riflemen left with him.

"Well, big shot," Hedges said, after they were gone, "where do you think all that got us?"

"Damned if I know," Fertig said thoughtfully. "All I know is that you have to put your pants on one leg at a time."

WHEN MORGAN RETURNED, Fertig was wearing the silver stars of a brigadier general. They had been shaped and hammered out of coins by a Moro silversmith, and they now glinted in the morning light, one on each shoulder strap of Fertig's stiffly starched khaki shirt. Morgan saluted them satirically. Fertig's hand whipped through the briefest of returns.

"At ease," he ordered Morgan and Morgan's men.

Fertig came down the porch steps and had Morgan introduce his officers. He shook hands with each of them, each man snapping to attention as the General came before him, while Morgan looked on, as if amused, one pace to the left rear.

The conference was held in the farmhouse with Fertig standing like a schoolmaster in front of a seated class. Hedges leaned silently in a corner, looking at them all, from time to time chewing on a straw.

"I have accepted command of this organization," Fertig said. "Henceforth, our designation will be the United States Forces in the Philippines. As of this date, you gentlemen are commissioned officers on active service within the United States military establishment. . . ."

He explained their privileges and responsibilities, said he would create a unified guerrilla resistance throughout the Islands, and then, to cover the fact that he had no plans, Fertig asked questions.

It was Tait who answered. Morgan sat negligently in a chair, with the half-smile of the contemptuous, while Fertig shot questions and Tait answered them. And it was Tait who had a suggestion.

"General, sir," he said, "I think we ought to send some people over to Misamis Occidental to look around. Folks over there tell us there isn't more than a platoon of Japs in the whole province. They say just this couple of soldiers is here, and a couple there, and a couple of civilians somewhere else. The Japs tell the people they're going to collect all their rifles and any kind of guns on the fifteenth.

"Suppose I take some boys over there now, General, and collect those guns before the Japs get around to it?" Tait asked. "That way, we can find out how many Japs there really are, and the least we get out of it is some more guns. I can find out what the people say when I tell them there's a general from MacArthur come to do 'em some good."

The province of Misamis Occidental lay directly across Panguil Bay from Morgan's headquarters at Baroy. Fertig could not recall whether there had ever been an American garrison there, but he knew the province had not been defended when the Japanese invaded Mindanao.

"You've sent no patrols over there in all this time?" Fertig asked.

"No, sir," Tait said.

"Take a company and go at once," Fertig said.

"Yes, sir," Tait said. He grinned and sat down.

"I gave you an order, Lieutenant."

"Sir?" Tait rose again.

"You may go," Fertig said.

"Yes, sir," Tait said doubtfully. He looked at Morgan.

Morgan, tilted back in a chair, hands steepled together, staring at the ceiling.

Holding himself bitterly at attention, Fertig said, "You may go, even now. Pronto!"

Tait's frantic eyes slid to Fertig, back to Morgan. The guerrillero stretched, half-stifled a yawn, and jerked his thumb toward the door. Tait left.

AFTERWARDS, Hedges said, "Wendell, one of these days we're going to have trouble with that bastard, and we might as well put a stop to it right now. *I'll* kill him, if you don't want to."

"Kill who?"

"Don't be funny. Morgan. Christ, you saw him laughing at us."

"It worked, didn't it?" Fertig said. "I'll admit, for a while I didn't know if we were going to make it stick. Just remember one thing, Charley— Morgan needs us, and we need him."

Hedges said a word.

"It's just his pride," Fertig said. "Damn it, give him credit He put this thing together. Sure, he made a mistake when he pulled out instead of fighting. But he did keep an outfit together, and he's ready to fight now. He doesn't want to step aside. If this was your outfit, you wouldn't want to step down, even if you asked somebody to come in and run it for you."

"If he pulls any stuff with me," Hedges said, "I'll fix his goddamn wagon."

ON THE NIGHT OF September 13, 1942, William Tait sailed for Misamis Occidental with thirty-seven men in two small fishing boats. The reports he sent back were unbelievable. He had collected guns at Tangub. He had met no Japanese thus far; the coast seemed clear. Morgan left to join Tait, and reports came back that the guerrilleros had embarked on a triumphal procession of fiestas that carried the two of them clear around the coast of Zamboanga province and all the way to the outskirts of Zamboanga City. It was fantastic.

It seemed there had been only 125 Japanese in Misamis Occidental, all of whom were now dead. In Misamis City itself, news of Tait and Morgan's approach had encouraged the townsfolk to free themselves. Accordingly, they captured the one Japanese in town—a petty civilian official—and tied him to a tree no thicker than a stake. They tied him at the end of a rope that permitted him to run in a little circle. Before he was dead, the Japanese had been stoned almost beyond recognition as anything human, and after he was dead, dogs ate him.

Elsewhere throughout the province, the remaining Japanese died in various ways, and Fertig reflected that, if nothing else had been done, Morgan and Tait had at least bound the province to the guerrilla by blood guilt. But equally important to him were other reports about Misamis Occidental.

It was the site of one of the oldest Spanish settlements on Mindanao and hence was one of the most civilized, a land of fat farms and easy ways. Apparently, it had been undamaged by the war. The Japanese had not invaded the province because it was of absolutely no strategic importance, and no American force had tried to defend it, for exactly the same reason. The Japanese, concentrated in Davao in the south, Lake Lanao in the center, and Cagayan-Iligan-Kolambugan in the north of Mindanao, apparently intended to gather up such outlands as Misamis Occidental at their leisure. They had sent a corporal's guard into the rustic province, offering no violence and meeting with none. They had left their token force there to make an inventory and had forgotten about it.

To Fertig, an intact, undamaged province would be full of materiel of all kinds; it would be the very place to build a solid basis for a serious guerrilla, if only the Japanese would give him time. With luck, it would be weeks before the Japanese learned what had happened there and weeks more before they did anything about it. He could not understand why the Japanese had not long ago moved on Baroy to crush Morgan. There had been many rumors of an imminent Japanese attack, but nothing had come of them. Surely, the Japanese must now have heard the rumor about the American general. Possibly, they thought it a rumor and nothing more; at any rate, the Japanese had made no move from Kolambugan, and Fertig wasted no time trying to speculate why they did not. He was grateful enough for any time that anyone wished to give him. He needed now to move into Misamis Occidental to establish himself before anyone should assume that Morgan and Tait were not guerrilla patriots but simply bandits.

While Morgan and Tait were overseas, as Hedges put it, Fertig patched together a truce with the Moro Datu Umpa. It was Umpa's suggestion: If Fertig would put an end to Morgan's senseless war with the Moros, the Moros would cease their attacks on Morgan's perimeter around Baroy. Datu Umpa promised some vague sort of future help against the Japanese at an unspecified time, but Fertig put no stock in this. Merely to have the Moros neutral would be a net gain. How long the truce would last, once he had left the area, Fertig did not know. There were a great many necessary things to know that he did not know.

I AM NOT A RELIGIOUS PERSON, Wendell Fertig told his diary, *but I have certain standards to which I adhere. Not for reasons of other persons' opinions but because after all and most important, I have to live with myself. During the months in the forest, I have become acquainted with myself and developed a feeling that I do not walk alone; a feeling that a Power greater than any human power has my destiny in hand. Like a swimmer carried forward by a powerful current, I can direct my course as long as my way lies in the direction of the irresistible flow of events. Never have I lost the feeling that my actions have followed a course plotted by some Power greater than any human agency.*

He paused to look upon his world: a small, forgotten valley held in a cup of jungled hills; a thing of rice fields, a few grass houses, coconuts and bananas. Fertig, sitting in the afternoon in a rattan chair on the porch of a bamboo house, looked down on it and saw an empire.

I am called on to lead a resistance movement against an implacable enemy under conditions that make victory barely possible even under the best circumstances. But I feel that I am indeed a Man of Destiny, that my course is charted, and that only success lies at the end of the trail. I do not envision failure; it is obvious that the odds are against us and we will not consistently win, but, if we are to win only part of the time and gain a little each time, in the end, we will be successful.

So he wrote, lost in a dream of grandeur among the rice paddies, but a feeling of certainty had been growing within him ever since the first days on Luzon.

During that fighting, Fertig had gone through all the stages of mind of a man at war. Before his first action, he had been absolutely certain that, while other men would be killed, death would not touch him. Afterwards, he knew that it was not only possible but entirely probable that he would be killed at any moment. Terrified, he found that, to keep his sanity, he had to become so involved in the thing that needed to be done at the moment that there was no time for reflection. Thus he came to the fourth state of a warrior's mind: that he would be killed and that it did not matter, that only the job of the moment was important. When he arrived at this view, his mind was truly free for his work, but then the cycle began again. Now he did not believe he could be killed, because he was in the hand of God. War had made him an active fatalist.

Surely, Fertig thought, God's hand was apparent. He had not been wounded when others around him had been killed on the Luzon plains and in the Bataan jungles. He had escaped unscathed to Corregidor, but, while it was clear to him that Corregidor would be surrendered, he was certain that he would escape. He would swim the three miles of swift current if necessary. He was a wretched swimmer. Therefore, he tried to strengthen himself. Seeing Fertig running in place, flexing his arms doing deep knee bends and push-ups while Japanese bombs and shells thundered down on the island fortress, his friends thought him mad. But Fertig had decided that Franklin was right: God helps those who help themselves.

He was not surprised when ordered out of Corregidor to join MacArthur's headquarters in Australia. To him, the orders were proof that he was a man set apart. The first aircraft that was to take him from the Rock crashed on landing. The second put down successfully on the shell-torn field at night, and Fertig climbed aboard. Taking off, it struck a hole and was demolished. Fertig emerged unhurt. Through a confusion of orders, he missed the submarine that came to remove men who, like himself, had priority orders to be evacuated. He escaped, finally, on the last Navy flying boat to reach Corregidor before the surrender, and, when the flying boat crashed on landing at Mindanao, Fertig felt increasingly sure that he was destined to survive.

He was certain of this even when he discovered that he would be left behind in the Islands.

There was just one aircraft left on Mindanao, and there was no place on it for him. Fertig gave the pilot the staff studies he had prepared on Corregidor for MacArthur's engineers, and a private letter to Mary. Because of the censorship, he could not say much. He began, "Dearest: Pineapples for breakfast!" and went on to say that he was well and that he loved her. He handed the letter to the Navy pilot and felt certain that it would reach Mary in the clear light of Colorado and that she would read it and know where he was. There was just one place in all the Islands where fresh pineapples were served. That was at the Del Monte plantation on Mindanao. Mary would understand this, and Fertig was certain that she knew he would survive.

Fertig reviewed the disasters that had overtaken Mindanao and found in them nothing but an inexorable fate that was stripping everything away to leave him standing alone.

It is a strange position in which I find myself, he now told his diary, *for I am not a particularly charitable man, and yet my action in taking command is a response to the kindness offered by people who could have taken full advantage of my helplessness.*

He thought of the aged Datu of Rogungan, a spear carrier in purple trousers; of don Salvador with his fears; of Mrs. MacMichael, who had given him sanctuary from both the Japanese and her own people. He thought of all the anxious Filipino faces, and of Morgan. It was an act of charity to Morgan that he should take command.

Never having been a general officer before, I have no idea what constitutes a general headquarters, he wrote.

"How long," an acid voice broke in upon him, "are you going to sit there in that goddamned chair?"

Hedges came into the hot light of the late afternoon. Fertig closed his diary and leaned back, stretching.

"Oh, sair, you are in much hurry," he said. "You are not a good Filipino. You do not know there is always tomorrow."

"You're damned right I'm not a Filipino," Hedges agreed. "And neither are you. Let's get going."

Fertig shoved his diary into his musette bag, and the two friends climbed down the porch steps—Hedges swaggering, wearing his captain's bars like chips on his shoulders, Fertig moving in long-legged thoughtful silence. Hedges gave brusque orders to the cargadores and the squad of soldiers waiting in the dirt yard. The little procession moved out—down the hill to the valley floor, and down the road toward Baroy. At Baroy, they would board ships of the Free Philippines Navy to join Morgan and Tait in Misamis Occidental, and proclaim the province free.

IT WAS DARK when Hedges and Fertig reached Baroy. Kinkie lamps shone from the windows of stilted bamboo houses, and there was about the village the immemorial odor of Southeast Asia: a scent of food frying in coconut oil, of charcoal smoke, feces, animals, flowers, dust, urine, chickens and wet leaves. Fertig loved the smell of Filipino villages because it seemed to him that it was the sweet smell of life itself. Heads appeared in windows of the houses as the parade passed; voices called Mabuhay! to the Americano general.

The General! There was a Graustarkian quality about the whole adventure, one that only a South American revolutionary could take seriously. Fertig was a general because a paper in his musette bag said that he was. The paper was an old court blank that said notice of delinquency in payment of real property tax. On the back of this document, Fertig had written in pencil:

Office of the Commanding General
United States Forces in the Philippines
Mindanao-Visayan force
In the Field

1 October '42

PROCLAMATION

1.   By virtue of the power invested in me . . .
By virtue of the power he had invested in himself, Fertig stated, he had assumed command of Mindanao as senior representative of the United States Government and the Philippine Commonwealth, and formally declared a state of martial law for the duration of the national emergency. He signed it:

BY ORDER OF THE COMMANDING GENERAL Wendell W. Fertig
BRIGADIER GENERAL, USA, COMMANDING

Then, in the lower left-hand corner, he wrote:
DISTRIBUTION

1.   To all commanding officers, USFIP

2. To all provincial governors
3. To all provincial officials
4. To all justice of the peace courts
5. File

He was particularly pleased with "5. File." Nothing is truly believed until it is printed, and, of all printed things, nothing is ever quite so much believed as something that is purported to have been filed. As soon as he could find a typewriter, if such a thing could be found, Fertig would have his proclamation duplicated and tacked on suitable trees and grass walls.

But, listening to the voices calling Mabuhay!, Fertig was keenly aware that he was a general whose silver stars had been hammered out by a Moro metalsmith; who had no transportation, no supplies, no information, no plans, and, for that matter, no army.

TWO HUNDRED GUERRILLEROS were waiting for him at the beach. A mist lay upon the black water, and Fertig could not see across the bay. He made his way over the damp sand and climbed into the huge hollowed-log hull of a native outrigger. When he and Hedges were seated, the soldiers shouted and heaved and slid the banca from the grating sand into the warm shallows and clambered wetly over the side. They piled in, helter-skelter, so many of them that the gunwales were barely awash.

The sail hung slack in the wet air. Their progress was barely perceptible. Behind what Hedges sardonically called their flagship, six other lateen-rigged fishing boats moved like dark ghosts across the silent bay. Fertig wondered if Caesar's heart had been in his mouth as he stepped across the Rubicon.

He looked at Hedges' familiar leer in the darkness and at the murmuring ragged soldiers and wondered if what he did not really most need was a psychiatrist. Two hundred men to hold a province of 250,000 inhabitants from an enemy that had wiped its foes from the skies, sunk the world's strongest Navy, broken the British heart at Singapore, chased MacArthur out of the Philippines, and captured all of East Asia in six months! He felt it would have been far wiser to have remained in the Rogungan Valley with the old Datu and his food, women, and good conversation.

"We'll be all right," Hedges speculated, peering into the night, "if we don't get stuck in a goddamn fish trap. The whole stinking bay is full of fish traps."

Wavelets bubbled about the banca's slow-moving prow, and lights began to swim through the night. There were many moving red glares of coconut-oil kinkies in the mist as the landing place at Tangub came toward them.

The banca drew closer, and, in the flickering glare, Fertig began to see the whole population of the wretched little fishing town of Tangub waiting there in all its fiesta finery. As the banca touched the sand, an orchestra broke into song. It was a vaguely familiar song, as interpreted on a wet beach by three guitars, an accordion, and a violin, all more or less in tune and time with one another. But what were the people singing?

"Somm-whaare, ovvaa that rain-bow . . ."

The whole town of Tangub was singing to him.

They were singing to the liberator; to the general from Australia who had come to save them. They were trying to sing to him in his own language, to offer him a song of his country, in order to tell him of their hope and faith and gratitude.

"For God's sake," Hedges muttered.

Fertig caught his breath with a sob as a tension broke within him. It was a tension that had been building ever since Mary and the children had been sent away before the war began. Throughout all of Bataan and Corregidor, through all the defeat on Mindanao, and the months of wandering and hiding, and the endless days of abysmal boredom, the tension had been growing. Now it broke, and there was nothing he could do about it. Tears streamed down Fertig's strangely young cheeks as the Commanding General stepped ashore.

BOOK THREE

The Dragon's Teeth

1

FIRST CAME THE ARMY staff car, bolting and bucking over the stony road with Hedges and Fertig bouncing up and down in solitary grandeur in the rear seat; behind them the ragged soldiers in the open beds of the army trucks, straw hats blowing off to sail into the banana plants, the soldiers shouting and howling to the villagers over the truck horns that kept hooting without meaning, the chickens scattering wildly out of the village streets, sometimes turning into flying balls of tattered feathers as the trucks smashed past with the soldiers laughing, mothers darting into the road to snatch their bare-tailed babies out of the way seconds before eternity; the villagers all agape and the struck pigs shrieking; and so, with a swirl and screech of brakes and a final blare of horns, into the plaza of Misamis City, where Morgan and Tait waited with an honor guard before the stone municipal building.

It was quite a guard of honor: a platoon of smartly uniformed and well-equipped Filipinos standing in company front beneath two flags that sagged from staffs of equal height: the American and the Philippine Commonwealth flags. When Fertig emerged from the staff car, the brightly dressed throng that swarmed through the plaza went mad with pleasure at the sight of the General who had come from Australia. The rumors were thick, and all of them good! American Negro paratroopers had poured down from the sky to liberate Surigao on Mindanao's northern coast! See—there was one of them now, greeting the General! Here was the General! The Aid had come! Naturally, there would be fiesta tonight! The war could wait; the war could be resumed mañana, with the General directing the victorious Aid!

And, naturally, there was fiesta in every town that Fertig and Hedges

visited on a flying trip that took them the length of Misamis Occidental and into Zamboanga province as far as Dipolog. It was a fantastic
four days, and Fertig's diary entries became a chaotic jumble of names
and places. There were important people to meet, everything to explain,
rumors to deny, couriers arriving and departing, and no time to do anything well. It was quite absurd; absolutely irrational.

The fantasy began when, after they had landed at Tangub, a Filipino
almost hysterically pushed through the crowd at the beach to cry out a
welcome to Hedges. It was one of Hedges' former drivers, and he had
incredible news: Hedges' motor pool was intact! The trucks and automobiles were hidden not far away.

But this was not the only miracle of Misamis Occidental. The telegraph
line was still in operation, with telegraphers at their posts. There was a telephone system in a state of disrepair but a telephone system nevertheless.
True, manufactured commodities had disappeared, but it seemed reasonable
to assume they might reappear as inexplicably as Hedges' trucks. The coconut-oil factory at Jimenez was shut but intact; the provincial capital buildings
at Oroquieta wanted only the return of their staffs. Swiftly, Fertig decided
that the first thing to do would be to make an inspection tour of the province in order to gain a cursory view of its contents and—more important—
in order to be seen by as many people as possible. Off he went with Hedges
at once, with Hedges' driver leaning on the horn, driving at the one rate of
speed a Filipino driver knows, which is as fast as possible. There was no way
to tell him to slow down for the pigs or to stop blowing his horn without
causing him to lose face. The driver sat at the wheel like a grim seraph of
determination, personally bringing The Aid to the province, with shouting
soldiers in trucks banging along behind.

Caught in the crazy excitement of those first four days, Fertig found
himself longing for the simple time when he, Hedges, and Offret had
blundered along the forest trails. Even in the misery of their aimless wandering, there had been companionship and time for shared thoughts. Now
there was none, for, at every town, every barrio, every sitio, men would
crowd around to speak to The One.

"Good sir," they would say, "the locusts are eating all the rice. What
are we to do?"

"Sir, I have five ballots for my reefle and three ballots for my peestol,
but I do not have a peestol. You will give?"

"Sir, this woman says she was raped by her father, but she did not resist because she always obeys her father. Was this a rape, as she says? What
must be done?"

"Sir, the people say the Hapons will attack tomorrow."

"Sir, I will borrow your money, only. But, sir! You are very rich!"

"Sir, how many copies of the proclamation shall we make? Where are the proclamations to be placed?"

"Sir, Lieutenant Chavez hears where a radio is buried, but the man who told him is a liar. Does he speak the truth?"

"Sir, the rice dealers would not sell the rice, and that is why we took it."

"Sir, may I go home to see my wife? I have not seen her for two weeks."

Soldier and civilian, man and woman, came crowding around the strange new general, each anxious to tell him news and rumor; to explain, excuse, request, advise, wheedle, suggest, demand . . .

Obviously, the endless suppliants could not each be answered if anything was to be done. But just as obviously, they could not be escaped, for Filipinos believe it is useless to look for any kind of decision from anyone who is not The One. Centuries had taught them that all subordinate functionaries are either thieves or incompetent relatives, or both, and the beliefs of centuries are not lightly put aside. Certainly, if Fertig were to escape being drowned in a flood of trivia, he would have to delegate authority, but he had no delegates. He was merely the embodiment of a rumor. If he was to convert rumor into fact, he would have to establish a civil government to deal with all nonmilitary affairs. The alternative was to rule as a warlord. Fertig toyed with this notion, only to discard it as undesirable, which to his mind meant impossible. Fertig had a good grasp of the area of the possible. Anything that was possible was probable, depending on the ingenuity of the commander. Anything that was not possible was undesirable; indeed, fatal. The thing to know, Fertig believed, was what could *not* be done. All else was probable. But what to do first? There was a vast number of things that each had to be done first, before any of the other things that must also be done first. Meanwhile, the suppliants crowded around, and it was Hedges who reminded Fertig of the way out.

"Don't try to do anything," he said. "You just make trouble for yourself by talking with them so goddamn much. If I were you, Wendell, I'd take the Spanish view. If you forget about a problem, it goes away after a while under its own steam. Or it curls up and dies. Hell, these people don't really expect you to do anything for them right away. You know the old Filipino expression, 'Sir, there is no time. Just from now on, only.' These people just want you to *listen* to them. They've been to Caesar and told him their problems. Then they'll go away and settle them in their own fashion. You know this as well as I do."

But opportunities thus to talk with Hedges became increasingly few. The two friends drifted apart as they traveled together; Hedges immersing himself in an inventory of every article and commodity that could possibly be used in a war, Fertig making an equally frantic inventory of people and motives and storing the information away in his photographic memory to be evaluated at a later time. Meanwhile, he issued orders to recruit an army and attempted to form judgments on urgent reports that ranged everywhere from wishful thinking to misstatements of fact. In the midst of it, over the telegraph line that still strangely worked, came this:

MISAMIS 6 OCTOBER XXX ENEMY SHIP ATTEMPTED LAND MISAMIS BUT HAS BEEN DRIVEN OFF BY OUR TROOPS XXX

Fertig read the message and felt his heart stop.

What kind of enemy ship? A canoe? A Japanese launch? The battleship *Haruna?* What was meant by "driven off"? Did it mean that whatever ship it was had scurried back to Cagayan or Iligan to alert the Japanese command that revolt had flared in the sleepy province of Misamis Occidental, and that the Japanese would come storming in to crush the guerrilla before it could begin? Or did the message mean—as well it could—that a ship had passed the island far out to sea and that someone had shot at it and then had construed the fact that the ship kept on its way to mean that an invasion had been repulsed?

Fertig preferred to believe the worst, for Misamis Occidental was altogether too good to be true. It was exactly the place to work in silence and carefully build the nucleus of a serious resistance. He had hoped at least for weeks in which to begin to make some order out of things. It now seemed the Japanese would not grant him days, or even hours. He drove pell-mell to Misamis City, oblivious of the taos in the barrios who took off their hats as the staff car arrowed at the head of a plume of dust down the narrow road, not hearing the thin shouts of the children who called Mabuhay!

In Misamis, there was news of the great victory.

It seemed that the motor vessel *Tular,* a small interisland steamer, had come directly into the sketchy harbor, apparently intending to moor at the pier. Guerrilla troops had manned the medieval Spanish stone cota[27] that overlooked the waterfront, and others waited in foxholes dug along the beach. Unsuspecting, the *Tular* moved toward the splintery pier, the engines at dead slow ahead, thunking dully in the midday silence.

Some idiot opened fire.

---

27. cota = fort

Then all the soldiers on the firing step of the cota banged away, and all the soldiers in the foxholes in the sand. The Stars and Stripes was run up the fortress flagstaff.

The startled *Tular* belched smoke, moved full speed astern, and swung slowly away, finally spitting out a random fire from a light cannon mounted aft. That made the *Tular* a warship to the people of Misamis, but the cannon shells hit nothing.

Fertig barely listened to the news. He pushed directly on to the cota, where he found his barefoot army hard at work. They were killing a carabao in the good old Filipino fashion, running after it, stabbing it with bayonets while the frightened animal bellowed about, the men yelling and lunging and scattering away from the swinging horns, and just as Fertig furiously entered the arena, Bill Tait slid lithely out onto the sand, grinning his friendly Negro grin, a two-by-four in his black hands. Tait went up to the bolting, shivering, bloody-shiny animal, raised the two-by-four, and, rising on his toes, swung the beam down and broke it on the bull's head. Then everyone cheered and dashed in with bayonets while the buffalo dropped, with Tait standing over it, doing a little jig and blowing on his stinging hands, grinning while men slapped his big shoulders. Then someone saw Fertig, and silence fell as suddenly as the buffalo had dropped.

"Captain Tait," Fertig said, "I want you and Major Morgan to report at once to my headquarters."

In the conference that followed, Fertig questioned the young guerrilla lieutenant who had been in charge of the cota when the *Tular* arrived. Bright-faced and proud, believing absolutely in his general and in The Aid, the lieutenant was delighted to explain.

"Sir," he said, "the ship did not show Hapon flag, so I ordered one man to fire one shot only, to see if it was hostile.

"I did not wish all to fire," the lieutenant said, "because it might be one of our ships, bringing The Aid."

He waited.

"But," he said, half-ashamed, "after the first shot, all opened fire many times."

"Splendid," Fertig said drily.

"Now you listen," Fertig said. "Next time, you do not do that, no? You do not shoot at a ship you do not know. If it is our ship, the ship might think, 'There are Hapons here,' and go away. If it is Hapon ship, it might think, 'There are guerrilleros here,' and go away. You are to remember, huh? If a ship comes, you are to let it tie up.

"You are to wait until the ship is all tied up. When the ship is putting its baggages ashore, then you will capture it, huh? You will capture the whole ship, huh, and all its baggages and all its crews. Next time, you are to remember, yes?"

Fertig's voice was stern, but kindly. Patiently, he led the young officer over the possibilities again, making certain there was no misunderstanding. The troubled lieutenant left his general's presence not knowing whether he had been praised or blamed but remembering what he had been told. He had barely gone before Fertig was issuing orders. Send a man to Iligan at once to learn from our people what damages the ship had suffered and what the Japanese planned to do about it.

Issue a proclamation to the people:

"The Mindanao-Sulu Force, USFIP, has won its first province and has decisively defeated the first attempt of the Japanese to recapture it . . ."

Of course it wasn't true, but the people of Misamis thought it was, and I'll be damned, Fertig thought, if we can—or maybe even should—try to tell them otherwise.

"Telegram to all former provincial officials," Fertig said to his Filipino aide, and he spent the rest of the afternoon trying as best he could to work as quickly as possible to salvage something out of the fiasco. He saw in it nothing but the complete wreckage of his dreams. The Japanese had now been alerted by an eager, barefoot young patriot.

All right, Fertig told himself, *forget it. There isn't anything we can do about it. Now they know. They would know sooner or later, anyway. Forget it.*

2

"LOOK AT THAT!" General Morimoto shouted, although his office was small and his audience limited to two silent officers. "Look at that map and tell me more about your outstanding success!"

Colonel Yashinari Tanaka, commander in chief of the Japanese forces of western Mindanao, stared at the military situation map on the wall. The civil affairs officer, Seiji Kogoh, knew as well as Yashinari and the General what the map would show. It was brightly decorated by more than seventy colored flags, each representing what Seiji-san insisted on calling a bandit area. It also sported more than 200 pins, each representing a small disaster. The pins were tightly clustered about the towns garrisoned by Japanese forces, and they were strung like posts along the island roads.

"Perhaps you agree that this is an accurate picture?" General Morimoto inquired.

An obedient silence answered the samurai who was the Imperial Japanese Army commander of Mindanao and Sulu.

"Say something!" General Morimoto shouted. "Is it accurate or is it not?"

Colonel Yashinari bowed and said it was. Seiji-san murmured that it seemed to be.

"Fools!" the General yelled. He bounced to his feet, snatched a tiny colored flag from his desk, stumped to the wall, and drove the flag into a blank area on the map.

"Why must I learn these things from spies?" he demanded. "Why must I learn these things thirdhand from dirty farmers in the market place? Why do I not learn them from my military commander and from my civil affairs officer? What have you to say? Is the map accurate *now*?

"It may interest you to know," General Morimoto said, resuming his seat behind the desk, "that the motor vessel *Tular* returned to Iligan today. It arrived with forty-two corpses and fourteen wounded out of a ship's complement of 160 men.

"Does that impress you?" he roared. "It impresses me! What impresses me is the fact that the *Tular* did not even dock at Misamis. It could not dock. It came into the harbor—your peaceful harbor of your peaceful province, Seiji-san—to put ashore the electrical engineers.

"And as it came into the harbor the fort opened fire!" General Morimoto said.

"The fort!" he said. "Where were your brave soldiers, Colonel Yashinari? Were they not in the fort?

"No, they were not," General Morimoto answered himself.

He pulled a sheaf of papers across his desk, scattering them, selecting one from the mess.

"Your soldiers were at that time in the bellies of dogs," he informed Colonel Yashinari. "And so were your civil affairs officials, Seiji-san."

The two officers said nothing.

"The American flag was flying from that fort," General Morimoto said. "Just when did you receive your last reports from Misamis Occidental, gentlemen?"

The two officers said nothing. To say anything at this time might irrevocably commit them to a situation for which hara-kiri would be the only means of atonement. They waited to learn more of what their general knew.

"For your information," General Morimoto said, "there is no longer a need to send electrical engineers to Misamis City. It seems that the city is now well-lighted. An American engineer is running the plant. Nor will we need the services of your traffic experts, Seiji-san. It seems that trucks and automobiles are again traveling through the province without our help.

"It is incredible," General Morimoto said with deadly calm, "that here, on an island that we have captured" (he bowed satirically to Colonel Yashinari) "and control" (bowing to Seiji) "we find a city brightly lighted at night, where trucks move normally, where forts fly American flags, where there is a thing they call the Free Philippines Government, and where the military commander happens to be a United States Army major general."

Still controlling himself, General Morimoto selected another paper from his desk.

"Major General Wendell W. Fertig," he read. "He has, according to the Thought Police, a uniformed army of 7,000 men."

General Morimoto stared at his officers with infinite contempt. Then he crooked his arm to look at his new American wrist watch.

"In one hour," he said, "you gentlemen will report back to this office with every scrap of information you might possibly have concerning Misamis Occidental, this so-called General Fertig, and your morning reports for the past month."

He jumped to his feet, his black eyes burning.

"Get out!" he yelled.

3

HIGH ON A MOUNTAINTOP, a small, thin man with a great blade of a nose peered suspiciously at the steep trail below. His dirty Navy uniform hung loosely on him, and his sight and hearing were failing. Sam Wilson thought his ears had been permanently damaged during the shelling of Corregidor, but he did not know that his deafness, and his increasing myopia, were due to malnutrition.

The tiny figure toiling up the trail came closer, and Sam Wilson recognized him as a tao who occasionally brought food. He moved the latch of his Colt automatic from fire to safe and put the pistol into its holster.

This day, the tao brought rice and small, plump bananas, and a great air of mysterious excitement.

"Oh, sair, not one knows you are here," the tao said quickly, "but *if* you are to come near my barrio and *if* one sees you, he is to say the Americano general say for you to come to Misamis!"

Sam heard the words as if from a great distance. They struck him like a knife thrust, which is itself painless but which carries the promise of the pain to come.

"What Americano general?" he asked emptily.

"Oh, sair, it is The Aid!" the tao exclaimed, clapping his hands. "A general comes with flenty, flenty guns! All Americano officer are to go to Misamis, sair, and yes, the general asks for you. Cargadores will carry your baggages, sair. They are waiting in my barrio, even now!"

Now the pain began—the pain of mingled hope and fear and the pain of having to make the decision that Wilson had always known he would one day have to make. As he stood indecisive on his hilltop, listening to the tao's happy voice, Sam Wilson had a vision of the Japanese leading his wife and sons to the chopping block.

AT THE SAME TIME, another man in another part of Mindanao smoothed out a crumpled bit of paper and read a water-blurred and faded message.

Letter to all guerrilleros, as senior United States officer in the Islands, Lieutenant Colonel Wendell. W. Fertig, CE, AUS, assumes command of the Mindanao-Visayan Force, USFIP, with the rank of brigadier general. All organized units resisting our common enemy are invited to serve under this command. Unified resistance is the key to success. W. W. Fertig, Brigadier General, Commanding.

"So!" Waldo Neveling said to himself, unconsciously stiffening to attention. "I absolutely agree."

For the first time in months, Herr Neveling hummed to himself, thinking what a pleasure it would be to work with this General Fertig— with a man who had a good German name and a good name for a general. General Ready!

Unified resistance, with all under one command, that was correct. One man should always be completely responsible for everything. That was the way to get things done. Everything must be organized. There must be order. Also, this Fertig was clever to say "our common enemy." That shows he knows what is what, Herr Neveling thought. He knows that all guerrilleros are not friends. He, Neveling, had heard of this Fertig before, in the mining business. That was what was needed! A practical man who understood Filipinos and could get work done. If Fertig was actually also a soldier, so much the better . . .

IN THE FLAT RICE LANDS of a broad river valley, United States Army Captain Ernest McClish read a copy of the message that Neveling had received, and he pondered the rumors that had raced ahead of it through the island. His problem was to decide what to believe.

Captain McClish was a whipcord, darkly handsome officer who dreamed of the days when cavalry charged with lance and sabre. He had wanted to be a cavalryman, but it seemed the world had changed. He was now reduced to practicing polo by himself, riding a little Filipino horse, driving a coconut down a barrio street with a homemade mallet. But this was simply his private offering to his dreams of the past. McClish had fought well early in the war and had refused to take part in the surrender.

Indeed, he looked upon the surrender as an opportunity to show the world what he could do with an independent command, and, after a series of adventures as complicated as any American's in those days on Mindanao, he had assembled a force of young American enlisted men—fugitives like himself. He now read the words "unified resistance is the key to success" with mixed approval and concern. Unified command was all very well, but who was to command? Who was this strange Fertig? If, as rumor said, he was actually a general from MacArthur's staff, McClish's course was clear. He would take orders. But what if—as rumor also said—this Fertig was merely another would-be guerrillero? In any event, did unification necessarily mean an end to independent operations?

But wholly apart from the somewhat esoteric questions of future strategy and operations, McClish had a practical problem to consider. He had just expended nearly all his little army's ammunition in an inconclusive attack on a Japanese garrison, painfully learning that riflemen cannot, from an open field, capture a concrete schoolhouse that is defended by a soldiery armed with machine guns. For such work, cannons are ideal or at least mortars and, failing mortars, then hand grenades at the very least. Perhaps, if the rumors were true, this General Fertig could supply McClish's army with cannons, as well as replenishing the supply of rifle ammunition.

"I think," he said to his young Americans, "we better send somebody down to Misamis to see what the deal is."

"I'll go," Private Robert Ball suggested. "Suppose Knortz and I hike down and take a look?"

ACROSS THE COGON GRASS plateaus, through the forests, and along all the trails of Mindanao, the messages and rumors of the American general spread. One by one, the word reached each of the Americans still free, for the number of such Americans was sufficiently small and the facilities of the bamboo telegraph sufficiently extensive for the fugitives to gain at least a shadowy knowledge of one another's identities, or reputations, and presumable whereabouts. In some cases, as in Sam Wilson's, the message was direct and personal. To Chief Elwood Offret, the word was, Come on, sailor, we've got some engines for you. Slowly, painfully, still weak from dysentery, the good-natured Offret set off on the long march that led to the sea, around the end of Panguil Bay, and up the farther shore toward Misamis and his friends. But by no means all the unsurrendered Americans were as eager to help.

Some, like Wilson, eventually went to Fertig because they were starving and defeated, and there seemed nothing else for them to do. Others came out of sheer boredom, unable any longer to look upon the same rank patch of squalid tropical growth for day upon endless day, knowing there was no place to go and nothing to do, and no apparent end to the everlasting sameness of their pointless lives. But many others, hiding in the hills, feared action more than they feared inaction; they were incapable even of feeding themselves but were content to live upon the pity and charity of simple Filipino peasants whom they still privately believed to be inferior to themselves. Such Americans, out of fear, did not acknowledge receipt of Fertig's call to arms. Worse, many Filipino guerrillero chieftains greeted Fertig's messengers with open scorn.

"Who ees thees Fer-teeg?" they asked derisively. "How many ammunitions does he geeve me? Will he send me gons? Where ees the mon-ey? How are we to know he comes from MacArthur? Why should he be beeg shot? Let him be The One in *his* sitio. Here, *I* weel be The One."

Underlying the refusal of many of the chieftains to join Fertig was the subtle suggestion that American leadership was not entirely necessary. Many Filipinos had had their fill of condescending Americano officers, and felt that, if the Americans would confine themselves to delivering material aid, the Filipinos would take care of the rest. The implication was that, when Philippine independence came after the war, a successful guerrillero would be an obvious choice for public office, and the less he owed to the Americans the more obvious a choice he would be. Less subtle about this were leaders like Salipada Pendatun, who was frankly anti-American.

Pendatun was a short, stocky, brutally handsome young Cotabato Moro. A trained lawyer, deeply involved in Moro politics and protected by a princely family, Pendatun created himself a brigadier general after the surrender, putting himself at the head of a large, well-armed Moro guerrilla. His starched khakis crackled as he walked; his insignia shone; he affected highly polished riding boots; and it was he who pioneered the use of a novel sort of artillery to take enemy strongpoints. The artillery consisted of carabaos laden with fused explosives. The carabaos were pointed in the general direction of the Japanese, and the fuses were lit. Then kerosene torches were applied to the genitals of the carbaos, and away they ran—hopefully toward the enemy.

The right hand of this enterprising warrior was a mestizo: a Colonel Andrews, chief of the prewar Philippine Air Force. Like Pendatun, Colonel Andrews was the very figure of pride, the kind of man who, even naked, would seem to be wearing a uniform. But Pendatun's icy anti-Americanism was superficial in comparison to Andrews'. Perhaps the mestizo had never got over a racial insult suffered during his training days at flying fields in the southern United States. For whatever cause, his hatred was deep and genuine. He complained that he could not sleep at night because of his disgust at the thought that American blood flowed in his veins. Thus, when Fertig's message reached Pendatun's headquarters, the young Moro and Colonel Andrews simply laughed.

In the wild hills around Lake Lanao, the Moro Datu Busran Kalaw was no more willing to put himself under Fertig's command than was Pendatun, for Kalaw, too, entertained delusions of grandeur. Like Pendatun and Fertig, he, too, had created himself a brigadier general, and he commanded a band of Maranao Moro swordsmen that he called the Fighting Bolo Battalion. Unlike Pendatun, however, Kalaw was not anti-American. His xenophobia was benign. Kalaw was merely anti everyone who was not a Maranao Moro.

Yet, while Fertig's messages met with every response from curiosity to open contempt, they—together with the rumor that an American general had come, bringing The Aid—had one immediate effect. It was to intensify guerrilla activities throughout the island. Anxious either to impress the new general with a record of accomplishment against the day that they should meet him, in order to seek privileges and supplies, or to prove their utter independence of Fertig, the guerrilla chieftains fell upon Japanese patrols and isolated garrisons with new vigor, thus creating new problems for the much-beset Japanese commander, General Morimoto.

It was not that General Morimoto did not know what to do. He knew very well how to deal with guerrilla bands; he had learned how years ago, in China.

Studying his maps and reports, General Morimoto decided to order all Japanese troops into garrisons that could easily be held by relatively few men. Then, stripping the garrisons to minimum strength, he would create a special mobile combat team from the surplus. It would be a force large enough to encircle a guerrilla area. It would attack from the circumference, herding ahead of it all the guerrilleros and the civilians, and when the Filipinos were pushed into a small enough space, they would be obliterated. Then the combat team would move to the next area, and so on until all seventy of Mindanao's centers of resistance were stamped out And the first target of the combat team would be Misamis, headquarters of the American general who obviously was directing the resistance.

The answer was simple, but there was one difficulty: to create a special force was virtually impossible. The Butu'un garrison could not be depleted. It had already been hit by an American named McClish, and reinforcements had to be sent to Butu'un from Cagayan. In the midst of this, a Moro named Pendatun had the effrontery to attack the town of Malaybalay, and reinforcements had to be sent there from Davao. No sooner would a convoy start up the road from Kolambugan to Cagayan than it would be attacked by guerrilleros under Filipinos named Jaldon and Limena and under an American civilian named Walter. Additional troops must be assigned to protect the convoys. Whenever troops moved down the Agusan River, they would be attacked by guerrilleros led by a Syrian peddler named Kahlil Kador and by a comedian named Zapanta, who had mounted a homemade cannon on a barge. Moreover, no men could be spared from the Lake Lanao area, which was being terrorized by a savage named Kalaw. None of the attacks were particularly harmful. The guerrilleros could not prevent the Japanese from moving wherever they wished, because the Japanese could always assemble a superior force in any one place at any one time. But the guerrilla activities, taken as a whole, were annoying, disruptive, and put Morimoto in the impossible position of a man trying to hold his trousers up while swatting at wasps.

Obviously, the thing to do was to ask General Homma in Manila to send reinforcements, but this, to General Morimoto's mind, was absolutely impossible. After all, Morimoto was in charge of the island of Mindanao which—on advice of his military commander Yashinari and his civil affairs chief Seiji—he had declared conquered and pacified. To admit now that the island was neither conquered nor pacified would be to admit that he, Morimoto, was either an incompetent or a liar, with the resultant loss of face in either event. Indeed, it would cause such loss of face that General Morimoto would, in all honor, be required ceremoniously to disembowel himself.

On the other hand, Morimoto wondered, could he afford *not* to tell Homma this strange news about an American general suddenly arrived from Australia? If this general had an army only half the rumored size, it was still too large a force for Morimoto to deal with unless reinforcements were sent from Manila. That is, he could not deal with such opposition while at the same time also dealing with the guerrilla bands that plagued him everywhere else on Mindanao.

But then General Morimoto had a happy thought. If an American general had come with supplies from Australia, it could hardly be Morimoto's fault; it would be the Navy's. Anything that would cause the Imperial Navy to lose face was perfectly all right with General Morimoto. Therefore, he could ask for reinforcements without fear.

But, General Morimoto thought miserably, what if Homma sent him troops, and what if he went into Misamis with them only to discover that it had all been a rumor; what if the 7,000 men of Major General Fertig were not even 700? What then of the Morimoto face?

The trouble was, he could not be sure. Angrily, Morimoto condemned Yashinari and Seiji for their failure to keep him accurately informed. Their concern for their own face had led them to submit false estimates to him, which he, with guilty innocence, had passed to Homma.

A badly worried man, Morimoto went from horn to horn of his personal dilemma and then—like the soldier he was—he made his decision. Fertig's strength could not be a rumor. No general in his right mind would burn electric lights at night in a wartime city, fly flags from forts, and move trucks on the roads in broad daylight. Not when the city in question lay 1,500 miles deep in enemy territory, vulnerable to land, sea, and air attack. It was true that all white men were inscrutable, but this did not mean that the things they did made no sense to them. The only possible explanation was that this General Fertig must know his force was superior to anything that he, Morimoto, could throw against him. Therefore, it was no rumor: The American was about to attack; therefore reinforcements were necessary at once.

But he could not send for them at once. No Japanese Imperial Army officer could think of screaming for help before he was attacked, particularly before he had accurately determined his enemy's strength. In all his cerebrations, it never once occurred to General Morimoto that there was no organized resistance on Mindanao, that the resistance he felt everywhere was merely universal, spontaneous, and (had he only known it) very nearly out of ammunition. Nor could he have possibly imagined why Fertig had ordered the lights turned on in Misamis. General Morimoto was not only a prisoner of the universally orthodox military mind, but he was also a victim—like nearly all Asiatics—of the inability to ask the question *why*. But, for all that, he was brave and skillful. Therefore, bit by bit, scrimping here and borrowing there, taking chances and overriding the objections of his local commanders, Morimoto began to patch together a combat team large enough at least to challenge the force he assumed that Fertig commanded. But it took time. Even to assemble a squad of soldiers takes a certain amount of time. And, once assembled, the squad must be trained and rehearsed—to undertake even the simplest of operations. And then it must be transported and fed, and, when the problem is far from simple and the number of men is many times larger than a squad—larger, indeed, than many platoons, if not companies—the time consumed can be enormous. Doggedly, General Morimoto set to work, and, while his slowly growing task force trained for an amphibious operation, a single Japanese aircraft would soar across Panguil Bay each morning precisely at eight o'clock to bomb Misamis City, returning with photographs which were rushed to Morimoto's office.

Meanwhile, on his side of Panguil Bay, Fertig anxiously sent men to commandeer the provincial supply of pop bottles, wrapping paper, coconut beer, and pieces of old motion-picture projectors. Out of junk and hope and rule of thumb, Fertig struggled to build a strength that could stand up to the power of his enemy. General Morimoto would have been astounded to know that he was not the enemy against whom Fertig was painstakingly preparing himself.

4

TO HEDGES, THE MATTER was very simple. He had said as much from the beginning. The man who blocked Fertig's path was the man on whom their lives depended. It was Morgan—the indispensable and impossible Morgan. Wherever Fertig looked for a source of power, Morgan's arrogance barred the way. Wherefore, and not for the first time, Hedges said, "I tell you, Wendell, sooner or later we'll have to shoot that son of a bitch, and I might as well do it right now."

The two friends were sitting in comfortable rattan chairs in front of a beach cottage, with their bare feet propped up on a low table. Fertig was about to reply when the uneven, grinding noise of unsynchronized Japanese aircraft engines ate into the hot silence of the morning.

"He's on time," Fertig said.

Automatically, Hedges checked his watch and wound it. During the past week, Fertig and Hedges had fallen into the habit of taking coffee at this beach cottage in a coconut grove two kilometers from Misamis, while the Japanese bombed the city. With that relentless lack of imagination, the Japanese military had acquired from their prewar German advisers, they always bombed Misamis precisely at 8 A.M., never at any other time. Everyone left town for the bombing and returned when it was over. The bombs, always aimed at the stone cota, had so far killed two chickens and a kinky-tailed cat, but, since many of the bombs proved duds, they were welcomed as a source of powder.

"We don't want to kill him, Charley," Fertig said, ignoring the shriek and dull thump of the bombs. "We want to use him."

"Use him?" Hedges echoed. "The bastard treats you like an office boy, and he hates my guts. And as for that goddamned Sinang of his, I swear,

Wendell, someday I'm going to wring her neck. I know for a fact she's been telling the boys that nothing's been changed; that Morgan is Number One, she is Number Two, and Tait is Number Three; and that, if you or I tell the boys to do something different from what she, Tait, or Morgan says, they're not to pay any attention to us."

"I know," Fertig said, seeing in his mind Sinang in her army khakis, wearing a .45-caliber pistol on her hip.

It was a strange costume for a woman so lovely, for a woman so much of a woman. She was Morgan's dark-eyed, long-haired beauty, and, no matter what Morgan did, Sinang clung to the one truth of her life: that Morgan was a man. She did not wish to understand Morgan's constant need for other women. She never forgave him for lying with them, but she put this matter out of her mind because she knew that Morgan knew there was no ecstasy like the wild bitterness they shared. She had followed him for years before the war, constantly enduring his cruelty. Her one dream now was to find ways to create her lover in fact what he already was to her: the commanding general of a Filipino army that would liberate the Islands. And Morgan had made her his second in command.

"She's poisoning Morgan's mind against us all the time," Hedges said. "She doesn't like the idea we're asking Ducklegs, Wilson, and the rest of them to come down here. She tells Morgan, 'The Americanos will get all the best jobs, and you will not be The One.'"

"Yes," Fertig agreed.

They fell silent as the racket of the Japanese plane grew around them. Then they saw the twin-engined light reconnaissance bomber the Americans called the Betty race low over the coconut palms, homeward bound across Panguil Bay for the airfield at the Del Monte Company's pineapple plantation.

"He couldn't hit a bull in the ass with a bucket of rice," Hedges said dispassionately. "You ready to go back to town?"

"All right," Fertig said, putting the coffee cup down on the sand beside his chair for the houseboy to find. "But just don't shoot Morgan today, Charley. We need him. The answer is to become bigger than he is."

"I mean it, Wendell."

"So do I," Fertig said. "Take it easy. I think we're a good team. Last week, I wanted to shoot him, and you said no. This week, you want to shoot him, and I say no. I think whichever of us is saying no is being smart."

"I hope to God you're right," Hedges said, "but we're going to have to do it someday."

Later that morning, Fertig found himself privately endorsing Hedges' suggested remedy. The two friends were sitting in a staff conference with Morgan. Fertig told Morgan that he had heard the soldiers were confiscating lead sinkers from the fishermen and that he wanted Morgan to stop it.

"They will not sell, so we take them," Morgan said briefly. "I need lead for bullets. Let the fishermen use stones. Why worry about stupid fishermen?"

"Because they are saying we are Tulisaffes[28] and they will not catch fish for us," Fertig said sharply. "We need bullets, yes, but we need fish also. Let the fishermen use stones. But pay them for the lead. More than we need fish or bullets, we need the people. We cannot confiscate anything, except from black marketeers. The people will never support us if we rob them."

Ostentatiously, Morgan yawned, and stared past Fertig at the bright sunlight falling on the thick leaves outside the office window. His fingers drummed on the desk with the irritation of a busy man trapped by a fool.

"You tell me who says he will not catch fish for us, and I will shoot him," Morgan said carelessly. "Then the rest will go out fishing, you bet."

Oh, God, Fertig thought, this is our morning for shooting people, but so far nobody has mentioned shooting a Japanese.

Aloud, he said, "And how many fish will the dead man catch? And how many men will go fishing and then come back, saying, 'Oh, sair, we fished much, but, too bad, we did not catch one thing; there was bad luck only'?"

"All *right,*" Morgan said angrily. "I tell the men what *you* say."

"Well, that will be fine, Colonel," Fertig said, leaning back, agreeing to pretend to believe that this was what Morgan would say and that it would indeed be fine.

Morgan got to his feet, and the conference was over, Hedges leaving for the motor pool and Morgan returning to the bivouac where new recruits were drilled. Fertig stood for a moment beside the office window, looking absently into the tropical day. Below him, a soldier was sitting with his back against the building wall, cleaning his rifle with a bit of rag and a brass curtain rod.

One of Morgan's soldiers, Fertig thought. There was no question about it: Morgan had the army, such as it was. He had not yet found it possible, as he once had hoped, to win the army away from Morgan.

But no army is ever as large as a people. An army was always simply the cutting edge of a popular will. The thing to do was to create a civil government that all the people in the province would support: a government deriving its power from the people, which would then feed, clothe, and

28. Tulisaffes = Tulisan, meaning thief, plus USAFFE, or United States Armed Forces Far East

equip an army. Morgan simply did not understand this, or—perhaps—he did. At any rate, when Fertig broached the idea of a civil government to Morgan, suggesting they issue a call for all former provincial officials to return to the capitol building in Oroquieta and that he and Morgan go there to talk with them, what had Morgan said?

"The civil-yans?" Morgan had asked, incredulous. "You want *them* to help? If I were you, *General* Fertig, I would have those fat civil-yans come to my office and stand at attention while I told them what to do."

That was pure Morgan. That was the former junior lieutenant of police, now in a position to give orders to the kind of men who had once been his masters. And Morgan had apparently taken care that the ilustrados knew of his contempt for them, for, wherever Fertig sought aid from the responsible people of the province, the answer was no. For instance, there was Judge Florentino Saguin, a tiny, delicately boned man of great charm, intelligence, and courage. Fertig wanted Judge Saguin to become the chief of state of a proposed Government of the Free Philippines.

"If you wish to form a government according to the best principles of law and order, I am anxious to help," the diminutive judge said with quiet dignity. "I love liberty so much I am willing to give my life for it. But I am willing to join only on condition that you and Colonel Hedges remain in this province and command the troops."

Other ilustrados put it bluntly, although all avoided mentioning Morgan by name.

"I cannot serve under former police officers who say they are now guerrilleros," Provincial Treasurer Pacana said, and former Philippine Army officers refused to join the guerrillas for this same reason. Nothing Fertig said could persuade the well-born ilustrados that Japanese victory was far more dangerous to them than an association, however remote, with Morgan. Nor would the Catholic Church help. Knowing the power of the Church, Fertig had gone to Father Calanan, the Jesuit priest of the city of Jimenez.

Well, now, Father Calanan explained in his rich brogue, the Church was neutral, y'see. Furthermore, the Irish missionary priests claimed a secular neutrality as well. But unofficially (Father Calanan said), the Church was at war with the Japanese because the little heathens were enemies of the True Faith. A blustering Japanese civil affairs officer, Seiji, had boasted to a Filipino priest, "No more Jesus Christ; all now belong Nippon." The Japanese flatly said his nation intended to extirpate the white man in East Asia, together with all traces of his beliefs. Therefore, unofficially (the Jesuit explained) the Church on Mindanao had decided that each priest was free to serve his parish as his conscience dictated. If a priest thought he could best do this by preaching a crusade, he did. In fact, some priests were personally killing Japanese in guerrilla ambushes elsewhere on Mindanao. But the Church Militant wanted no part of the bigamous, amoral Morgan.

It was not only the white-gowned Irish priests and the careful, smooth-faced ilustrados of Misamis Occidental who were distrustful of the swaggering guerrillero and his hardbitten men. The businessmen and the Chinese merchants complained that Morgan's soldiery stripped their bodegas and jeered when the merchants asked for payment.

Fertig felt the hostility of the fishermen was far more serious than the complaints of a plundered Chinese. Heretofore, the fishermen had been the principal source of the Army's explosives. They would cut loose and tow ashore the Japanese mines, and amatol from the mines, mixed with low-grade miners' dynamite, became powder for the Army's cartridges. And more important than powder, of course, was the fact that the whole population depended upon fish for meat.

Moodily, Fertig stared at the soldier cleaning his rifle and then returned to his desk. It was true that much had been accomplished in the past week. Hedges had gathered up public-notice forms, schoolbooks, Manila wrapping paper, and bits of tissue from nearly every town in the province, in order that Fertig's headquarters could issue a multitude of orders, proclamations, directives, and regulations. They were painfully typed on the one rickety typewriter someone had found for the general's use, and, when the ribbon wore out, the orders were typed by means of carbon paper. When the carbon paper wore out, a substitute was devised by smearing the back of a piece of paper with charcoal. Issuing a great many orders was necessary, Fertig thought, to lead people to believe that he was running a military organization. There was no question but that the Filipinos had been impressed by the flood of official-seeming documents, and best of all, the bamboo telegraph reported that the Japanese general, Morimoto, had been even more impressed. News of Morimoto's reaction was considered particularly accurate because its source was the lover of Morimoto's Filipina mistress, a cousin of one of Fertig's couriers.

Fertig leaned back in his chair and sighed, neither pleased nor displeased by the fact that both the Filipinos and the Japanese were equally unaware that the orders were just window dressing of a store that had nothing to sell. The city lights that so puzzled General Morimoto were part of the same sham. Fertig had ordered the lights turned on at night simply because his staff worked night and day, and he reasoned they might as well have light to see by. If the Japanese wanted to bomb or storm Misamis, he couldn't stop them, anyway. But then he found that the people were saying that the Americano general ordered the lights turned on to show that Americanos had come who would not run away or surrender, that they were different from the Americanos who, at the beginning of the war, had ordered the lights turned off.

Therefore, there was light, and a great semblance of busyness. Couriers bustled about, and troops mounted guard beneath the flags of the United States and the Philippine Commonwealth. Recruitment went on in the city and in the barrios, lead was poured into handmade sand bullet molds, and Misamis woke from its 400-year-old sleep to take on the aspect of a city of purpose. It was an atmosphere Fertig studiously cultivated, for, as he explained to Hedges, "If we look and act like an army, we might actually become one." For all the superficial activity, however, Fertig was bitterly aware that he had not touched the deep sources of power in the province. To be sure, the people held fiestas and cheered when the general appeared, but the kind of men who came to the recruitment offices were generally master-less men, adventurous youths, men who wished to get away from their wives, and the kind of men who seemed to have nothing better to do. The ilustrados, the merchants, and the majority of the simple peasantry still held shy. It seemed to Fertig that they were waiting for some voice other than his.

Irritably, Fertig cursed the whole pack of them: Morgan, the ilustrados, the Church, the merchants, and the guileless peasantry.

From somewhere in the surrounding day, a thin sound of happiness came into the dim, cool spaces of Fertig's bare office.

The sound grew closer, and, looking from his desk, Fertig saw that it was a wedding party, moving toward the cathedral.

There was the demure bride with downcast eyes, her indomitable mother sitting beside her in the calesa, proud in her cherished mestiza dress. In the following carriage, the anxious young groom had the foolish look of one about to be sacrificed, and all the wedding party came laughing behind in their fiesta finery. Everyone waved as an army truck roared past; then all held handkerchiefs to their faces against the dust.

Like most countries of Spanish tradition, the Philippines seemed to be made for the pleasure of indolent men. Religion, the Filipinos said, was something for women to believe in. But it was a woman who carried the boy to the font, who dragged the groom to the altar, and who usually buried the husband in holy ground and who, when she died, left the family fortune to the Church. If the Church was a sop thrown to the women, it was also true that women were the support of the Church.

The wedding was barely out of sight when Fertig wrote out a general order:

"As of this date all members of this headquarters will attend Mass."

Later that day, Hedges flung himself into Fertig's office. He waited until Fertig's secretary was gone. He closed the door.

"Mass?" he demanded. "What the hell for? You're no Catholic, and I'm not either."

A faint smile momentarily lightened Fertig's bearded face.

"Women go to church," he said simply. "We want to make friends with both the Church and the dalagas. I'm going to try to make a deal with the padres: We'll take all our men to Mass if the padres preach the guerrilla.

"We want the priest to say, 'Look, the American general and his men are Christians. They come to church. The Hapons say there is no Jesus Christ. The general is fighting the Hapons. It is the duty of all to support the General who is fighting the enemies of God.'

"The women will go home and start jumping up and down on their men, all about how it is the will of God that all should support us."

Fertig paused, regarding Hedges with the bland benevolence of a poker player who might or might not have reason for his confidence. He looked positively boyish behind his beard, and Hedges suspiciously said nothing.

"There's another thing, Charley," Fertig said mildly. "I think we better round up every brass curtain rod in the province."

Hedges glanced sharply at Fertig. Experience had taught him to be wary whenever Fertig wore such a seraphic look and spoke in such an apparently artless way.

"Go ahead," Hedges said, refusing to be drawn. "Drop the other shoe."

"I saw a soldier squatting in the dirt outside," Fertig said. "A hell of a thing. We can't look like an army with people sitting around this way."

Stubbornly, Hedges waited.

"Well," Fertig said, "at least he was cleaning his rifle. But he could hardly work the patch through. It kept jamming in the barrel. What he needed was a ramrod slotted for a patch, not an old curtain rod.

"Curtain rods," Fertig said absently, looking at the ceiling, "are too thick. They just barely fit the barrel. Matter of fact, I checked one out this morning, and it turns out they're almost *exactly* .30 caliber."

"You go to hell," Hedges said happily. "I'll get your damned curtain rods."

But, where Hedges joyously saw bullets, Fertig sat back with his faint smile, seeing an end to the confiscation of sinkers; hence an end to the complaints of the fishermen, hence a resulting increase in the number of fish in the market and in the number of mines brought ashore. More important, he saw a woman giving up her precious curtain rods, aware of her sacrifice to the holy war against the enemies of God. Later, when the rods were returned to her, cut in little pieces to be sharpened, the point would be unmistakable. Then the woman could see that, without her, the Japanese would not be killed and that to sharpen a piece of brass was just as much fighting for her children's souls as pulling a trigger.

It would take a woman a long time to rub a bit of brass on a flat stone until she had sharpened it into a point sharp enough to satisfy her. But Fertig knew the depths of a Filipina's devotion. She would work patiently all day, hour after hour in the dripping heat, scratching away until her fingers bled, to produce three bullets. Twenty miles away across Panguil Bay, Japanese supply ships were unloading more bullets in half an hour than a woman could sharpen in ten years. In unit-production terms, the sharpening of bits of brass on stones would be more cumbersome than the unsatisfactory sand molding of lead. But it would produce more bullets, because there were a great many women, and in any event, the loyalty of the women was more important than the number of bullets they made.

In the privacy of his office, Fertig told Hedges of his thoughts, and when he had finished, Hedges said, "Wendell, I swear to God I don't know why we haven't thought of it before, but how about the good Lady Carmen? If you want the Church and the women to help, by God, old Carmen is The One to make them jump."

"She is the patron, huh?" Fertig mused, rubbing his goatee, and thinking how, in almost every province, there was usually one ruling family of Spanish descent. He had heard of the Ozamis family before the war, but he had also heard of them since.

"The thing is," Fertig said, "I hear that, when the Japs first came here, they stayed at the Casa Ozamis."

"Oh, horseshit," Hedges said. "The way I heard it, dona Carmen helped them little, and unwillingly. I heard the Japs left her alone on orders from Manila. Anyway, it sure won't hurt us to find out.

"She inherited this province from her old man," Hedges went on. "She's run it ever since. When the taos get sick, dona Carmen sends the doctor. When they go broke, she sends the rice. In return, they work for her. The taos love her. She's got the ilustrados buffaloed because she's so damned rich. Maybe she hasn't been helping us for the same reason she wouldn't either help or work against the Japs. Maybe she thinks she's protecting her people by being neutral. But, if you want the women and the

Church to help, by God, they're all going to wait to see what dona Carmen will do. The women will do whatever she says, and she's the biggest contributor to the Church. You tell her frankly what you told me and see what she says. I don't know why in hell we didn't go to her the day we got here."

"Maybe it's because she didn't ask us," Fertig said drily.

That night, the messenger reported that dona Carmen would be home and asked that the General come to dinner. Fertig trimmed his goatee and pulled on a starch-stiff khaki shirt that had been cleaned so many times it was almost white. He dressed as anxiously as a boy going to his first high school dance and gave an extra shine to the new shoes for which he had given a Chinese merchant a fountain pen. The shoes had been too big for the Chinaman, and, since Fertig had no ink for the pen, it had been an even swap.

Jolting over the seacoast road from Misamis to Jimenez, Fertig felt the incongruity of what he was doing. After months of wandering and hiding in the wet muck of jungles, it was fantastic to be driving in a motor car to a dinner party through a province that was a memory of the lazy days of the Old Philippines, to be going to dinner in a defeated country in order to persuade a rich spinster to start a war. Nothing in Fertig's kaleidoscopic experience in all the past months had prepared him for such a thing. And nothing that Hedges had said prepared him for dona Carmen Ozamis.

She seemed to float toward him through the soft evening as Fertig climbed stiffly from the car. She came toward him, a slim hand extended, jewels flashing at her wrist, her head tilted to look up at him, her brown eyes large and dark in the cream-tinted light of her face. She was slender and her hair was midnight black and she was beautiful.

Fertig felt the sweat begin to form at his armpits and said that he was charmed. Covertly, he darted an angry glance at Hedges, who had described this vision of aristocratic Spain as a purse-proud old woman. Hedges wore a look of happy innocence.

In a trance, Fertig followed dona Carmen through the iron gates of the Casa Ozamis and up the wide, curved staircase that led to the living quarters of the thick-walled house. He passed through a drawing room where portraits of ancestors, lighted by lamps of Czechoslovakian cut glass, stared haughtily at him from dark-paneled walls. Fertig moved onto the polished floor of a spacious dining room where silver and bone china gleamed on damask, to find himself being introduced to dona Carmen's six younger sisters.

He was, Fertig knew, seeing before him a typical tragedy of the high-born Spanish mestizo family in the Islands: seven lovely girls for whom there were no eligible Spaniards or mestizos. Two other guests were in the room: white-gowned Father Calanan and a Filipino, Dr. Contreras. Following medieval custom, priest and sage ate at the board of the patron of the province. Fertig was conscious of the soft, firm touch of dona Carmen's light fingers on his arm.

"You must please sit here, General," she said.

And she placed him in what had been her father's chair at the head of the table. She would sit at his right.

Throughout the banquet that followed—a banquet that began with asparagus soup and wound on, in a leisurely way, through fish, poultry, meat, and salad courses to conclude with coffee and liqueurs—Fertig was conscious of the languorous eyes of the seven sisters who lived without a man. He found it difficult to know which was reality: the Mora who had sullenly thrust a pot of undercooked rice and pieces of monkey at him or the exquisitely gowned, sophisticated ladies of this luxurious palace, who smiled across a flower-strewn table and fluttered their fans. It was incredible that both the Mora and the Ozamis sisters would be a part of the reality of Mindanao, but this was just as true as the fact that Fertig's life was bound up with theirs.

Hedges was completely at home. He had found himself a place between Paulita and Nieves, the most vivacious of the sisters, and the girls would look at Fertig, hide their pretended confusion behind their fans, put their heads together with Hedges, and laugh.

"Paulita wants to know if your beard's real, and I told her it was, seeing how you're mostly goat," Hedges said.

But dona Carmen looked up at Fertig, the candlelight glinting in her dark hair, and said it was such a beard as men had worn. Then Father Calanan broke the spell—if spell there was—by telling an Irish story, and the moment—if moment there had been—was gone.

The candlelight, the food, the civilization of the casa, and the elegance of its mistresses were a precipitous return to the kind of life that Fertig had all but forgotten, and, looking at dona Carmen, he felt a throat-tightening need to protect these women and the life of the casa. Something of his need deepened his light voice when it was time for him to say the things he had come to the casa to say. The table was still as Fertig spoke of his hopes for a unified resistance and the need for a civil government that would stand for the decent laws of free men, to which the army must always be subservient.

When he finished, there was a little silence. Dona Carmen placed her delicate fingers on Fertig's khaki sleeve.

"Your Colonel Morgan," she said. "It is too bad that Colonel Morgan could not be here tonight. I have heard much about him, and it would have been a pleasure to meet him."

Her soft words sent a dagger into Fertig's heart. Carried away by his own mood, Fertig had forgotten Hedges' warning that dona Carmen's mind was like a trap. In speaking of his needs, Fertig had carefully avoided mention of Morgan. But dona Carmen obviously was not the unofficial owner of Misamis Occidental by accident.

"Colonel Morgan could not come," Fertig said steadily. "I am afraid it will be some time before he returns."

He had spoken because he had to say something, but, even as he did, an idea that had long been somewhere in the back of Fertig's mind now emerged, full-blown.

"Frankly," Fertig said, "I am not satisfied with the progress we are making in the other provinces. I am sending Colonel Morgan, as my chief of staff, to other guerrilla areas, to tell the people what I have told you and to bring the guerrilleros into line."

Fertig was aware that Hedges was regarding him with utter astonishment; out of the corner of his eye, he saw Dr. Contreras and Father Calanan look at one another.

"Ah," dona Carmen said.

She glanced at the white-gowned priest, who returned an almost imperceptible nod, and Fertig felt his heart beat again.

"You wish us to help, si?" dona Carmen said, looking deeply into Fertig's eyes once more, her fingers tightening on his arm. She smiled quite suddenly; a vivacious, Spanish smile. "Of course we shall help!"

Her soft accents sent a thrill through Fertig, who wondered if, in these few words, she had made him a gift of Misamis Occidental without realizing it. For it was obvious that authority, cloaked by kindness, came easily to her, so easily that it was conceivable that she was quite unaware that even her merest opinions, voiced however lightly, were laws to both the ilustrados and taos of her province. Indeed, it seemed to Fertig that the Irish priest's barest of nods might not have been a sign of churchly blessing but the acquiescence of the Church to the whim of Caesar, to the decision that dona Carmen's confessor had immediately recognized in her swift glance at him.

Late that night, driving back to Misamis, Hedges spoke low and quickly in order that the driver should not hear.

"Since when did you send Morgan anywhere?" Hedges asked. "By God, it's going to be news to him."

"She wanted to know who was in charge," Fertig said. "What else could I say? Besides, when she put me on the spot like that, she gave me an idea. You know the kind of answers we've been getting from some of these guerrilleros. They've been saying, 'The hell with you, Bud.' I figure we've got to put the fear of God into those birds, and Morgan is just the kind of evangelist they need."

Rapidly, Fertig sketched out his idea. He needed to get Morgan out of his way and to get the other guerrilleros into line. Therefore, he would tell Morgan that the peaceful province of Misamis Occidental was no place for a man of Morgan's talents. There were no Japanese to kill. He would paint a picture for Morgan of all the new unmarried girls that Morgan could expect to find in the barrios of other provinces, of all the fiestas that would await the conquering hero. There would be plenty of girls, plenty to drink, and plenty of fighting—and Morgan was one of those few men who actually enjoyed combat. Moreover, Morgan would be seen everywhere, and all would see the fighting leader of the resistance. He would be the one whom all would remember after the war. Morgan could thus regard his mission as political spadework for the postwar elections. Meanwhile, he would preach the gospel of unified resistance, carrying letters from the American general from Australia. The letters would promise arms and supplies to all guerrilleros who followed the general's tactics and who would put themselves under his command. There would be no need to mention that the arms and supplies would take the form of homemade shotguns and reloaded ammunition: Something was better than nothing. Morgan would be the proof that an American command existed, proof that, if anyone hoped to get anything from the Americans, he would have to deal through Morgan. If the leaders did not go for it, their people might, for, with automatic riflemen at his back, Morgan would be no furtive courier but proof of the gathering power.

"What I won't tell Morgan," Fertig said, "is that, everywhere he goes, the other guerrilleros who don't know our setup will think he is the messenger boy. Even if he says he is The One, they won't believe him because, if he was The One, he wouldn't be carrying letters. What he will really be doing is spreading the word that the Americans are back and in charge."

"And if he does," Hedges mused, "then you can turn around and tell Judge Saguin and the rest of them, 'See, I am the Incharge. Morgan is the small boy. I tell him to go, and he goes.'"

"Exactly," Fertig said. "This, and with dona Carmen behind us, ought to do it."

"Well, for God's sake, let's send Morgan to China," Hedges said. "Send him so far away that Sinang will go chasing after him. And tell him to take Tait along."

5

PERHAPS, AS FERTIG later said, the Mindanao guerrilla was finally born at dona Carmen's supper party. Morgan and Tait sailed the following night for the far shore of Panguil Bay, and, as Hedges presumed, Sinang could not endure her lover's absence. She drank and sulked and ordered soldiers about to compensate for the fact that she could not wholly possess the man she loved, and, two days later, with a helpless, suspicious glare at Fertig, she buckled on her pistol and set out alone, promising to kill Morgan if she found him in another woman's arms.

With Morgan, Tait, and Sinang out of the province and with dona Carmen and the Church behind them, Fertig and Hedges set to work. Meanwhile, beset by problems of his own, General Morimoto postponed his attack upon Misamis from one week to the next, and the weeks became the two months of November and December 1942—months during which Fertig and Hedges built a power that began to reach out beyond the province of Misamis Occidental until, by Christmas Eve, its presence was felt throughout Mindanao and even upon the neighboring islands, holding men like Dimaponong Uy in the grip of it.

On that Christmas Eve, Dimaponong lay on his belly beneath the dry, withered stalks of a banana plant. His face was the color of cold tea with milk in it, and his hands wet the walnut grips of his rifle. He was completely oblivious of the million things that lived in the dusty leaves and that now fed on his sweating, naked legs and arms. He did not feel the bites because there was no room in his mind for anything but his orders. If he did not keep repeating his instructions to himself, he would begin to shake. He was very much afraid that, if the shaking came once more, he would finally lose control of his sphincter muscles. Dimaponong had heard of men who lost control, and, when he first started to shake, he discovered that it could happen to him.

He looked from beneath the leaves and down the road the Japanese would use. He saw everything more clearly than he had ever seen anything before. Indeed, he saw the hot white road and the dark green trees and light green grasses at the road's edge as though it was all a picture, and he had the curious notion that he might already be dead. He concentrated on what Somang had told him.

"You are to remain in this place," Somang had said. "Now tell me what you are to do."

"I shoot all my ammunitions," Dimaponong said. "Then I am to run."

"Idiot," Somang said impatiently, "when are you to shoot your ammunitions? What are you to do next? Where are you to run?"

Never in his life had anyone called Dimaponong an idiot, particularly a fellow townsman, and he looked with bright anger at Somang, whom he had known since childhood and whose fields were adjacent to those of the Uy family. He was not afraid of Somang, who was a man like himself, despite the fact that, because of the war, this townsman of his was called a lieutenant.

"I will shoot my ammunitions at the last man in the column," Dimaponong said sullenly. "I will shoot when I hear the BAR shooting."

"And then what?"

"Then," Dimaponong said, "I run."

"Before you run," Somang insisted with a sudden gentleness, "what do you do?"

"I will pick up all the empty cartridge cases," Dimaponong said, still sullen. "Then I will run through the grove to the jungle, and, when I come to the stream, I am to go uphill."

"You are to remember this, yes?" Somang asked seriously. "It is all right? You are afraid, no?"

He put a hand on Dimaponong's shoulder and felt the trembling.

"Oh, sir," Dimaponong said, his defenses pierced, "I have much fright. Today I will die. But I will die brave."

It did not occur to Dimaponong until now, lying alone under the leaves and watching the road, that he had called his townsman sir. But, when he thought about it now, it did not seem unnatural. Then he saw the first of them coming up the road.

They were small, muscular men, dressed in gray-green clothing that sagged and bulged. Some had towels tucked into their belts, and they had tied wisps of grass into the netting over their helmets. Perhaps because they were still so close to the village, they came in column, carrying their thin rifles slung over their shoulders, except for the first three, who carried their rifles across their chests in their hands and who peered this way and that into the underbrush along the road. The first of them looked directly at Dimaponong, who in an ecstasy of fear wildly pulled the trigger of his Enfield.

His brown finger pressed yellow against the trigger, but the Japanese walked on, peering into the underbrush, and behind him came the next two, and then the column of men marching, their faces haggard with the anxiety of men who must move, armed, along a road in the hot silence of an alien land.

Terrified, Dimaponong pulled the trigger again, and again. It seemed to him that everyone was shooting, and he heard a tumult in his head, but his eyes saw the Japanese column marching past him at sling arms as though in a dream.

There was a sudden, blurting rush of explosions. Lieutenant Somang Tamparong's Browning automatic rifle had opened up, and, on the road, men were falling and running to throw themselves into the ditches, and puffs of dust sprang from the road, and the air was filled with the heavy sound of the Springfield and Enfield rifles of the guerrilleros and the *pt-sssrrng, pt-sssrrng* of ricocheting bullets. It seemed to Dimaponong that a man was screaming. He had never heard a man scream before.

A Japanese came running heavily straight for the banana plant under which Dimaponong lay, and hurtled into the ditch. The Japanese shrieked as he fell on the suyoks that Somang had ordered planted there, and Dimaponong swung the muzzle of the Enfield and pulled the trigger. This time, the rifle jumped in his hands and slammed against his shoulder, and Dimaponong dully realized that he must now have switched the safety lock from safe to fire. He kept working the bolt and pulling the trigger after the rifle had stopped jumping, but Dimaponong's whole life was filled with the image of the Japanese not five yards away from him. The grass-decked helmet had fallen across his eyes, but, from beneath the helmet, the Japanese seemed to be asking for something. His mouth kept slowly opening and closing. He seemed to be making no sound until, in a perfect instance of absolute silence in the midst of all the sounds of the road, Dimaponong distinctly heard the Japanese cough and saw the open mouth suddenly fill with bright blood.

Then Dimaponong realized he had fired all five of his bullets, and scrambling to his knees he turned to run into the safety of the jungle behind the banana grove. He had gone two steps before he stumbled, and, falling, he remembered the cartridge cases. The empty cartridge cases that must be reloaded!

Any man (he heard Somang's voice saying) *who does not bring back the cartridge cases will go back to the plow.* To go back to the plow was to lose all face, and Dimaponong went plunging again to his place of ambush, searching frantically among the litter of stalks and leaves for the glitter of the brass tubes, his brown fingers tearing among the leaves while the air around him crackled with the flat whipcracks of the Japanese rifles and the sharp smacking of bullets striking trees.

Two, three of them—there was the third—he fumbled them anyhow into a pocket of his short trousers. There was the fourth! One more—where could it be? A banana frond snapped above his head and fell on his back, and Dimaponong yelled like a child. At the same time, he saw a glitter, and cramming the cartridge case and a handful of dirt into his pocket, Dimaponong started again for the jungle, pausing to scoop up the rifle he must have thrown away, and now, running with the rifle, he dashed through the shadows of the grove, the air around him whispering and cracking. He fought his way into the tangled jungle and did not stop until he had stumbled into the stream.

He paused with the cool water about his ankles and fought for breath. As it returned, he was conscious of a stench, and something wet and slippery running down his legs. Dimaponong stood in the stream and looked fearfully around. He was alone. He laid his rifle on two dry stones. He took off his trousers and took the cartridge cases and the dirt out of his pocket, and he washed himself and his trousers in the shallow water. They will see my wet trousers and know, Dimaponong thought, so he lay in the stream to soak his shirt as well. I will tell them I fell in the stream, he thought, and he put on his wet trousers and picked up his rifle and made his barefoot way up the stream bed toward the place where he would meet the others.

From a purely military point of view, the action in which Dimaponong fired his first shot was unimportant to the point of negligibility. The entire action, from the moment Lieutenant Tamparong felt the smooth rush of bullets spurting from his automatic rifle until Dimaponong found the last of his five cartridge cases, took place within three minutes. Fifty guerrilleros, hiding on a prepared ground of their choice, ambushed a patrol of twenty Japanese, killing four and wounding three. Twenty-three of the guerrilleros had been so excited they had forgot to fire their rifles, although they believed at the time that they were shooting. Three men had thrown their rifles away when they ran. One man forgot to run, and he returned to the camp hours later to say that he had seen the Japanese build a fire to burn their dead. He said they had also thrown onto this fire one man who was not yet dead but badly wounded. When they saw him struggling to crawl from the burning logs, one of the Japanese ran quickly up to the pyre and struck the wounded man over the head with a clubbed rifle.

Having burned their dead, the Japanese marched back to their garrison in the village. No guerrillero had been killed; none had been wounded. But, a courier reported to the guerrilleros, many may have died in the village, because the Japanese were questioning the townsmen. He, the courier said, had heard men and women screaming and the sound of shots as he left the town.

Colonel Charles Hedges stood in the center of the circle of guerrilleros, hearing the courier's report and that of Lieutenant Tamparong. He roundly cursed all those who had failed to fire, although—as an experienced officer—he had expected this. He ordered the three men who had thrown away their rifles to return to the scene, find their guns, turn them back to the army, and to report tomorrow to the army farm. They would go back to the plow, and three of the men now farming would be given a chance to fight the Hapons who butchered helpless townsmen and enwhored the women of the villages.

"Who thinks he killed a Jap, huh?" Hedges demanded, glaring at them all.

No one spoke, but, after a while, Dimaponong Uy raised his eyes and said, "Good Sir, I think perhaps I kill one, only."

He told how he had heard the man cough and had seen the blood. Fixed by Hedges' penetrating stare, he went miserably on to the end of it.

"I tell my companions I fell into the stream," Dimaponong said to the Colonel to whom no man could lie, "but it is not so. Oh, Great Sir, I too much frightened I shit my pants!"

Hedges threw back his head and laughed so hard his straw hat fell off.

"Well, by God, you're man enough to admit it!" Hedges said to the shamefaced Dimaponong.

Hedges whacked him fondly across the back, and, clutching the puzzled Dimaponong by the arm, he presented him to the others.

"Here's the only son of a bitch I found yet, outside of the Lieutenant, who had the goddamn sense enough to do what he was told," Hedges said.

Incredibly, Dimaponong realized the Colonel was praising him.

"Here we got a bunch of goddamn old women who forget to shoot and a bunch of binabays[29] who throw their guns away, and one man with

---

29. binabays = homosexuals

guts enough to hang in there and actually kill one of the bastards," Hedges said.

"Now listen here, Dimaponong," Hedges said, loud enough for all to hear, "we have no medal, huh? But, by God, you deserve one, huh? I am giving you a medal right now. From now on, any man who does well in combat gets the Hedges Medal, huh? That means he can take my own Springfield and one bullet, huh, and go down to Iligan at night to shoot the Jap sentry off the bridge. You take my rifle tonight, Dimaponong, and, if you knock the bastard off the bridge and into the river, you will be a corporal tomorrow. OK, huh? Can be, yes?"

"O, Great Sir, yes, salaamit, can be," Dimaponong stammered, trembling again but not with the emotion of the morning. He squared his shoulders in imitation of Hedges' jaunty swagger and threw Hedges a Boy Scout salute, which Hedges briskly returned. From that moment, Dimaponong's dark eyes followed Hedges, as the very terrible Colonel Goddamn shouted at the others, "Great Moro warriors, horseshit! Bunch of old women! Get out of here! Tomorrow, I'm going with you myself, and God help anybody who throws his goddamn rifle away. So help me, I'll shoot you myself . . ."

"That Colonel goddamn, he has very short intestines," a guerrillero whispered to Dimaponong.

But Dimaponong, in whom a mystery had grown, looked coldly at his companion and swaggered away.

IN ANOTHER PART of Mindanao that Christmas Eve, Abundio Cabcaban sprang to his feet when he heard the repeated, hollow *tunk-tunk, tunk-tunk* of a wooden gong. Quickly, he ran to the gong that hung in his yard and struck it with a knotted stick, waiting until he heard the thinner sound of the gong of Diosdado Butsalac, the roadmender, reply. Then he untied the instrument and carried it into his house, where he tucked it into the thatch. Wordlessly, Abundio embraced his wife, Buenaventurada, who had already sent eight-year-old Policarpo to drive the carabao from its wallow and up the trail leading to the nearby jungle. He watched his wife, carrying tiny Serpia on her hip and the woven banigs on her head, follow their son and the carabao. When the Japanese arrived, Abundio was alone, digging with a stick, squatting at the edge of his rice paddy, shaping the mud wall of the low dike that would hold the water when it was time to flood the field.

"You are guerrillero," the Japanese interpreter told him.

"Yes, sir, thank you, sir, I am not guerrillero," Abundio said. "They are bery bad mens. They steal my chickens."

The Japanese slapped him; Abundio had forgot to bow.

"I am friend of Nippon," Abundio said, tears in his eyes, bowing many times.

"Where is your wife?"

"Yes, sir, thank you, sir. My wife is gone to Butu'un only."

Butu'un was the market town, now garrisoned by Japanese. The interrogation went on.

Sir, he said, his children had gone with his wife to the market in Butu'un. Yes, he had a carabao, but, too bad, it was gone, too.

Where had it gone?

Oh, sir, no one knew. The guerrilleros had taken his carabao.

Why had he not kept them from taking his animal?

Oh, sir, they came with guns.

They slapped him again.

Oh, sir, he said, I am a friend of Nippon, you make a great mistake. If only brave Nippon soldiers would protect poor people with their guns, then the guerrilleros, those very bad men, would not come to steal the chickens and the carabaos.

You will come with us to Butu'un and point out your wife, they told him.

Yes, sir, Abundio said, wondering what someone might have told the Japanese about Buenaventurada and the Women's Auxiliary. But he could not go, because he must fix his dike if there would be rice for the brave Nippon soldiers to eat, and besides, his wife would return at any moment.

You are lying, they said. You are farmer by day and guerrillero by night. When Abundio denied this, bowing frequently, they slapped him again. One of the Japanese soldiers slammed his rifle butt down Abundio's shin, scraping it and bruising Abundio's foot, and the interrogation went on.

Eventually, they left because they could not waste all this time on what the Japanese commander called a village dolt, and Abundio thoughtfully watched them go.

He waited until they were out of sight, and then he rose from the mud into which they had beaten him. He painfully climbed into the branches of the breadfruit tree in his yard and scanned the countryside as far as he could see. When he was sure they had really left and that none was hiding down the road to see where he, Abundio, might go, he climbed down from the tree, pulled the gong from beneath the thatch, and struck it in the signal that meant the Japanese had passed through his sitio. He searched beneath the mudslime of the carabao wallow until he found the wet bundle that was his sinamay,[30] which he had wrapped tightly around his rifle. Despite the pain in his ribs and in his shin and foot, Abundio moved at a light trot along the trail that led to the jungle, because it would take time for Buenaventurada to wash his uniform and for him to clean his rifle and then to run to the assembly point where, even now, plans were being made to ambush these Japanese when they returned, hot and tired, down the road toward their barracks at Butu'un.

WHILE THESE EVENTS were taking place in the lives of Dimaponong Uy and Abundio Cabcaban, the war was being fought in yet another way on Christmas Eve on the island of Mindanao. In a village near Baroy, Subang Daud was digging carefully, almost with love, driving the worn iron shovel straight down into the earth with his hard, bare foot. The muscles of his back and arms swelled and slid as he lifted the heavy, wet earth. Whenever he came to a stone, he dug around it with his fingers and pried it loose and threw it to one side of the neat pile of dirt beside the excavation. He kept the walls of the pit straight and paused from time to time to wipe sweat from his eyes and to drink from one of the soldiers' canteens. While he dug, women lit cooking fires in the shade of the trees and began to prepare the food they would eat at sundown. There would be fiesta tonight, but no one could eat until the sun had set.

BY NOON, SUBANG had finished, and regarded his work with satisfaction. But, as he stood there with his chest heaving, shiny with sweat, someone said, "We do not want him buried here. Only good people are buried in the holy ground, and he has brought shame to all."

Subang was tired and giddy from working in the sun, and he stood there, angry and hot-eyed, talking with them, but they told him to fill the pit he had dug. Such work should not go to waste, he told them. Sooner or later, someone else would die, and then this grave could be used. One man looked at another, and then all decided that Subang spoke with wisdom. The pit could remain until someone could use it. While this discussion went on, the women continued to pluck chickens and peel camotes in the shade of the trees.

It was midafternoon when the second pit was finished, and, as Subang stood up at last and threw his shovel down, the school principal called

---

30. sinamay = rough hemp fiber uniform

to him. As Subang looked around, the principal shot him with a rifle. The shock of the bullet knocked Subang backwards into his grave, and a woman came from the shade to stand over him. She picked up a handful of the new earth and said in Spanish, "May you rest in peace."

Subang looked up from the bottom of his grave at the woman sprinkling earth on him, and, maddened by the thought that a Christian should be muttering magic at his death, he sprang from his grave and rushed at one of the guards, wrenching the guard's bolo from him. Blood from Subang's wound stained the guard's clothing. But, before Subang could strike, a second guard slashed from behind, missing Subang's neck but cutting deep into the shoulder and knocking Subang scrambling to the ground. Before the guard could slash again, Subang scuttered on all fours out of the way, rose to his feet and dashed toward the trees, blood spurting from his shoulder and spattering the dust. Before Subang could reach the forest, the school principal fired once more, completing the execution of Subang Daud. While all this was taking place the women who watched placidly continued their cooking.

The crime for which Subang was executed was not that he had stolen a pair of trousers, although he had, and he was wearing them at the time he was caught.

"It is not the trouser involving here," a courier subsequently explained to Commanding General Wendell Fertig. "It is the oath, only. The Moros have swear they are not to steal again until the beectory. All are shamed when their townmate breaks the oath. It is the Moros who bring him to us. They tell the judge of their shame and say, if the man is killed, then all can be sure he will not repeat the offense."

IN DIPOLOG, which means The Other Side, because there had once been a Spanish barracks across the river from Dipolog 200 years ago, Sol Samonte was fighting the war alone on Christmas Eve 1942. Samonte, a deft man with an intellectual delicacy in his Malay features, was working in an open shed with a thatched roof. He was trying to combine quicksilver, taken from household thermometers, with his memory of high school chemistry in order to arrive at fulminate of mercury. If he succeeded, his fulminate would replace the heads of kitchen matches as the percussive in the caps of rifle cartridges. Matchhead percussion caps were not dependable, and the supply of matches was as small as the supply of mercury from the thermometers. Since fulminate of mercury is a most unstable compound and since the powder for the cartridges consisted of flash powder from Chinese firecrackers, mixed with dynamite and amatol, newly commissioned Lieutenant Samonte was left to work alone by common consent. So far, he had blown up three rifles, and, once, he had nearly blown up himself.

In a similar although much larger shed near the town of Jimenez, there was an ordnance factory. Here, on Christmas Eve, bare-chested brown men squatted on the packed-dirt floor, tinkering tiny ejector springs for the Enfield rifle bolts. Enfield ejectors were always breaking. New springs were fashioned by men whose only tools were hammers, chisels, and rat-tail files. They would first chisel a sliver from the heavy steel strap of an automobile spring. Then they would work this down into the shape of an Enfield ejector spring with the files. It might take a man two days to make such a spring by this method, but there was no other method, and the men who worked at the ordnance factory labored with the patience of the women who sharpened bits of brass on stones.

On Christmas Eve, as on every other day, men worked in a building they called the rice mill, although no rice was ground there. It, too, was an open shed and stood outside the capital city, Oroquieta. It was the combined mint and treasury of the Government of the Free Philippines, and here men carved printing plates of hardwood. They mixed inks made of soot and dyes and cut heavy kraft wrapping paper into small squares. The hardwood was difficult to carve, and the woodcuts had to say everything in two languages.

"Kining sapi-a kailisan sunala sa lydng bili tapus ang kagbut ug dili kakubsan ni kaayran," the plates said. "Ma-bug-at nga silot ipahamtang sa maga kawat pag sundog ning sapi-a."

"This note," the plates said in English, "is redeemable at face value after the emergency and will not be devaluated or discriminated against. Counterfeiting of this note will be severely punished."

The wooden plates wore down rapidly, but the printing process went on without pause, and all the squares of paper were carefully numbered, and the numbers were entered in two separate ledgers in order that the money would someday be redeemed by the United States Treasury. The General Fertig had promised that it would. The people believed that the General Fertig, whom many now called Tai Tai, always spoke the truth. Tai Tai literally means Old Old, but the people used it in its common meaning, which is witch doctor. Fertig was their magic-maker.

Throughout the province of Misamis Occidental, which was the entire extent of land actually in possession of the Government of the Free Philippines at that time, men swarmed up trees and poles to expand the

telephone and telegraph systems. Since there were no regular glass insula-
tors, they used pop bottles. Since there was no copper wire, they stripped
iron wire from farm fences or bought it from those who stole it from the
Japanese army stores. The telephone batteries wore out, and there was no
way of recharging them until someone discovered by accident that, if a telephone battery was soaked overnight in tuba, the coconut beer, life would
return to the battery. No one knew why this should happen, although everyone had great faith in tuba, but happen it did, and the soaking of batteries in
coconut beer became Standard Operating Procedure for the United States
Forces in the Philippines, Brigadier General Fertig, Commanding.

Near the foot of Panguil Bay, on a wooded hillside some distance from
the barrio of Bonifacio, beneath a huge mango tree, the Force Radio Section
was trying to invent the radio. The Section consisted principally of Gerardo
Almendres, a slight, determined high school boy who had once sent away
for an International Correspondence School course. He had been able to
buy the school's books before the war but had not been able to buy the
radio parts with which to practice. For two months, Almendres had been
working through the hot days with bits and pieces of old radio receivers and
parts of the sound equipment taken from a motion-picture projector that
had been buried in a swamp. The result was, as all said, the goddamnedest
mess you ever saw. The inwards of what should have been a sending set the
size of a small valise were now spread across the four walls of a nipa house,
resembling in magnified detail the exploded diagrams of the International
Correspondence School of Scranton, Pennsylvania. Wires ran everywhere
to mysterious devices whose use Almendres could only try to guess.

The youngster was assisted in his researches by a Filipino who had
once sold radios as a traveling salesman and by another who had once
listened to a radio. From time to time, their contraption hummed for a
moment or so, and they all wondered if, when it hummed, it was working.

Elsewhere in the province, men tried to find a way to make soap from
coconut oil and wood ashes. If soap could be made, it could be traded to
the Island of Negros for sugar, which could be used in the manufacture
of alcohol, which could be used as fuel in the automobile engines. At
the navy yard, which was simply a section of the beach near the town
of Misamis, men installed light machine guns on iron pipes in the bows
of the two launches that constituted the fighting ships of the Navy of
the Free Philippines. In the capital city, Oroquieta, Judge Saguin presided
over the government that, among its many duties, paid the army and the
navy, printed stamps as well as money, regulated commerce and interisland
trade, pegged prices, collected clothing, and shot men who stole trousers.

6

THE SUN FELL INTO THE SEA, and Christmas Eve 1942 became one of those tropical nights that made it difficult to believe there could be such a thing as ugliness. A light breeze stirred as the day's heat began to give way to the cooler evening, and the breeze brought the sound of a woman's laugh into the office where a red-bearded man sat alone.

A Man of Destiny, Fertig thought wryly, must issue a Christmas message to his people. How would General MacArthur put it? Something antique, orotund, and rather grand. Fertig tore a page from a pad of lined school composition paper and typed across it the capital letters:

ORDER OF THE DAY 25 DECEMBER 1942

"A year ago," he wrote, "the outlook was black with impending disaster as the tide of Japanese aggression rolled over the peaceful islands of the Philippines. The flood has passed, and now the irresistible surge of awakening power of a united people is sweeping the enemy back. Now our radio speaks from the United States, 'You are still in the service of United States and under command of Gen. MacArthur. Stop. You are not forgotten.' Not deserters, but fighters!"

Fertig decided he was not exactly lying. If he had a radio, it would say something of the sort. It was no lie to say a united power was awakening, even if it had not yet got out of bed. Why admit the Filipinos were not united? And there was no harm in calling them an irresistible surge— would you call them a resistible surge? And if the Japanese withdrew their patrols, as seemed to be the case at present, the effect was that the Japanese were being swept back.

"You have withstood a year of war," Fertig typed, "continuing to grow in unity, strength, and love of country while the end of Japan draws nearer with each passing day. With such people, nothing is impossible, for the war has given birth to a united people—not Visayan or Tagalog, not Ilongo or Ilocano, not Moro or Christian, not tao or ilustrado, not civilian or soldier, but Filipinos All."

He ran the platen back, underlined Filipinos All, and hoped this wish came true. He continued:

"I salute you on the 25th December 1942. The first Christmas as a people freed by right of your own fight and defeat of an alien enemy.

"Dedicate your Christmas prayer," he wrote, and then crossed the four words out. The Moros would not be offering Christmas prayers. But they would be praying tomorrow, as on all other days, and since Christmas Day was a national holiday that the Moros recognized more or less as Protestants take brief note of St. Patrick's Day in the United States, the Moros might not be offended by mention of the fact it was Christmas.

"Dedicate this Christmas to prayer that the steady thrust of the northeast monsoon will rise as the surge of a baguio[31] to sweep our beloved islands clear of the invaders."

Fertig paused. It was a fine sentence in Filipino-English, but would the ultranationalist politicians and guerrilleros want to hear an American refer to "our" beloved islands? Fertig decided the hell with them.

"The tiny ants kill the python—not one single bite, but many," he wrote. "Christmas Greet . . ." He scratched out all of this. The evil fairies who brought bad luck lived in anthills. One guerrilla patrol refused to make a night attack because of the danger of treading on anthills in the dark. In any event, Filipinos might not like to be compared to ants of tiny bite, particularly after having been called an irresistible surge and equated with monsoons. And it did no good to call the Japanese a python when the Manobos, like Datu Soong, and probably a good many recent Christian converts, still worshiped the Great Snake.

"Christmas Greetings," Fertig concluded his Order of the Day. "Greetings, soldiers of the army, the soil, the people. Greetings, Filipinos!"

He signed it, and dropped it in his Out basket, for the Message Center clerk to find before dawn.

Fertig stared at the homemade calendar on his wall. Above it a lizard darted to seize a beetle larger than it could possibly swallow. He put another piece of paper in his typewriter and wrote, "Dearest:—"

He looked at it. Was that what he really wanted to say? It was a serious

---

31. baguio = tropical cyclone

question. Fertig had a momentary vision of a tall woman with masses of dark hair. She had been the center of his life for twenty years. The vision faded; it was by no means as compelling as the reality of the tropical night and the faint scratchings of the lizard and the beetle. She was not the center of his life now. She had nothing to do with it. "Dearest:—" looked mockingly back at him.

"One of those nights when I feel the need of writing a letter," Fertig typed. "Every few weeks I have written one of these, scattering them among the people, some of whom may survive the future rigors of the war. At least one of the many should reach you. They are historical, in part, for much has happened in the past few months . . ."

He told her how their old friend Charley Hedges had proved to be a tough guerrillero, leading a pack of Moros; of how he had made himself a general and how his command was reaching throughout the island of Mindanao to the islands beyond.

He read what he had written and found it cold. *I am writing to you because I need to write a letter because I am making history.* It was not what he wanted to say, but, like most Westerners, Fertig found it difficult to speak from his heart. Western tradition says of the emotions, *keep them to yourself.*

"To you again, my dearest, all my love," Fertig wrote, trying to reach toward his love across the barrier of himself. "I will either come out of this a live hero or a dead one, for there is no chance of surviving a capture. It is best this way. Actually, I have supreme faith that I was born to scourge the Japs, not to die at their hands. The feeling has grown more intense when I remember that they have hunted me for half a year. It seems as though my whole life had prepared me for this. 'Wake up and Live' offers the pattern, provided the opportunity is there. I am commanding general of one-third of the Philippine Islands, and my command is growing all the time. May the gods continue to smile. Actually, this thing has moved so well that I begin to feel as a Man of Destiny. May my luck hold."

The Man of Destiny still had not said what he wanted to say. He tried again:

"I like to dream of you and the girls safe in the sleepy little town of Golden. I will be back with you, and how I shall rest, and how. Adios, my darling."

Something still remained to be said. He got it out at last, in pencil, below the meticulous typing.

"I love you."

Fertig folded the letter into thirds, and into thirds again, and sealed it in an envelope and put the envelope in a tin box. He looked up to see the lizard and the beetle still struggling silently above the calendar. The beetle was slowly and powerfully moving its horn legs, but it could not escape the lizard's terrible tongue, nor could the lizard, its clawed feet braced, pull the beetle toward its too-small mouth.

BOOK FOUR

Harvest

1

"SIR," THE FILIPINO CAPTAIN SAID, not making a request but stating a fact, "you should give me an American to command my company."

Fertig regarded the slim brown officer with astonishment. "For why?" Fertig asked. "You are better trained and more experienced than any of them. They are lieutenants, yes, but they have not had command. Few are soldiers; most are mechanics. You are the soldier. To you, they are the small boys."

"Yes, that is true," the captain said without conceit. "But I do not need a good one. You understand, any of the Americano lieutenants. I will be The One; I will say, 'We will do this.' But my men will not know that I say. They will be more confident if they believe an Americano is the Incharge."

"More confident?" Fertig asked. "You wiped out two Japanese patrols. You do not lose one man. Not one was wounded. How could your men be more confident?"

"Oh, do not make mistake," the captain said. "I have command, sir. My men obey. But they would do more if we had an Americano. He would be a kind of anting-anting for them, sir."

He smiled the thin smile of a man who must put up with superstitious people.

Fertig promised to see what he could do, and the captain left. Both men were realists. One of the realities was that most Filipinos still believed, in that winter of 1942-43, that Americans possessed superior wisdom and powers. Whether this view was right or wrong was not important. What *was* important was that most Filipinos believed it. Most of them actually felt uncomfortable to see an American working in a subordinate capacity

to any but the most obviously gifted Filipino. Despite the white man's hor-
rendous loss of face in East Asia, enough of this feeling persisted among
the simple taos of Mindanao to make it necessary for Fertig to commission the white men who joined him.

In the cast of Chief Elwood Offret, he did so gladly.

Offret was one of the first of them to come to Misamis in the early
days of the organization. He came from Momungan, still twisted by the
dysentery that was never wholly to leave him, but rolling along on his sea
legs with loyal good humor.

"By God, it's good to see you," Fertig said, wringing Offret's hand.
He did not add that he'd never really expected to see Offret again. The
bamboo telegraph had spoken of Moro raids and Japanese terror in the
Momungan area.

"I have a job for you, Chief," Fertig said. "You ever run a coconut-oil
factory when you were in the Navy?"

"Coconut factory?" Offret said.

"As commanding general, I have authority to commission officers,"
Fertig explained. "I'm offering commissions as second lieutenants, Army
of the United States, to American personnel who join this command.
Now let me tell you this, Chief: If you accept any Army commission from
me, that commission is going to stick. When The Aid comes, you can go
back to the Navy if you like—but at equivalent commissioned rank. I'm
not doing this just because we hiked all over Mindanao together. I can use
you, and you'll need a commission because the Filipinos expect it."

Offret's countenance showed the suspicion that Navy chiefs have his-
torically held of the officer class. The idea of a Navy machinist becoming
an Army lieutenant to run a coconut-oil factory was bizarre, but Fertig
explained that the factory was powered by an engine, and Offret said, if
the plant had an engine in it, he guessed he'd be able to figure it out and
make it work.

Fertig felt much more secure in the case of Cecil Walter, a civilian
and general manager of the Anakan Lumber Company. Walter couldn't
have been left out of the organization under any circumstances. He was a
leathery man in his fifties, as hard a man-driver as Hedges and every bit as
ready with his fists. He had been cited for bravery under fire in the First
World War, and he had already begun a guerrilla of his own in the Anakan
area. Walter had been in the Islands for years, the head of a working force
of 2,000 men, and he was fluent in the earthier phrases of the dialects.
Fertig had known him before the war as Walt and was delighted to have
this tough, no-nonsense warrior join him. Walt was also Hedges' personal

friend, and, between them, Walter and Hedges mounted as vicious a close-in infantry action as men have fought. Their soldiers not only ambushed Japanese along the coastal road but patrolled the streets of Japanese garrison towns at night.

Sam Wilson was a different matter. Fertig was shocked by Sam's appearance when the onetime Manila millionaire reached Misamis, still in possession of his heavy wooden crate and billowing mattress. Sam's frame was a scarecrow's. His hearing was faulty, and his eyes were failing him. He refused to say what his crate contained, and he wanted nothing to do with the guerrilla.

"But, Sam, you're just the man we need," Fertig told him. "All your life you've made money, and I want you to make some more. You know printing, and you know finance, and that makes you The One. I need you to take charge of printing our money and accounting for it."

"Wendell, the Japs have Susie and the boys," Sam said, shaking his head. "I just can't take the chance. You know what they'd do to Susie if they found out I was working against them. The only reason I'm here is, I was starving to death where I was."

He was the only man with whom Fertig pleaded. He did so coldly, stifling his sympathy for Sam's predicament. In the end, Wilson accepted Fertig's pledge of absolute secrecy, in which neither he nor Fertig believed for a moment. If ever there was a man who sacrificed himself for a cause, that man was Sam Wilson, who did so each day. He went at his work with the courage of despair, living in inward agony at the thought he had condemned his wife and children to death by torture. But he did a meticulous job. Indeed, he drove himself and his men to a constantly greater efficiency, like a man sprinting on a treadmill. And the more Sam tried to lose himself in work, the more work Fertig found for him to do.

Many of the young American servicemen who began to arrive in Misamis had less than two years' service. They were Air Corps armorers without bombs; radio operators without radios. They had not been trained to fight, nor to command. If Chief Offret had been suspicious of the officer class, most of the young Air Corps specialists positively hated it. Moreover, Bob Ball, who visited Misamis with Major McClish, told Fertig that, while he was a radio operator, he really knew nothing much about radios.

"Look, General," Bob Ball explained, "if the damn thing didn't work, I told the crew chief, and he had somebody put another one in the plane. If I'd touched the thing myself, the crew chief would have busted my head. Radio operators go to operators' school; technicians go to technical school."

Impertinent, untrained, inexperienced youngsters with no education beyond high school were not what an Army examining board would
consider officer candidates. Moreover, men who resent orders are hardly
qualified to give them. On the other hand, those who arrived at Fertig's
headquarters during the winter of 1942-43 had already been screened by a
different sort of examination.

The stories fell into a pattern. They were men like Kenneth Bayley,
who two years ago had been an eighteen-year-old boy living on a farm
near Plainview, Texas. Bayley illustrated a general rule: It was chiefly the
city-bred Americans who had surrendered, perhaps in the belief that, if
they kept together, someone would have to look after them; while the
country boys escaped to the country, where they felt sure they could look
after themselves. There was another rule, too: The young Southern and
Western farm boys thought more highly of personal liberty, and of the
word *patriotism*, than the more sophisticated personnel from the North-
eastern American cities. Further, Southerners and Westerners had a far
keener sense of racial pride than their Northern countrymen, and all of
these factors found expression in such statements, as "Ah doan kyar whut
yo' gonna do, but sonofabitch if Ah'm gonna let no bunch of slant-eyed
yellow bastards put mah ass in no jail."

That was the first frame of mind of those who escaped.

Off they'd gone, into the jungles, into the cogon, with none of Fertig's or Hedges' knowledge of the terrain, customs, dangers, or languages.
Young Bayley was neither the best nor the worst of them, nor were his
adventures anything other than typical. The story he told Fertig was this:

When the Japanese approached the field hospital where Bayley was
burning with malaria, he and thirteen others hobbled away into the hills.
Bayley heard that seven of the thirteen had since died, but he never learned
how or where.

He first accepted shelter from a Filipino, only to be warned next day
by a Manobo that the Filipino had really betrayed Bayley's presence to
the Japanese, who were on their way to seize him. Fleeing, he ran into a
group of Moros who professed friendliness but who—he learned from a
Filipino schoolteacher who seemed to be either the Moros' guest or prisoner—were planning to murder Bayley for his guns.

During the next seven months, Bayley, who had never been away from
home before he'd joined the Air Corps to see the world, traveled a long,
long way from both the Air Corps and Plainview, Texas. He toiled through
jungles and lived with naked primitives, whom he came to respect as being
as friendly, hospitable, and decent as any people he'd ever met. They were,

he discovered, his different equals. But savage Magahats speared Bayley's best friend to death—a youngster named John Grant, who had escaped from hospital with him.

Moving aimlessly, looking for food, Bayley drifted from kaingin to kaingin in the hills. Sometimes, there was only corn to eat, sometimes only camotes. He saw primitive women rise from childbed one day to resume their backbreaking chores the next; he would never forget the way milk dripped from the ripe breasts of a new mother as she thumped a heavy log pestle into a huge mortar, pounding the breakfast palay for her family.

He met Americans who roved the country, looking for food and women, telling the Filipinos all kinds of stories to better their own condition—in some instances, at the expense of other Americans. In a land where civilization and savagery had lived side by side, but which was now everywhere a complete chaos, Bayley found that race disappeared. What remained was human good and evil, and no one could say that any race was predominantly one or the other. The world was composed of such natural dangers and evil men that no good man could be free except to help another. Bayley found himself so far from home that his home had no reality any more; he no longer had any idea of helping his nation win a war. Instead, he became a part of the only world he now knew, and his one thought was, as he told Fertig, "to alleviate the situation and better conditions for the local people and everyone concerned."

In becoming a part of the local scene, he came to the second stage of mind of those Americans who became guerrilleros of Mindanao.

He joined the first guerrilla he found—that of the Moro Salipada Pendatun.

From the first, Bayley had his reservations. He found Pendatun well educated but cocky, egotistical, and a born Commander of furious energy. In the beginning, Pendatun seemed happy to have Americans join his command; he went out of his way to provide Bayley with medicines and food. Since Bayley had been an Air Corps mechanic, he was put to work in Pendatun's motor pool. But Bayley quickly learned that Pendatun and his staff used their few precious vehicles and their tiny supply of gasoline for pleasure driving. He also found Pendatun fighting a foolish sort of war— to Bayley, it seemed more of a lark than anything else. It consisted of a few guerrilleros now and again firing random shots at the town of Malaybalay, where the Japanese were entrenched in force. If the Japanese felt like it, he said, they would fire a few hundred shots back—several thousand, sometimes. But the Japanese never left Malaybalay, and the guerrilleros never got in, and as far as Bayley could discover, few of the shots hit anything.

Meanwhile, Pendatun's attitude toward the Americans changed. Bayley felt this was because Pendatun's staff—particularly his chief of staff, the mestizo Colonel Andrews—insisted on it. Daily, Bayley felt more discouraged. For his money the only real officer in Pendatun's army was Colonel Frank McGee, a West Pointer who had served with distinction in the First World War. Pendatun's staff treated Colonel McGee with contempt. And Bayley became increasingly disturbed by arrogant Moro officers who ordered him—once at pistol-point—to turn vehicles over to them for their trips to village dances. The mestizo Andrews was the worst offender. The end came when Bayley heard Andrews voice his notorious complaint that he couldn't sleep at night because of the thought he had American blood in his veins. This was more than another American, Leonard Merchant, could stand.

"Why goddamn it," Merchant said, drawing himself up and squaring away, "if it hadn't been for some drunken American dog-face with two dollars he didn't know what to do with, you wouldn't *have* any American blood in your veins."

Andrews went for his pistol; the American was saved—or, perhaps, Andrews was—by the intercession of other Americans and some Filipinos, but Pendatun had Merchant removed from the motor pool and a Filipino put in charge of it. And Bayley knew the time had come to leave. This time, Bayley was on his way toward the western seacoast of Mindanao in search of a rumor—a rumor that said an American general had come from Australia to take charge of the guerrilla and had issued a call for all unsurrendered Americans to report to him.

Thus, on Christmas morning 1942, Bayley awakened to find himself lying on a bamboo floor. As the gathering light made objects clear, he discovered he was staring at a naked woman who sat cross-legged facing him, intently searching for lice in her pubic hair. He regarded this apparition without surprise, having by now become accustomed to households where, when children defecated on the floor, the dogs would eat the mess and then, for good measure, lick the cooking pots. The night before, the pots had held meat—the flesh of a three-day-dead horse, most of which had been found awash in a river. The rest of the horse had apparently been eaten by crocodiles. Sometimes the cooking pots held deer, but most often monkey. Monkey was tough. Food was scarce. In addition to the Japanese, there was a plague of rats and locusts. People were eating rats and locusts.

A kindly family sheltered the twenty-year-old Texan on Christmas Eve. They plainly regarded the horse as a gift from the gods but generously urged the best portions on their guest. They also explained, by means of explicit signs, that they wished him to impregnate their young daughters in order to produce white children, whose presence would honor the whole tribe. Bayley declined the invitation as gracefully as he could, and on Christmas morning, after breakfasting on a cold, unsalted paste of rice and water, he continued the travels that had begun two years (or was it two centuries?) ago in Plainview.

The man whose blood would have honored a Manobo family was emaciated and dirty. His hair was long. He was malarial, and there was a boil the size of a silver dollar on his ankle. Leeches had burrowed into the boil. He no longer wore a uniform but rather a costume consisting of an old Filipino Constabulary shirt that was too small for him and a pair of woolen olive-drab trousers. Since his Army shoes had long ago rotted away, he was barefoot. He had no underwear, and the woolen trousers galled him. His crotch was raw, and this, together with the boil, made each step painful. But Bayley's rifle and pistol were clean, and there was ammunition for them in his pouched web belt, and, more important to him than anything else in this world, he was free. He was at complete liberty to choose how best to risk his life to help other people. That was the third frame of mind of those who became guerrilleros of Mindanao.

Singly or in twos and threes, Americans like Bayley crossed the wild mountains and virgin forests, making their way toward the rumor. They came furtively to the coastal road. Filipino patriots smuggled them past Japanese outposts. They slipped by Japanese launches in native bancas, disguised as fishermen with wide, conical hats. They came out of the sea, the jungle, and the cogon as filthy and as exhausted as Bayley, nearly all of them malarial and suffering from dysentery, skin diseases, and malnutrition—gaunt, ragged men whose home was no longer Grand Junction, Plainview, or Macon. Some came to help. Some came simply looking for more food and less danger. But all of them were as astounded as Bayley by what they found in Misamis Occidental.

Their astonishment began when armed guards asked to see their travel orders. Travel orders! The thought was incredible—and so were the guards. They were armed with bolos, homemade shotguns, .22-caliber rifles, air rifles, sticks. They were the Home Guard, or voluntarios. General Fertig had revived the Spanish system of requiring each man to devote so many days' labor a month to the state in lieu of taxes, and the labor that each man owed, who was not in the Army, was to guard the roads and trails.

If a truck was available—a truck!—the newly arrived American was driven to Fertig's headquarters. Jolting over the stone road, he passed well-tended farms and prosperous villages such as he had not seen since before the war began. He saw recruits practicing open-order drill; found women enlisted in a Women's Auxiliary Service, busily making bullets, uniforms, and bandages. Everywhere, he sensed a feeling of purpose and controlled power. Organization was at work here, and, as an American, he could understand the value of that. In Misamis City, Philippine Commonwealth and United States flags flew from staffs of equal height, and smartly uniformed, heavily armed warriors guarded the entrance of the old Spanish stone building that was the headquarters of the Commanding General.

The General proved to be a tall, straight, sandy-haired man in starched khakis. There was power in his posture, and in his gray eyes. His hair was close-cropped, and his red goatee, touched with gray, was neatly trimmed. The General's expression was more interested than kindly, more stern than compassionate; there was that about him that looked at a man seeking competence rather than friendship. In this officer's presence, it was difficult to remember people eating locusts or the way the leeches would burrow into rotting sores. No matter how recently a man had come from the jungle or how long he had been there, no matter how much a man might have considered himself no longer a part of the regular military service that had lost a war, there was something about Fertig that drew a man suddenly back into a vision of the service he had once known, something that took his rags off his dirty skin and washed him and put him into a clean uniform and called him to attention and made him salute, realizing that he was not saluting the officer but rather that he was saluting something he had all but forgotten but in which he now believed suddenly and strongly again.

Bayley felt it. Ball felt it. They all did. Ball took one look at Fertig and muttered: "Well, for Christ's sake, a real officer at last."

It was not that Ball disliked his guerrillero chieftain, Captain McClish. He had every respect for McClish's bravery. It was simply that Fertig gave Ball a larger view of what might be possible.

For his part, Fertig distilled what he could use out of the stories the Americans told. Bayley had essentially said two things: first, that Fertig must find some way to gain control over Pendatun's guerrilla and make real use of Colonel McGee; second, that starvation in the Bukidnon must be turned to account. Surplus corn from Misamis Occidental, packed over the trails by cargadores, could buy the allegiance of Bukidnon guerrilleros.

Meanwhile, as Bayley and the others told their stories, Fertig brushed aside the fact that none of them had heard of *The Officers Guide*. What they had was more important than what they lacked. What they had was something that set them apart from all other Americans on Mindanao: their freedom. To Fertig, any American who had had the courage to refuse to surrender or the guts to escape and had proved able to stay alive thus far, was potentially able to help other people. That potential basically qualified him for a commission.

As they talked, Fertig measured each man with the experienced eye of one who had spent his adult life hiring unschooled men to work in mines. He looked beneath their rags and sickness for purpose and hardness. If he did not always find it, it must be said that his method of selection was arbitrary. To Fertig, a handsome man like Ball—a man with a firm chin, an open, direct gaze, and proud carriage—was, for all his impertinence, a better risk than an ugly, slouching man with shifty eyes and loose lips. Fertig chose purely on the basis of whether he liked a man's looks as the man answered questions. It was hardly an infallible method of what the Regular Army might call personnel recruitment, but it worked well enough. Fertig by no means took all of the young Americans who came to Misamis.

To those he did, he explained, "This is purely a volunteer organization. You do not have to join. If you do not wish to do so, I will have you sent out of Mindanao by the first available transportation. Since we have no communication with Australia, I do not know when that will be. If you join us, you can quit whenever you please. If you quit, I'll have you sent out as soon as possible with the provision that you will never be allowed to return."

Then, Fertig explained why it was necessary for him to commission white men.

"You will have one hell of a responsibility," he said. "You're going to have to live up to the idea these people have of you. Since you have neither the training nor the preparation for this job, I'm going to make it easy for you: You will do what you are told, and I will do the thinking for this command."

Most of them took it and liked it

"Imagine me a goddamn second lieutenant in the Signal Corps," Bob Ball said. "What do you know about that?"

Fertig knew he was taking a risk. What most Filipinos expected, another Filipino would resent. Fertig was making trouble for himself, for he knew he would have to ride herd on these Americans. But the reluctant and those whose looks he did not like Fertig sent to another part of Misamis Occidental to await repatriation. One Air Corps sergeant who proved to be a psychopathic liar and spreader of false rumor, Fertig jailed.

Fertig's most pressing need was to consolidate his control over the

province the Japanese so obligingly did not invade; to direct the combat being waged elsewhere by guerrilleros who acknowledged his over-all
command. He also needed medicine, arms, laws, face, bullets, wire, powder, string, cloth, and, since none of these things were readily available, all
had to be searched out or devised. If any of the young Americans possessed any of the alleged Yankee ingenuity, they would have every chance
to exercise it. If they turned out to have no particular skills, there was
plenty of simple work for them. They would be put to supervision of the
endless housekeeping that the Army calls fatigue detail.

Most important of all, Fertig needed to establish communication with
Australia. Therefore, any man who knew anything about a radio must be
sent to Bonifacio, where Almendres and his Filipinos were trying to invent
one. If a man could invent a radio, Fertig was willing to create him colonel.
Then, in late December 1942, according to a report from Lieutenant Ball,
Almendres' homemade transmitter began to show signs of life. Ball said
it hummed.

2

BALL PAUSED, MOPPED his face, and everyone waited, tense, straining to hear a chirping birdsong of dots and dashes in reply. But all they heard was the steady chuffing of the diesel engine that generated the electricity. There was nothing for them but the inhuman heat of the still air, sickly sweet with the burned coconut-oil gases of the diesel's exhaust.

When the tension became unbearable, Ball tried again. His set young face ran sweat as he pounded over and again the dots and dashes representing groups of numbers determined by Fertig's pocket code cylinder. Translated, the message read we have the hot dope on the hot yanks in the hot Philippines. The frail house shook as Ball rattled the key, banging away as if he expected the very sound of his urgent violence to carry to Australia if the message did not.

There was no question that the transmitter was on the air. It was a crazy tangle of wires strung around the four walls of a nipa shack under a mango tree, but it worked. Young Almendres had puzzled it out, by trial and error and by reference to the International Correspondence School diagrams. An American civilian, Roy Bell, schoolteacher and radio ham from the island of Negros, had solved the problem of the aerial. But, because the set lacked a crystal, having instead a wire erratically coiled around a joint of bamboo, the signal did not keep to one frequency. It went rasping and sliding across all the kilocycles. Nevertheless, it was a signal, and the Jerry-built transmitter was a monument to a truth that Fertig had learned in a hundred mining camps: "There is almost nothing a man can't make for himself, once he realizes there is no outside source of supply."

Each day, the transmitter shrieked into the hot tropical air, but no answer came.

"Keep trying," Fertig said. "When they hear us, they'll reply."

But, by virtue of a radio phenomenon called skip distance, Australia could not hear Fertig's radio. But this did not mean that no one was listening.

"GOD DAMN!" a United States Navy signalman said, tearing off his earphones, to escape a screeching, wailing noise, like that of a handsaw keening through green hardwood knots.

The signalman muttered, waiting impatiently for the racket to stop. Then he called the station whose traffic he had been receiving, asking them to repeat the message drowned out by the handsaw noise.

The signalman manned a set in Radio Station KFS, San Francisco, monitoring military communications from the Pacific theater of war. There was no doubt at KFS that the wailing signal, which interrupted traffic on all frequencies, was a Japanese jamming the air. How did KFS know? It was simple enough. Decoding Center had recognized the coded number groups at once. But the Army had suspended use of those old code cylinders with the surrender of Corregidor, as a matter of prudence. Therefore the signal was sent by a Japanese, using a captured cylinder, trying at once to jam the air and to suck KFS into replying. It was a Jap, trying in the cornball Jap way to use American slang. The hot dope on the hot Yanks, indeed!

Maybe, the signalman thought, *we ought to double-cross that Jap by telling him to stand by for an answer. Then he'd have to shut up, waiting, in order to stay in character. Of course, we'd never answer, but, while the Jap was waiting, he wouldn't be jamming the air.*

The signalman suggested this, but his lieutenant said no. To give any answer, the lieutenant said, would be to tell the Japs that their jamming was successful.

MEANWHILE, THE SLOW days of January 1943 dripped by in the stifling heat of Mindanao, and each day was a month to Fertig as he waited for the answer that never came.

What's wrong with those people down there? Fertig asked himself. *Were those West Point prima donnas so ashamed of having surrendered the Philippines that they were afraid to acknowledge the fact that some men were still fighting? Did they think that, if they helped those who had not surrendered, the Japanese would kill the prisoners who had?*

Slowly, as the days passed, the suspicion grew in Fertig's mind that

MacArthur's headquarters was deliberately ignoring him. Was this the Army's way of punishing those who had refused to obey the orders to surrender? To treat them like men already dead?

But, damn it, they can't ignore me! I'm doing their work for them! They don't know what I have here! But I can't hold this thing together, forever, all by myself . . .

The need to be heard, to have attention paid him, wore the edge of Fertig's patience, the more particularly now that he knew his transmitter was sending a signal. More to the point, Fertig needed official recognition to nail down his assumed authority. He had no practical control over Mindanao's local commanders. Busran Kalaw and his Maranao Moros were a dubious quantity in the Lanao Hills. The Dansalan Moros, equally enigmatic, told Fertig that, if they should wipe out the Japanese in their area, then they, the Moros, would be free to raid Christian settlements again, "and this would not be good for the movement." While Fertig was trying to deduce what *that* meant, Salipada Pendatun made matters clear in Cotabato province. Pendatun suggested sardonically he might be willing to give Fertig a job. Even within his own nominal area, Fertig often found that he could only try to persuade his subordinate commanders to act, rather than order them to do so. For the guerrilla was less of a military establishment than an alliance of free men. Moreover, to force a proud Malay leader to do something against his wishes could cause him to lose face, and, in any event, Fertig had no force to use. Worse yet, certain American officers, fugitives like Fertig from the surrender, openly refused to join the guerrilla. One was Fertig's age and may have refused out of pride, but the refusal of *any* American—civilian, officer, or enlisted man—weakened the Filipinos' picture of America and of Fertig as the Commanding General from Australia.

Goddamn it, Fertig asked himself, *when will those thickheads answer me? The minute I can show somebody a directive to me from MacArthur or, better, show him a case of rifles, a first-aid kit, hell, even a roll of Australian toilet paper, he'll know on what side his bread's buttered.*

But it was not MacArthur who gave Fertig official recognition in January 1943. It was the Japanese. They announced their aircraft had destroyed Fertig's headquarters, killing him. The remnants of Major General Fertig's forces, the Japanese said, had been driven into the hills to starve to death.

A ruse, to lull him into a false sense of security? The prelude to the long-expected attack? In January 1943, the peaceful province of Misamis Occidental was certainly grotesque. No army in its right mind would tolerate creation of an enemy government in its midst. The failure of the Japanese to have acted long ago was inexplicable. They were scarcely unaware

of Fertig; they had bombed his headquarters daily for three months. And
now this. Fertig's spies in Cagayan reported that a Japanese ship, instead
of bringing reinforcements, had taken Japanese troops away—reducing
the Cagayan garrison to 185 men. Was that ship, now en route to Misamis,
part of an invasion fleet?

The Japanese were like a typhoon in the distance. Fertig read the Japanese report of his death and shrugged. The important thing about the
broadcast was that it fixed in the minds of the people of Mindanao the
idea that the Japanese considered him to be the guerrilla commander. That
gave him face, but not enough.

HALF A WORLD AWAY, men were fascinated to read of Fertig's death.
The Japanese propaganda broadcast had been reprinted as a legitimate
communiqué by the English-language newspaper that was still allowed to
appear in Tokyo. By various means, copies of the newspaper arrived in
Washington, and the item concerning Fertig came to rest upon a desk, a
desk that received copies of any information that might be remotely connected with the Philippine Islands.

"Major General Wendell Fertig," an intelligence officer mused. "Odd.
No major generals by that name."

But where had he seen a name like it just a day or so ago? The officer
searched the files and found an official copy of a calm but insistent letter that a Mrs. Mary Fertig, of Golden, Colorado, had written to the War
Department. She was, it seemed, the wife of a reserve lieutenant colonel
named Wendell Fertig, reported missing in action since Corregidor. According to her letter, Mrs. Fertig thought the War Department had made a
mistake. She believed her husband alive, and what was more she thought
she knew where he was.

"Poor woman," the officer thought. "She just can't accept it."

But *why* should she think she knew where her husband was? And why
should a man (assuming it was the same Wendell Fertig) reported missing from Corregidor be reported killed nearly a year later on Mindanao?
Almost every disaster has its survivors; resistance movements follow every
surrender. It was a standard Japanese gambit to announce the death of
resistance leaders in order to destroy any emergent popular hope for such
leaders, a gambit they had used for years in China. The Japanese mag-
nification of Fertig's rank was doubtless propaganda also. But assuming
that this Fertig had escaped and was leading a resistance movement on
Mindanao, why should Mrs. Fertig have written to the War Department

prior to the Japanese announcement? If she had received some message from Mindanao, how had it reached her? Since the Army could not afford to overlook any possibility of establishing communications within the Japanese-occupied areas, the intelligence officer arranged to have a man call on Mrs. Fertig in Colorado.

At this same time, a routine report from Radio Station KFS was also on its way to Washington. Among other things, it complained that a signal, purportedly from unsurrendered Americans in the Philippines but most probably from the Japanese, was interrupting traffic. KFS wanted an intelligence appreciation of this signal, suggesting that means be found to end Japanese jamming.

WHILE THESE EVENTS were taking place in the United States, a small open boat rose and fell over the long hills of the Coral Sea. The three white men and two Filipinos in the boat were still alive but weak, giddy, and painfully sunburned. Numbly, they stared at the low, distant line of an immense land mass. It was the end of the longest open-boat voyage since Captain Bligh's, and it had been made, without any aids to navigation other than a weather map and a miner's compass, through the entire Imperial Japanese Navy. But the men in the boat had no room in their minds to dwell upon such aspects of their accomplishment. They simply watched Australia come toward them over the edge of the world, and Charles Smith's dry lips framed the words *Well, there it is.*

Days later, the report of the interrogation of Jordan Hamner, Charles Smith, and A. Y. Smith was also on its way to Washington. The report stated the three men had sailed from Mindanao, where Filipino guerrilleros were ambushing Japanese troops. Hamner and the two Smiths had been assisted in their escape by Wendell Fertig, a mining engineer who commanded a guerrilla in the province of Misamis Occidental and who was trying to build a radio to establish communication with the outside world. The three men felt that, if any aid could be given Fertig, it should be sent at once. Confident that he would succeed in putting a radio on the air by the time Smith reached Australia, Fertig had given Charles Smith a radio call-sign known only to the two of them. It was MSF. Easy to remember. Mindanao Smith Fertig.

From this point, matters moved as quickly as they could, considering the fact that the United States was trying to wage war simultaneously in the Arctic, Europe, Africa, the Near East, China, Burma, India, and the South Pacific. In the general scheme of things, Philippine Island affairs had a lower priority than the American garrisons in the Caribbean. As far as the Chiefs of Staff were concerned, MacArthur was expressing a personal wish when he said, *I Shall Return.* Japan was to be defeated by aerial bombardment, made possible by United States Navy capture of the Central Pacific Islands sometime during 1944–45. MacArthur, although he did not know it, was expected to do nothing more than defend Australia if he could. The Philippines would be returned to the United States by peace treaty at the end of the war. Yet *any* military information was always welcomed by army intelligence, and so a telephone rang in Golden, Colorado, and a woman answered, "Yes, this is Mrs. Fertig."

"Mrs. *Wendell* Fertig, this is Mr. Jones," the receiver told her. "I have something of importance to discuss with you, Mrs. *Wendell* Fertig."

The voice drew out the first name, putting little spaces of silence around it.

"Mrs. Wendell Fertig," it said, "do you think Patricia and Jean would like to go to the movies tonight with their grandmother?"

"I beg your pardon?" Mary asked faintly, while her husband suddenly seemed so close to her that she could almost feel his arms around her.

"I'm sure you understand," the voice said flatly. "You will draw the blinds and turn off the light over the door. You will be alone? I will ring the bell once, at nine o'clock."

"Have you heard . . ." Mary began.

"Goodbye, Mrs. Fertig," the voice interrupted.

At nine, there was a step on the porch, a short ring, and a tall man in civilian clothes stepped quickly into the house, closing the door behind him. An army officer's identification card flickered in his hand.

"Where do you think your husband is?" he demanded.

"He is on Mindanao," Mary said automatically, vaguely angry as any woman would be at a stranger's implication that she did not know for a fact where her husband was.

"How do you know?"

"Because I got a letter from him," Mary said sharply, more than a little nettled by her visitor's abrupt manner. She was almost as tall as he, and she came from Irish pioneer stock. In her country, when a stranger came riding up to the campfire, he was invited to *Git down an' set,* and a stranger was expected to show a polite restraint before showering his host with personal questions, if, indeed, he asked such questions at all. Moreover, Mary was tense with the excitement of this visit, telling herself *Wendell is alive; they've heard from Wendell . . .*

"You got a *what?*" the officer demanded. "A *letter?* From *Mindanao?*"

"Certainly," she said, and then realized that Mr. Jones must have thought her mad, that anxiety had given her delusions. Obviously, there was no postal service between Golden and any point within Japanese territory.

"May I *see* this letter?" Mr. Jones asked very carefully.

He turned it over and over in his hands. He held it to the light. He put it down on the table and stared at it. It was just a letter. It had been put in the ordinary mail.

"What is there in this letter that leads you to believe your husband is on Mindanao?" Mr. Jones demanded.

He looked at it again. It said the writer was well, hoped the war would end soon, looked forward to seeing his wife and children, whom he loved.

"Right at the beginning," Mary said. "It says, 'Dearest, Pineapples for breakfast!'"

"You and your husband have a private code," Mr. Jones said.

"No, we don't," Mary said, beginning to feel thoroughly annoyed by intelligence officers who engaged in elliptical telephone conversations in a sensible place like Golden; who visited only in houses with drawn blinds, and who at the same time imagined that civilian clothes effectively disguised a military bearing. Why, she thought, they don't even know enough to take off their academy rings. She wondered what Mr. Jones would say if she asked him where he'd stood in the West Point class of 1927.

"Mindanao is the only place where they grow pineapples," she explained. "Before the war, Wendell would always take his vacation at the Del Monte Club on Mindanao to eat pineapples and play golf. He loves pineapples but only fresh out of the field at Del Monte. When he says he has pineapples for breakfast, that is his way of saying, 'Don't worry about what the papers say, I'm on Mindanao.'"

"Very well," Mr. Jones said, "let us say that your husband *is* on Mindanao. What reason do you have to believe he is still alive and free?"

"Look, Mr. Jones," Mary said. "I don't have any *reason*. I *know* he's alive, and, if he's alive, he's free. Wendell isn't the kind of man who surrenders to anybody. He can take care of himself. Why, he's been all over the Islands, prospecting and mining. Wendell knows the country and the people. He's lived off the country by himself. Don't you worry about him."

"But this letter is postmarked Australia," Mr. Jones said, shifting his ground.

"Well, I guess somebody must have mailed it for him," Mary said tartly.

And so, indeed, someone had. It was the letter Fertig had handed to the pilot of the last seaplane to leave Mindanao. Perhaps because the war was then still so new, it had not occurred to the pilot to send it through the military post office that would have censored it. Instead, he had dropped it in a corner postbox.

Mr. Jones tried hard. He sought significance in the farewell, "Adios my darling." He kept after her for two hours but failed to discover a code for the simple reason there was none. When he slipped out of the house, he took the letter with him for laboratory analysis. He ordered her to say nothing about his visit to her children or to her mother-in-law or anyone else. The fate of a great many men depended on her silence, he said. She promised to say nothing. It was not until much later that Mary Fertig realized that Mr. Jones had asked her everything she knew about her husband but had told her nothing in return.

DAYS LATER, a decision was reached in Washington.

"We'll take a chance," the intelligence officer said, shoving a file of reports aside. "We'll assume the Japs are lying, that this Fertig has become a nuisance to them, that he's built a radio, that it's his transmitter and not a Jap's that's lousing up KFS traffic. Tell KFS not to answer that mystery station directly. But, as soon as the noise stops, send KFS calling MSF. Let's see what that does. If it's Fertig, we might not be able to help him, but he can at least help us: We'll tell him to get the hell off the air."

That night, when the familiar banshee wail of Fertig's transmitter filled the KFS receivers, the signalman notified his lieutenant.

They waited for the sound to die.

KFS CALLING MSF KFS CALLING MSF, the signalman rapped in open Morse.

Then they heard the improbable shriek of Fertig's transmitter, repeating its coded message about the hot Yanks.

"Try again," the lieutenant said.

KFS CALLING MSF, the signalman sent.

They kept trying until Fertig's set went off the air.

"Well," the signalman said, "that isn't the one."

"No," the lieutenant said, "it's a goddamn Jap, after all." He turned away, relieved. He had been worried that he might have been wrong.

3

IDLY, FERTIG PICKED up a loose bit of copper wire and worked it back and forth with his hands, thinking, as he always did whenever he touched copper, what a peculiar stuff it was. Malleable, ductile, the first metal man smelted . . . He twisted the wire and asked the radio operator, a former navy signalman named William Konko, otherwise known as the Mad Russian or as Army Signal Corps 2d Lieutenant Konko, USFIP, if there was anything new.

It wasn't much of a question, and Fertig regretted it the minute he'd asked it. Obviously, if there had been any news, they would have told him.

"No, sir," Konko said. "Nothing. I worked Mr. Bell for a while, and he didn't have anything."

Konko referred to Roy Bell's ham set on the island of Negros. It was the only station with which Fertig's transmitter had made contact, and they talked back and forth like two children calling to one another in a dark cellar.

"But I tell you what," Konko said. "We got good reception. Last night I heard San Francisco."

"Oh you did, did you?" Fertig said.

"Yes, sir. I picked up KFS. That's a Navy monitor in 'Frisco. I could hear 'em calling stations I remember, Pearl, Dago, and a lot I never heard of. Like last night they kept calling MSF. You know who that is, sir?"

"No," Fertig said, twisting the wire, trying to remember the call letters of military stations.

It was a curious stuff, copper. It was one of the few metals you would never want to find in a free state, because, if you try to blast it, you would only spatter it, and there was almost never a good way to cut it out. He

coiled the wire around his finger, thinking of the times and places he had
mined copper, and remembering the trouble Charlie Smith had had with
his copper mine at . . .

Charlie Smith!

Fertig tore the wire loose and threw it at the wall with a shout, and the
men in the nipa shack stared at him as if he had just gone mad.

"Now, just a minute," Fertig said as steadily as he could, fighting down
a wild clamor inside him. "You're sure? M-S-F? Did you write it down?
Did you log it anywhere?"

"No, sir," Konko said. "I didn't write it down. Why? I mean, you want
me to log the stations I hear?"

"Are you sure it was MSF you heard?" Fertig demanded.

"Yes, sir. Pretty sure."

"You get on that set, and you start sending MSF calling KFS," Fertig
said. "Find that frequency and get on it right now."

"Yes, sir. Why . . . ?"

"Just start sending," Fertig interrupted.

Why, for God's sake. The one trouble with citizen soldiers, and particularly with American citizen soldiers, is they always want to know *why,*
Fertig complained to himself. Being told what to do isn't enough. They
always want some damned reason.

But Charlie Smith! Had that sawed-off little Texan got through? If
there was one thing that had always irritated him about Charlie, it was
that, once Charlie got an idea, he had no room in his head for anything
else. Fertig remembered how Charlie, 'way back at Momungan, when he
and Hamner had come out of Deischer's camp, had talked about going
to Australia.

Charlie never talked about another blessed thing. He had convinced
himself that all there was to sailing to Australia was just heading south
until he ran into it. He'd wanted Fertig and Hedges to come, too, and
when Fertig asked him whether he'd ever sailed before, Smith had said,
"No, Wendell, but I figure I'll sure as hell learn on the way." Fertig could
still hear him saying this, and he remembered Smith's look of absolute
determination.

And Fertig, seeing that nothing could be done to change Smith's mind,
had helped him fit out a twenty-six-foot native cumpit, a kind of whale-
boat. He'd felt at the time he was helping to send Smith and Hamner to
their death, but, since that was the way they wanted it, Fertig had helped.
Smith figured he would sail when he could and motor when he couldn't,
and he'd taken one look at a weather map and decided there were so many

islands on the way that they'd never be more than a day out of the sight of land of some kind. They'd know when they came to Australia, because it would be the biggest piece of land. So Fertig had helped find them fuel for the cumpit's engine and wished them well. Since there was always a chance that they *could* get through, Fertig had pretended to believe they would and had arranged a call sign . . .

MSF CALLING KFS, Konko sent.

And back the answer came, loud, crisp, and clear:

KFS TO MSF XXX IF YOU KNOW DOUBLE TRANSPOSITION USE AS KEY FIRST NAME OF SECOND NEXT OF KIN AND CITY OF RESIDENCE SECOND NEXT OF KIN AND ENCODE THE FOLLOWING INFORMATION XXX

When Konko finished copying the message, he was grinning all over, and there were minutes before the brown and white men in the nipa house beneath the mango tree could think of anything coherent to say to one another.

"That's us!" Konko kept saying. "Hey . . . hey . . . that's us!"

Second next of kin: that would be his first-born child.

PATRICIA, Fertig wrote on a schoolchild's notebook paper.

City of residence? Who knows? They were probably back in Golden, but, if for any reason Mary had moved, say, into Denver . . .

GOLDEN, Fertig wrote, taking the chance. If it wasn't Golden, the whole message would be garbled, for double transposition is the Army's simple but effective code based on a double substitution of letters in the alphabet, arranged in five-letter groups, with the order of the substitution determined by the key. The information KFS wanted, like the name of Fertig's first-born child and her home city, was personal trivia that a Japanese interrogation was not likely to have discovered. He wrote it out and handed the message to Konko.

Acknowledging receipt, KFS said:

WE HAVE NO TRAFFIC FOR YOU XXX MAINTAIN NIGHTLY SCHEDULE AS FOLLOWS . . .

That night, at the assigned time, KFS told Fertig, WE HAVE NO TRAFFIC FOR YOU, but Fertig didn't care. The main thing was that he had got through; he had reached the outside world, and no doubt the world was now busy thinking of him, checking out his answer, preparing to reply. Fertig did not expect miracles.

Yet, year by year, the next two days passed. By the end of the first day, Fertig's wild exultation had become impatience. By the end of the second, impatience had become intolerance. By the third day, it had become anger—a desperate anger. He could hardly believe that the lost world, so briefly rediscovered, had no further interest in him nor in the story he was bursting to tell. Surely, by three days, those Stateside idiots should have satisfied themselves as to who was manning the station MSF.

"My God!" Fertig asked Ball and Konko. "What are they doing out there?"

Ball's suggestion as to what they might be doing was interesting. Konko said they had probably decided the guerrilla was such a big military secret they wouldn't even allow themselves to think about it. But then, on February 5, 1943, KFS suddenly said:

DESIRE FURTHER INFORMATION PATRICIA.

"Oh, for Christ's sake!" Fertig shouted. "They know damn well who we are! They'd never have known MSF if Charlie Smith hadn't got through and told them! What are they doing? Pinning medals on each other?"

Furiously, he encoded a message about his daughter's childhood, her nickname, and the names of her young friends. Surely when "they" checked this out, there could be no further doubt. KFS acknowledged receipt, and silence set in again.

The following day there was a message for Fertig—a message he read in a black fury that brought forth all the brutality of which he was so unexpectedly capable. If Marcario Peralta had been in Fertig's office at that moment, Fertig would have drawn his pistol and shot Peralta down where he stood. For it was not a message from KFS, but from Roy Bell.

The message said that, although he, Bell, had not been able to reach Australia, he had picked up a guerrilla station on Panay Island, and Mr. Bell was asking whether Fertig was aware of the situation there.

Fertig had supposed he was. Months ago, Marcario Peralta, an ambitious young Filipino lawyer who had risen to the rank of major before the surrender, had put together a guerrilla on Panay. But his guerrilla was only one of several; it was the old story of every resistance movement: There had been the inevitable vicious, internecine battle for power during which each guerrillero chieftain seeks to dominate the others. Therefore, Peralta had written to Fertig, suggesting that, if Fertig would recognize him as the sole legitimate guerrilla commander of Panay, then he, Peralta, would put his unit under Fertig's over-all command. It was a simple request for Fertig to give him face, and Fertig agreed. Nothing more concrete had passed between them, for each was busy with his own affairs, although Fertig regarded the Peralta organization as something that might be useful at a later time. So, Fertig thought, Peralta was in his camp. But Mr. Bell's news changed all that.

Peralta had recently found an Army radio transmitter hidden in the jungle. He had radioed MacArthur's headquarters that certain officers, including one Wendell Fertig, were trying to usurp his command. Wherefore, Peralta requested that MacArthur recognize him, Peralta, as the sole commander of Philippine guerrilla forces. And three directives to Peralta from MacArthur were the result. Mr. Bell's station furnished the text.

The first directive banned the printing of military scrip. The second limited command of guerrilla forces to those already in control of them. The third designated Peralta as "military guerrilla chief of temporarily occupied enemy territory."

Fertig was appalled at the absurdity of the three directives.

How in the hell could those dumb bastards in Australia send orders when they didn't know what was going on?

Coldly mastering his rage, Fertig read the directives again. The first made Fertig's printing of emergency money a flat disobedience of Supreme Headquarters. Worse, it made Fertig out a liar to his own people, for he had promised that the emergency money would be redeemed at face value by the United States. It had never crossed Fertig's mind that the United States would ever boggle over spending a few thousand dollars to help a captive people become free.

Well, the hell with it, Fertig decided. I'm not printing military scrip. I'm printing real money. If those chair-borne commandos at Headquarters want to come up here and eat cold rice and dodge Japs with me while we sit down and argue whether it's money or scrip, I'll be glad to arrange it.

The second directive was gibberish. Command was always limited to those you controlled. And I control, Fertig thought, everything I *can* command. And that's the way it's going to be.

The third directive was also meaningless, because it could not mean what it implied: that Peralta was designated leader of everything the Japanese had conquered in all of East Asia! Moreover, Fertig reasoned, it could not apply to Mindanao. Mindanao was not "temporarily occupied enemy territory." To Fertig, it was unsurrendered territory belonging to an undefeated, sovereign government, on which a Japanese army was trapped.

I got the goddamn Japs cornered, Fertig told himself mirthlessly, thinking of something Hedges had said long ago. With my 6,000 men, I've confined 150,000 Japanese to the biggest towns, the best harbors, the only decent roads, and the best farmland on Mindanao. I have them in a position where the only thing they can do is take what they want and go wherever they wish, whenever they please.

So much for MacArthur's directives to Peralta.

Yet it was now more important than ever to reach MacArthur himself, so that MacArthur could send some instructions that did make sense.

If I only had somebody to talk to, Fertig thought. *If Hedges were here, I could talk with HIM. Charley would tell me what a goddamned fool I am. Charley is the one man I CAN be friends with, because everybody knows Charley and I were friends before this thing started.*

But Hedges was fighting in Lanao, where he was badly needed to keep the coastal Moros in line, and Fertig could not afford to be friendly with anyone else. He most certainly could not share his problems with doña Carmen; it was dangerous enough to take an occasional dinner at the casa because of the possibility of entanglement with women and because it was not the best of politics to appear to be identified exclusively with ilustrados. He could not eat with his fellow American officers, lest the Filipinos complain. Already, some were saying he favored Americans, but none had told him so to his face. Nor could he mess with his Filipino officers, lest the Americans complain. Already some of them were, behind his back, calling him a gook-lover. To eat with Filipinos one day and Americans the next would give the impression he was trying to appear not to have favorites, which would imply that he really did.

Therefore, Fertig ate and slept alone. He was friends with no one, for to hold himself apart was to wrap himself in the mystery of command. The commander who was a buddy or pal to his men, softened them, just as a man who pats a hunting hound converts a useful animal into a worthless pet. Fertig held himself as deliberately aloof from his officers as an old-time sea captain—and for exactly the same reasons. It is impossible to give orders to friends.

The days passed, and the silence persisted, and Fertig could stand it no longer. If he couldn't get attention one way, he'd get it another. As commanding general of a United States army in the field, isolated from other commands, he had a right to deal directly with the Secretary of War. Then, by God, the fun would begin . . .

AS SENIOR AMERICAN OFFICER IN THE PHILIPPINE ISLANDS, he radioed to KFS to pass to the War Department, I have ASSUMED COMMAND OF MINDANAO AND VISAYAS (and *that,* he thought, would take care of Peralta) with rank of brigadier GENERAL XXX AS LEADER OF THE GUERRILLA FORCES WE HAVE REACTIVATED THE USFIP AND ESTABLISHED CIVIL GOVERNMENT IN THE HANDS OF DULY ELECTED COMMONWEALTH OFFICIALS XXX MONEY IS BEING PRINTED BY THEM AND LOANED TO USFIP XXX FERTIG

KFS acknowledged but had no traffic for Fertig. Not until February 9, when KFS at last broke its stolid silence.

NAMES OF TOWN AND STATE WHERE PATRICIA LIVES
WILL BE USED AS CODE PHRASES FOR DOUBLE TRANSPOSI-
TION XXX SEND TEST MESSAGE AT ONCE, KFS said.

Fertig did not reply at once. It was some time before he could think
of anything that was not blasphemous. For, if KFS had broken his earlier
code—and their acknowledgment implied they had been able to do so—
then it was obvious that Fertig knew double transposition, that there was
no need to send a test message. Nor was anything gained by changing the
code phrases, because a closed code . . .

But there was no point in arguing. The point was that Fertig was no
farther along than he had been a fortnight ago. He wrote Golden Colorado and encoded the test message from it, and once again KFS fell silent.
On February 11, KFS had traffic for him: Fertig's call sign would henceforth be WYZB. And that was all.

During all this time, a war was being waged on several continents and
sundry oceans, and, in a vicious, stealthy way, it was being fought without
quarter, by ambush, terror, and assassination on the island of Mindanao.
It never occurred to Fertig that the ambush of Japanese patrols on Mindanao might be the farthest thing from the minds of the Chiefs of Staff
in Washington.

Yet the vast machinery of the Army, sending trucks to Russia, pilots
to England, and a shipment of athletic supporters to the Aleutians, was
also considering the problem of Wendell Fertig. And so, on St. Valentine's
Day 1943, KFS radioed Fertig additional procedural instructions and told
him that the next station he would hear would be KAZ, with which he
would henceforth deal. KAZ was the net control station for the Southwest
Pacific Command. And, in the body of the message, someone had inserted:

**PATRICIA SISTER MOTHER AND
GRANDMOTHER WELL**

It was the first word that Fertig had received concerning his family
since the fighting on Bataan. Fertig read and reread the few words, blurred
by starting tears. The simple fact that someone cared enough to send him
those words helped him through the next week, until, at last, KAZ called.
Immediately, Fertig replied by repeating his radio message to the War Department and demanding that the command situation of the guerrilla areas be clarified at once. KAZ's reply was prompt.

KEEP YOUR SHIRT ON YOU ARE NOT FORGOTTEN

A week later KAZ sent the message from MacArthur:

COMMAND AREAS WILL BE PROGRESSIVELY ESTAB-
LISHED BASED ON EXISTING MILITARY DISTRICTS XXX COM-
MANDER OF DISTRICTS WILL OPERATE UNDER CONTROL
THIS HEADQUARTERS (SOUTHWEST PACIFIC) AND ASSIGN-
MENTS WILL BE SUBJECT TO REVIEW ON BASIS OF PERFOR-
MANCE XXX LT COL W W FERTIG (CE) INF IS DESIGNATED
TO COMMAND THE TENTH MIL DISTRICT (ISLANDS OF MIN-
DANAO AND SULU) XXX HE WILL PERFECT INTELLIGENCE
NET COVERING NINTH MIL DISTRICT (SAMAR-LEYTE) XXX
NO OFFICER OF RANK OF GENERAL WILL BE DESIGNATED
AT PRESENT XXX LT COL PERALTA WILL COMMAND SIXTH
MIL DISTRICT (PANAY) AND IS RESPONSIBLE FOR ORGANI-
ZATION OF INTELLIGENCE NET COVERING SEVENTH AND
EIGHTH MIL DISTRICT XXX MACARTHUR

Reading this, Fertig felt the weight of the Moro silversmith's stars on his collar.

Lieutenant Colonel Fertig of the Corps of Engineers was now Lieu-tenant Colonel Fertig of the United States Infantry.

Couldn't those thickheads understand that he did not want to be a general because of the pay or out of vainglory but because it was abso-lutely essential for the Filipinos to believe they had an American general leading them?

Didn't those idiots at Headquarters know that face was the most important fact in Asia? That there had to be *one* commander and not a swarm of lieutenant colonels knifing each other in the back? Would MacArthur have tolerated the existence of *two* Supreme Commanders of the Southwest Pacific Theater of War?

But a secret corner of his mind told Fertig he *did* want that rank. He wanted it more than he had ever wanted anything in his life, because he felt he had already won it. He wanted the rank *and* he needed it.

He had called an army into the field after the Regulars had quit. Maybe that's what irritated them. They surrendered; he fought. For this, not even a normal promotion based on length of service in rank, much less based on merit in the field. Not even a full colonelcy!

Yet contact had been made. He had an assignment, and there was an implied promise in MacArthur's directive. He must now send acknowledg-ment. It was a historic occasion, and he, Fertig, would send something appropriate:

URGENTLY REQUEST VIA FIRST AVAILABLE TRANSPOR-
TATION NECESSARY DRUGS TO TREAT VENEREAL DISEASE
RECENTLY CONTRACTED BY KEY PERSONNEL XXX FERTIG

4

EXCITED MEN SWARMED into the muddy barrio, materializing from nowhere in that way Filipinos have of suddenly cluttering an empty landscape. They surged into the village street, calling to one another in order to be heard, laughing at whatever was said whether they heard it or not. The rain made no difference. There could have been a typhoon, and no one would have cared. The oldest inhabitant of Pagadian was borne along with the rest. Never had he imagined there were so many people in the world. He did not understand precisely what was going on, for he was an old man who did not always understand things any longer, but, in a dim way, he knew he should be happy. He looked at the book of paper matches that someone had given him. It bore the photograph of a white man who looked like an eagle, and printed in Visayan and English was the legend I SHALL RETURN—MACARTHUR.

The old man could not read these languages, but he knew the value of matches. What puzzled him was that others would put the photograph to their lips and laugh while tears ran down their cheeks. Tremulously, he kissed the picture, too, and when, for some reason, he found that this brought tears of exultation and tears for memories, he understood at last. This was The Aid of which men spoke. The Aid was an anting-anting that would keep all men from harm. It was an anting-anting as strong as the white stone he had found years ago in the stomach of a crocodile. When he returned to his house, he would put The Aid beneath the crucifix, beside the white stone in its leather pouch.

Soldiers jostled the old man aside, splitting a path for Fertig through the uproar of Pagadian. Fertig did not see the ancient stumbling back, because he was fascinated by the one who stood beneath the protection of a nipa porch, holding a copy of *Life* magazine, not reading it but rapidly riffling the pages so that those who eddied and shoved behind him could glimpse the fluttering pictures over his shoulder. Then, rolling the magazine abruptly, he turned to meet new customers milling in. Holding *Life* high, he shouted that the price for viewing the rapidly turned pages was 50 centavos. For ten pesos, he would permit a man to rent the magazine exclusively for half an hour.

Ten pesos! Before the war, a man in Manila could call for his girl in a calesa, take her to dinner, to the movies, and home again in the calesa, for two pesos.

But to Fertig's amazement, ten pesos instantly changed hands, and the renter at once went into business for himself, turning the pages more rapidly yet and recovering his investment almost immediately, while the original owner fumed.

Fertig's fiesta spirit mounted as he shoved through the fiesta of Pagadian in the rain; it had been building in him from the moment he received the news; it churned in him as he climbed over the mountains from Misamis. The Aid! At last, The Aid!

By God, they'd even sent magazines!

Men shouted Mabuhay! as Fertig's soldiers made a way for him to the schoolyard, where rain-and-sweat-wet cargadores heaved heavy boxes into carabao carts. The paper matches and the few magazines that had been distributed were enormously important, but here—in those boxes—was what Fertig and all others had poured into Pagadian to behold. The fact that there was nothing to see but anonymous wooden crates made The Aid all the more exciting. Men cheered when the cargadores strained with an exceptionally heavy crate. They were like children who believe they know what the Christmas packages contain but who can scarcely wait to make sure.

The odd thing was, they *did* know. In that indefinable way that rumor spreads in the Islands, it was accurately reported everywhere that a submarine had brought carbines, ammunition, medicines, and radios to General Fertig. Even the Japanese General Morimoto knew this before Fertig had covered the thirty miles between Misamis and Pagadian—a matter of only two days' travel. In fact, General Morimoto had already issued a public announcement that blandly ignored his previous announcement of Fertig's death.

"The Japanese are like the fishermen," General Morimoto proclaimed. "We have stretched our net around the Philippine Islands to protect you from harm. However, the net is too big, and the holes are too large to stop the small fish. Through the small hole came an American submarine, but with only a few supplies. These supplies we know came from Australia, because they are new carbine ammunition. They are things that could not be made by Fertig in Misamis. Therefore, they have been brought in from Australia. However, they are very small quantity and will not hurt the Japanese. The only thing I wish, should anyone find American cigarettes, bring me a package so I may smoke."

But the people who came to Pagadian knew better than to believe this stupid lie, for there were not a few only but plenty, plenty wooden boxes. So many that they had entirely filled two trucks, weighing the trucks so heavily that they sank in the mud and, too bad, could not be moved. But no matter: there were plenty carabao carts to move The Aid over the mountain trails.

And Fertig, reaching the schoolyard, stopped as though suddenly paralyzed.

Was *that* it? *That?* Could that be *all* of it?

The message had spoken of four tons of supplies. To a man who has nothing, four tons of anything seems a very great deal, particularly when he has not yet seen it Although the engineer in Fertig knew quite well what four tons meant, the lonely bankrupt in Fertig had magnified the gift beyond reckoning. Hope had multiplied the number in geometric progression as Fertig had slipped and skidded over the mountains in the rain, but now reality confronted the engineer.

Four tons was a head load for 160 men.

At most, it was a burden for twenty-five carabao carts.

Divided into the strength of Fertig's half-armed army, it was precisely 1.3 pounds of Aid per man. Perhaps a handful of .30-caliber cartridges apiece.

But even as reality turned Fertig's dreams into bitter lees, hope began to make a wine of them again. Four tons of anything was better than nothing. Judiciously used, much could be done with them. And the effect of this token Aid upon the Filipinos was obviously electric. But then Fertig caught sight of the two men who were watching the unloading of the mired trucks and the loading of the carts, and the first breath of hope became a gale. One was a short, stocky American in wet new khakis. The other, dressed in the simple attire of a tao, surveyed the scene with the slight smile of the faintly amused as he idly flipped and caught a silver trade dollar. They were two men whom Fertig had never expected to see again.

"Chick!" he called, striding forward. "Charlie!"

"Hello, Wendell," the man with the dollar said softly, reaching out his hand. "You call, we haul."

"I remembered you needed shoes," the stocky American said. "I brought you three pairs, Wendell."

The last time the three had met together was at a party in Manila before the war, when they had been civilians, and, for a long moment, the war fell away as they shook hands in the rain.

"Damn it, Charlie," Fertig said, "it's wonderful to see you again! I thought you couldn't wait to get out of here?"

"No, I said I'd be back," Charles Smith said.

For the stocky American in the new khakis of an army captain was the same Charles Smith who once had wanted no part of the guerrilla, nothing to do with the Army; who only wished in his one-thing-at-a-time way to reach the safety of Australia. But now, a civilian mining engineer no longer, he was back in the Islands to serve as a liaison officer, commuting to and from Australia by submarine, daily facing the danger of death by torture when he did not face that of being drowned like a cat in a bag.

"They talked me into it," he explained, but Fertig knew that no one could ever talk Charlie Smith into that which Smith did not want to do.

"Besides," he said, "I told you I'd find you a pair of shoes, so I figured I might as well bring them myself. But wait till you hear what Chick did. Chick actually got the Japs to send him, Katzie, and the boys home from Manila!"

"The Japs did *what?*" Fertig asked, looking sharply at the dark-haired, brown-eyed man in the Filipino clothes.

"First class," Lieutenant Commander Charles Parsons murmured. He smiled one of his soft smiles. "After all, I was the Panamanian consul."

"So you were," Fertig said, remembering Manila before the war. It had been the custom of small nations to appoint consuls from among the businessmen of Manila, rather than send out their own nationals, and Chick Parsons—sometime army private, boxer, shorthand stenographer, later a mining-stock promoter, sawmill operator, molasses exporter, co-owner of the Luzon Stevedoring Corporation, Uncle Chico to most of Manila's children, and the roughest Number Four ever to appear at the Polo Club—had, among many other things, also been the Panamanian consul. Therefore, when the Japanese entered Manila, Parsons promptly ran up the Panamanian flag; spoke nothing but Spanish when the Japanese arrived; announced that, because of the war, the consulate was closed; demanded repatriation to Panama; and brusquely ordered them off the territory of a neutral nation.

The Japanese were puzzled. But no one in the foreign missions betrayed El Chico—not even the Italians or Germans—for all of the white foreigners were horrified by the unspeakably bestial way the Japanese tortured and humiliated the British and American civilian men and women they interned.

At length, Parsons said, the Japanese sent him and his family home to Panama, and the rest was simple: A step into the Canal Zone, and then Parsons was off to Washington with a plan. He could pass anywhere in the Islands for a Filipino. Needing no disguise and armed only with his courage and his profound knowledge of the Islands, the languages, and the people, Parsons would gather intelligence, coordinate guerrilla activities, and supervise distribution of supplies by submarine to guerrillero chieftains. He was now a naval intelligence officer.

"Chick, it's wonderful," Fertig said when Parsons finished. "After we made radio contact, I hoped that Headquarters would get some help in here, but I never imagined that I'd be lucky enough to get you and Charlie."

Beaming at them, Fertig saw friends at court. They knew him; they knew the Islands; they would impress MacArthur with Fertig's needs.

Parsons grunted.

"You won't get much from us, compadre," he said. "Anything I bring comes from the personal interest of Douglas MacArthur. Not from the War Department. Uncle Sam is sending more stuff to Brazil than to MacArthur. Mac has to beg for anything he gets. And as far as MacArthur's concerned—and he's the *only* one really interested—you're just too damn small and too far away."

"The hell you say," Fertig said.

"That's the story, Wendell," Charlie Smith said. "That's all she wrote."

Fertig listened in a trance as his friends told him how it was in the world outside. What help, indeed, could a few barefoot Filipinos on Mindanao expect while Europe was enslaved, while Russian armies were being obliterated, while the Japanese were closing in on India and the Germans on Suez? MacArthur's only duty was to try to save Australia—if he could.

Fertig looked across a wet field of cogon to see gray mists twist up from the forests to smother the mountains. The Aid that Parsons brought was a mockery. It was the dish of water the Japanese set just beyond the lips of a man they had stripped and tied to a sheet of galvanized iron, to fry slowly to death in the sun.

The carabao carts filled and began to move along a track in the cogon to disappear beneath the wet eaves of the jungle. Fertig stood silent in the rain, watching them lurch creaking away, each making the track more difficult for those that followed.

"Look," he said at last. "You people are hungry. I'll get the boys to find you some chow."

5

"YOU MIGHT AS well know it, Wendell," Charles Smith said. "We're supposed to find out whether you're competent to command."

"Competent?" Fertig said, "Why damn it, who do you think is *in* command? Do those thickheads in Australia think I could be running this outfit if I was incompetent? Do they think if anyone was *more* competent that *he* wouldn't be running this show?"

Parsons took his Chinese trade dollar from his pocket and flipped and caught it.

"Take it easy," he said, watching the coin spin in the air. "Nobody's said you aren't doing a good job. It's just that nobody down there knows what's going on up here. Down south, we heard you and Peralta had been captured."

"Bullshit," Fertig said.

"All right," Parsons said gently. "I know it is—now. I'm just trying to tell you we were sent in to find out what's going on."

The three men were sitting together, late at night, in Fertig's headquarters at Misamis City, and Fertig was finding it difficult to accept the fact that other men were inspecting his work. Ever since their arrival, Smith and Parsons had been poking about, looking at things, asking questions.

"You know," Parsons continued in his soft, mild way, "you didn't do yourself any good at Headquarters when you set yourself up as a brigadier general, Wendell. You can guess who blew up over that."

"What do you mean?" Fertig asked.

"Pat Casey was all for you, but Willoughby wouldn't hear of it," Smith interrupted. "When they got your radio to the War Department about your taking command, Willoughby said, 'Fertig can't command men he can't see.'"

"Baloney," Fertig said. "MacArthur commands men he can't see. Does Willoughby think generals command platoons? Tell him to read the book again. Goddamn it, men in the Civil War assumed brevet rank in the absence or death of their superiors—and the brevet rank was confirmed later."

He stopped short, conscious that Smith and Parsons were regarding him with an alert solemnity that had nothing to do with friendship.

"It's just common sense," Fertig said. He was angry with the Army's rotten habit of setting friends to spy on one another.

"It's not a question of whether I want the rank," Fertig said, speaking carefully now, through Smith and Parsons to MacArthur. "It's just that I need it, as a matter of practicality. Every damned bandit in the Islands is promoting himself major, colonel, general. You and I know, and every poor Filipino knows, there's no rank in the Philippine Army equal to that of brigadier general in the United States Army. If we're going to run this show, there has to be a United States general officer here, somebody with so much rank that no Filipino can question it. And if all the Regular generals surrender, which they damned sure did, then, by God, somebody *else* has to be the general. MacArthur is an old Filipino. He ought to know there has to be The One who is the Incharge."

"He does," Parsons said, flipping his dollar. "He is The One."

Fertig looked at Parsons as Peter looked at Judas. He felt in the position of a man damned if he did and damned if he did not. For he knew very well that, if what he had done did not meet with approval of Supreme Headquarters, an officer would be sent to relieve him. On the other hand, if Smith and Parsons were to report Fertig's command in good shape, then one of the ambitious sycophants around MacArthur would press for appointment as Fertig's relief, on grounds that Fertig was not, after all, a Regular officer and that the job was too big for a former mining engineer to handle. Fertig knew several such officers in MacArthur's headquarters who would look forward to command of the guerrilla as a step to a general's stars. He felt his only hope lay in making his position, and his ideas, absolutely clear.

"Chick, I know MacArthur is my superior officer," Fertig said. "I want him to give me orders that make sense. Therefore, I want you and Charlie to know just what we're up against. The biggest trouble we have isn't with the Japs. It's with these little Hitlers who ambush one Jap patrol and then get big ideas about building their own military empires. The only way I can control them is to have more rank than they and to control the source of food and supply. How much or how little you send is really secondary. *Any* Aid can help me get the guerrilleros in under one roof.

"Anything," he said, holding up a hand to prevent Smith from interrupting. "Anything at all. Magazines with this month's date. Those *I Shall
Return* matches. Paper. Bullet molds, lead, powder, percussion caps. Any
little thing that helps give the people reason to hope. That makes them feel
they are not alone. That proves I am in touch with MacArthur and that
says, 'Anyone who would get The Aid must go to General Fertig.'

"Now as far as the Japs are concerned," Fertig continued, "the over-all
strategic objective is very simple. It is, *Kill the bastards.*"

Fertig rose from his chair and stood in front of them.

"We kill them whenever we can," he said. "We can't fight set battles.
We can't defend any place. When the Japs come, we run. But we kill them
whenever we have picked the ground, have surprise, and outnumber them.
We never wait for counterattacks. We just hit, and run like hell.

"Well, we dry-gulch 'em," he confessed, vaguely ashamed. "We can't
do anything else. It's the kind of game any American kid knows how to
play, and, if it's done right, there's no way to stop it unless the Japs are
prepared to murder every Filipino in the Islands."

Fertig paused, uncomfortably aware that he was talking like an infantry instructor to recruits but at the same time knowing how terribly
important it was for Headquarters to understand.

"We tell the people," Fertig continued, "'You are farmer by day, guerrillero by night. If Hapons come, you are farmer. You do not hurt them,
and, if you must help them, you help them little, making many excusas.
But, as soon as the Hapons leave, you are guerrillero again. When the
Hapons come back, tired, and confident that nothing will happen to them
this day, then you shoot from the ambush you have prepared.'

"And it works," Fertig said. "The people must have immediate victories, no matter how small, in order to believe in themselves. They need to
prove, 'We can do it, we have already won once.' When they go out and
bushwhack a gang of Japs without losing a man, they come back saying,
'The Hapons are not so much; we are mightier than they.'"

Support of the people was absolutely fundamental, Fertig explained,
for it was the civilian population who bore the burden of casualties.
None of Fertig's soldiers had been killed so far, since they fought only
with every possible advantage. It was the civilians whom the Japanese
butchered, and, as long as the Japanese were bestial, popular support
of the resistance was assured. And, as long as there was resistance, the
Japanese would continue to be bestial. The worst kind of Japanese, from
Fertig's viewpoint, was that single captain on the east coast of Mindanao
who was actually being kind to the people in his area, who seemed to

have taken literally the Japanese propaganda about the benevolent co-operation of brother Asiatics.

"In this case, we have to use terror ourselves," he told Smith and Parsons. "It's tricky, because you have to show that the enemy is evil, while you are good. If you become evil, then you are the enemy, too. So, in this case, we send men to the people to say, 'You are either for us or against us. Things are good here for you, yes, but not so everywhere else. You must act for the good of all Filipinos. If you are for us, you will do all that we ask. If you do not, then you are against us, against all Filipinos. If you are against us, then, too bad, but we must kill you.'

"We give them a choice," Fertig said grimly. "Meanwhile, we practice sabotage and assassinate Japanese in that area to provoke the Japanese into making the kind of reprisals that *will* put the people on our side. But, except for that one area, the people are all for us because the Japanese everywhere else act like weasels in the hen house."

For his part, Fertig felt his principal role was to see that the guerrilla army merited the support of the people. Therefore, there was no army that moved from place to place. Rather, the army was the people. Fertig had divided the island into areas, each defended by its own population, not only because Filipinos, like most men, were even better defenders of their own barrios than of their neighbors' but also because such a scheme simplified the logistical problems. Each area had always raised its food, seldom creating a surplus. To quarter additional troops in any area would put an intolerable burden on the community resources and would necessitate delivery of supplies from outside areas. To further insure the people against an undue burden, each guerrilla command therefore had its own farm land, and its command posts were established well away from the barrios. But not all areas were self-sufficient, now that the Japanese, the rats, and the locusts had come. Therefore, Fertig was sending hundreds of tons of rice, corn, and sugar from Misamis, all of it painfully carried over back trails by cargadores. These supplies, plus whatever extra arms and ammunition Fertig could devise, tentatively nailed down the precarious allegiance of the local commanders.

"I couldn't move an army and all its supplies, even if I wanted to," Fertig explained. "The Japs have all the principal roads, watercourses, and seacoasts. But, the way we're set up, I don't have to move an army. All I have to do is make sure we're keeping constant pressure on the Japs everywhere, so that no matter where they are or which way they turn, somebody is kicking them in the ass. Now, to do this, you need two things: control over all the organizations, and accurate information.

"Generally," he said, "our information is good. Practically every bar girl in the Islands keeps us informed on the Japs. The Japs can't move a step without somebody seeing them, and the people tell us. I know I can trust the information, because the people who send it are betting their lives on the accuracy of their reports. But the problem is, to get that information to the local guerrilla commanders in time for them to use it. The bamboo telegraph is fast enough, but secret messages must go by safehand courier. On foot. And you know what that means—it can take weeks to send a message fifty kilometers. That's why I say those radio sets are just about the most important things you brought."

He would have gone on, but Parsons said, "What MacArthur wants is information. Not twenty Japs dead in some gulch. Those radios we brought you are for information. You are to establish a flash line of watcher stations along the coasts and pass the word to us of Jap ship movements. We will have subs waiting for those ships. One torpedo in half a second can blow up more ammunition than the Japs would shoot at you in a year. Another can kill more Japs on a troop transport than all the guerrilleros in the Islands could ever kill."

"You're talking like an American, Chick," Fertig cut in. "Damn it, this isn't America. This is a land where the Japs come to a man's house, huh? They slap his face and tie him up in a chair so he can watch them rape his women. Then they steal his food and leave. By God, that man wants to see those Japs dead.

"Chick, do you honestly think any Filipino is going to say, 'The Hapons rape my wife. It is too bad, but I will have revenge: I will tell the Americanos of the small ship of the Hapons that left Cagayan yesterday with much copra, and so I am repaid'? Can you see any Filipino, or anyone else in that man's shoes, thinking like that?"

"No, I can't," Parsons said. "But you are to avoid contacts with the Japs and use those radios to send us information on ship movements."

"Damn it, Chick," Fertig said, "I am trying to make clear that any guerrilla has to keep the pressure on, everywhere and all the time, killing Japs. Otherwise, no public support. The public wants to see dead Japs. Without public support, no guerrilla."

"And I am trying to tell you that your duty is to build a coastwatcher net and stay out of fights with the Japs," Parsons said. "If you do this, then Headquarters will send what Aid it can."

"Look, Wendell," Smith said, not unkindly but as a physician might overlook the understandable but not-to-be-condoned arguments of a sick man. "Down there, they have their own view of guerrilla operations. You and Chick and I might think the Filipinos can win the war if only we send them the guns. But Headquarters doesn't think so. They think that, if the Japs can run a Regular American Army out of here, no gang of gooks is going to beat them.

"Headquarters," Smith went on, "is afraid that you *will* kill so many Japs that you'll become a nuisance and that the Japs will move in and clean you out. If they do that, then there will be no possibility of getting information out of here—information Headquarters needs. Hell, MacArthur knows the guerrilleros want to fight. His plan is, when he returns, to arm the guerrilleros so they can shoot up the Japs' rear while the Army attacks from the front."

"You know that's bullshit, don't you, Charlie?" Fertig asked quietly. "You know better than that, don't you, Chick?"

"I'm just saying what they think down south," Smith said.

"Well, I hope you can help them change their minds," Fertig said slowly, picking his way with care. "That might be a good textbook theory of guerrilla operations they have down there, but it isn't in accord with the facts up here.

"I'll put in the watcher net," Fertig continued. "But I can tell you we'll have to post troops around each radio station to give warning when the Japs close in on them. Because the Japs will put direction finders on those radios and come after them. Broadcasting intelligence isn't avoiding contact with the enemy; it's a means of attracting it. You might explain, Chick, that, if we put in these radios, we'll need a few hundred thousand rounds of ammunition, BARs, carbines, Tommy guns, mortars, and grenades."

"And you'd never, of course, use these in an offensive way?" Parsons murmured.

"Of course not," Fertig said blandly. "Farthest thing from my mind."

"Speaking of face," Parsons said softly, as though anyone had, "about this civil government of yours . . . You know that MacArthur brought the President out with him. Officially, the Philippine Government is in exile, waiting to return. But here you've set up a Free Philippine Government in the Islands."

"The Free Philippine Government is loyal to and obedient to the Commonwealth Government in exile," Fertig said.

"Yes," Parsons said, "but some people are a little worried. They wonder if, after the war, the people will say to themselves, 'Shall I vote for the one who ran away or the one who remained?'"

"We're not going to win the war tonight," Smith said. "You two look as tired as I feel, so let's all hit the sack."

BUT FERTIG REMAINED AWAKE after the others had gone to bed. He leafed through the stack of magazines that Charlie Smith had brought him. They were incomprehensible. Had he lost his need for reading? Perhaps the magazines were meaningless. Fertig had a dim memory of having once been interested in the kind of things the magazines set forth, but they did not interest him now. Fertig wondered if the fault was not in himself. He looked at pictures of a world that was unspeakably foreign and remote. There were pictures of people Fertig could not really remember at all, people engaged in ludicrous trivialities. There was a photograph of people sitting at a banquet in street clothes. The caption said that, because of the war, the people at this banquet had relentlessly decided not to wear evening clothes. The price of admission to the banquet was the purchase of war bonds.

What was this supposed to mean to him? That, in distant America, they gave you a banquet as a reward for the patriotic sacrifice of saving your money? On another page, Fertig learned that hordes of schoolgirls screamed in ecstasy whenever a spindly crooner with the wise-guy face of a city-smart Italian mooed into a microphone. Was this a picture of the future mothers of America? And what did it have to do with the kind of screams that could be heard on Mindanao? The photographs of the men in training camps were all very well, but they were still in training and 10,000 miles away, and Parsons had said that none of the men now training would be seen in the Pacific until Germany was destroyed, and no one could guess when that would be. Fertig turned the page and discovered that Lucky Strike Green Had Gone to War.

Angrily, he threw the magazine away. It represented no America that he could recognize. God pity the poor Filipinos who looked at an American magazine and saw America in it. Fertig knew of an America that set friends to spy on one another, that cavalierly sought to dictate terms and policies to a foreign people it did not understand and whose circumstances it ignored, apparently on the assumption that what was good for America was obviously good for everyone else. America was men who had lost the war, trying now to enforce their ruinous policies on everyone.

Yet Fertig knew that America was larger and better than the magazines could ever portray and that one group of men in one Army headquarters was hardly representative of all Americans. America was also a gaunt kid like Bayley, coming sick out of the bush, rifle in hand, ready to help as best he could. America was Charlie Smith and Chick Parsons, casually risking the worst of deaths. America, for all its crooners, was still also the land that produced hard-handed men like Walter and Hedges: men who took no nonsense from a swarm of Moro tribesmen with filed teeth who would have scared the wits out of that banquet hall of bond buyers; men who killed a Japanese soldiery that really would have given the schoolgirls something to yell about. And more than anything else, America was something that no magazine could ever portray: It was essentially an idea. The idea that men could be free.

Perhaps the Filipinos who clutched at *Life* found the sacrifice of Lucky Strike Green to be as grotesque as Fertig did. Perhaps they saw nothing in *Life* but a token, some tangible evidence that there was still a land where men were free and that that land was interested in their agony.

In the midwatches of the tropical night, Fertig heard the steady musketry of rain battering away at the nipa roof, and the sounds of his friends' sleeping. Exhausted by the varying emotions of the day, Fertig turned to his diary.

I am so tired. For more than a year, I have borne burdens which continue to increase in complexity and during that entire time I have had no one with whom I could discuss the seriousness of my problems or share my burdens.

He shut the book, blew out the lamp, and went to bed. Unlacing the new shoes that Smith had brought him, Fertig reminded himself that he must be very careful in whatever he said.

6

PARSONS AND SMITH spent more than a week in Fertig's province, taking notes that would serve as the basis of official reports. Fertig kept out of their way as much as he could, volunteering nothing, confining himself to precise answers to his judges' questions. He felt like a man on trial for his life, and he was not present when Charlie Smith reached the first, tentative verdict.

"I tell you. Chick," Smith said, "three months ago, when I got out of here, I'd have said it was impossible."

"You know what Willoughby said," Parsons murmured. "He said, 'There is no resistance in the Islands, and no possibility of any arising.'"

"Well now, *there's* a fresh point of view," Hedges said mildly, slouching happily back in a chair with his feet up on another. He had come with Cecil Walter to meet with Smith and Parsons, whom both he and Walter had known before the war, and to attend a meeting of guerrilla leaders.

Hedges yawned, stretched, comfortable as a cat, and looked benevolently upon Walter, who stirred a cup of black coffee.

"Kind of gives a man the strength to go on, don't it, Walt?" he asked.

"And who the devil is this Willoughby?" Walter said, not really caring but smelling the fragrance of the first good coffee he had had in months and looking over the verandah into the colors of the garden below. The four men were billeted in the Casa Ozamis, and Walter had not been in such a house as dona Carmen's for even more months than he had not had good coffee.

"Willoughby's just MacArthur's intelligence officer, is all," Hedges said.

Walter, suddenly aware of the conversation, put his cup down before it reached his lips.

"Not really?"

"Yes," Smith said. "Really. Very really. Willoughby says, because there's no possibility of resistance, there is no reason to send in guns and ammunition."

"Why, the man's an ass," Walter said, dismissing him.

"Whitney sent the guns," Smith told him. "He and Willoughby don't get along. They're each bucking for the job of being MacArthur's Number One Boy. The way it's set up, Willoughby is intelligence, and Whitney handles Philippine affairs. Willoughby thinks any information coming out of the Islands is intelligence and ought to go to him and nobody else. Willoughby's idea of an intelligence report is that, if you get one, you want to lock it up so nobody will see it. Whitney's idea is that he's in charge of Philippine affairs, so any information coming out of here ought to go to him first, for evaluation and action. It's Whitney who put the carbines and the ammo on the sub."

"For two reasons." Parsons added. "First, because he knows you can use them, and second, to annoy Willoughby."

"That sounds like a great little outfit you have down there," Hedges said.

"Don't make too much of it," Parsons said. "We're only telling you rumor. Actually, Willoughby and Whitney are damned smart men."

"And I'm Queen of the May," Hedges said. "Goddamn it, Walt, save some of that coffee for somebody else."

"Seriously," Parsons said, "when Willoughby, MacArthur, and the rest of them pulled out, it didn't look as if there'd *be* any resistance movement. You remember the Filipinos were deserting, regiments disappearing overnight."

"That's why I don't see how in the world Wendell got this thing together," Smith said. "But he's got all kinds of Filipinos working together. By God, he even has agents in the Jap headquarters in Manila."

"General Homma's mistress is one of them," Hedges said. "Every Irish priest in the Islands is another. Wait until you see Father Haggerty, Chick. He's an American Jesuit. He'll tell you how it works. The stupid Japs show some respect for the priests' official neutrality, and the padres come and go through the Jap lines and everywhere, saying Mass, dealing out the sacraments, and whatever the hell else it is that priests do. Looking after the goddamn flock, as they say.

"But, in the business," Hedges said, "the priest picks up intelligence information from our agents and passes on instructions and orders from Wendell. Why, Father Haggerty is the unofficial intelligence officer of this whole goddamned guerrilla, and him and the other padres have probably sent more Japs to hell than they've ever got any of you Catholics into heaven."

"What stops me," Smith said, "is how Wendell knows what to do."

"It's simple enough," Walter said. "He runs the guerrilla like a government, like an army, and like a business."

Hedges laughed.

"Business is right," he said. "You know all those women you saw lined up at Headquarters the other day? You know what they were doing? They were waiting for their goddamned permanent waves. Wendell may not be the smartest man in the world, but he catches on fast. One day, he got to wondering why the hell any woman with hair as long, thick, and beautiful as a Filipina would want to cut the damn stuff off and frizz it up in curls. But Wendell didn't waste time trying to figure it out. He just decided that all women were contrary, so you might as well take advantage of it.

"He had the boys round up every hair curler in the province," Hedges said. "Now, if a woman wants her goddamn hair curled, which they every silly one of them do, she's got to come to the army to get it done. It was the same thing with the band. We captured the best dance band in the Visayan islands and brought 'em here. Now we rent 'em out to barrio fiestas. We probably got the only army in the world that is financed by dance music and hair curling."

"Actually," Walter told the two visitors, "Wendell just uses common sense, as any miner, logger, or construction man would. He uses whatever he can and tries to find some use for whatever there is. Women want their hair curled, and the army needs money. So we're in the beauty business. Now tell me, Chick, what would you think of using the Negritos in the guerrilla?"

"I don't know," Parsons said, thinking of the sky-black pygmies who so seldom allowed themselves to be seen. "Offhand, I'd say it would be pretty hard to bring 'em in."

"I don't think Wendell would have thought of them either," Walter said, "if he hadn't heard what happened when a Jap patrol surprised a bunch of them digging up camoteng cahoy in a jungle clearing. For once ,the Negritos didn't hear anyone coming, but all of a sudden, there the Japs were, and they took the camotes away from the Negritos.

"When the pygmies started to bitch, the Japs just laughed, and slapped them away, and sat down and cooked the camotes for themselves. Two minutes after the Japs started to eat, it was all over. Every mother's son of them blue in the face, grinning like an idiot, and deader than hell. The

Negritos had been trying to warn the Japs that camoteng cahoys look almost exactly like edible camotes, but you have to peel and dice them and put them in a basket in a fast stream for three days to leach the cyanide out before you can eat them. But the Japs just beat up on the Negritos, stole their chow, sat down to eat, and died.

"When Wendell heard the story," Walter said, "it gave him an idea. He got word to the Negrito chief through a friendly Manobo. He gave him two twenty-centavo pieces to play with, and, in return, Wendell now has every pygmy in the hill watching the jungle for us—moving like smoke through the woods and warning us when the Japs are coming. But that wasn't enough for Wendell. He also got them to dig up all the camoteng cahoy they could find and trade it to us. Our agents mix them in with the other camotes and sell them to the Japs in the markets. The result is, we not only poison a few Japs, but we have them scared of buying or stealing food in the markets."

"Walt has the key to it," Hedges said. "Wendell just uses whatever works. He can't worry too much *how* it works, as long as it does. Hell, he's no genius. He doesn't know any more about how to run an army or a government than you do. But Wendell says *he* doesn't have to know, as long as he can find somebody who *does*. You know these Philippine Army officers, how they all sit down and memorize the damn book like it was the Bible? Memorize every army regulation, comma by comma? Well, Wendell leaves all the administrative work up to them.

"They love it," Hedges continued. "This is their life. So here we have an army set up along the lines of a regular outfit. Complete with military police, judge advocate's section, and staffs for supply, training, intelligence, and operations. Hell, we even have a communications section, a medical section complete with a field hospital, and a training camp for officer candidates. Of course, the hospital is just a quiet place to die, because there's almost no medicine and damn few surgical tools, and the communications section includes a raft of guys beating on wooden gongs, but what the hell. It's beginning to look like an army. The only time Wendell fiddles with any of this stuff is whenever something *isn't* working. Then he finds out why, and, if there's an AR standing in the way, he ignores it and makes up a rule of his own that *does* work, on the basis of what the hell we *can* do.

"It was the same thing with the civil government," Hedges said. "Wendell leaves all that up to the Filipinos. All he does is make sure they have good men in the jobs. Then he lets them alone to do their stuff, until somebody screws up. Take price control. We have to put controls on to control the black market. The Filipinos, like any other damned bureaucrats, came up with a long list of prices—so much for needles, so much for thread, so many centavos for this and that. Naturally, it didn't work. So Wendell told them just to peg the price of corn and rice—the two staples—and forget about the rest. And sure enough, once the price of rice was pegged, all the other prices fell into line."

"It was so simple," Walter said. "So damned obvious, when you come to think about it."

"The black market was plenty bad when I left," Smith said.

"Not now," Walter told him. "The big crooks are taken out and shot. The little crooks go to Happy Valley."

Happy Valley, Smith and Parsons learned, was Fertig's camp for Japanese prisoners, collaborators, and criminals. All the public knew about it was that it was somewhere in the hills, guarded by Moros.

"One Jap and seven collaborators busted out of it one night," Hedges told them, "and the next morning, the rest of the prisoners saw eight fresh heads stuck up on poles outside the wire, looking in at them. A little crude, but it worked like a charm. Since then, no problems with the prisoners."

DURING THE NEXT few days, Smith and Parsons heard Fertig's officers tell them that Willoughby could not be more wrong: that there was resistance everywhere there was a Japanese.

On the other hand, they learned that Willoughby was right in saying there was no possibility for resistance, in the conventional military sense of the word. Moreover, the resistance attempted by Filipino guerrilleros was often pitiful, not always wise, and, in some cases, ruinous.

To resist in any way in Manila required bravery, Parsons learned, for the penalties ranged from a savage beating for failing to bow to a Japanese soldier, to tortures characterized by the most perverse sexuality. Compared with these, the chopping block and the sabre stroke seemed a blessing. Yet, he said, despite the worst the Japanese could do, groups with brave names, such as the Hunters, operated within the city. One of the most aptly named was the Live Or Die, primarily an organization of young intellectuals. Nearly half of them died— many in the torture chambers of Fort Santiago, the medieval Spanish fortress whose dank, lightless dungeons were beneath the level of the Pasig River. But the survivors continued to collect intelligence to pass to guerrilleros outside the city; they assassinated Japanese, swam into the harbor at night to fix homemade explosives to the hulls of Japanese ships, composed and distributed propaganda, and organized what relief they could send to the American and British civilians shut up m the internment camp the Japanese had made of Santo Tomas University.

But there were uglier matters. Despite the general truth of the popular saying that there was a hero in every barrio, Smith and Parsons also learned there were guerrilleros who made treaties with the Japanese. They would remain peacefully in the hills, harming no one, if the Japanese promised not to attack. Thus, in some area of many islands, there was no real resistance in any sense of the word, merely an armistice which the Japanese would abrogate when they found the time for it. There were also counter-guerrilleros—irregular forces in the pay of the Japanese, recruited from the old Philippine Constabulary, which the Japanese now called the Bureau of Constabulary. Worse, there were guerrilleros who sold information of rival guerrilleros to the Japanese. To be sure, the number of spies, traitors, and collaborators was minuscule compared with the total population of the stricken Islands, but the point was that no one could be altogether certain of his neighbor. Who could be sure that the man who seemed to be simply a muddy tao who wanted to join the resistance was not a Japanese spy? Because of this uncertainty, as well as because of political rivalries among guerrilla leaders, liaison among the resistance units was short of ideal.

Further, Smith and Parsons learned that many resistance units suffered a lack of intellectual leadership. For the most part, they were composed of uneducated peasants who had nothing to lose but their lives and who had no plans beyond those of the imperative moment. If such bands survived, they did so on the basis of animal cunning. Too often, the wealthier, educated people would refrain from active resistance in the hope that the Japanese would therefore not rob them.

"Some of these ilustrados are just damned traitors, trying to save their own hides at the expense of their own people," Fertig told his official visitors. "Some are actually pro-Jap. But you want to be careful before you report a man to Headquarters as working for the Japanese. Some are good men who think they can help reduce the suffering if they can work with the Japs and persuade them not to rape and torture.

"Such men are wrong," Fertig said, "but they mean well, and damn it, they're brave. It takes guts for a man to go to the enemy to try to get a better deal for his own people. For he knows the Japs will treat him with contempt, because they hate traitors as much as we do. He knows that his own people, not understanding what he's trying to do, are apt to catch him and put him to death as painfully as the Japs could."

Then, Fertig said, there were Filipinos like Lieutenant Ignacio Cruz, a young college graduate who volunteered to help the Japanese persuade unsurrendered soldiers to give up.

Impressed by the young man's protestations of hatred for the white man and admiration for Japan, the Japanese gave Cruz a short course of instruction and sent him on his mission. Once outside Japanese lines, Cruz found unsurrendered soldiers, organized them into three guerrilla companies under his command, and found means to tell them when and where the Japanese would patrol. But, in order not to arouse Japanese suspicions, Cruz accompanied these patrols in Japanese uniform, discovering only one difficulty in his new vocation: "It is very hard to conceal your fears when you know your own men are going to begin firing," he confessed.

"The real point of Cruz' story," Fertig told Smith and Parsons, "is that Roxas put him up to it."

"Roxas?" Parsons asked softly. "We heard he was working for the Japs."

"That's exactly what I'm driving at," Fertig said. "After the war, we'll have to go easy before we call a man a collaborator. Roxas is a member of the puppet government, but he's doing everything he can for us."

Here was news indeed for both MacArthur and the Philippine Government-in-exile to consider. For Brigadier General Manuel Roxas, prewar political leader and heir-apparent to the Philippine presidency, was by all odds the most important Filipino in Japanese hands. In prison camp at Malaybalay, Roxas advised young officers like Cruz to become double agents. Later, taken to Manila, Roxas managed for months to stay out of the puppet regime, pleading ill health. When this pretense could no longer be maintained, he joined the puppet government to begin his deadly game.

To their astonishment, Smith and Parsons discovered that Fertig had a link to Roxas. The intermediary was Jose Ozamis, only male of the Ozamis family, brother to dona Carmen and her sisters, and prewar senator from Mindanao. Pretending to embrace the Japanese, don Jose had become vice commissioner of sports in the puppet regime. The commissioner was a Japanese whose idea of sports was one of indoor exercises. Therefore the Filipinos derisively called don Jose the commissioner of vice, for one of his jobs was to find girls for the Japanese Army brothels. He promptly staffed the brothels with young Filipina patriots. The girls' reports told an accurate story of troop units, command changes, Japanese hopes and fears. From such reports and from information gathered through his position in the puppet government, don Jose gathered intelligence to pass to resistance units in Manila and in the provinces and islands beyond. He was linked to Fertig through a young relative-by-marriage, Dr. Antonio Montalvan who—as a public-health officer assigned to Mindanao—came and went between his station and his home office in Manila on Japanese travel passes.

"We are damned lucky in the kind of Filipinos we have working with us," Fertig told Parsons one night during Parsons' inspection visit. "There are no braver, more intelligent men than Tony Montalvan and Jose Ozamis. Judge Saguin would be a great man in anybody's country. That little aide of mine, Rex Reyes, could run the army all by himself if he had to. Mortera is a first-class fighting man, and Andres is another. Tony's brother, Jesus Montalvan, is as deep but as honest as they come. He's my Nick Capistrano of the political side—never the man who holds office but the one you must see if you want to run for anything from dogcatcher to senator. He represents dona Carmen's wishes—and all dona Carmen wishes is that honest men run for office. If you wish to run, you must be passed for honesty by don Jesus."

Parsons nodded. He had already recognized Fertig's flair for understanding Filipino politics and for adding the intelligence of the educated ilustrados to the basic patriotism of the taos. Parsons appreciated the Filipinos himself and thought it only logical that one of them, Nicholas Capistrano, was Fertig's right hand.

Nick, as everyone called him, was a wealthy mestizo in his thirties—tall for a Filipino, with a round moon face and Chinese eyes. He was a graduate mechanical engineer who owned the electric-light company of Misamis City, the Misamis Lumber Company, and a nipa wine distillery. He knew many of the local dances, as not all ilustrados did, and had a most un-Spanish sense of humor that appealed to Parsons' own. He wore a general air of kindliness about him, in which there was no sign of weakness. Rather, he seemed to be kindly in a curious, skeptical, politely aloof, almost mysterious sort of way.

"Don't worry about Nick," Fertig told Parsons, who wondered what the mestizo's precise status might be. "He's my corps of engineers, my labor-relations expert, and the one who gets done whatever needs doing.

"Nick has an American mind," Fertig said. "If I ask a Filipino 'Can we do this?' most of them will say, 'Oh, yes, sair, if you say so'—and then they'll wait for me to tell them how. But if I ask Nick, he'll grin that slow grin of his and say, 'Why not?'—and go off and get it done. He won't take a commission, and he won't take pay, but he's the one who summons up the labor gangs and cargadores, who keeps our mechanical equipment going, and who arranges for the collection and distribution of the army's food. And where Nick ends, Josefa begins."

Josefa Capistrano, Parsons discovered, was Nick's wife, the extremely wealthy goddaughter of Vice President Osmena. She was a Chinese mestiza of lustrous beauty whose skin had that creamy tone that only the skins of highborn Chinese women have. No matter what the circumstances, Josefa always looked as clean and delicate as a flower at dawn, but anyone who imagined that she was merely decorative would have made a great mistake. There was a driving ambition beneath that limpid loveliness. Josefa had organized the guerrilla's Women's Auxiliary Service, which she intended to build into an organization that would be recognized by both the United States and Philippine governments as a regular military force,and that would serve her as a political organization after the war.

Parsons was as impressed as Smith by the complex structure Fertig had built out of diverse elements and the debris of defeat. As a naval intelligence officer, he was even more impressed by the possibilities inherent in an organization that had the priesthood as its couriers and had agents in both the Japanese civil and military commands. But he found men on Mindanao who regarded the whole thing as a farce. One was a United States Army officer who refused to have anything to do with Fertig's guerrilla and who predicted the entire edifice would disintegrate at the first serious Japanese attack. There was a third, far more important view, however, of which Parsons was entirely unaware. This view was Morgan's. It was growing like a cancer in Morgan's mind, but, as yet, even Morgan would not admit that it existed.

7

WOMEN THREW FLOWERS in his path and rushed to put leis around his neck, and men cheered, and Morgan walked slowly through it all, golden, sleek-haired, white teeth flashing, glancing with bold mockery at the pretty dalagas whose eyes met his and who then demurely turned their heads in the most provocative of invitations.

Morgan laughed, waved his arms to the throng, and only Tait, walking proudly beside her, heard Sinang murmur, "He is The One. For the people, he is The One."

Fertig met them at the head of a guard of honor, and afterward there was fiesta for the handsome young chief of staff who had so successfully carried out a hazardous mission of foray and recruitment throughout Mindanao to the northern coast and thence across the sea to Leyte and back. But pleading the pressure of affairs, Fertig had not lingered long at the fiesta for the return of the conquering hero. His departure fed the doubt that had always been in Sinang's mind.

During the days that followed, her suspicions grew. Much had changed during Morgan's long absence. There were new faces in the headquarters in Misamis City. White faces. Most of them were very young, but all of the white men were officers. There were also new brown faces in Headquarters—and some of them belonged to men who in the past had refused to join Morgan. They were the smooth, careful, and intelligent faces of men far above Morgan's station, and these men, too, were officers. But most disturbing of all was the bleak hostility that Sinang found in the sombre features of Crisanto, who followed Fertig closely as a shadow with a Browning automatic rifle in his arms.

"Crisanto is with Fer-teeg and against us," she told Morgan.

"Woman, woman," Morgan pleaded, "when will you learn? We are not *against* Fertig. He is not *against* us. I fight while he plays big shot. The people know this. Fertig knows this. Everyone knows this but you. All know that, without me, there is no Fertig."

"Soon, without Fer-teeg, there will be no Morgan," Sinang said bitterly. "Everyone knows this but you. Crisanto was one of the first to join us. Now he calls Fer-teeg Tai Tai. When Crisanto was with us, he did not call *you* Tai Tai."

"Crisanto is a stupid tao!" Morgan shouted. "For the love of God, let your suspicions die!"

FERTIG WAS ENTIRELY aware that Sinang was murmuring, as the Filipinos say. It was not something he knew on the basis of documentary evidence. Rather, he knew it instinctively, having picked his way for nearly a year through a quaking bog of Filipino politics, jealousies, loyalties, involved family connections, and nuances. He suspected it from the way Sinang looked at him, and he knew it from the way Crisanto looked at her. Few men stare at a beautiful woman with disgust, without reason, and the mental processes of Fertig's bodyguard were simple enough. Crisanto's hero worship was perfectly obvious.

For all Sinang's maneuvering, however, there was no change in Morgan's outward manner, but Fertig had expected none. Morgan would always be swaggering, priapic Morgan, and the question was whether Morgan would see that his larger chance lay in accepting Fertig's leadership, or in a palace revolt.

"One day, you're going to have to shoot that bastard," Hedges kept saying, yet Fertig would not give up his idea that much could be made out of Morgan and that Morgan was a patriot.

"She's just a damned pest," Fertig told himself, brushing Sinang under a rug in his mind. He had other things to think about during the month of May 1943, and he was tense and drawn. Smith and Parsons were as strained as he. Each was furious with the other. Each had sent a report to Headquarters over Fertig's radio, but neither had showed his report to the other, nor to Fertig. Smith sent his in a secret Army code. Parsons sent his by Navy code. Parsons felt he was the commander of the penetration party and that Smith should have filed his report through him, to be sent to the Office of Naval Intelligence. Smith retorted he was representing Army intelligence and that Parsons had no right to hold out information from the Army, much less give him orders. Both men berated Fertig for having allowed the other to use the radio. At any other time, Fertig would have regarded the whole affair as comic opera, but there was nothing comic about it. Those reports carried an evaluation of his competence, and, if Headquarters found him lacking, the adventure would be over.

But Fertig did not want the adventure to end. He had taken on a job, and he wanted to see it through, and he did not believe anyone else could. Everyone was nervous. Sinang, Smith, Parsons, himself. The cause of the general uneasiness was the absolutely certain report that the Japanese would throw a divisional attack on Misamis Occidental on June 19. This intelligence came from agents who had seen the actual orders. There was ample time to run away, but Fertig could not run and still remain in the eyes of the Filipinos the American general who had come to fight. It was the other generals who had run, or quit. More important yet, he would have to receive the attack to test his theory of guerrilla, upon which all of his hopes for resistance in the Philippines depended. The penalty for failure of the theory was death. The reward for success was not known.

Outwardly maintaining his mask of paternal omniscience and inwardly fussy as a hen, Fertig sent food to the hills; issued orders to remove and conceal the telephone and telegraph facilities when the Japanese attacked; designated escape routes and assembly points; sent specific instructions to each local commander. And, in the midst of this and the thousand nagging daily tasks—such as ordering a guard mounted over the fuel supply to prevent the young Americans from drinking it faster than the tuba alcohol could be produced—he was now required to weaken himself to establish the watcher stations that Headquarters demanded.

For however much Fertig told himself that Morgan was basically patriotic and that Sinang was merely a nuisance, Fertig had nevertheless built an organization of his own—a sort of praetorian guard. Now, just as he felt equal to Morgan's power, he had to send most of his trusted men to guide and guard Parsons and Smith to the isolated locations where the coastwatcher stations would be established. And since an American officer would be in charge of each of these radio stations, there was a further diminution in the number of men upon whom Fertig could depend.

And all the while, Sinang was being—Fertig thought grimly—her own sweet self.

BUT MORGAN listened to her coldly, as his pride demanded.

He slept with other women, as though to prove his independence.

But Sinang talked incessantly, pleading with him, ignoring the other women, trying to make him see what was happening to him. And Morgan began to pay attention. It seemed to him that perhaps there was something in what she said.

As Sinang talked on, it occurred to Morgan that Fertig's warm greeting *had* been a little less warm than it seemed. In fact, it might not have been warm at all. Looking back, it now seemed to Morgan that perhaps Fertig had always been a bit patronizing. The memory of his first meeting with Fertig came back clearly, and the mestizo scowled.

Yet it was true that Fertig had done much, and, with a guilty fear, Morgan wondered if it had not been more than he, Morgan, could have done. It was also true that Fertig seemed to be in the constant company of the white priests, the new Americans, Hedges, and the men from Australia, Parsons and Smith.

Were the Americans planning to shove the Filipinos aside?

Moreover, Hedges, whom Morgan detested, had concluded a pact with Morgan's old enemies, the Moros of Lanao. Under the terms of this pact, the Maranao Moros of Lanao province had formed the Maranao Militia Force—a separate guerrilla of Moros under Hedges' personal command but an army of Moros in any case. Their mission was to protect their own areas, but, since the Moros regarded all of Mindanao as properly theirs, Morgan wondered what boundaries the Maranao Militia Force might recognize. There was a rumor that Hedges had promised the Moros their own government after the war.

Then, through the efforts of Parsons and the schoolteacher of the Moros, Mr. Edward Kuder, Salipada Pendatun had strangely accepted a commission as major under Fertig's command. Powerful arguments and concessions must have been used to bring Pendatun and his Cotabato Moros into line, and Morgan could not imagine what these might have been. One of them, he suspected, was The Aid. Two submarines had come during Morgan's absence from Misamis City, and some of The Aid must have gone to Pendatun.

"Who gets The Aid?" Sinang asked, trying to make Morgan understand. "You started the movement, and you are the chief of staff, but do you get The Aid? The Americanos get the best shoes, the best cars, the best positions. That Hedges is not the chief of staff, but he has a better car than you. You ask Fer-teeg for a new Tommy gun, and he says, 'Oh, too bad, but there is no more.' But do you know what he gives to the Moro Pendatun?"

This was not precisely what Fertig had said to Morgan's request for a Thompson submachine gun, but it now seemed to Morgan that it had been.

"You see," Sinang said, "already you have become the small boy."

She took his hands in hers and turned her beautiful, love-stricken face to his.

"You see?"

"It is not so," Morgan muttered thickly, as though to himself. "I made him the general, yes. But he does not fight. He does what generals do. He talks to the civil-yans and pretends he is big shot. I am the one who fights."

"I think you should talk with Colonel Andrews," she said.

Morgan said nothing. He did not wish to believe Sinang, and he did not wish to harm the movement. Moreover, he was not so sure that he no longer controlled it.

But Sinang kept whispering to him, and, as the end of May 1943, drew near, Morgan delicately began to sound out his position. His sensitive antennae told him that he was still the overwhelmingly popular hero to the soldiers and that he could count on the support of many officers in event of trouble. But his political sensitivity told him, as surely as Sinang's told her, that he was somehow diminishing in importance. He thought it best to discover precisely how he stood with Fertig, without disclosing himself or approaching Fertig in any way. He would use his aide, Captain Fertalvero, as the means.

Hedges is Fertig's dog, Morgan reasoned. He will do nothing his master does not permit. I will send Fertalvero to Lanao to give Hedges orders from me. If Hedges obeys, then it will be because Fertig has told him that he must obey me. This will prove Fertig is loyal to me. If Hedges does not obey, then it will be because Fertig has told him not to obey me. By what Hedges does, I learn what Fertig thinks.

A week later, a much-shaken Captain Fertalvero returned with the story of what had happened.

He had coolly entered Hedges' quarters, unannounced, and told the American that Colonel Morgan had sent instructions to guide Hedges in his relationship with the Moros. The eruption of Colonel Goddamn had no doubt been heard by the Japanese, live miles away in Iligan.

"Look, you young squirt!" Hedges roared, bounding up from his chair to send it spinning into a farther wall, "I don't give a good goddamn who you represent or who sent you here!

"You walk out that goddamn door and come back in and salute your commanding officer in the proper fashion!

"And if you don't want to do that, you just keep right on going the hell out of here, because I'll come after you, and sooner or later, somewhere along the trail, I'll catch you and finish you off! Git!"

Captain Fertalvero went out like a shot. Minutes later, Hedges' clerk reported that Captain Fertalvero wished to speak with the Commanding Officer.

Grimly, Hedges returned Fertalvero's salute.

"Yeah?" he asked.

"Since you are the commanding officer of Lanao province, sir," a badly confused Fertalvero said, "I want to know if you have any instructions for me."

"Well, now," Hedges said dangerously. "Now that's a fine thing. First you bust in here without knocking and tell me what the hell *I* have to do, and now you come crawling back in here and tell me that I have to tell *you* what to do. What the hell *do* you want, anyway?"

The question was rhetorical. Hedges knew very well. An old Filipino himself, he had seen clearly through Fertalvero's visit. He had seen through it the instant the young Filipino had first entered the office, and he welcomed it because he intended to shoot Morgan at the first available opportunity. He hoped that such an opportunity had now come. What Morgan had failed to understand was that Hedges was not Fertig's dog but was a man with a mind of his own—with a mind that by no means agreed with Fertig's mind where Morgan was concerned. Hedges was not a man to count up allies in the event of trouble. He would accept any odds anyone wished to offer.

"Sir, I have been acting as Colonel Morgan's adjutant," Fertalvero began to explain.

"Adjutant? What's Morgan done now? Has he been setting up a staff so that he has a headquarters just like the General's?" Hedges demanded.

"Yes, sir, but I do not think it is the same staff as the General has," Fertalvero said.

"Now you take the wax out of your ears and listen, Fertalvero," Hedges said. "Let's cut out the comedy. I know why you're here. Now you go back and tell that brown-eyed bastard exactly what I think of his tactics. No, by God, don't you tell him. As a matter of fact, I think you better get the hell out of here and go on back and keep your mouth shut, and I'll make a point of telling that slopeheaded skirt-chaser what I think of him, myself. Now get the hell out of my office before I lose my goddamned temper."

"You see?" Sinang said anxiously, when Fertalvero had told how it had been.

"If a man is brave and has a gun," Morgan quoted strangely, "he joins Morgan."

Sinang looked at Morgan aghast.

"I made him the brigadier general," Morgan said carefully. "I think maybe I will make him the major general. But without me, he is nothing. Nothing. What difference does it make what rank he is? Let him be God if he wishes. He is not a Filipino. After the war, he will go home. But I shall remain. For the Filipinos, I will be The One."

"Who told you this?" she asked furiously. "Fer-teeg? You believe this? He tricked you to go out of the province so he could take it for himself. After the war! After the war, you think those civil-yans that Fer-teeg has put in office will come to you with their hats in their hands, and say, 'Welcome, don Luis, will you please be the Presidente, por favor?'"

But Morgan was silent. Fertalvero had told him what he wanted to know. Sinang had been right, but what Morgan now thought he could not tell anyone. Not even Sinang. But he came close to telling that night, when he and Andrews were drunk.

"When I had won control of Baroy, I asked the Old Man to come because I needed an American for a front," Morgan said.

"The Americans think they are so big," Andrews said. "But I cannot sleep at night because . . ."

"Yes, yes," Morgan said, as drunkenly. "But I think they . . . the Hapons."

He stopped, owlishly.

"The Hapons?" Andrews suggested.

"I forget," Morgan said. But through the fumes in his mind, he knew one thing clearly. He knew exactly what he was going to do when the Japanese attacked.

Then there would be time to deal with Hedges.

"The Americanos get the best shoes," he heard Andrews saying.

For some reason, this made Morgan giggle. Thinking he had said something funny, Andrews laughed, too.

They looked drunkenly across the table at one another and laughed.

8

WHEN THE FIRST RADIO message came from McClish, Bob Ball had a vision of the flat river country and the faces of his friends. He had served with McClish in Agusan province, and he had seen an attack across those plains before. He would never forget his first view of the little brown men in gray-green with the wisps of straw in their helmet nettings, moving carefully across the gold-brown fields, looking very small and far away but pressing closer toward the barrio, and the red gouts of flame and the rolling gray smoke and dust as the mortar shells burst, the flimsy houses beginning to burn, and the guerrilleros falling back, buying time as best they could with a painfully hoarded rifle fire but always falling back, and the Japanese always coming on. Ball could see, again, the people hurrying ahead of the attack, the women in a wobbling scurry with their babies in their arms, with one woman's white dress dark where the baby had wet on her and the woman worried about this among all her other fears; the older girls towing the younger children by their hands; the boys trying to drive the carabaos, and the men shouting to them to forget the carabaos; some of the men gasping as they trotted their terrified grandparents pickaback toward the shelter of the trees and into the back country; everyone afraid to use the road because of the possibility of airplanes; the flash and dust of mortar shells and the smoke of the houses and the anxious face of the priest who was the last to leave and who had stayed to bless the men who could not stop the Japanese.

"*No* answer?" Ball asked, horrified. "Jesus, General, the man's in a sweat."

"Just do what you are told, Lieutenant," Fertig said evenly, "and stop trying to tell me how to run the goddamned war."

"No answer at all?" Ball persisted when the next and more frantic message from McClish arrived.

Under heavy attack from two directions, McClish was retreating and desperately needed eight cases of .30-caliber ammunition. It seemed little enough to send.

"Goddamn it," Fertig snapped, "don't answer him, period."

McClish might as well have asked for eight carloads of diamonds, but Fertig could not tell this to Ball, nor to anyone else. It would be fatal to admit he had no ammunition to send his local commanders. It would be equally fatal to lie, to tell McClish that nonexistent ammunition was en route.

Fertig slammed out of the radio shack, angry with himself for having lost his temper. He had not intended to tear Ball's head off and wished he could apologize. But generals never explain or apologize, and lieutenants should simply follow orders. Fertig saw Sam Wilson, looking more sick and nervous than ever, making his way across the Headquarters compound.

"Is the mint packed up and ready to move?" Fertig asked.

"For the eighteenth time, yes!" Wilson cried.

"Sam, I just asked you."

"You asked me and asked me, and I told you and told you. 'Are the receipts signed? Are the accounts current? Are you ready to go?' Yes, Yes, Yes!"

"You don't have to blow up about it."

"And you can stop asking me. You told me, and we're moving it."

Fertig kicked angrily at the dust and went off in search of Hedges. He found him talking to one of the young Americans who had escaped a few days before from a Japanese prison camp. It seemed to Fertig that all who had escaped from Japanese prisons were still in a state of shock. Some could hardly wait to throw themselves at the Japanese in a suicidal attack. Others lived only for the day when they could have a Japanese to themselves, tied to a tree. This one was sick and hysterical, but Hedges either did not realize it or did not care.

"Christ, what the hell do you want to go to Australia for?" Hedges demanded. "If you want to fight, we got a war right here for you. The Filipinos have been taking care of us, and, by God, I think we ought to stick with them. They helped you out of a mess, and now it's your turn. I can't see any goddamned use in constantly running away."

The former prisoner stepped back as though struck.

"Don't you say that," he said. "Don't you accuse *me* of running away, you bastard."

"Nobody's accusing you," Hedges said bleakly, moving toward him. "If the shoe fits, put it on. And forget that bastard stuff, buddy, or I'll put so many holes in your belly, you'll leak all over your diapers. Lay it on the line or back down, boy."

The former prisoner's mouth fell ludicrously open as he saw Hedges' right hand draw back, poised over his pistol, as he began to understand the staggering fact that Hedges actually intended to shoot him without further provocation or the slightest compunction.

"Oh hell, Charley," he muttered weakly, surrendering for the second time on Mindanao.

Fertig thrust himself between them.

"If you're going to kill each other, do it somewhere else. There are no fights in my camp. Go kill a Jap if you're so damned anxious to fight.

"You," he told the former prisoner, "are going out of here on the next sub, and you're never coming back."

"You want to see me, Wendell?" Hedges asked.

"No," Fertig said.

He turned his back and walked away. His head was throbbing with an ache so intense he almost groaned. He had never had a headache before, and he wondered if something had broken behind his eyes. He went to his quarters to lie down, but lying down did nothing for his headache.

Fertig returned to his office. Everyone's nerves were on edge. McClish was not the only man with problems. Pendatun was being forced back and back from Malaybalay and was turning into a great sender of radio messages. First, he would say he was retreating. An hour later, he was holding. Fifteen minutes later, he needed supplies. By midmorning, he was thinking of attacking. By midafternoon, he had discovered an urgent reason to retreat another five kilometers. Pendatun was a Moro with the wind up, but, wind up or not, he had problems. Radio reports from Lanao province indicated the Japanese had dive-bombed every single one of the guerrillero command posts, down to and including those of companies. This spoke volumes both for the increasing accuracy of the Japanese Air Force and for the quality of Japanese espionage. From the air, one grass house looks much like another. How had the Japanese known which to bomb? The answer was simple: Somebody told them.

None of the reports in Fertig's office were good. The last week in May 1943, the Japanese opened a series of attacks all along the seacoasts of Cotabato, Agusan, Surigao, Misamis Oriental, and Lanao provinces. The Japanese were moving strongly up the central road that split Mindanao in two from Davao in the south to Cagayan in the north. They were following the path of their invasion the year before, concentrating on the seacoasts and following the roads and watercourses inland. But this time they were not rapidly seeking out American armies. They had brought Filipino labor gangs to Mindanao and were forcing the laborers to harvest the standing rice and corn, the ripe bananas and coconuts. The Japanese Army was not exclusively supplied with food from Tokyo. Wherever a Japanese army went, its mission was to live off the conquered lands and send the surplus to Japan. But, in Mindanao, the Japanese not only looted as they came, but ,after they stripped the farms and villages, they burned the fields and houses. Along the coasts, Japanese launches confiscated the fishermen's catch and machine-gunned the log canoes.

So far, the Japanese attacks had not penetrated deeply inland either from the coasts or from the roadsides or watercourses, but, for that matter, neither did Mindanao's civilization. The Japanese offensive seemed to have two purposes: to loot and then, by destroying the fields, to starve the people. For little food was grown in the back country, and practically none grew in the jungle.

The Japanese pressed on everywhere in such strength that it was almost impossible for Fertig to winnow the rumors for facts. One rumor said General Morimoto had asked Manila for two divisions to wipe out the Mindanao guerrilla. Another said 20,000 Japanese were now involved in the developing offensive. Another put the figure at 150,000, with more on the way. Still another rumor said the Japanese were reserving something special for Fertig's province of Misamis Occidental, and Fertig's instincts told him this rumor was doubtless a fact. His province seemed to lie like a land that is still bathed in sunlight, while a line squall hurtles down upon it. There was that same anxious tension in Fertig's headquarters that men feel before such a storm. Tempers more placid than Hedges' were now as highly strung.

Having nothing but advice to send his hard-pressed local commanders, Fertig sent them that, in the form of detailed instructions.

He told McClish and the others to get the people out and to slide away from the attacks but to send a few soldiers each night to infiltrate the fields. These soldiers would hide in the bamboo thickets near the rice-paddy dikes, and, when the harvesters appeared at dawn, they were to shoot to kill and then run before the Japanese guards could put in a counterattack. Each commander was to develop special teams to stage hit-and-run raids at dawn and dusk, not on the fields themselves but along the routes to and from the areas where the laborers were quartered. Special furloughs and increased rank would reward those guerrilleros who raided successfully—particularly if they captured carabaos loaded with sacks of palay. Meanwhile, Fertig ordered agents sent into the areas from which the Japanese were recruiting the labor gangs. The agents were to tell the people that the Japanese were deceiving them; that, as soon as the rice was harvested, the Japanese would kill the workers; that, if the Japanese did not kill the taos, they would nevertheless confiscate all the rice and, in any event, there would be no rice for the men who cut it. Then the agents would tell the people, "If you steal our rice, we will have to kill you. We will shoot you first, before we shoot the Japanese."

These measures were tried and proved successful in slowing the Japanese offensive. As laborers became more difficult to recruit, the Japanese were forced to cut the rice themselves. To guard against night intrusion, the Japanese were forced to set up perimeter defenses, to use battalions where squads had been sufficient before. As the offensive slowed, the guerrilleros gained time to harvest the fields themselves before the Japanese appeared. But still the Japanese pressed on, and the position of uninvaded Misamis Occidental became more conspicuous day by day. Fertig's headaches increased in severity and frequency, and, for the first time in months, he came down with dysentery. He was sick, worn, and tired on the last day of May 1943, when he sat down to tell his diary things that he could not discuss with anyone.

The end of another month of peace in our province. Fritz has pulled out and left me. Parsons and Smith are away on business. Pendatun still argues. Limena still revolts. Hedges has gone back to Lanao. The Japs are active everywhere, but the organization here is a month older and more established. Why the Japs have not come to Misamis is beyond me. Each day, I have expected them. They could have started here as well as anywhere else when the recent campaign began. Is it because the local Jap administration has concealed the extent of our activities? It is noted that the Japs always speak of us as outlaws, which may account for the fact they have not bothered us. They refuse to consider us an organized force. The Japs announce they are encouraging outlaws to surrender, and their commanding officer has said the Moros are pacified. They have withdrawn all aerial reconnaissance. It is hoped that they will continue to disregard us. Australia does not envision our position here at all. They simply consider us as unorganized bandits. Our only hope of changing that is to get Parsons back there.

Fertig could not believe the Japanese were stupid. Perhaps he had succeeded in bluffing them into thinking he was stronger than he was. Double agents had labored to spread the word that Fertig's force was equal to an American division supplied with modern weapons.

But, if this bluff had worked, its end result could only be to draw on

Misamis Occidental a Japanese attack stronger than an American division could handle. If it had not worked, why had the Japanese not begun with an offensive in Fertig's province?

There was no logical answer.

Fertig looked uneasily at his wall map, wondering where the Japanese would land when they came. There was no place to run and no place to hide, for, if Misamis Occidental had offered Fertig a remote area in which to build his organization, it was also vulnerable from a military point of view. Converging attacks across the narrow throat of land between Panguil and Pagadian bays would amputate the Zamboanga Peninsula from the rest of Mindanao and cut Fertig's overland means of escape into the unexplored center of the island. Simultaneous landings along the northern shore would shove Fertig off the narrow coastal plain and into the inhospitable mountains. When this happened, it would be all over, save for the mopping up, for there was nothing to eat in the hills and, if Fertig was not starved, the guerrilla in any case could no longer be maintained. For no guerrilla can succeed if divorced from its base in the local population and denied hope and material aid from an outside source. A guerrillero in the hills is, indeed, nothing but a bandit.

Perhaps I should have prepared defensive positions in the hills, Fertig admitted to his dairy, but position warfare has never been my forte.

Perhaps it was too bad that it was not. Fritz Worcester, a Naval intelligence officer, had been trying to tell him to prepare a safe retreat. So had Mellnick and McCoy, two Regular officers who had escaped from Davao prison camp. Mellnick, formerly a field artillery intelligence officer, and Commander McCoy, an Annapolis graduate, wanted no more part of his guerrilla than Worcester did. They frankly told Fertig what they thought of country boys who promoted themselves to the rank of general officer, advised him that he had no chance, and demanded transportation to Australia by the first available means. Fertig considered their public behavior so damaging to Headquarters morale that he finally wrote them a formal letter of instruction that confined them to house arrest. But he could not lightly dismiss their professional opinions. Now, on the last day of May 1943, he privately agreed with them.

Unless a United States offensive starts very soon, he confessed to his diary, we are lost, for we cannot meet the full force of the enemy.

ON THAT LAST DAY of May 1943, Fertig's thoughts were precisely shared by General Morimoto. He had canceled the observation flights over

Fertig's area because he now had all the photographs he needed and there was no point in wasting aviation gasoline. Copies of these photographs had been distributed to company commanders, together with large-scale maps and specific orders regarding routes of approach, boundary lines between companies, and hour-by-hour objectives. Unlike other Japanese operations on Mindanao, Operation Big Voice was not simply an opportunistic looting expedition. Its specific mission was to locate and silence Fertig's radios, utterly destroy the guerrilla, and kill Fertig. It was a meticulously planned attack, for General Morimoto had no doubt he would run into a well-armed, well-entrenched enemy. He would have preferred to make the attack with more men, but no more could be spared—not with Japan fighting simultaneously in China, Burma, the South Pacific, readying an invasion of India, and maintaining occupation armies to digest the territory she had already swallowed. But Operation Big Voice would have the benefit of offshore naval bombardment and close air support, and its troop strength was adequate if not overwhelming.

It irritated Morimoto to think that, because of circumstances beyond his control, the date of the attack had to be moved back again and again, but news of the American submarine's arrival had at last forced a definite date from Manila. The new target day was June 26, which was dangerously close to Mindanao's lowland rainy season. But, if all went according to plan, the exercise would be over before the real rains began, and, once it was over, the orderly looting of Misamis Occidental could begin. Then Morimoto could truthfully report the island secure.

During the next three weeks, while Morimoto's officers and men rehearsed their landings, Fertig just as anxiously reviewed his plans with his men. The province was divided into guerrilla commands, with each commander responsible for definite areas running inland from the beaches. A linked series of consecutive ambush sites had been selected in each area. What Fertig had in mind was an extremely flexible defense in great depth or, as he put it, a pillow.

"The guerrilleros are like a pillow laid over the land," he told his officers. "When the Japanese strike, they make a dent, but, as soon as the fist is withdrawn, the place struck can no longer be found.

"When they come, give ground," he said. "But slide aside and infiltrate behind them, so that the only ground a Japanese occupies is that beneath his sandals. When he moves a step, he gains new ground, yes, but loses all that he had." In Filipino-English, the sentences punctuated with interrogatory *huhs,* followed by pauses to make sure everyone understood, Fertig told his men to wait until they were sure of the direction of the Japanese before they surrendered ground. He told them to remember that one shot would pin down a Japanese patrol for at least fifteen minutes while they tried to figure out where they were and what they had run into and what they would do about it.

"When you see what they will do, huh, you will use your head, yes? Hit them fast and get out, huh? Eight minutes is a long, long time for a fight. Plenty, plenty long. You are to fire and run like hell."

He told his officers to have the men run, each by a different route, to the assembly area behind and to one side of the ambush site. Command posts must be up close, he said, and assembly areas should be no more than 500 meters from the ambush. Post the assembly areas on the flanks because, as soon as the guerrilleros hit, the Japanese would try to envelop them. Slide to the flank, set up the next ambush, infiltrate from the rear.

Fertig envisioned an infantry action in which the Japanese would wander into a hopeless morass of endless small-arms skirmishes, in which his men would gladly trade territory for the advantage of movement and surprise attacks. They would wipe out small Japanese patrols, delay the larger patrols, and melt away in the presence of enemy forces in excess of company strength. He had no thought of winning a decisive victory but rather of exhausting the Japanese to the point where they would sit down in fortified camps. When this happened, the people elsewhere could go on about their business, and the guerrilleros' mission would be to keep the Japanese sitting still while the guerrilleros continued to grow in strength, to install the watcher stations, and to collect sufficient supplies from Australia to permit an attack on the camps.

Fertig issued his orders orally in English to officers who then translated into the dialects, and he followed his verbal orders with explicit instructions printed in block letters. He inspected the beach defenses, the ambush sites, the assembly areas, and reviewed his tactics, looking for flaws. Apparently, the only thing wrong with them was that every American professional officer of his acquaintance said they were impractical, and impossible. As June 26 drew near, Fertig felt that his best was none too good. Yet, if all *did* go according to plan, the Japanese would hit a pillow.

On the night of June 25, he received word that a Japanese force of warships and transports was moving in the direction of Misamis Occidental. He thought nothing of it. It was probably bound for the South Pacific. Quite possibly, the force did not exist, for every time a Filipino fisherman saw a Japanese launch, rumor magnified it into a task force, and the rumor became a report. He had been receiving such reports for days, and still the Japanese had not come. And if they came, what more could he do? Fertig went to bed early that night and, for the first time in a week, slept well.

WHILE FERTIG SLEPT, the Japanese moved into position off Panguil Bay, off Pagadian Bay, and off the northern coast of Misamis Occidental. The ships were dark and silent, waiting for the dawn. In one of them, a middle-aged Japanese Army captain lay awake, thinking of the ironies of life. He wondered if he would recognize Wendell if he saw him again. He had not seen him since they had been classmates in high school in La Junta, Colorado. He remembered Wendell very well, for Fertig had stood first in their class and had been a rangy forward on the basketball team. Once he had cheered for Wendell, not because it was his duty to do so but because he had wanted to. Now, if he met Wendell, he would have to kill him, not because he wanted to but because it would be his duty.

The Japanese captain's musings did not lead him to reflect upon the general inanity of war. On the contrary, he felt this war was necessary for Japan and that Japan would win it—although, having been raised in the United States, he could imagine neither how nor when the victory would take place. He felt truly sorry for Fertig, whom he remembered as a tall, slender, gray-eyed, sandy-haired boy who had seemed so full of promise: the star athlete and honor student.

But life is full of ironies, and, when dawn came, nothing went according to Morimoto's plan, or Fertig's. Everything began to go wrong the instant a Japanese cruiser split the gray-milk light with the lurid orange flash of its broadside, for a moment disclosing the dark shapes of the destroyers, the transports, and the milling landing launches.

9

FLYING WEST OVER Iligan Bay, guiding on the dark form of 8,000-foot Mt. Malindang, Lieutenant Kiyo could see sparks flickering all along the curve of the distant black shore. Pale light was gathering behind him as the climbing sun bore upon the low clouds above, when Lieutenant Kiyo heard the disembodied voice of his air-control officer, calling over the rasp of static, speaking to him from the cruiser.

The cruiser was slowly steaming north, the black tip of an arrowhead of wake. The two smaller arrowheads between the cruiser and the shore were destroyers. Lieutenant Kiyo could see the orange flares as the ships fired, followed almost instantly by winking lights along the gray beaches. Looking to his left, he saw the narrow finger of Panguil Bay, gray-silver in the dawn, and, deep down the bay, there were lights flashing where another task force was landing at Tangub. The intermittent glow in the farther darkness, where it was still night, would be the landing at Pagadian Bay.

Lieutenant Kiyo slid the sky up along one cloud-wet metal wing and watched the island move out along the other as he turned in obedience to the metallic voice in his headset. He test-fired his guns, feeling the aircraft shudder lightly beneath him, and then the sky and the island slowly swung back into place, and the horizon climbed rapidly, island and sea rushing toward him faster and faster. Lieutenant Kiyo shouted to clear the mounting pressure in his ears. It seemed to him that he was a hawk of the Sun Goddess, stooping out of the dawn to seize a sea-flower edged with fire. There was no time to try to compress this image into the seventeen syllables of a poem as the land mass, hurtling toward him, became a reality of gray sand and dark green coconut palms.

He flattened out, feeling the aircraft leap as the bombs fell; pushed the metal cowling back down beneath the horizon line; pressed the triggers and watched the sparkling tracers flitting into the trees; and, racing suddenly lower than the trees along a narrow beach, he saw tracers erupting into spouts of sand. He rose in a tight, soaring turn to watch the other aircraft streak along the beach and rise to follow him.

He fell back down through the air toward the island, the aircraft pulsing to the guns, and, this time, Lieutenant Kiyo had a fleeting vision of a few random holes smoking along the shore, of a coconut tree here and there out of line breaking the symmetry of the groves. He kicked his rudder to swerve and fire at what might have been a man darting across an open space where trees were smashed.

Lieutenant Kiyo led his squadron back and forth, rising and falling, until their ammunition was spent and the fuel gauges approached the point of no return. The clouds were breaking apart when Lieutenant Kiyo flew toward the rising sun, while, below him, the tiny wakes of launches arrowed inshore from the transports.

The warships stood silently aside. There had been no fire from the ground, and, except for the thing that might have been a man among the trees, Lieutenant Kiyo had seen no sign of his enemies. Despite the shellfire and the bombs, the coconut groves were more or less intact, if somewhat tattered and askew. He wondered what he should say to the air-intelligence officer when he returned. In China, Lieutenant Kiyo had seen bombs falling upon villages, houses flying apart and burning, and people running into the fields and falling as tracers struck them. All this could be reported. But there was nothing to see when trees were machine-gunned and bombed, and the only thing Lieutenant Kiyo could think of to say was that he had accomplished his mission, meeting no opposition. Vaguely oppressed, Lieutenant Kiyo flew east, home to the pineapple fields of Del Monte, feeling not at all like a hawk and even less like attempting the poem that had occurred to him at dawn.

THE COMMAND POST of Third Lieutenant Primitivo Bacarisas was located in a coconut grove two kilometers south of Tudela, a town halfway between Misamis City and Jimenez. Lieutenant Bacarisas had been sleeping on a grass mat in a tightly shuttered house with his head wrapped in cloth to prevent the Wak Waks from stealing his soul, when the first Japanese shells burst upon the beach 200 yards away. The grass house swayed in the wind of the concussion, and Lieutenant Bacarisas, jolted awake, wildly tore the cloth from his face and threw open the shutters in time to see the red blast of the second salvo striking the beach. In the instants before the shock wave arrived, Lieutenant Bacarisas leaped from the house in the uncertain light, wrenching his ankle, shouting to his men.

Everyone was shouting, but Lieutenant Bacarisas, who had once been a poor tenant farmer but who was now an officer because, among other virtues, he had a great voice, shouted louder than the rest.

"Atras,[32] you sons of putas!"[33] he cried, seeing dim figures sliding away through the trees. "Come back! The Hapons are not there, they are coming to the beach!"

There was no time for a proper muster, but, gathering those he could see, Lieutenant Bacarisas formed them into a ragged line.

"We go to the beach!" he shouted.

"Yes, sir!" a soldier shrieked. "But the Hapons come with battlesheeps! With their cannons, they will kill us, only!"

"If they kill us, we will die!" Lieutenant Bacarisas shouted.

He stared wildly at them in the dawn, frantically searching his mind for the proper order. Inspired, he pointed to the sea.

"Charge!" he yelled.

Without waiting to see who obeyed, Lieutenant Bacarisas turned and plunged toward the beach himself, feeling the sudden pain in his ankle, forcing his ankle by an effort of will not to give way, running in a staggering limp through the ranks of the coconuts toward the foxholes that had been dug in the sand at the edge of the trees.

He turned to see perhaps a third of his men following some distance behind him. They were moving tentatively; the rest had vanished.

Lieutenant Bacarisas shouted, but his voice was lost in a vast rush of sound and red roar as the beach seemed to blow apart.

There was sand down his neck, and the air was filled with a vast ringing, but, after Lieutenant Bacarisas felt his breath come back and discovered that his fingers, his arms, and his legs moved and that there was no pain except in his ankle, he crawled rapidly through the stinging smoke and dropped into a hole.

Despite the quaking ground and the uproar all around him, Lieutenant Bacarisas found time to think.

Too late, he remembered that, as commander of the detachment, he should have remained at his command post, sending men to the beaches, maintaining communication with them by means of runners, so that he could be able to give some direction to the battle that would take place when the Japanese troops began to come ashore.

32. atras = turn around
33. putas = whores

But they would not come, he thought, unless I lead.

He crouched unhappily in a hole six feet deep and two and a half feet wide, while sand spilled from the lip of the hole down his neck every time the ground shook.

Those cowards, Lieutenant Bacarisas thought of the shadowy forms running inland through the trees. Truly, the cannons are very terrible, but the Americanos were right: The foxhole cannot be hurt unless one of those shells falls into it, and, if one does, you will never know it happened.

There was a long moment of silence, during which Lieutenant Bacarisas' ears rang emptily.

Cautiously, he raised himself and peered out. The Japanese warships were no nearer than they had been when he had come through the coconut grove.

Cursing, Lieutenant Bacarisas raised himself out of the hole. The nearest foxhole was empty. So was the next. The ringing in his ears increased. It became an irregular roaring, rather than a ring, and suddenly he knew what it was. Fifteen fast-moving black dots were swinging down out of the dawn sky, and Lieutenant Bacarisas jumped into the empty foxhole that should have been filled with the hard, tough body of Amado Balatayo.

The whole world filled with a rising shriek and sand poured in upon Lieutenant Bacarisas as the bomb burst. He heard the clattering roar of the engines, the howl of wind through the open gun ports, and felt the backwash of the propellers as they raced overhead.

"Mother of God, they can look right down into this *foxhole,*" Lieutenant Bacarisas muttered to himself. "The cannons, yes, a man can hide from the cannons, but not from the airoflane. From the airoflane, the pilot can piss on you!"

When the last of them went by, Lieutenant Bacarisas scrabbled out of the hole in the sand and ran limping back through the mess of tilted trees and fallen fronds, calling for his men.

"You know, I will lead from behind, next time," he promised himself. "The first retreater, I will shoot."

FERTIG CAME AWAKE with the first rolling bumping of the distant thunder. He dressed rapidly in the gray light and was hurrying across the headquarters compound when the aircraft came lowering on a long slant out of the south.

"No!" he told Crisanto. "You are not to shoot! They are too high!"

Crisanto lowered his automatic rifle and watched them hurtle over-head while Fertig counted.

"Fifteen," Fertig said.

He watched the sweep second hand of his wrist watch move through an arc. Fifty seconds later, the light morning breeze brought back the faintest muffled kettledrumming of bombs.

In five seconds, a sound wave moves somewhat more than a mile. What was there approximately ten miles north?

"The Japs are landing at Tudela," he told Crisanto, who marveled to think the Tai Tai could read the mind of the Japanese by looking at his watch.

Striding into the headquarters building, Fertig found his Filipino aide, Lieutenant Reyes, talking rapidly into a telephone. Reyes put the receiver down as Fertig approached. "What do we know?" Fertig demanded.

"Plenty Japs everywhere," Reyes said. He smiled his tough little smile. "They're landing at Tucuran, Tangub, Aloran. Aloran says they are moving up the beach, toward Oro quieta."

"How about Tudela?"

"Sir, I do not know."

"Who's on the phone?"

"It is Aloran, sir."

Fertig scooped the receiver from Reyes' desk.

"This is General Fertig," he said. "Who is speaking? Hello. Hello. Goddamn it, answer me. Hello."

He thrust the telephone back at Reyes.

"Here," he said. "The damn fool hung up. Get him back."

"What's the deal, Wendell?" Hedges asked, coming into the room.

"I'm trying to find out, myself."

"Sir, there is no answer," Reyes said.

"All right, try Jimenez."

"I think I better haul ass back to Lanao," Hedges said. "I've got all the stuff loaded."

Hedges referred to his share of the four tons of medicines, radios, and ammunition that the second submarine had brought—the submarine that had arrived two weeks earlier. He had come from Lanao province to take delivery, and the crates were now loaded on carabao sleds, ready to be inched to the seacoast for shipment across Panguil Bay to Hedges' head-quarters at Kolambugan.

"Wait till we see what's happening," Fertig told him. "It seems they're landing all along the coast."

"Sir, there is no answer at Jimenez," Reyes reported.

The little Filipino's tough grin was gone; his face was dark and empty.

"Try Tudela," Fertig said.

"I figure the Japs will be so busy putting men ashore that I can get a couple of bancas across without sweat," Hedges said. "They'll be using all their launches at the landing sites, and I'll just sail out between two of the landings."

"They're using air," Fertig said. "Don't lose any supplies. Get your men moving while I try to find out what the hell's going on."

"Sir," Reyes said, "I think the telephone is not working in the north. Tudela does not answer, either. I think the line is dead."

Fertig looked at his watch. The morning sun was strong, for dawn springs upon the tropics like a tiger, but there had not been time enough for a Japanese soldier, advancing at a dead run from the beach, to move far enough inland to cut the telephone lines. Perhaps they had been cut by a bomb, or shell.

"I must know exactly where the Japs are landing," Fertig told Reyes. "Where? How many? Where do they go? What weapons do they have? When you talked with those people on the telephone, what did they say?"

"Sir, you know how it is. Those people, they say 'Flenty, flenty Japs.' I say, 'How many? Ten? Hundred? T'ousand? Maybe six men only?' They say, 'Maybe pipty t'ousand.'"

"Fifty *thousand?*"

"I know, sir, I know," Reyes said. "They do not know."

"Get to those people at Aloran by telegraph," Fertig said. "And send for Colonel Morgan."

Reyes disappeared, and Hedges edged toward the door.

"Take care of yourself, Charley," Fertig said.

"You too, Wendell."

"And don't lose those supplies."

"Don't worry about it."

Fertig picked up the telephone as Hedges left, and tried to call south, through to his base radio section at Bonifacio.

The line was dead.

It was bad that the line was dead, for the Japanese were landing at Tangub, between Fertig's headquarters and the radio section at Bonifacio.

"Sir, there is no telegraph to Aloran," Reyes said. "There is only the line to Aurora."

"What do *they* say?"

Aurora was south of Bonifacio, on the road to Pagadian Bay.

"They're landing at Tucuran. Aurora does not know how many. But one force moves toward Pagadian and another toward Aurora."

They're putting a pincers on the radio section, Fertig thought. Moving south from Tangub and north from Pagadian Bay.

"Tell Aurora to report whatever they learn as soon as they find out," Fertig said.

"Sir, I have told them that."

"Fine. Now where is Colonel Morgan?"

"Oh, sir, Colonel Morgan is gone. He was in his car when I told him you want to see him. He said, 'Tell the General I have gone to fight at Tangub.'"

That, at least, was something. As chief of staff, Morgan's nominal place would seem to be at Headquarters, but, since Morgan was a fighting man rather than a staff officer, it had been agreed that he would guard the southern approaches to Misamis in event of Japanese invasion. Fertig was glad that Morgan had moved so promptly. A land route of escape to the interior of Mindanao should be held open as long as possible between Panguil and Pagadian bays, and, if anyone could hold it open, Morgan could. If the Japanese forces converged at the foot of the peninsula, Fertig would be trapped.

Very well, Morgan was in the south. But where was everyone else, and what was happening? Battles are won or lost before they begin. Once they are begun, there is little that generals can do about them except watch—particularly if the generals have no reserves. If all men on both sides of a battle do exactly what they are told, the battle is won by the men equipped with the wiser orders, and the victorious general is regarded as a genius. But if, as is usually the case, almost every soldier on both sides takes the liberty of personally amending his instructions, the victorious general is simply a lucky man. In any event, the rapid communication of accurate intelligence is the key to whatever control a general may hope to claim over a battle, and Fertig spent the next feverish hours dispatching runners to commanders he could neither see nor reach by telephone, telegraph, or radio.

His greatest fear was for the base radio section, for its transmitter was the only link to MacArthur's headquarters. It was not until midmorning that a runner arrived with report that Fertig's young American officers had ordered the radio section dismantled, packed on carabao sleds, and moved to an evacuation site that had been prepared in the hills.

"The Hapons were very near, yes?" Fertig asked.

"Oh, yes, sair," the runner said. "The Hapons were not yet come. But maybe bery soon they will come."

"Did anybody *see* the Hapons?"

"Yes, sair, not one," the runner said. "But maybe bery soon one will see flenty Hapons on the dailan."

Fertig cursed silently. *Very soon* could mean in an hour, perhaps tomorrow, maybe next week. It was clear to him that the radio section had panicked and pulled out without orders to do so, without waiting to find out what was happening or in which direction the Japanese were moving, without telling anyone or asking permission. They had run at the first sound of distant firing. Still, for the time being, they were safe.

He wrote orders in block letters for the radio section to halt wherever it was, reassemble the transmitter, and get on the air at once. Without it, he could not reach Australia, and he could not maintain communication with his guerrilla commanders in other provinces of Mindanao. He handed the orders to a fresh runner and prepared to move his headquarters.

At this time, Fertig was located southwest of Misamis City, on the road that led toward Tangub and Bonifacio. Headquarters was a group of nipa-thatched buildings hidden among trees off the road, and Fertig had moved there weeks ago in anticipation of an aerial attack on Misamis City. But now, in view of the landings, it was important to set up a mobile field headquarters. Fertig sent his truck to an evacuation site. With it went the Filipino Captain Lagman, carrying the administrative records. Other records were sealed into tin cans and buried near the Headquarters area. Fertig packed his diary, secret radio codes, and intelligence data into a curious brief case the submarine had brought. Anyone who did not know the trick of opening it would set off a small explosion followed by a violent magnesium fire.

Carrying this brief case in one hand and a Springfield rifle in the other, his chest crossed by the leather straps of map case and binocular case, an ammunition belt buckled around his waist, canteen and pistol suspended from this belt, Fertig climbed into his staff car, already loaded with his blanket roll and backpack. The driver, Placido, once a bus driver and possessor of the title of the best thief on Mindanao, sometime jailbird and great friend of Crisanto, slid under the wheel. Crisanto sat beside him, and Reyes slipped into the rear seat with Fertig. The field headquarters of the Commanding General of the Tenth Military District began to move north to permit Fertig to see for himself those things he could not learn from a broken communications system. He left behind a skeleton staff to relay messages from Morgan and the garrison at Aurora. Morgan's fighting abilities, plus the rough mountainous terrain in the south, should—Fertig thought—delay the Japanese long enough to permit an inspection of the north.

The road that Fertig had traveled as a liberator nine months earlier was filled with women carrying bundles on their heads, with anxious men driving slow-moving carabaos ahead of them, some families moving south and some north along this road with no one apparently knowing where he was going or why but greatly believing in the necessity for moving somewhere. The people held cloths to their faces as Fertig's car moved through the press, and no one called Mabuhay! to the General. Fertig had a glimpse of an olive-skinned man in a white drill suit, wearing a Panama hat, stepping daintily through the dust that coated his black patent-leather shoes and stained the cuffs of his white trousers. He was one of the civil servants, a minor official of the Food Supply Administration. He politely raised his Panama hat as Fertig's car swerved along with Placido leaning on the horn. The civil servant had the appearance of a man out for a Sunday stroll.

The streets of Misamis City were deserted. No one leaned from open windows to throw flowers down upon the General's car. The windows were shuttered. So were the bodegas. The noon sun beat down upon an empty plaza whose emptiness was not that of the time of siesta but was a kind of ominous vacuum, oddly emphasized by the sudden intrusion of three riflemen, who moved furtively past the locked bodegas on the north side of the plaza. Seeing the car approach, the three men darted into a narrow passageway between two buildings, and vanished.

A thin clatter of distant rifle fire came into the sunlit silence of the plaza. A plume of smoke rose straight above the western hills until it was bent by the trade winds. The smoke was very far away, but it was the smoke of a large fire, and Fertig wondered what village it was.

In the half-empty offices of the old headquarters in the stone municipal building, men were hurriedly preparing to leave.

"Sir, the Japanese landed at Tudela, and they are coming here. That is all we know," a Filipino captain told Fertig. "And yes, the Japanese are at Labo, also."

Labo was a town a few kilometers northwest of Misamis City. Fertig told the captain to post men at the edges of the city to intercept couriers and direct them to him. He spread a map of the island across a table. From what everyone had said thus far, it appeared the Japanese were deployed in a vast pincers movement, closing on the province from north and south, pressing in from the sea in the east to send smaller pincers out to seize specific objectives. But now, if they had also worked into the northwest, Fertig was nearly encircled in Misamis City.

"How fast are they moving from Tudela?" Fertig asked. "Are our men tying them up?"

"Sir, I am ashamed," the captain said. "We have not many soldiers remaining. Too bad, but yes, they are running away. At the beach at Tudela, one man only remained, but since he could not fight all the Japanese by himself, he, too, buqueed."

To buquee meant to take to the buckwheat, which was old Army slang for running away, which was a libel on the actions that morning of a certain Filipino third lieutenant. But libel or not, the effect was the same. It was not only the men of one platoon who had buqueed. Throughout the province, desertions were high. The first Japanese salvos had radically reduced the strength of Fertig's army without wounding a man, although Fertig had no way of knowing this at the time.

Fertig remained in Misamis City for an hour, until couriers reported the Japanese were seen cutting through the greening rice fields from Labo, moving slowly on the city without opposition. There was no point in Fertig's remaining. There was even less point in trying to go farther north. Fertig returned to his skeletonized headquarters southwest of the city, driving in a light rain. There, he learned that the fugitive radio section had halted as ordered but that, when it attempted to set up its transmitter, rain short-circuited and burned out the transformer. His radio was as effectively off the air as if the Japanese had captured it.

The telegraph line was still open to Aurora. But there was no news from Aurora. The trails were open to runners to Tangub, but there was no word from Morgan. Just before dark, couriers from Misamis reported the Japanese had stopped short of the city, apparently pausing for the night; that many civilians had died in the shelling of Tudela; that the Japanese seemed to have opened a campaign of terror in the north, bombing and strafing towns and villages. Rumor said the Japanese had landed at Sinonoc, advancing on Jimenez, and that those that landed at Aloran were attacking Oroquieta, the seat of Fertig's civil government. Chick Parsons, Sam Wilson, and Fritz Worcester were all staying with dona Carmen in the Casa Ozamis in Jimenez, and Fertig wondered if they had escaped. The casa and the stone cathedral were the two largest buildings in Jimenez, and Fertig had a vision of the stones of a crumpled wall lying among the smashed flowers of the garden, of tilted floors littered with fragments of Czechoslovakian glass, and of fires starting and the clothing on bodies beginning to burn.

The rain had stopped, but it was black night. There was no way to learn, nothing he could do. Fertig went to bed, only to have a brutal headache return. For hours he lay awake, waiting for the headache to go, hoping for sleep and at the same time hoping that a courier would come somehow through the blackness to tell him something—anything. The headache left, but no one came, neither while he was awake nor after he fell asleep.

Nightfall of the first day of attack found Hipolito Mercado and Felipe Ruiz, fellow townsmen from Cebu and soldiers of the Bureau of Constabulary, squatting back to back at their sentry post, watching the darkness and listening to a woman sobbing. It was a hoarse sobbing that had a mindless quality to it, monotonous and mechanical—a noise far from anguish and beyond hope. Every now and then it became a kind of tired shout, and, on these occasions, Mercado and Ruiz could also hear the Japanese laughing.

"They still play with her," Mercado said, looking into the darkness and away from the sounds.

"She is very unfortunate," Ruiz said noncommittally.

The two soldiers squatted silently, each remembering coming on the family hiding in the thickets near the rice dikes, the woman crossing herself and the man with the glazed look, staring only at the ground, and the wide eyes of the children.

"Felipe," Mercado said.

"Yes."

"We do the right thing, yes?"

"Of course. Why not? What else?"

"She is a Filipina."

"She was the wife of a bandit."

"He did not look like a bandit. He looked like, like a . . ."

"What *does* a bandit look like?" Ruiz asked. "He can look like anyone. He can look like you, or me. This is a place of bandits."

"And the children?" Mercado asked. "They were bandits, too?"

Ruiz said nothing.

They heard that tired shout again, and the men laughing.

"Suppose she was the wife of a bandit," Mercado said. "Let her be the mother of all bandits. Very well—we have captured her. Now, do you want a turn? When they brought her in, Lacorda, that tough guy, he thought he would have some, too. What happened to Lacorda? I think now he is not so tough."

Ruiz said nothing, remembering very well what the Japanese had done to the soldier Lacorda, who had thought he would be given a turn with the woman the Japanese had caught.

"Felipe."

"Yes."

"What is happening with her is happening with the Islands. That is the Prosperity Akko. The prosperity for the Hapons, only."

"The sooner the resistance is over, the sooner these things will not be," Ruiz said. "The real traitor to the people is the one who wishes to continue the resistance."

"*You* say the word traitor, not I," Mercado said.

"We are not the traitors," Ruiz said. "I will not fight my countryman, but against bandits only. A man who fights bandits is no traitor. The bandits are the traitors."

"The bandits call *us* the traitors," Mercado said. "They say, 'We will shoot the BC[34] before we shoot the Hapons, for the BC are traitors, and traitors die first.'"

Ruiz shifted uncomfortably.

"But the children were not bandits, Felipe," Mercado said. "A year-old boy is not a traitor, Felipe."

"Where are you going?" Ruiz asked, feeling Mercado rise in the darkness.

"You know. You are my town mate. You are a Filipino. They are not bandits, and we are not traitors. Come with me."

"'Polito, the bandits will not believe you. They will kill you."

"I am not a child. I am not a woman. Why should they kill me? Bandits kill only women and children, have you not heard?"

"Do not be a fool, 'Polito. If the bandits do not kill you, the Hapons will kill you slowly when they find you."

"It seems that I must die," Mercado said, moving away in the darkness. "Will you die with me?"

"I order you to come back," Ruiz said, thoroughly alarmed. "You give me the orders?"

"Come back or I will shoot."

"You *will*, Felipe?" Mercado's voice said from somewhere in the darkness. "My own town mate?"

Ruiz rose, wildly staring after the shadow of Mercado that now darted away into the night. He raised his rifle, then lowered it uncertainly. He did not want to do it; he did not want to see the Japanese do it. There was a swift, soft sound of running in the night and the monotonous noise of the woman.

Ruiz threw the rifle to his shoulder and fired rapidly until the clip was empty.

The Bureau of Constabulary sergeant came bounding up, and Ruiz excitedly explained what had happened.

---

34. BC = Bureau of Constabulary (Filipinos serving the Japanese)

"My own town mate!" he kept shouting. "He has fooled us! He was a bandit!"

"Shut up, you idiot!" the sergeant roared. "Which way did he go?"

"There! That way!" Ruiz shouted, pointing with his chin in a direction Hipolito Mercado had not taken.

THE BEST THING TO DO—in fact, the only thing to do—was to put on a bold face and walk right up to them, Father Healy decided. There were four of them across the way: an officer and three soldiers. As Father Healy was about to leave the shade of the galvanized-iron porch roof of the school building, the Japanese officer said something to his men and came alone across the sunny street toward the priest.

"Good morning, Father," the Japanese captain said in American-accented English.

"God bless you, my son," Father Healy said, somewhat startled but thinking that this Japanese was, perhaps, one of the few Japanese Catholics.

"And can you tell me," Father Healy went on, "who is it that I see for permission to return to my parish?"

"Where is your parish?"

"At Tangub."

"Then what are you doing here in Oroquieta?"

"And what should a priest be doing anywhere, except his holy duties?"

The Japanese smiled.

"Perhaps if I say you can go to Tangub, you can tell me where we will find General Fertig," the Japanese said.

"General Fertig?" the priest mused, his round, youthful face as puzzled and innocent as his blue eyes.

"Wendell Fertig," the Japanese captain said, having no difficulty with his /s.

"Well, now, I've heard of him to be sure," Father Healy said. "But I've never had the pleasure of meeting himself. I have no idea where he could be, at all."

The Japanese regarded the Irishman with amusement.

"The next time you see Wendell," he said, "you will tell him, 'Be very careful. Do not be captured, for the Japanese believe that, with your capture, the fighting in the Philippines will end.' Tell him to take care, for the Japanese have put a price on his head.

"Father," the Japanese continued, speaking quickly and earnestly, "I am trusting you with my life. If the Kempetai knew that I said this, they would execute me. I will not tell you the name I was known by when I was young, for it is best for me if you do not know. But I grew up in Colorado and went to school with Wendell. One summer, we picked cantaloupes together. My parents never became American citizens, and I returned with them to Japan. I *am* a Japanese. But I do not want to find Wendell. Tell him to be careful."

"To be sure, I'll tell himself!" Father Healy exclaimed.

"That is," he added quickly, "if ever I meet the man."

"You would not meet him on the way to Tangub, of course," the Japanese said.

"I wouldn't think so at all," Father Healy said.

The Japanese captain laughed. He wrote something on a pad and handed it to the priest.

"Good luck, Father," he said. "This is your pass."

He stepped lightly away with the happy air of a man who had transferred his own heavy burden to the shoulders of another, and Father Healy watched him go with some misgivings. Had he fallen into a trap? Father Healy wondered. Would the Japanese shadow him, using him as a dupe to lead them to Fertig's headquarters?

Father Healy left Oroquieta that afternoon in a roundabout way, and, when he was sure that no one was following him, he began the long walk to the back trails that led down the line of mountains to Fertig's headquarters. He carried the Japanese captain's pass in his pocket, and he carried in his head a detailed description of the Japanese strength in Oroquieta, and the reports of a frustrated guerrilla commander. Father Healy had no adventures on the way, beyond the routine difficulties of the trail. Another traveler, Hipolito Mercado, was also on that trail, rapidly rotting at the end of a grass rope, suspended from a tree. The note, pinned by a thorn to Hipolito Mercado's bare ankle, said:

THIS HAPPIN TO ALL DAM TRAITOR BC.
ANYONES WHO CUT HIM DOWN WILL GET SAME.
SINGED, PRIMITIVO BACARISAS,
3D. LT., U.S. FORCE IN PHILIPPINES.

It was midmorning, and a light rain was falling. The rain did nothing about the heat. Nothing would ever mitigate the heat of Mindanao. Men sweated in this heat during the dry season, and, during the rainy season, the sweat did not evaporate. Six Americans sat in a house in the hills, sweating, listening to the rain.

"Ten days from now, the trails will be impassable," Fertig said. "It's coming a little earlier each day and lasting longer. If we can get through the next ten days, we can last another month."

"Just what *is* between us and Pagadian Bay?" McCoy wanted to know.

"Jap patrols," Fertig said. "I don't know how many. Last night, one patrol of a 120 men got within six kilometers of my camp before we found out and moved out of there. How were you people able to find me?"

"We just asked the way," Parsons said.

"That's what scares me," Fertig said. "Nobody should have known. Nobody *could* have known, because I didn't know myself that I'd be here today until early this morning. I've been moving every day, on the theory that, if I'm confused, the Japs will be, too."

"Rumor said you were in the area," Parsons said. "We headed south and kept asking. Today, somebody told us."

"Thank God they're not telling the Japs," Fertig said. "If those people last night had known how close they were to my camp, they wouldn't have turned around and headed back to Bonifacio.

"The real problem," he said, "is that you never know what's around the next bend. At any moment, you may run into some lost Jap patrol. Mostly, they're following the well-established trails, and you're generally all right if you stay off them. But you never know."

There was nothing that anyone could think of to say to that. Prior to the Japanese attack, it had been arranged for Fertig's five visitors—Mellnick, Smith, McCoy, Parsons, and Dyess—to leave for Australia aboard a submarine that, hopefully, would be found waiting for them off Pagadian Bay on the night of July 10. It now appeared that the way would be difficult.

"Look," Fertig said, spreading a map of the province of Misamis Occidental before them. "You'll have a rough walk over the mountains. It would be bad enough even if it wasn't raining. If you're going to make that rendezvous, you'd better leave today. Stay clear of Bonifacio and stay out of Aurora. When you work down toward the bay, stay away from Pagadian."

He indicated a point on the map several miles out to sea. "You'll be picked up here," he said.

"Out there?" Mellnick asked, incredulous.

"That's how it is," Fertig said. "In view of the Jap landings, the Navy got panicky and decided not to risk losing a submarine by coming any closer. You'll be on that water a long time. But you'll have the advantage of knowing when and where the sub is coming, while the Japs won't. To reduce the time you'll be on the water, I'm sending you out in the *General Fertig,* even though it will make you more conspicuous."

He pronounced the name wryly. To Australia, he was still Lieutenant Colonel Fertig, but, here on Mindanao, he wore his stars and used the title Tait and Morgan had given him. The *General Fertig* was a sixty-foot steam vessel, once a lumber company's workboat but now the flagship of the Free Philippines Navy. It was not much faster than a sailing outrigger, but at least it was not dependent upon a breeze. Armed with a machine gun salvaged from a wrecked fighter aircraft, it could hold its own with a Japanese launch. Fertig saw no reason to say that Japanese destroyers had been reported in the bay.

"But you don't know how many Japs are between us and the bay?" McCoy persisted.

"No," Fertig said. "I don't know how many, and I don't know where they are—except by rumor. Not only that, but I don't know where my own men are, and I can tell you why I don't. It's because I obeyed orders."

He looked squarely at his judges and his critics.

"I could have had communications within this province if I had kept those radios. Knowing the attack was coming, I could have placed the radios with my commanders in this province. But I put them into those goddamned watcher stations. The watcher stations are in isolated areas. The Japs aren't attacking any isolated areas. The Japs are *here,* and my best men and the radios are *there.* Consequently, the radios are no use to me at this time, when I need them most. When you get back south, tell those people to send radios that I can use within my own command."

Grimly, Fertig told his visitors that, while he could talk with Australia over his base radio transmitter, which had been recently located and repaired, his entire knowledge of Japanese movements in Misamis Occidental came from reports brought by runners. The news came late, and all of it was bad.

"When the Japs started shelling, the first thing that happened was the people tore down the telephone and telegraph lines and took off with them for the hills," Fertig said. "They weren't supposed to move those lines back until the enemy was actually in sight, and, when they did move them, they were supposed to set them up again. Instead, they just ran. Base radio section panicked, too, and it took me two days to find *them.* So the first thing to go was communications."

It was now the fourth day of the Japanese attack, and Fertig said he was just beginning to piece together the story of what had happened on the first day. Few ambush sites had been prepared, he said, and even fewer were used. The beach defenses, intended to slow the enemy, had been abandoned before the Japanese neared the shores. Fertig said his men had taken far too literally his instructions to fade back in the face of attacks in superior strength. Troop units had melted away in a matter of minutes, before the enemy's strength had been ascertained. Desertions were high, and, hours after the first shells burst, Fertig's complicated organization was a complete shambles, with the government running and scattering even faster than the army. He had no idea what had taken place after that; no idea what was taking place around him now.

"I do have the runningest boys," Fertig admitted. "They run away with the greatest of ease. The only good thing about it is that it's apparently confused the hell out of the Japs. They came slamming in here to fight a static force, only to hit something as evanescent as drifting smoke. They're fumbling around looking for us, and our boys are running before they arrive. One trouble is those damned airplanes. The boys see an airplane go overhead and immediately pull out of an area it would have taken the Japs weeks to reach on foot."

It seemed to Fertig that Mellnick and McCoy were looking at him askance. In a few days, they would be in Australia, telling the story of the Mindanao guerrilla. Conscious that he was speaking through them to MacArthur, Fertig said, "These people simply will not maintain a defense line, and there's no way you can make them try. Worst of all, that goddamned Morgan has deserted. He told me he was going to Tangub to fight, but instead he took his men across the bay to Baroy, spreading the word that if and when I'm killed, he'll be the commanding general. He pulled out and left the back door wide open. At least, it cleared the air. From now on, I can treat him as a traitor and deserter and not as a loyal officer."

"From now on," Mellnick said. "You think you'll be able to weather this one out?"

"It doesn't matter whether I think so or not. We have to try to weather it, so we might as well assume that we will."

"What have you heard from up north?" Parsons asked. "Nothing. You're the first people I've seen from up north. I was going to ask you."

"Then you don't know McClish is on his way here?"

"No. What's he coming here for?"

"He's bringing a Navy guy named Richardson, who's been working with Kangleon on Leyte. Kangleon wants you to help him."

Fertig smiled sourly at the word *help*.

"McClish arrived right in the middle of it," Smith said. "He had no idea what he was getting into. He came to Jimenez by launch, just after the Japs had landed. He tied up at the seaward end of the dock before he found out the Japs had the land end. He and Richardson abandoned the launch, jumped into the swamp, and had a hell of a time getting out and working around the Japs."

"The Japs took Dipolog, using troops from Cebu, Davao, and Cotabato," Parsons said. "They're in Oroquieta and Jimenez. We got out of Jimenez with the Ozamis girls, Fritz, and Sam and later connected up with McClish and Richardson. Sam said to tell you the mint was safe. He said all the documents were moved out of Oroquieta except the files in the treasurer's office. But Sam's not worried about them because he has duplicate accounts with him."

"Sam would have," Fertig said.

"The Japs aren't moving fast up north," Smith said. "They're playing it safe, with a screen of BCs out front. I guess one reason they're moving slow is because the BCs are scared to death."

"They ought to be," Fertig said. "I'd feel sorry for them if I could. The boys told me one of them came to us the other day, with some song and dance about how he wanted to join us because the Japs were killing defenseless civilians, innocent kids, and were raising hell with the women. The boys figured, if he could turn his coat once, he could turn it again and that he was probably a spy anyway. So they strung him up and stuck a note on him. If he was telling us a straight story, that's his hard luck. He shouldn't have joined the Japs in the first place. We have no use for BC deserters."

The six men talked through the forenoon and ate a lunch of rice, stewed corn, salt fish, and coffee. It was raining hard when it was time for Fertig's guests to leave. He walked a little way down the trail with them and stopped to shake hands. He kept his good-byes stolid and matter-of-fact; as if they were merely catching a train that operated on schedule in a country at peace instead of embarking on a journey that led across brutal mountains, filled with lurid dangers, to take a leaky workboat out upon a sea patrolled by enemy warships to meet a submarine that might not be there. Standing tall in his rain- and sweat-wet khakis, radiating a confidence he did not feel, Fertig was a picture of competence: a tough man with a red beard and a pistol on his hip. For a long moment, he watched them move down the trail.

If they're killed, he thought, it won't be fatal for me. Someone at Headquarters will send in another penetration party. They won't have anyone as good as Chick and Charlie to send, but they'll send somebody. It will just mean further delay in getting The Aid.

Fertig wondered what Mellnick and McCoy would tell MacArthur.

Their worst predictions, and those of Fritz Worcester, had come true. Fertig's card house lay in ruin; his theories disproved. His men were running and deserting; he had lost communications and control; his only safety lay in constant flight. Perhaps, after listening to Mellnick and McCoy, Headquarters would not send The Aid to Mindanao. If that was the way it was to be, then it did not matter to Fertig whether or not Mellnick and McCoy reached the submarine.

Fertig turned and squelched back to his fugitive headquarters through the rattle of a hard rain striking leaves. He held himself straight, but, at every step, his shoes sank to their laces in the liquid mud of the trail. Above the rain clouds, there was the grinding noise of a Japanese aircraft engine, and then there was only the sound of the rain.

BOOK FIVE

Morgan

1

ON THE FOURTH OF JULY 1943, the Headquarters of the United States Forces in the Philippines consisted of one grass house, a number of lean-tos, nineteen worried Filipinos, and Wendell W. Fertig, Brigadier General, Commanding. The twenty men had walked all morning in a hard rain to come to this area, which was the site of an old kaingin on a minor trail that led into a mountainous rain forest. At nightfall, however, the rain stopped, the skies cleared, and the moon was bright enough to read by. General Fertig employed the moonlight for purposes of literature.

My second Fourth of July as a refugee from my friends, the yellow bastards, he wrote to himself. *Last year in the forests of Lanao and this year in the cornfields of Misamis Occidental. I did not look forward last year to eight months of comfort. Perhaps this year will break as well for me. I hope the third Fourth will be under more auspicious conditions, back with my own family.*

This morning, I moved my camp since Japs were reported on the road at Belingson. They continued on through Tambulig and were shot up by a small ambush near Salug. Some casualties were inflicted. No information after that. Reports are that Liargo patrols returned back to Aurora. Looting was rampant in Misamis, Clarin, and Tudela, with the civilians doing it. Report says Jesus Montalvan was captured in Oroquieta. I still doubt it. At 12:30, report was no Japs in Bonifacio. Base radio was moved and was off the air all day. Although they may have been back on for the evening schedule.

Since there was nothing more to be said, he shut his diary. The night hung all about him in a vast silence of golden light and black shadows. He stared into the night, lightheaded from fatigue. His belly was sore from recurring cramps of dysentery, which he was trying to cure with a diet of baked camotes. His clothes were still damp from the day's rain, and the warm air was rank with the odor of rotting leaves.

A shadow separated from the deep black of the trees and became a man in the moonlight as it crossed the clearing that led to Fertig's house. It was a man who brought further news:

Captain McClish was patrolling with three men in the direction of Bonifacio, trying to locate the Japanese patrol rumored to have been shot at near Salug. Meanwhile, an unknown number of Japanese had reached a schoolhouse not three kilometers away. Perhaps this was the Japanese patrol in question. In view of this development, should Headquarters move once again?

"No," Fertig snapped, exasperated by rumors and reports. "You are not to move, huh? I will be The One to say."

Turning to his bodyguard Crisanto, Fertig said, "Tell Placido he is to come with us."

While he waited for Placido, Fertig slid a full magazine into a Browning automatic rifle. He stuffed two more magazines under his belt. The bullets felt solid and reassuring, and the magazines, pressing on his belly, helped to ease the empty ache.

Together with his driver and his bodyguard, Fertig made his way along the rain-soaked trail that led through low hills of woods and kaingins to a shallow valley of cornfields. At the lip of the valley, he met nine men with rifles, men who had been attached to the guerrilla company assigned to the area. The company had been living in the schoolhouse when word came of the Japanese approach. Then everyone had run, leaving the records of the company behind. No, the nine men had not seen the Japanese. No, they did not know how many Japanese there were, but the report had said plenty, plenty. Therefore, they had all run away rapidly. They had no idea where their officer had gone nor what had happened to their companions.

"We will find the Hapons," Fertig promised them. "You will lead the way."

Fertig felt completely detached, walking through the night toward his enemy. He was neither angry, nor sick at heart, nor courageous, nor full of fears. He was merely tired, as an engineer would be tired of a problem that was presented to him in inexact terms. Perhaps the problem was insoluble, but Fertig at least wanted the truth of its terms. Precisely what *were* his men running from?

The schoolhouse was a low, unpainted wooden structure on short pilings, and its galvanized-iron roof was the color of milk in the moonlight. It sat in the middle of fields of standing corn, and, from the edge of the fields, all that could be seen clearly was the roof. Briefly, Fertig outlined his plan. The nine soldiers would surround the building on three sides, three men to each side. He, Crisanto, and Placido would approach from the front. The soldiers at the rear of the building would fire one shot when they were in position, to attract the attention of the Japanese. Placido would instantly rush from the front, dive beneath the porch, and set fire to it.

Fertig and Crisanto would give Placido covering fire with their automatic rifles as he ran to and from the building. It would be necessary to burn the school not only to drive the Japanese out but because the records of the guerrilleros had been left behind. If the Japanese were to keep these records, they would read the names of the soldiers, and later they would kill the families of the men whose names were on the rolls. Thus, in attacking the school, the guerrilleros were protecting their own families.

Was this clear?

It was.

Were there any questions?

"Sair, suppose the Hapons have *out-posts?*"

"You will walk with much care," Fertig said. "If there are *out-posts,* you are to send one to me, huh? He is to speak. I will tell him what to do, huh?"

By the time the schoolhouse loomed before him, Fertig's clothes were soaked through from brushing against the dripping cornstalks. The building lay in a pool of moonlight. Fertig sank into the shadows of the corn, kneeling in the mud at the base of the stalks. He saw the schoolhouse door open, and a Japanese come out.

The Japanese stood on the wide porch and unbuttoned his trousers. An arc of urine glittered in the moonlight. The Japanese buttoned his trousers and re-entered the building, shutting the door behind him.

Fertig heard the murmur of Japanese voices, and the rustle of cornstalks as Crisanto and Placido slid carefully into the shadows beside him. Fertig lifted the Browning and sighted on the door. The light was strong. He could set the blade accurately into the shallow U of the battle sight. He swung the rifle through an arc that covered the front of the schoolhouse. At all times, he could see the blade sight set into the U.

He lowered the rifle and smiled at Placido. Everything had gone well. There had been no Japanese sentries in the cornfields. Judging from the tired sound of the voices in the schoolhouse, those inside were settling down for sleep. Placido's hard face was absolutely without expression. Fertig could not tell whether Placido was wearing a mask to conceal his fears or whether Placido plainly and truly did not care what happened. It did not matter what Placido thought or what happened to him.

Fertig's head was clear ,and the pain was gone from his belly as he concentrated on the shooting. He would not have to lie prone to fire the automatic rifle, using a bipod and bearing down on the strap to keep the bullets from rising, because he had filed a deep V-shaped notch in the bottom of the muzzle's flash-hider. Automatic rifles that had this done to them stayed on target and could be fired like any other rifles, thus doing away with bipod and strap, thus reducing the weight that a man must carry, meanwhile increasing the accuracy of the piece. Carving notches in BAR flash-hiders was a simple application of a rule in high school physics governing the pressure of gases in a confined space. It was standard operating procedure in Fertig's guerrilla, although the Regular Army might have regarded it as defacing United States property. Fertig thought of these pleasant matters and of nothing else at all as he waited for the sound of the first shot to come from the rear of the building.

There was the heavy *blang-crack* of an Enfield firing and the bullet striking wood, and the schoolhouse door burst open and Japanese came spurting out.

Fertig aimed low and pressed the trigger, the rifle on fully automatic, feeling the bullets blurt smoothly in the soft, thudding way a BAR shoots, his ears battered by the sound of Crisanto and Placido firing beside him.

The first Japanese fell suddenly, absolutely. There is nothing else like it in the world, and it can never be done by anyone who is not dead. There was no lurch, histrionic staggering, or putting out of hands to break the fall. The Japanese was moving forward when he was shot, and, dead but carried by momentum, he fell from the schoolhouse porch, striking the ground with his face, and lay with his face flat in the mud, one arm bent behind him with the palm of his hand up and open on his back, with the other arm caught beneath his crotch, and with his legs in a tangle above him on the steps.

One Japanese cowered back on the porch with his hands out as if to hold the bullets back. His rump bumped the wall. This seemed to remind him who he was and what he was doing, but, as he straightened, he fell, still moving. Since he was still moving, Fertig fired again. The remaining Japanese had plummeted back into the building.

Placido lurched forward, and Fertig grabbed his arm.

"No can be!" Fertig told him.

Instead of drawing the Japanese attention, the shot from the rear of the schoolhouse had merely flushed them out the front. Now they had been blown back in again. If Placido were now to dash across the schoolyard, the Japanese would be ready for him, shooting from cover.

A heavy gust of rifleshots erupted from behind the schoolhouse, together with a sound of hilarious shouting.

The shooting stopped, but the shouting continued, and Fertig could distinguish the excited cries of the guerrilleros.

"Shut up!" he shouted.

"Tell them to shut up," he told Crisanto.

Crisanto yelled the order in the dialect He kept yelling until the shouting stopped.

In the startling silence that followed, there was a sound of stertorous breathing, the noise a man makes who no longer has the strength to groan. The schoolhouse was silent, and its roof reflected the light of the moon. The sound of breathing came from a dark pile of clothing lying in the schoolyard. There was another body lying to the right of it.

"Placido," Fertig said. "You will go to our companions. Then you will return back, huh, and say what has happened."

Fertig saw the pile of clothing shudder. The sound of its breathing stopped. Then there were no sounds except those of the night. The house stood dark in the shadows of its eaves.

Placido returned to say that four Japanese had bolted out the back door, only to be cut down by guerrilleros' rifle fire. The guerrilleros felt that perhaps there were no more Hapons in the building, for they had not started shooting until the Hapons had come out the door. All now waited to be told what to do, but all thought the Hapons had been killed.

Fertig felt there might be more Japanese inside. Minutes dragged past, but no sounds came. It was most unlike Japanese to remain silent under attack. Perhaps it was true; all had been killed. But the sound of the shooting most certainly had been heard by other Japanese in the area. Therefore, Fertig could not afford to sit still all night, wondering and waiting for events. On the other hand, because of the records in the building, he could not pull out his men and leave well enough alone. He would have to spend a man to learn the facts. He would spend Placido. He sent him angling in toward the schoolhouse from a corner where there were no windows.

No one shot at Placido. Fertig saw his driver climb the porch, step around the body of the man who had been holding out his hands, and look cautiously inside.

"Sair, there is not one," Placido called.

WHEN FERTIG RETURNED to Headquarters, he found McClish waiting for him. McClish was young, brave, energetic, and disappointed.

"We couldn't find them anywhere," McClish said. "We looked all over hell. We met some people who said they'd shot them up, but they didn't know a damned thing. They said they figured they'd killed plenty Japs because 'We fired all our ammunitions.' But they didn't wait to find out if they'd hit anyone; they just shot and ran. About two hours ago, we heard somebody shooting in your direction, and we beat it back here to help out. I guess what we heard was your scrap."

"I wouldn't be a damned bit surprised if we hadn't both been chasing the same bunch," Fertig said. "What it all boiled down to was eight stinking Japs. To hear the people talk, you'd have thought it was an army."

"So you didn't have any trouble?"

"As far as I can figure out, they never fired a round at us," Fertig said. "We fired a total of seventy rounds. You never can tell what Japs will do. We fired a shot to draw their fire. Instead of staying under cover and protecting themselves, they came piling out the front door. They ran into fire, turned around, went piling out the back door, caught it again, and that was that."

Fertig sat on the edge of his bamboo bed, unlaced his heavy field shoes, stretched, and yawned.

"When you catch them with their pants down, they get more panicky than Americans or Filipinos," he said. "But if you tackle them when they're ready, God help you.

"We collected the Jap guns and ammunition, got our records back, and got out of there," he said wearily. "I wanted to get out before the Japs sent people up to see what all the shooting was about. I outposted our back trail, but nobody came. I never will understand why, when a Jap patrol is shot up, the Japs so seldom send the main body to help."

"Maybe it's because they're split up and are wandering all over," McClish said. "Maybe there isn't any main body between here and Aurora."

"In that case," Fertig said, "now is the time to catch them. We'll just have to get the boys to go to work."

He yawned again, comfortably tired, as after a good day's effort. His stomach cramps were entirely gone, there was no indication his headaches would return, and, if in his mind's eye Fertig saw the bloody and contorted bodies of eight Japanese, they meant absolutely nothing to him. Bodies were simply a predictable, logical, and ordinary part of the world in which he lived. He said good night to McClish and slid at once into the first deep sleep he had enjoyed in weeks.

But shortly after dawn, Fertig's aide Reyes shook him awake. There *was* a main body of Japanese, and they had discovered the bodies of their eight comrades. Once again the Headquarters of the United States Forces in the Philippines broke camp to move to a farther hill, with its commanding general squelching along behind the guides, chewing a breakfast of cold baked camotes as he walked in the rain.

2

MCCLISH WAS RIGHT. Fertig would have to move out of Misamis Occidental; out of the Zamboanga Peninsula altogether. Fighting on a peninsula, against an enemy who commands the air as well as the sea, is apt to be a fatal pastime. Fertig had already discovered this on Bataan. But where could he go?

McClish wanted him to come to Agusan province, explaining, if they were driven out, they could still retreat into the unexplored interior of Mindanao and, if need be, all the way to the east coast. The night before he left to return to his command in Agusan, McClish vehemently urged Fertig to leave with him, only to hear Fertig say in his distant, most pedantic way, "I shall take this matter under advisement."

Fertig saw no reason to tell McClish that, as much as he admired the handsome younger man's vigorous bravery, he had no confidence in McClish as a strategist; no confidence that McClish had real command over his own men, and every reason to believe that McClish did not understand Filipinos and had made a mess of his relationship with them. Moreover, much of the lower Agusan was a river plain, offering few advantages to guerrilla forces and every advantage to a mobile enemy. To Fertig's mind, the only reason McClish's force was still in existence was that they had not made themselves enough of a nuisance to encourage the Japanese to finish them off. Nor did the Agusan really offer room to retreat, for there would be no food in the savage interior of the island, and the east coast was still a confusion of bandit gangs who owed allegiance to no one.

To escape south to Pendatun in Cotabato was out of the question, not only because the Japanese attack had sealed off the root of the Zamboanga Peninsula but also because to go to Cotabato in defeat would be to fall into Pendatun's hands. Pendatun was ambitious; such a move would cost Fertig not only his face but perhaps his head.

To return to Baroy would certainly be suicidal, for Morgan was there, and his speeches left no doubt that he considered Fertig's death a foregone conclusion, if not his fondest wish.

Of all the possibilities, McClish's suggestion seemed best, but something stronger than logic kept Fertig where he was. It was curiosity. He felt he could not leave until he saw the end. He had labored for nine months to build an organization in Misamis Occidental, and he could not leave until he saw his theories disproved or vindicated. It was not until mid July that Fertig, ceaselessly moving his campsites, began to see a pattern emerge.

At the end of three weeks of attacks, the first, most important fact was that no guerrilla leader had been captured by the ubiquitous Japanese patrols. Smith, Parsons, Dyess, Mellnick, and McCoy had managed to find a way around the Japanese at Pagadian Bay and had successfully kept their rendezvous with the submarine. True, the *General Fertig* had been lost, together with whatever the submarine had brought. It was caught in a Japanese destroyer's searchlights as it reentered Pagadian Bay, but Fertig felt that the escape of the penetration party was worth infinitely more than the loss of his ragtag navy's flagship.

Next, messages began to move freely, if slowly, among the guerrilla areas. Putting the messages together in the light of his own experience at the schoolhouse, Fertig deduced that the Japanese force was far smaller than rumor had it. He had suspected this from the beginning, for it seemed to him that men throughout history had always overestimated the strength of an aggressor; as though the thought of doing evil was so fascinating that men would never imagine anyone attempting it unless certain of success. But, from all accounts, one cruiser, two destroyers, and fifteen aircraft had supported a landing of some 3,000 Japanese on the east coast of Fertig's province. Compared to the paper strength of Fertig's forces, this was little more than a corporal's guard—particularly after the Japanese moved inland beyond the range of their cruiser's guns and after their aircraft were withdrawn. One of their patrols stopped dead for two days although there was nothing in front of it—as aerial reconnaissance would have clearly shown. The Japanese apparently lacked liaison among ground, sea, and air forces. Nevertheless, the Japanese, with or without air cover or artillery, could assemble a single force at any one place that would be far stronger than anything Fertig could put in its way, and small or not, the Japanese attack had smashed Fertig's organization to bits.

In mid July, rather than fleeing from what was a militarily indefensible position, Fertig slogged through the wet hills, maintaining communication with his radio section by runner while he hunted for guerrilla units. He discovered that the hundreds of desertions had strengthened his command in the sense that those who fled were now ashamed to return, thus reducing the guerrilla forces to those who might actually fight.

Meanwhile, as the Japanese moved farther inland without resistance, they divided their massive formations into smaller units and divided the units into patrols and the patrols into searching parties, growing ever more careless in the absence of opposition until their very carelessness betrayed them. The sight of small numbers of Japanese reminded Fertig's guerrilleros of principles that Fertig had tried to teach them.

Slowly, in groups of two and three, guerrilleros coalesced into groups of five and ten, growing into larger units of twenty to thirty, and, by mid July, into companies of a hundred or more, who could not resist the temptation of ambushing isolated Japanese squads. Without central direction from Fertig, or anyone else, guerrilla organizations reformed and began to fall on Japanese throughout the province, harassing, ambushing, inflicting casualties.

Despite small daily losses and the fact that they had accomplished neither of their objectives—silencing Fertig's radio and capturing him—the Japanese began to withdraw troops from Misamis Occidental. Fertig wondered why. Perhaps the men were needed elsewhere; the Allied campaigns in New Guinea had begun. In any event, withdrawal was the Japanese plan, not Fertig's. He was grimly pleased to hear the Japanese announce for the second time that he had been driven into the hills to starve to death.

Day by day, the resistance increased, and, as it did, the Japanese—although reduced in total numbers—increased the size of such patrols as they did send out. Probing units were built to battalion strength but at the loss of all hope of speed and stealth. Unlike a squad or even a platoon, a battalion can scarcely be concealed, and it moves like an ox.

Slowly, as with the men of other provinces who had long known Japanese occupation, the people of Misamis Occidental came of age. They learned, not as a theory but as a matter of fact, that a Japanese battalion could move wherever it wished but that, once it had moved, the ground it left behind immediately became guerrilla country again. The pillow defense that Fertig envisioned began to appear. At the same time, Fertig's young radiomen were similarly maturing. At first, they had run from rumors, but now they fled more slowly, eventually growing bold enough to move only minutes ahead of the Japanese patrols, instead of days ahead. They became expert at tearing their equipment apart, loading the heavy diesel generator onto a carabao sled, and moving to a new location to reassemble the set and return to the air in a matter of hours. When their skill reached the point where they waited until the Japanese approached within rifleshot, Fertig's radiomen were able to maintain daily if erratic contact with the watcher stations, with commanders in other provinces, and with Australia.

Fertig regarded their performance with mixed feelings. He thanked God that the Japanese electronics industry was rudimentary. The Japanese obviously lacked dependable radio compass direction finders, which would have enabled them to pinpoint the guerrilla radio station, surround its area, and close in. But this good luck was purchased by the bad luck of constant movement, snatched meals, interrupted sleep, eroding fear, back-breaking labor, and the endless misery of living in a rain forest in clothes that never dried. A safer place must be found.

Some relief came by the end of the third week of July, when the Japanese tired of trying to patrol everywhere. As Fertig had predicted, they withdrew to establish garrisons in the seacoast towns. When this took place, Fertig's communications improved. The telephone and telegraph apparatus reappeared and began to bind the guerrilla together again. True, many civilians who had not been able to escape to the back country had been savagely treated, but those who had were safe. The Ozamis sisters were in the good hands of their dependents. The rumor of Jesus Montalvan's capture proved false. Not one of the government officials had been taken. The coastwatcher net was secure, although one of Fertig's American officers had shot himself—not because he was in danger of immediate capture but because he was unable to endure lonely monotony. Sam Wilson's fugitive mint was operating, money was circulating, and the government once more began to govern. It was able to govern simply because people accepted on faith the orders and judgments that came to them by word of mouth. Trade, too, was restored. It moved slowly, on the shoulders of cargadores who labored over the back trails, working their way around the enemy. Everywhere the Japanese were not, Fertig's organization began to breathe again.

It was clear, however, that food would be a problem. The Japanese held the seas, and fish were the Filipino's greatest source of meat. It was also plain that harvesting the coastal plain's rich corn and rice fields would henceforth mean a running battle with Japanese gleaners, sent forth from the towns. Yet, by the end of the month, Fertig's forces were in control of all the province save the garrisoned cities. In less than a month after complete disaster, the guerrilla was once more a going concern, leaner but more sinewy than before. The Japanese were now a known quantity; instead of being terrified by a new reality, the people of the province had learned to deal with it. Fertig wished that Parsons, Smith, Mellnick, and McCoy had waited to see his predictions come true.

On the night of July 20, Fertig was living neither well nor badly on a hillside in the rain, as safe as men reckoned safety in Mindanao at that time, ten kilometers from the sea and three kilometers from a Japanese force that was hunting him, when Hedges unexpectedly appeared with a guide.

"When the hell are you going to get out of here, Stupid?" Hedges greeted his commanding general. "Did you know there's a whole regiment of slopeheads just east of here?" Grumbling, Hedges came in out of the rain, banging the water from his ragged straw sombrero.

"I mean it, Wendell," he said. "You fool around here much longer, and you're going to get caught, sure as God."

"Did you come all the way over here from Lanao to tell me this?" Fertig demanded.

"You're goddamned right," Hedges said. "Did you expect me to broadcast it? I want you to come back with me. I have a banca waiting for us on the coast. You know as well as I do you haven't any room here, while I have all of Lanao behind me."

Hedges spoke with authority, for he had logged Lanao province before the war and knew the country intimately. Moreover, he felt certain that the Moros in the farther hills would protect the rear while he and Fertig lived on the beach. It seemed that Hedges had a taste for living on beaches, in the open air and sunlight, away from malarial jungles, and it did not bother him at all that the Japanese in Iligan shelled his headquarters every day. He said their marksmanship stank.

"What I'm looking for is a place about three miles back from the sea, about 200 feet up, with a view of all approaches," Fertig said.

Hedges swore he knew the very place; a cut-over hillside in an area protected by dependable Moros.

"There aren't any such animals," Fertig objected, remembering that these very Lanao Moros had deserted General Fort, stealing his food, guns, and ammunition—leaving him to surrender. General Fort had imagined himself the Moros' friend.

"I've never seen a Moro outfit that I'd trust out of sight," Fertig said.

"Hell, you don't have to trust them," Hedges explained. "Just kick 'em in the ass, and they'll love you. They'll call you their mother and their father. But give an inch, and they'll slip you six inches. They'll jump anyone if they think they have him buffaloed. But they're bluff. If anyone calls them, they back down. They'll stay honest as long as you let 'em know who's boss."

"I'm talking about Moro troops, not individual Moros," Fertig said.

Hedges shrugged.

"Give them the same leadership, the same guns, and they're as dependable as anybody," he said. "The Japs tried to land three launches at Kolambugan, and my boys shot the hell out of them. The Japs never got ashore."

Fertig barely heard him, for Fertig was busy with another thought that had nothing to do with the dependability of Moros in the presence of Japanese. The great advantage of moving to Hedges' area might not be so much access to Moro hills, nor that he would again have the acid optimism of a devoted friend to sustain him, but that Hedges' Moros might be absolutely dependable against Morgan.

"That son of a bitch Morgan," Hedges said. "He's been talking to his officers to find out where they stand. But some of them have been talking to me. Most of Morgan's crowd is just marking time. They're waiting to see what you're going to do, before they make a move one way or the other. Which reminds me. What *are* we going to do about that bastard?"

"Let him hang himself."

"How soon?"

"I don't know yet. We'll talk it over when we get to your place."

"Well, now, that's better," Hedges said, putting on his waterlogged straw hat. "Let's get going. You ready to leave?"

"It will take me a minute to pack," Fertig said drily. "We're taking the radio section with us."

PACKING TOOK MOST of the night. Fertig sent a runner to fetch the barrio teniente, who was told by Nick Capistrano to have eleven carabao sleds at the radio station before dawn. A runner was dispatched to the radio section to tell them of their imminent departure. Konko would be left behind with one sending set to maintain Headquarters traffic while the base section was moved. Orders were issued for the motor pool—now scattered and hidden—to follow how and when it could, a thing easier to order than to accomplish in view of the liquid mud of the roads and the fact that the route around the foot of Panguil Bay was in Japanese hands. Scouts were sent to make certain of the trails that led from the hills to the sea, and Fertig sat up until nearly dawn, reviewing his Filipino staff in their instructions. He told them he would direct them from Lanao, just as he had been directing the Lanao, Agusan, Surigao, Bukidnon, and Cotabato provincial guerrillas from Misamis Occidental. He told them it did not matter where his headquarters was located, nor would it matter if he were captured. They were now familiar with guerrilla tactics, and, as far as the day-to-day operations were concerned, they had only to follow these routines, tactics, and principles. If he, Fertig, should be captured, they would receive orders from Colonel Robert Bowler, who commanded a guerrilla in Bukidnon province. He said nothing of his ostensible chief of staff, Colonel Morgan. He told them he had confidence in them, that it was only because he had confidence in them that he was now able to move to Lanao.

The departure, however, was somewhat less brisk than Fertig's goodbyes. Three carabao sleds, not eleven, appeared at the radio section at 4 A.M. The promised cargadores who were to carry the headquarters baggage failed to materialize. Six hours passed before the necessary number of animal and human beasts of burden were found, assembled, and loaded. Fertig accepted it philosophically.

"Forget it, Charley," he told the fuming Hedges. "You know damned well they're setting a new record for speed in the Philippines."

"Honest to God, I don't know how you've stayed alive so far, Wendell."

"The Japs are slower," Fertig said.

This was by no means true, but Fertig sought to minimize the anxiety everyone felt. The young radiomen, Ball and Mitsos, were plainly worried, and Fertig regarded the unprecedented delay in moving camp as a bad omen. It was late afternoon before Fertig's little procession picked its cautious way along a route that led through brush, across bare hillsides, and into cornfields to the seacoast where Hedges had left his banca. The twenty heavily armed men that Hedges had brought with him marched ahead. When they reached the shore, they discovered the boat was gone.

"The banca?" a fisherman said, scratching his head. "Ah, yes, it has returned back. I think the patron had much fright, and, besides, the men were hungry. Too bad, but yes, the banca is gone. If you had only come last night, the banca would be here now."

"Then you will be The One," Fertig said. "We will go with you. You will take us in your banca, huh?"

"Yes, sair," the fisherman said. "But too bad, I have no boat. The Hapons . . ."

"Goddamn it, we can't stand here on the stupid beach all night," Hedges interrupted.

"Who has banca, huh?" he challenged the fisherman. "You take me to him, huh?"

But it was hours before another sailing vessel could be found, and it was well after dark before its owner could be located and then persuaded to drag it from its hiding place in a mangrove swamp. The fishermen had heard rumors of Japanese everywhere; Fertig's own party had been mistaken for Japanese as they approached the beach. When, at last, the banca, a deep-bodied, two-masted sailing vessel, was dragged forth and its masts stepped and manned by a makeshift crew, Fertig's cargadores were too exhausted to load the ship. Time hung still while the cargadores slept on the sand, while the soldiers and the American officers mounted a nervous guard on a silent, rain-swept beach. It was late night before Fertig and Hedges cleared the coast, creeping slowly under sail in a light, wet wind across the shallow end of Panguil Bay, retracing through bamboo fish traps the way that they had taken months ago to seize a province and start a war.

Vainly, Fertig pleaded with the patron to shape a bold, diagonal course for the Lanao coast, but the patron's fear of Japanese launches was so great that no threats or orders could move him. His one idea was to sail directly across the narrowest part of the bay, to get as far- as possible from Misamis Occidental in the least possible time, before turning north, hugging the far coast. He ran aground off Lala.

Everyone went over the side to lighten ship, standing in the warm, chest-deep water, shoving the heavy outrigger off the mud, while the patron jittered in an ecstasy of fear.

When the ship was again afloat, the patron still insisted on hugging the coast that led past Baroy. Not even Hedges could persuade him to stand well offshore, and, for reasons of face and politics, Fertig dared not explain why the east coast of the bay was as dangerous to him as the west coast was to the patron. But, when Baroy came hard aboard the starboard beam, everything was made clear.

Lights winked in the darkness, instantly followed by the whipcrack smack of bullets striking the hull, the duller sound of the rifles, and the hollow droning of bullets tumbling and keyholing through the night as they glanced up from the sea.

"Lower the goddamn sails!" Hedges bellowed.

Fertig, crouching behind the low gunwale, flashed the guerrilla identification signal with a pocket torch.

"Don't shoot!" Hedges shouted to his men. "Those are guerrilleros!"

The sails fell in a wet smother.

Fertig's signals drew another burst of fire.

He threw himself into the bilge of the banca as splinters flew around him.

"The son of a bitch was waiting for us," Fertig heard Hedges mutter.

Fertig knew very well who Hedges meant. Morgan must have heard the rumor of Fertig's projected move to Lanao almost as soon as Fertig had decided on it. Perhaps the delay in getting under way had not been accidental. In any event, the sound of Browning and Springfield rifles could never be mistaken for Japanese weapons. They were guerrilla weapons, and Morgan commanded them.

Hedges stood up to shout at the shore while Fertig again flashed the recognition signal. An automatic rifle blurted back at them. There were a few uncertain shots, then silence.

"Get the sails up," Fertig told the patron. "Take us ashore."

"The Hapons will kill us!" the patron shrieked.

"If they do not kill you, I will kill you," Fertig promised him. "You put up the sail, or I will kill you now."

"I told those bastards to stop shooting. If anybody fires one more round, I'll hang the whole goddamned bunch of them," Hedges said.

He stood in the bow, a rifle in his arms, as the banca slowly gathered way.

"By God, we'll finish this thing now," Hedges said.

They listened to the light slap of the bow as the banca ghosted in toward the dark mass of foliage that rose abruptly behind the beach.

3

"WHEN THE BANCA comes, we shot, but when it shows the signal, the men said, 'It is not the Hapons, it is not the Moros, it is guerrilleros!'

"I said maybe it was a trick, and we shoot again, but we heard Colonel Hedges shout, and we knew it was not so. Of course, after we heard the Colonel, we could not shoot again," the lieutenant explained.

Morgan nodded; his face seemed blotched and puffed. "Of course not," he said wearily. "It was a mistake. We had the wrong informations. What did *he* say?"

"The General said we were bad shots."

"What?"

"Yes, that is all. He said next time, we must shoot to kill. He said, 'We have no ammunitions to waste.' He said, 'If you do not know the boat, you need fire once, only.' Then he asked for you."

"He is coming here?"

"Sir, I think so."

Morgan rose.

"If he come here, you are to say I am making an inspection. You are to say, I shall return."

But, by the time Fertig and Hedges arrived in Baroy, the lieutenant had gone, too. He waited for Morgan to leave and then walked rapidly into the night in another direction. He had no wish to remain with Morgan, whom he understood very well, and certainly no wish to meet again with General Fertig, whom he could not understand at all. To be accused of bad marksmanship, instead of treason, was a sobering experience.

4

HEDGES' HEADQUARTERS PROVED to be the largest sawali[35] house in a pleasant little village of such houses that smelled of fish, dogs, and chickens. It was a village that slept principally under coconut trees but which sprawled slightly across a gray sand beach to dip its toes into the warm sea. The people were amphibious Moros. Those who lived beneath the trees kept chickens and worked inland farms; those whose houses stood on stilts in the tidal flats were fishermen and wove nets. It was a village where women wore multicolored scarves; embroidered, tight-fitting jackets sewn with seed pearls; and trousers so voluminous they seemed to be skirts. They dyed their lower lips carmine and reckoned their wealth in terms of polished brass trays and vases. Their dark, lean men dressed in malong, turban, or fez; carried krises in wooden scabbards at their waists; and walked with an air of truculence. The colors of the women's scarves and the men's malongs, moving across the bamboo houses and contrasting with the rich greens of the dense foliage that now grew thick about the village after the rains, were something that those of Fertig's young Americans who had not served in Moroland had never seen before. They stared at everything. They had never seen women more lovely nor men more virile.

FROM THE PORCH of Hedges' house, Fertig could see the moon glinting on the water, turning silver the sun-weathered grass roofs of the stilted houses. There was a fire on the beach and the sound of nose flutes, wooden xylophones, and three-stringed fiddles playing in quarter tones

---

35. sawali = split bamboo thatch

while a storyteller chanted a tale that had come from Araby 700 years before. In such a setting, it was difficult enough to believe in the war, much less in Morgan. The enchantment persisted the next morning, when the muezzin's call wakened Fertig and called the faithful to prayer.

But the enchantment ended abruptly when the first Japanese shell came trundling through the hot, still air.

There was that rumble that was not quite a rumble, that whistle that was not quite a whistle, the indefinable but unmistakable sound of an incoming shell, followed by the splitting of a huge tree cracking at the precise moment someone slammed a giant manhole cover down over a hollow pavement. Then they heard the distant sound of the cannon that had fired.

"See what I mean?" Hedges said cheerfully, looking at the drifting smoke. "Hit in the trees. The Japs can't shoot for shit."

But then a battering line of shellbursts marched toward Hedges' house, and, shouting at his houseboy to pack the gear and get out, Hedges ran toward the beach, ordering his men to the shore defenses in the event that this bombardment should prove the prelude to a seaborne assault that Hedges' spies in Iligan had long predicted.

Running through the house with his own gear in hand, Fertig saw the houseboy carefully place a five-pound can of Karo syrup inside Hedges' bedroll. Instead of evacuating the baggage he had packed, the houseboy simply put it on the porch and ran after Fertig to the relative safety of the beach.

"They're earlier than usual," Hedges grumbled. "They usually wait till after breakfast."

They watched the shells burst red and black among the gray and green of the coconuts. A house began to burn, and Hedges gazed at this with the happy absorption of a man enjoying a good fire, until he noticed the house was his own.

"Hey!" Hedges shouted, above the shriek of incoming shells. "Goddamn you, Paul, you don't have the brains God gave a gnat! When I tell you to take care of things, I don't mean to leave them all over hell!"

Fertig, who had been looking across the curve of the bay, fascinated to find himself so close that he could see the Japanese gun emplacements clearly without glasses, turned to watch Hedges' houseboy scurry through the barrage to retrieve Hedges' pack, carry it across the beach, and place it in a barroto drawn part-way out of water. Having done this, the houseboy squatted on the sand to watch his village burn. Shells were falling among the houses, and a fragment struck a bronze gong.

"Ring the bell and win a cigar," Hedges muttered happily, but Hedges' mood turned to fury as he caught sight of the barroto with his baggage, floating out to sea.

"Jesus H. Christ!" he roared. "Paul! You get that goddamned boat back! If you do not, you keep right on swimming, huh! You go to Iligan and give up to the Japs! Because, if you no come back with it, I shoot you myself!"

"Imagine!" Hedges said to Fertig. "Of all the people in the Islands, I have to pick the stupidest to be my house-boy!"

As in a crazy dream, Fertig saw a houseboy phlegmatically pull off his undershirt, swim out, rescue a drifting barroto,[36] tow it to shore, tie it to a coconut tree, and, having done this, squat again impassively on the sand, once more devoting his entire attention to the excitement of the exploding shells and burning houses. Paul watched without expression.

A line of shells marched down the beach itself, and even Paul threw himself flat. The concussion picked up the barroto, spilled its contents, and, when Hedges next looked up to survey the scene, he was furious to see his belongings scattered on the beach. Obediently, the houseboy collected them once more, and Hedges was mollified to find they were apparently unhurt.

The shelling ceased as abruptly as it had begun. No Japanese launches appeared. No one had been hurt, for all had run at the sound of the first shell. Nothing had been destroyed, other than one-third of the village. But grass and bamboo houses can be quickly built; Hedges' view was that this gave the people something to do. If the ground was strewn with fallen coconuts, this saved men the trouble of climbing the trees. Since these facts were clear to Hedges, he could not understand why Fertig seemed anxious for them to leave an area that Hedges regarded as both fascinating and salubrious.

"Relax, Wendell," he said. "It's the same here as it was in Misamis when they used to send that plane over every morning. No worse. Same thing exactly. They always shoot in . . . "

Hedges stopped, staring at his bedroll, which Paul the houseboy was carrying ahead of them toward the largest of the remaining houses of the village.

"The goddamn thing's wet!" Hedges cried. "Paul, unroll those blankets!"

Then it was discovered that concussion from the shells had opened the can of syrup.

Propelled by the most majestic volley of curses yet heard on Mindanao, the unfortunate houseboy fled. But he did not go far. He stopped

36. barroto = a hollowed-log canoe

at the nearest sizable anthill—an anthill of the variety on which enemies of the villagers had once been pegged—and Paul spread the blankets on it. He sat on his haunches while the cleaning process took place.

Fertig and Hedges could see him squatting there in the sun, waiting with that infinite emptiness of the Asiatic, which is so often mistaken for patience but which is actually a kind of suspension of thought in the face of unavoidable, unpleasant exigence. The houseboy was quite literally doing nothing at all, a feat few white men have been able to accomplish. It was simply the will of Allah that he should sit there until the ants had gleaned every atom of syrup from the blankets. The disappearance of the last ant would somehow re-engage the clutch of Paul's mind, and then the houseboy would be aware that one moment of his life had ended and another had begun. He would fold the clean, sun-hot blankets and return to his master, as Allah had ordained. Fertig stared at this Asiatic tableau while Hedges dwelt on the advantages of his seacoast headquarters with all the enthusiasm of the Miami Chamber of Commerce.

"It's a good deal," Hedges explained. "These people have been sea pirates for a thousand years. I have some Moro boat crews here that just love to tackle Jap launches. In any kind of breeze, their vintas can sail rings around a launch. They move across the sea like a bunch of goddamned lice.

"The boys tell me that, one of these days, the Japs are going to attack from the sea under cover of an honest-to-God barrage, and I'd like to see them try it. I'll put in a counterattack with my boats. We'll catch the slant-eyed bastards in a crossfire between our vintas and the boys in the foxholes on the beach, and I'll bet you anything you like that not one goddamn Jap gets ashore alive."

"Three fighter-bombers could clean you out in five minutes," Fertig said.

Hedges shrugged in his so-what way, as though to imply that, since nothing could be done about an air strike, there was no point in thinking about it. He preferred to dwell on the fact that life was pleasant on the beach; that there was plenty of coffee; plenty of pineapples, coconuts, chickens, betel nuts, bananas, and fish. If rice was growing scarce, there was yet enough, and it must be remembered that, in wartime, one cannot have everything. And most important to Hedges, he had not had a malarial attack since establishing residence at the seashore.

Fertig found the whole situation as preposterous as Hedges' self-assurance. He thought his friend a trifle mad, that Hedges had been living so long with Moros he had become almost a Moro himself. There was no doubt that Hedges was entirely at home in the midst of a nest of betel-chewing pirates who loathed Christians and had a reputation for casual violence. It was also easy to see that the people readily accepted the infidel Hedges and his second-in-command, a tough, blond, crew-cut young sailor named DeWitt Glover, a former shipmate of Chief Offret's. Glover had endeared himself to the population of one Moro village by challenging a datu to walk with him down the village street while Japanese aircraft machine-gunned it. The datu agreed, only to back down at the last moment, leaving Glover to parade alone, taunting the datu and derisive of the bullets striking around him. "That Glover has very short intestines," the datu said afterward, paying Glover the highest Moro compliment. "He is a very dangerous man, and I will not cross him."

Fertig's opinion was that the datu was only slightly less crazy than Hedges and Glover. But it was also his opinion that none but eccentrics could wage a guerrilla, for the conventional mind would never accept the odds against any guerrilla's success. Fertig felt that he himself was not precisely conventional, but there was a difference in his mind between practicality and foolishness. However pleasant the beach, it was plainly not practical.

He would move the radio section at once to the cut-over logging area in the hills that rose steeply behind the coast.

The order was given, and it was wholly in keeping with the general fantasy in which Fertig found himself that the order was not instantly obeyed. With the infinite adaptability of youth, Fertig's radiomen had acquired, literally overnight, an interest in remaining where they were. It had been aroused by the kindness of the population. It was not that the Moro girls were immodest; they were merely helpful. They sincerely believed that men sicken if they do not enjoy regular sexual intercourse, and it seemed that none of them wished the Americans to become ill.

Plenty of coconut tuba, plenty to eat, sea breezes, an atmosphere recalling the Arabian Nights, plus the attentions of golden-skinned Malay maidens, led Fertig's Americans to adopt Glover's and Hedges' nonchalant view that matinal bombardment was no more than a minor nuisance. To exchange paradise for a hill in a wet jungle seemed pointless. They protested the radio could as well be established on the beach. It was with considerable difficulty that Fertig persuaded them that, since they were soldiers and officers, theirs was not to question; theirs was just to move to a new location in the jungle. Eight days later, the thing was done, and Fertig returned to the routine insanity of his war. A message from Konko in Misamis Occidental indicated the Japanese were withdrawing from contact with guerrilla forces everywhere on Mindanao. The Japanese withdrawal was part of the insanity.

IT IS A TRAGIC, comic-opera war, Fertig told his diary, thinking of the ambush that had failed, of Hedges' ridiculous bravado in living in sight of Japanese artillery, of fifteenth-century Moro pirates, of blankets cleaned by ants and homemade shotguns and old schoolmates and bombastic speeches to half-crazy men all mixed together for reasons of pride on a volcanic island in the Sulu Sea. Yet it was more tragic than comic, for the events were serious enough. The Japanese menace might have subsided, but the menace remained, and the problem of Morgan remained. The Morgan problem could grow dangerously, for Fertig concluded that Morgan was not simply peculiar but insane. Morgan had become an insane murderer.

Very carefully, in order to lay a groundwork for a scheme already in his mind, Fertig wrote Morgan a letter, directing him to report to the new headquarters in Lanao if Morgan wished to continue as chief of staff to the United States Forces in the Philippines.

It seemed to Fertig wholly in keeping with the unreality of the time to be writing such a letter to such a man. If ever his grandchildren asked him what he had done in the war, Fertig thought, he would tell them, "I sat in a logging camp in a jungle and wrote letters to a half-breed village police chief who went off his trolley."

5

DATU BUSRAN KALAW, lord of the Maranao Moros of Lake Lanao, a swarthly, birdlike man with the small bones of the blueblood Moros, came into camp wearing the stars of a general and the manner of Machiavelli. He somewhat grandly disposed his bodyguard of dark-faced swordsmen in a semicircle behind him. Then, politely inclining his turbaned head in a bow that came perilously close to sarcasm, he protested that Fertig was his mother, his father, his sun and his moon, his greatest protector, the defender of the Islands . . .

"Cut the shit, Busran," Hedges advised him. "If you got anything to say, say it. If you haven't, take your gang and get out of here before I run your ass up the trail. This isn't one of your goddamned bitcheras."

The advice was wasted, for, like all Moro leaders, Busran regarded oratory as the very stuff of life. He favored Hedges with an evil smile and went on to complete the intricate fabric of his compliments to Fertig. With the air of a king, he presented Fertig with an ancient kris, inlaid with gold and silver.

Fertig accepted the kris without comment. He understood the gift to be Busran's opening gambit to the intricate Filipino game they learned from the Spanish: the game of regalo, in which each participant tries to give the other such a gift that his opponent will be under obligation to him. Wherefore, he took one of Sam Wilson's one-peso notes from his pocket, scribbled his signature on it, and handed it to the Moro princeling. Busran flushed, and wet his thin lips.

"The peso is nothing," Fertig said blandly. "I have given you my name, the most precious thing I have."

Busran stared and nearly burst into laughter. He appreciated a shrewd bargain that was a joke on himself. Truly, the infidel had returned a gift without price but which demanded that he accept it in the best of faith. It could not have been done better by a Moro. Visibly pleased, Busran got down to business. The business was a note addressed to the Datu Sangulia. He handed it to Fertig.

"I have sent my resignation as chief of staff today. Advise Major Busran. Morgan, General of the Fighting Guerrilla."

Busran brought out another paper. It was a proclamation, dated July Fourth, issued when Fertig had been hiding from Japanese patrols in Misamis Occidental. It stated that Morgan had assumed command of Mindanao and the Sulu Sea islands, replacing General Fertig, who had stepped down to become administrative officer of the 10th Military District. This was signed, "Morgan, Commanding Officer of the Guerrilla."

"For your information," Fertig said, handing the papers back to the Moro, "if Colonel Morgan resigns, he will have no place in the guerrilla. In any case, he is not the commanding general. You are not to take orders from him."

Fertig said the last sentence in a manner that implied there was no doubt in his mind that Busran would take orders from Fertig, although Fertig privately regarded his visitor with profound suspicion.

Busran's last military exploit, before setting up as a guerrillero, had been to rearm his followers with arms and ammunition stolen from General Fort. There was still a question as to Busran's essential loyalties. Moreover, Busran was by no means the only Moro guerrillero whose allegiance was questionable. Sangulia was another. Still another datu had enlisted one son in the Japanese forces and one son with the guerrilla, and quite candidly stated that, when he was sure how the war would end, he would recall the son on the losing side and join the probable victors himself. Hedges, whose devil-may-care intransigence had won him an Indian sign over the Lanao province Moros, had managed to gather most of them under one porous roof by playing off one datu's jealousy against another's, with the result they had all joined as equals into a confederacy called the Militia, which owed a verbal allegiance to Fertig's organization. Thus, Busran was a general to his own men but was a major in the Militia, which was a semi-autonomous ally of the United States Forces in the Philippines. Fertig guessed that Busran's allegiance would persist exactly as long as Busran thought it advantageous. The question at the moment was what Busran intended to do about Morgan's letter and proclamation.

"Colonel Morgan has invited us to meet with him in Kolambugan for a bitchera," Busran said speculatively.

"Colonel Morgan does not need to meet with others to learn what he should do," Fertig said evenly. "He has only to ask me, and I will tell him."

"He wishes to be The One, and he looks for help from the Moros," Busran said.

Fertig said nothing.

"But he will not have the help of the Moros," Busran said. "Not one will help him, for, when there was no need, Morgan killed many who were not bad friends with him. Then he took a Moro wife, thinking to make all well. But then he left her, and she has gone back to her father."

Fertig said nothing.

"I think," Busran continued, "that Sangulia and I should write to Colonel Morgan that we will be willing to take our soldiers anywhere in the Philippines if General Fertig orders us to do so."

He paused to allow Fertig to appreciate the subtlety of his suggestion. Fertig did. He appreciated every nuance of what was apparently an uncomplicated statement. First, Busran would be implying that the Moros would attack Morgan if Fertig told them to do so. At the same time, he would also be implying that the Moros would attend the conference or obey any other order that Morgan might issue if Morgan were acting in the capacity of chief of staff, relaying General Fertig's commands. Meanwhile, Busran would also be professing official ignorance of Morgan's overt acts of rebellion. Thus he would be offering Morgan the choice of saving face, or of losing it, by the manner in which Morgan would reply.

For his part, Fertig wondered what the price of Busran's allegiance would prove to be. He did not inquire but ended the conference without having told Busran what to do. He would judge Busran by his actions. The Moro was still in camp the following morning, when a courier arrived with a letter. Signed by General Morgan, Commanding Officer of the Guerrilla, it told Fertig to appear at a conference to be held in Kolambugan on August 10.

Fertig muttered to himself as he wrote out the answer. *Any conference I might care to hold with you will be held only at my order. Fertig.*

He had scarcely dismissed the courier before the contents of his note were known throughout the camp, and Busran returned—this time leading a delegation of local commanders, including the datus Sangulia and Umpa.

Speaking for the group, Busran asked whether Fertig would object if the Moro leaders attended Morgan's bitchera.

"Perhaps," Busran suggested, "we can point out to Colonel Morgan that he will be making a big mistake."

Fertig could not be sure that Busran's intended visit was for the purpose of pointing out errors. But he could hardly refuse Busran permission to go without losing face himself, for he would be implying that he did not trust the Moros.

"When you see Morgan," Fertig told them all, "you are to say there can be only one general. That General MacArthur has said I will be The One. If Morgan does not obey, he will be punished. If he resigns, I will appoint another chief of staff. Either way, he is finished. You are to say his only path is to report to me if he wishes to continue as chief of staff. As long as he obeys, I have a place for him, for he is a brave man."

The Moros seemed unimpressed. Fertig reached into his brief case for an old copy of *Life* magazine the first submarine had brought.

"Before you depart," he said artlessly, "you may wish to see this, for it will remind those who wear the white turban of what they saw in Mecca."

The magazine's cover showed King Ibn Saud of Saudi Arabia, brave in all his finery. Inside was a long article on the King, replete with pictures of his palaces and—holiest of holies—photographs of Mecca itself. Fertig called the Moros' attention to the photograph of the King, flanked by a *Life* photographer and an editor, and to King Ibn Saud's statement that Islam was the ally of America.

The effect on the Moros was startling. Forgetting all dignity, the datus talked excitedly among themselves, and their followers came pushing around to glimpse the sacred pictures. Fertig made a mental note to radio that day for Australia to send him every available copy of the May 31 issue of *Life* at the earliest possible moment. A hundred or more Mindanao Moros had made the pilgrimage; judging from the reaction of Busran's people, the *Life* article was potentially worth more among the Moro population than a million promises from MacArthur.

The Moros departed with the light of Allah in their eyes, but, while Fertig felt reasonably sure they were firmly on his side at the moment, there was no guarantee they would be on his side tomorrow. The Moros were really no one's friends, but opportunists. While the *Life* article might undercut Japanese propaganda among them, it had little to do with helping the Moros decide whether to support one of two quarreling Christians. They would go to Morgan's meeting to see how many guerrilla officers would take Fertig's part and how many would obey the orders Morgan was issuing from Baroy. But Fertig felt the Moros' weight would be decisive if they chose to put it in the scales.

Meanwhile, he could do nothing but wait, remembering the Chinese proverb that says he who strikes the first blow loses the quarrel. To follow

Hedges' suggestion of using force against Morgan would be to admit that his position was insecure. Moreover, he might well fail, but, even if he were successful, Fertig's position would never be the same thereafter. No one would ever forget that an American had attacked a Filipino patriot. On the other hand, no one would wish to remember a Filipino who attacked an American who was helping Filipinos.

The more he considered it, the more Fertig was convinced that the proper thing to do was to pose as the patient parent, silently waiting with a paddle for the erring child to come home and confess its disobedience. Better than Morgan, Fertig understood that political power is another phrase for public esteem, that, in East Asia, patience is always a virtue while action is often considered ridiculous.

Two days after the Moros left Headquarters, Fertig had his answer.

"I and my people are much disappointed in what transpired in our organization," Morgan wrote. "When I organized the forces in September, last year, I have only the welfare of the United States and the Philippines at heart. I did not have the least intention of making myself a big shot. Being part American and loyal to America, I did not like to put the Americans down. So against the protest of my fellow officers, I requested you, a U. S. Army officer, to head our organization and placed myself as your Chief of Staff. By this arrangement, I thought I could bring about the cooperation of the Americans and Filipinos in this fight against our common enemy.

"Everything went well at first. I went on my trip to organize and coordinate all guerrilla forces under our Headquarters. I even sent my instructions to Col. Hugh A. Straughn in Luzon, thus carrying your name in practically all parts of the Philippines. I even made plans to make you the major general of our guerrilla forces upon the request of the various guerrilla leaders and the people. I defended you against hoarse criticisms from people who do not like you. I explained to Major Meider (who is antagonistic to you) and to Major Villamor why you are heading our forces. But during my long absence you practiced nepotism and sectionalism openly. You and your fellow Americans have the best cars, best accommodations, best clothes, best shoes, and best positions. Some of your American officers behave arrogantly toward Filipino officers and men. Tires and other supplies were taken from my house to accommodate your American friends. When you received your appointment as District Commander for the Tenth Military District, you sidetracked me by appointing Lt. Col. Robert Bowler as your second in command. When some Tommy guns arrived from Australia, I was entirely neglected although an American civilian was given one. I realized that my position as Chief of Staff is treated with contempt. I made recommendation for commissions which in many cases were not approved, but recommendations made by your American friends are given more weight. You gave me a rotten car while American officers inferior in rank than I have nice and better cars. I did not have any share of clothings and shoes although American enlisted men have their shares. There is no honorable way out, but to resign as Chief of Staff. I blame not you but your advisers for most of these faults. Your Filipino advisers are injecting politics in the Army while your American advisers are utterly ignorant of local conditions and have done you more harm than good. I am expecting you here in Kolambugan for conference as per letter dated 4 August. Col. Luis Morgan, Chief of Staff."

Fertig read the letter twice and then read it sentence by sentence. Some of Morgan's statements were absolutely true. Some guerrilla leaders were opposed to Fertig's leadership. They would be opposed to anyone's leadership but their own. When things had been going badly, they had been glad to dump their problems into Fertig's lap. Now that things seemed better, they wished to take the credit for it, pointing out that the guerrilla was, after all, a Filipino movement in which the Americans were invited guests. Fertig decided this was a human reaction, rather than a narrowly Filipino one, and that his being an American merely gave their dissatisfaction with themselves a convenient focus. Other statements in Morgan's letter were partially true, and some were wholly false, but Fertig felt the most important fact about the letter was that it had been written at all.

"What do you think this means?" he asked, handing the letter to Sam Wilson.

Wilson said he thought it was a declaration of war.

"I think it means the Moros turned him down," Fertig said. "If the Moros had thrown their hand in with his, he wouldn't have needed to write any letters. When he signs this thing 'Chief of Staff,' he's asking for his job back. Hell, he doesn't expect me to go to any conference with him. He's asking me for a chance to talk things over."

"He sure has a peculiar way of putting it," Wilson said.

"That is his pride," Fertig said. "I'll tell him to come here tomorrow."

So confident was Fertig that Morgan would obey that he told his diary that night:

Received a letter from him setting forth his grievances, which are those of a spoiled child. He was not given the same treatment as others, etc. I took the letter as an invitation to conciliation, while Sam took it otherwise. Unless Morgan goes amok, we have him. He will come for conference tomorrow on my terms that he leave his bunch of cutthroats behind. No good can come of the conference for he is an egomaniac and a murderer. I go with open eyes and return, as the next entry will show. Ambition is the curse of Filipino officers.

6

MORGAN HAD TOO much white man in him to run amok and too much Malay in him to swallow his pride. The white man insisted there was still hope, if he would bide his time, and the Malay told him that he must go boldly into the greatest danger, if he was to have any face at all.

For Morgan had examined the alternatives, his thought paralleling Fertig's. Many officers and men sincerely believed that Morgan, rather than Fertig, should command the Mindanao guerrilla. If Fertig killed him, Fertig would lose face, and the movement would be damaged perhaps beyond repair. Therefore, Morgan had nothing to fear. On the other hand, he had everything to gain, for, after the conference in Kolambugan, where it was made clear to him that he could expect no help either from the Christian provincial government officials or from the Moros, it was apparent that his only hope was to come to some temporary arrangement with Fertig, perhaps an independent alliance. After this, he would see what might be done . . .

Dressed in an immaculate uniform, carrying himself with all of his old arrogance, Morgan set out for Fertig's headquarters accompanied by Tait, who had his own reasons for wishing to attend the meeting.

Guards saluted as they approached, but Gentry stopped them just inside the door of the newly built grass-and-bamboo headquarters building.

Former Army Medical Corps Sergeant Robert Gentry, now Lieutenant Gentry of the guerrilla, was a small, thin wisp of an American, with light-blue eyes and sparse white brows. He was quite young, and he wore the scraggly blond beard of the immature male. But nothing else was immature about Gentry. He had skipped away from the surrender and had joined Morgan in the early days, long before Fertig had. Gentry and

Morgan were well-acquainted with each other's deadly courage. They nodded. Morgan smiled. Gentry did not.

"Take your pistols off and leave them here," Gentry said bleakly, motioning toward a clerk's desk with the muzzle of a Thompson submachine gun. "Sidearms are not worn in the General's office."

Contemptuously, Morgan unbuckled his gun belt.

"So *you* have a Tommy gun," Morgan said slowly, smiling no longer. "I have asked for one, but I have never seen one. Let me see the Tommy gun."

Gentry removed the magazine, jacked the bullet out of the chamber, ostentatiously checked the piece to make sure it was unloaded, and handed it muzzle first to Morgan.

"So even you don't trust me," Morgan said in that same slow, dangerous tone.

"I sure as hell don't," Gentry said as flatly as a fact could be stated. "If I had my way and the Old Man told me to go ahead, I'd give you the full magazine right in the guts."

"Man, what's got into *you?*" Tait inquired.

"In my book, the Old Man's too easy on the pair of you," Gentry said, yanking the submachine gun out of Morgan's hands. "If I had my way, I'd shoot the both of you here and now."

"The General will see Colonel Morgan," a clerk interrupted, and Gentry, reloading his weapon, keeping his eyes on Tait, stood carefully aside to let Morgan pass.

"What have you to say for yourself?" Fertig demanded, not rising from his desk as the door closed.

Morgan glanced around the room, his eyes falling on Crisanto, who stood in one corner with an automatic rifle in his arms. Crisanto stared back at him, and Morgan knew that Sinang was right. Crisanto was most certainly with Fertig, and Morgan understood Crisanto even better than he understood Gentry. He looked around for a chair, but there was no chair. He flushed.

"Sir," he said, "I have always been loyal to you and never at any time have I been guilty of mutiny."

"Who said you had?" Fertig asked.

"I have supported you whenever anyone questioned your decisions."

"Well, Morgan, you certainly have shown your loyalty and support in same damned funny ways, especially during the attack on Misamis Occidental. I would not call that an expression of loyalty."

"Sir, the rumor said you had gone to Australia with Commander Parsons. That is why I returned back to Baroy."

"When I came to Baroy, I was greeted by an ambush on the beach. I would not call that an expression of loyalty."

"Sir, that was some dumb junior officer and his stupid soldiers. They did not know you were there."

"That does not support the story I received from my G-2 officers," Fertig said shortly. "Your men told them you said, 'If the Old Man tries to land here, we will show him who is boss.' Of course, I may be mistaken, but I have every reason to believe that is what you said."

Morgan flushed again. Remembering Gentry in the hall and conscious of Crisanto standing in the corner, he said nothing.

"All right, Morgan," Fertig said, "let's cut this short. I am willing to forget what may have been a temporary lapse on your part, because you have done a magnificent job. If you wish to continue with me, there is no reason why you cannot."

Fertig could practically see Morgan's mind working, and he felt he had made a mistake.

"I do not see why we cannot go together, since I am willing to serve under you," Morgan said.

Then, his light eyes narrowing, Morgan said, "However, I should have a battalion assigned to me as my personal bodyguard troops. Also, the area around Baroy should be considered my own place, since I owned it by driving out the Moros before you were invited to take command."

"Goddamn it," Fertig said, driving his fist down on the desk before him, "you might as well get one thing straight for once, Morgan.

"You will either follow orders as they are given to you, or you are no longer serving under my command. There will be no troops assigned as bodyguards for any particular officers. That merely establishes you in a position to foster serious mutiny against this organization.

"Further, as chief of staff, you are too important a man to want to dominate a small area such as Baroy. I can only conceive this request must have been suggested to you by . . ."

Fertig stopped short. It would be better to allow Morgan to wonder how much Fertig knew, rather than to tell him.

"My answer to you is *no*," Fertig said. "You are to serve as chief of staff of this headquarters, here, as long as you wish to do so and so long as you do so in a satisfactory manner. Whenever I feel that you are failing in this duty, I will relieve you.

"Aside from that," Fertig said, "I want to talk with you very seriously for a moment."

Fertig paused. He looked contemplatively at Morgan, seeing once again, as he always had, the man that Morgan could so easily become. He would never be free of Morgan's enchantment. Morgan was everything he admired in a man as well as everything he detested, and, if the good in Morgan was overcome by the bad, Fertig felt it would be his fault. Seeing Morgan standing before him, Fertig could not accept his own judgment that Morgan was an egomaniac and a murderer.

"In September 1942, we started with a very small organization," Fertig said softly. "In the past eleven months, we have grown to 8,000 men, and we have established control over a substantial part of Mindanao. You, as chief of staff, are in a position to reap great benefit, for, after the war, I shall return to the United States while you remain here. There is no reason why, if you conduct yourself properly, you should not become one of the great leaders of the Philippine Republic when it is established. You should not let anything interfere with your postwar career."

Morgan looked past the grim figure of Crisanto. Crisanto was his countryman; Crisanto was his future. Morgan looked past him through the open window, saw the sunlight on the roof of the forest that slanted down to the sea below the logging camp on the hill. In the silence, there was a dry scurry of lizards in the new thatch, and then the happy call of a child from the village below the camp.

"Sir," he said at last, "you insulted the Filipinos when you said, if you were killed, Colonel Bowler would take command. As chief of staff, I should be second in command. Besides, it is my movement."

"No insult was there," Fertig said. "Look at it sensibly. I do not say it is right or wrong, but this is the word: The United States Army is not going to give the same support to a Filipino police lieutenant as it is going to give a lieutenant colonel of the Army of the United States. You and I know each other, but the Army does not know either of us. The Army knows only that an American colonel is one of its own men and that a Filipino policeman is not. Suppose the Philippine Army was asked to choose between a Filipino colonel and an American policeman. Which man would the Philippine Army support? I do not say it is justice. I say it is the way."

Morgan was silent.

"You make mistakes, Luis," Fertig said. "You are wrong here, and you know it. Just as you were wrong when you authorized the burning of all houses which had been occupied by the Japanese. Of course, the houses were to be burned after the Japanese had departed, because you could hardly burn them while the Japanese held the village. You did not think that to establish a scorched-earth policy *after* the Japanese had left could only result in harming ourselves. That was not only stupid but tragic. You are a combat soldier, yes, but you have much to learn about command."

Fertig leaned back and waited. Seeing what Morgan was and what he could be, it seemed to Fertig that the Philippines waited with him.

"If I can't have my own battalion to support and protect me, I think it may be better for me to resign as chief of staff," Morgan said sullenly.

Fertig sighed.

"Very well, Morgan," he said. "That is your decision, and I will accept your resignation, although this is not normal procedure under normal conditions. However, since these times are certainly not normal, if you request to resign, I shall replace you at once. Thereafter, my decision will be made as to where you will fit into the organization if you wish to continue with us."

"Will Colonel Hedges be the chief of staff?"

"I never take action on a matter that has not yet come up," Fertig said. "I think you should go back to Baroy, there to think this thing seriously before you make any move."

"Then sir, con permiso, I will return back to Baroy."

"I shall expect your decision next week. Give much consideration before you act. Be sure you are sure! You will not again change your mind," Fertig said. "Now I shall publish throughout this command a statement of your actions and my reply to them and a résumé of our discussion today, so that no one will be in any doubt as to your status. You are not the commanding general of anything. I am the commanding general. You are still the chief of staff. You will decide. Is that clear?"

Morgan said it was.

"Captain Navarro has been sent to Baroy to relieve your friend Captain Ecarma as commanding officer of the troops there," Fertig said. "You will find Captain Navarro there when you arrive."

Fertig stood up. Morgan saluted and left. In the anteroom outside the office, Gentry indicated that Morgan and Tait could reclaim their gunbelts. Tait did not wish to see General Fertig. Gentry followed them to the door.

7

HOW MUCH IMPRESSION the interview had on Morgan was made clear the following morning, when Fertig received news that Morgan had not gone back to Baroy but had made a trip to visit Busran Kalaw in private, offering Busran position as chief of staff and the chance to be promoted to general officer if the Moro would acknowledge Morgan as commanding general of the guerrilla. Tait, however, had gone straight to Misamis Occidental to take part in the fighting against Japanese patrols. Tait was carefully absenting himself from both Morgan and Fertig until the issue was resolved.

One of those who helped resolve it was Datu Pino. For years, Pino had been a legend: a dark, wiry little Moro with acid-blackened teeth, hunted first by the United States Army, then by Philippine Scouts, then by constabulary. He had been hunted constantly, but he had never been captured, and he had managed to exist in the wild country west of Lake Lanao. He was a bandit lord of great cunning and cold-blooded savagery, and he came into Fertig's camp with a turbaned horde of adherents armed with knives, swords, Japanese and American rifles and bayonets, spears, and—of course—the inevitable krises in the horizontal scabbards.

"Great Sir," Pino told Fertig through interpreters, "it is my greatest desire to kill Morgan and all his men."

Incredibly enough, it turned out that Morgan had asked Pino to join him. But inasmuch as Morgan's men had killed members of Pino's family during the fighting between Christians and Moros in early 1942, such a thing was impossible for Pino to consider. He told Fertig he was wholeheartedly behind him in his struggle with Morgan. Perhaps he would also help against the Japanese, Pino said. But he would be happy to take his

men at once to Baroy, cut off Morgan's head, and bring it to Fertig in a
sack—if, in turn, Fertig would do something for him.

"And what is that?" Fertig asked, thinking that Pino might have in
mind asking for a pardon for his crimes.

"We will kill Morgan and all his men if my men and I can have all the
guns, ammunitions, moneys, womens, and foods in Morgan's camp."

"I am indeed grateful for your offer of help," Fertig told the bandit
chieftain. "But it is not my intention to destroy my command by civil war.
Therefore, I cannot allow you to loot what is still my own camp.

"But you are a brave and loyal man," Fertig continued. Datu Pino
gravely acknowledged that this was so. "Therefore, I give you permission
to keep all the Japanese weapons and ammunitions you capture in fair
combat," Fertig said. "You need not, like the others, turn them in to the
army for redistribution."

Datu Pino looked hurt. Fertig was giving him nothing, for the idea of
giving up anything that he had captured had never crossed Pino's mind.
Surely Fertig was a fool for thinking Pino so foolish.

"But, in addition," Fertig went on, "I will pay you for each Japanese
you kill. Twenty centavos in plata, and one bullet, for each dead Japanese."

Datu Pino brightened. His command had killed a Japanese officer of
ancient family, and the Japanese commander in Dansalan had got word to
him that the Japanese would pay the Moros for a return of their captain's
bones. Since then, Datu Pino's men had been earning a small but steady
income by selling the Japanese bits of carabao bones they represented to
be those of the unfortunate captain. Perhaps carabao bones could be sold
to Fertig as well.

"Twenty centavos in plata and one bullet, huh, for the ears of each
Japanese," Fertig said. "It must be the right ear, huh, and yes, the left ear,
also. Both ears, and then there will be pay."

Datu Pino felt nothing would be simpler to arrange, and the bitchera
closed on terms of mutual regard, with Pino swearing undying loyalty to
Fertig, eternal animosity toward Morgan, and the early delivery of many
matched pairs of ears.

My God, Fertig thought, staring after the departing bandit, what a
fool's paradise Morgan is living in! Here he was, completely surrounded
by hostile Moros and with his back to Panguil Bay, which could easily
be crossed by the Japanese on any morning of the week, and yet plot-
ting a palace revolution! Fertig had not been altogether idle since coming
to Lanao. Unknown even to Hedges, he had worked out a plan to trick
the Japanese in Misamis into attacking Morgan, while the Moros applied

pressure on Morgan from the interior. It was a plan so far advanced that it could be put into effect at any moment, but Fertig would use it only as a last, desperate resort.

Following Pino's visit, the events of the next few days moved rapidly. Gentry, who spoke the dialect and knew all of Morgan's officers, was sent to Baroy. He returned with news that, in event of a showdown, many of the Filipino officers there would support Morgan, that a somewhat smaller number would support Fertig, and that the rest would try to remain neutral until a decision was reached, whereupon they would enthusiastically join the winner.

Morgan next wrote to Fertig that he would withdraw his proclamation of July Fourth, in which he had made himself a general, accepting full responsibility for any actions taken by subordinates under those orders. But the following day, Morgan notified all his officers to follow his instructions until the trouble with Fertig was ended. Then, Morgan sent word to Fertig that he wished to be named second in command for one week— not chief of staff but second in command—whereupon he would resign to become chief of the Philippine Constabulary. Meanwhile, without waiting for Fertig's reply, Morgan wrote out an order stating that the infantry regiment in Lanao province was herewith detached from the guerrilla army and transferred to the constabulary under his command. Thereafter, Morgan exploded into a blizzard of correspondence, signing letters and orders as Station Commander of Constabulary (which was his actual, pre-war rank), as Chief of the Philippine Constabulary, as Chief of Staff, as Second in Command, and as Commanding General. Abandoning all interest in ordering actions against Japanese patrols and garrisons, Morgan furiously wrote letters, sought to exact oaths of allegiance from his officers, repaired more and more frequently during the day to the consolations of his harem, and increasingly drank himself into a stupor.

Whereupon, his support dwindled. Tait ostentatiously kept himself remote and immersed himself in fighting, but, one by one, Morgan's other officers found excuses to come to Fertig's headquarters. There, they swore their loyalty to Fertig, who accepted most of Morgan's officers at their face value, thanked them for their views, and sent them back to their posts. Others, however, he deprived of command and ordered home to wait the end of the war.

I continue to believe that the only thing to do is take no notice of him officially, Fertig told his diary, as he found increasing evidence that Morgan's position was evaporating. *The farther this affair progresses, the more I am convinced that Morgan is insane. In any case, my position strengthens day by day, so there is no point of making an outright break with him at this particular time. Actually, these constant maneuvers and trial balloons of Morgan's merely emphasize the fact that he has backed himself into an untenable position and is now trying every maneuver to escape. I intend to keep him in that unfortunate position, because the longer I keep him squirming, the less effective will be any action that he may take. Here is Morgan, who had hopes of becoming the greatest commander in Mindanao, sulking in his camp, waiting for me to recognize his activities. It must be devastating to an egocentric. Odd, isn't it, that ,during the one lull given us by the Japs, the Number Two of our organization is making the trouble. Without Morgan, our present situation would be almost pleasant.*

Queer, this war, Fertig continued. *I am sitting in my nipa shack on a Lanao hillside looking toward Mt. Malindang across the smooth blue bay. The second growth forest of dark green gives way to the verdant green of the coconut groves along the coast. The surf is hidden by the palms, but, across the narrow bay, the white lines breaking along the Misamis coast can be seen. The American radio program from Chungking with Dinah Shore singing "The One I Left Behind." Love and happiness seem far away in spite of the beautiful scenery and the quietness. So does war, with the pleasant air of the hillside. Perhaps I am more lonesome than I realize, and the constant friction of subordinates merely emphasizes the fact that, although I have many vociferous supporters, yet I never know just who will support me without reservation.*

The day after this diary entry, Fertig received tangible evidence of support from a powerful source. It came in the form of a radio message that said:

> 20 August 43
> To: Fertig From: MacArthur #112
>
> In recognition of your meritorious services as District Commander and extraordinary heroism in action during the period 8 May 42 to 6 August 43, I have awarded you the Distinguished Service Cross. Announcement of the award is published in GO 47 Hqs. USAFFE dtd 18 August. I congratulate you on the distinguished service to your country and to the Filipino people that has so well earned for you such recognition and hope that in it you will find inspiration for even greater future service. Quezon congratulates you on promotion.

The citation meant everything to Fertig. It meant that Chick Parsons and Charles Smith had returned safely to Australia and that their reports, together with those of Mellnick and McCoy, had been favorable, for the actions of unsuccessful commanders are seldom called meritorious and heroic True, Fertig had not been promoted to the rank he had assumed, but he had been promoted to a full colonelcy, and personal messages from both President Quezon and General MacArthur carried as much prestige among Filipinos as any possible promotion. Fertig lost no time publishing his citation, and the personal messages, throughout the guerrilla organization. Reading them, the guerrilleros—civilian and soldier—came to the same conclusions that Fertig had. Any aid sent by MacArthur would come through Fertig. Quezon had spoken. MacArthur had spoken. Fertig was The One; Morgan was nothing. Even Morgan understood.

HANDSOME AS EVER, beautifully uniformed, but no longer swaggering, Morgan reappeared at Fertig's headquarters. There was a sadness about him that shocked Fertig. It was a sadness that showed behind his eyes and around his mouth; the sadness of a man who no longer truly believed in himself.

"Sir," Morgan said, "I have always been loyal to you, and I will always continue to be loyal to you."

"It is good to hear you say that," Fertig said. "Do you wish to be reassigned in this command?"

"Reassigned, sir?"

"During your absence and since you did not inform me as to your decision, Colonel Hedges was appointed chief of staff. Therefore, your former position is now filled."

For a long moment Morgan studied the man he had raised to power. Then he asked for a general amnesty for himself and all who had taken his part in the prolonged, undeclared mutiny against Fertig's leadership. Further than this, it was difficult for Fertig to understand what else Morgan had in mind, except, perhaps, the hope that he would one day have an opportunity to slit Fertig's throat.

"Colonel," Fertig said, giving Morgan back his rank and his face, "I am glad you wish to remain in this organization. For you are the very man we need. No one knows the guerrilla better than you. You have traveled much and have seen with your own eyes the conditions throughout the Islands.

"General MacArthur has asked me to send an officer to Australia," Fertig said. "Someone who can help him plan The Aid; to say what the guerrilleros need; to arrange for medicines, radios, the new guns; to help evaluate information coming from the other islands."

"But my place is here," Morgan said.

"Your place is to help the Filipinos," Fertig corrected him. "In Australia, there are many Filipinos. Filipinos who have escaped, Filipinos who were born in Hawaii and in America. Even now, there is a Filipino division training in Australia. You would teach that division jungle warfare, and you will return to the Islands not as a constabulary officer, not as a guerrillero, but as a Philippine Army officer leading the liberation."

Fertig leaned back, somewhat amazed at his own eloquence. He had been thinking of this plan for so long that it seemed to him as if he *had* been ordered to send Morgan to Australia, as if everything he said were true.

"Sir, I will think about this," Morgan said.

"If you are loyal, as you say you are, you will not think about it," Fertig snapped. "If you are loyal, you will do what you are told."

He stopped, suddenly remembering that Morgan was merely temporizing to save what face he had left.

"Besides, Luis," Fertig said hastily, striving for a tone of locker-room camaraderie that never came easily to him, not even with friends, "there are no dalagas left in Mindanao that you have not had. Think, Valiente, of all the blond women in Australia! You know how it is with blonds: They all want the man with the dark hair, the brown skin, and the Spanish accent! Just as many of the senoritas desire blue-eyed, blond lovers."

Morgan permitted himself to smile. It was not a great success of a smile.

"You would be foolish not to go," Fertig went on. "I, too, would like to go where there is beer and where there is whisky and women. But of course, that would not be the reason for you to go. That would be the pleasure. The reason is that you have a job there for you to do. It would be a fine job for you. It would do much for you after the war. More important, it would do much good, here, now, on Mindanao. You are the one who began the guerrilla, and you are the one to tell General MacArthur what we need. To be on the staff of General MacArthur himself is more important than to be on the staff of General Fertig. It is a promotion. But you must decide now, before the submarine comes."

"When does the submarine come?"

"You know I cannot tell even you that," Fertig said. "I do not even tell Colonel Hedges. A secret is something only one man knows. When two men know it, it is no longer a secret; it is a broadcast. But I can say it is soon."

Morgan knew that Fertig spoke the truth, for, despite the fact that Fertig would not name the day, it was obvious that a rendezvous was near. Morgan could see clerks frantically working to prepare copies of all orders and records of guerrilla operations to date; drawing up duplicate troop rosters and finance statements, all of which would be sent to Australia in order that a complete record could be kept in a place safe from Japanese attack. After the war, if there was such a thing as after the war, the records would be used as the basis for determining claims for back pay and redemption by the United States Treasury of guerrilla currency.

Further, Morgan had seen men coming into camp with quantities of fresh limes, bananas, avocados, pineapples, and jungle fruits—the surest indication of a submarine's arrival, for these would be traded to submariners for cigarettes, razor blades, fresh bread, soap, and candy bars. Others had also correctly guessed the meaning of the first bunch of bananas that moved toward headquarters, for into camp came a swarm of provincial officials, finance officers, and curious visitors who hoped to be present and actually see the submarine arrive. Here, too, came American civilian families who had sought refuge in the hills, taking no part in the guerrilla. Surely they would not have left their hiding places had they not been told to report to Fertig's headquarters for repatriation.

Other signs were clear to Morgan, too. The steady dwindling of his support. Tait's desertion. The laughter of the Moros. Fertig's promotion and citation. The very busyness of Fertig's headquarters was a mockery to him. He had come to make a truce with Fertig, hoping to salvage something from the ruin. He had never imagined that the penalty of failure would be exile. He licked his lips and looked at Fertig, whose gray eyes were as empty as the sky.

Morgan knew he was trapped. Inwardly, he cursed this white man who, by doing apparently nothing, had maneuvered him into a corner and had then named the only possible escape. Morgan knew that exile was no promotion, knew that Fertig knew it was not, knew that Fertig knew they would both politely pretend that it was for they both knew very well that Mindanao was no longer large enough for both of them. Morgan could either kill himself, try to kill Fertig, or accept exile.

"Sir," Morgan said in a voice that was strange to him, "if I am to go to Australia, I must first go to Baroy to put my affairs in order."

"Then you accept duty in Australia?"

"Sir, since it is a promotion as you say, I cannot refuse." The two men regarded each other with somber understanding.

Fertig wanted to say he was sorry. Instead, he said, "Unfortunately, you cannot return back to Baroy. You know how it is. No one who enters the area before a submarine comes can leave until the submarine has gone. That is the only protection we have for the rendezvous, for the only secret is the exact time and date and place of arrival. But, if you will leave your personal instructions with Reyes, I promise you that I will see that they are carried out."

9

COLONEL COURTNEY WHITNEY was General MacArthur's aide and officer in charge of Philippine guerrilla affairs. It was his duty to arrive early at Headquarters to make sure that all information relating to the Philippines was placed on top of all other papers awaiting MacArthur's attention, for the General dreamed only of a triumphant return to the scene of his defeat. Reading the overnight messages, Colonel Whitney came to NR 309, From Fertig to MacArthur.

"Partial list of repatriates," the message said. "Lt. Col. Luis P. Morgan, with complete file of orders issued during his mutiny, talkative when drinking and un-American. 1st Lt. Sam Grashio, AC, 0-412503, veteran of 21st Pursuit Squadron of Bataan Field, escapee, malaria. CMM Elwood Offret, USN of PT Squadron Three. SM First Class Paul A. Owen, USN, of PT Squadron Three. Both ill with dysentery. Cook 2d Class Francis Napolillo, USN, of PT Squadron Three. Requires eyeglasses. CQM Dewitt Glover, USN, chronic malaria. Sergt. William Bonquist. Outright fabricator and menace to security. Sergt. Mathew Henry, AC, prisoner for malversion of funds, released on Jap invasion of May 1942, later arrested for attempted sabotage of organization. Cannot stop talking, syphilitic, and possible psychopathic case . . ."

Since it was one of Colonel Whitney's duties to evaluate guerrilla messages and recommend action on them, he typed, "G-2, 309 Fertig, in re Fertig evacuees:

"Fertig seems to have converted our provision for repatriation into a means for banishment from his area of recalcitrant and otherwise undesirable characters. He has better (extralegal) means of handling such men than we have here, even when trial would be impossible in the absence of evidence on which to proceed . . .

"Action recommended: Dispatch to Fertig of the following reply: 'Policy of repatriation recently arranged permits, subject to your selection and discretion, the evacuation of American servicemen who have escaped enemy imprisonment and whose services are not needed by you and/or Americans who having rendered faithful service under your command are unfit for further service due to wounds, injuries, or illness not the result of own misconduct. Disciplinary cases may best be handled by you in your area where pertinent evidence is available. Accordingly, the evacuation of Morgan, Bonquist, and Henry (your 309) at this time is disapproved. It is desired that any further selection for evacuation be within the aforestated policy.'"

Hours later, the message was on its way.

10

THE SUBMARINE WAS a beautiful, deadly sight, black and low in the water, silhouetted in the night against driving rain squalls that slithered down Mt. Malindang across the bay. When Fertig arrived at the beach, Hedges had already left with the launch *Rosa Linda,* and Fertig could see the boat nuzzling alongside the submarine and the small figures of men passing bulky packages down into it. Fertig set out in a second launch, deeply laden with more than a ton of fresh fruit. The white-faced sub-mariners, whose skin was such a startling contrast to that of the sun-bronzed American guerrilleros, cheered as the launch drew close. Fertig thought they were cheering for him until he made out the words.

"Holy Christ, lookit the goddamn pineapples! What are them round green things? Don't let Rogers see the bananas—he'll eat 'em all! Hey, you guys, go easy with that stuff—it ain't money!"

Navy Commander Wallingham met Fertig on the bridge and took him below into a strange new world of clean linen, drip coffee, sandwiches, ice cream, and cookies. He took him back into a world of clean machin-ery, relative comfort combined with lean fighting power and crisp com-mand. It was a world that called powerfully to Fertig to leave the muck of Mindanao and the green mold that grew on leather; to return to a world of order and the accents of his countrymen and quit the mess of Moro intrigues, Filipino squabblings, and insect-infested bamboo houses. He had only to say two words, and he would be magically translated from a dubious battle, waged with makeshift weapons, rickety trucks, and leaky launches, into an efficient command that had an inexhaustible arsenal and treasure behind it. But he could not say those words. Instead, he gave Commander Wallingham letters for Mary and for General Casey, his old commander who was MacArthur's engineer officer. The letters to Mary were letters to a dream; his letters to General Casey were private arguments to a friend at court.

The men who were to be repatriated climbed down into the submarine and filed past Fertig toward the crew's quarters, where they were to sleep on empty torpedo racks. Offret had trouble saying good-bye, for he was plainly torn between his delight on being returned to the Navy he loved and his feeling of loyalty to the men with whom he had shared so much. Fertig hated to see Offret go, for sick and worn as he was, the Chief had always done what he was asked and had endured everything without complaint. Hedges did what he could to make Offret's leave-taking happier.

"Why any man would want to join the chickenshit Navy when he can live like a goddamned prince beats the hell out of me," Hedges said. "But I guess if you're born stupid, there's nothing else you can do. Anyway, after all I taught you, they'll make you an admiral."

Offret, Glover, Napolillo, Owen, Grashio—Fertig was distressed to lose men who had become important in his command, who had helped to transform a band of armed farmers into soldiers. But, because he felt the same pull himself, Fertig knew how much a return to the regular service meant to them.

Fertig watched Bonquist and Henry file past. And then came Morgan, dull-eyed, his tan skin greenish in the dim yellow light of the submarine's entrails. Fertig said nothing to Morgan, and Morgan said nothing to him, but followed the others mechanically aft, to the empty torpedo racks.

On the way back to the beach, Fertig felt the qualms of a small boy who has stolen a day from school. Out there in the night, in that unseen thin steel shell moving blindly beneath the water, were his hopes, some friends, the only tangible evidence of the outside world, and Morgan. Morgan, his greatest failure.

Fertig wondered what Morgan would think when he found no job waiting for him in Australia. Probably, nothing. Morgan couldn't really have believed there would be one. More to the point, what would Headquarters say when Morgan appeared? Fertig pulled a crumpled piece of paper from his pocket and read again the message that a runner had brought him hours ago, when they all were on their way to meet the submarine.

"What's eating you?" he heard Hedges ask.

Fertig handed the message to Hedges.

EVACUATION OF MORGAN BONQUIST AND HENRY DISAPPROVED MACARTHUR

"When did you get this?" Hedges asked.

"After the submarine left, of course," Fertig said. "Unfortunately, it arrived too late."

Hedges grinned. "You don't think they're going to believe that," he said.

"Of course not," Fertig said. "But that's what they'll expect me to say. I'll tell them what happened and give them hell for not getting their messages here sooner."

Hedges laughed, but Fertig felt no joy in his shabby victory, if it was a victory. Perhaps Hedges had been right all along. Perhaps if he had been as ruthless as a Malay; perhaps if he had shot Morgan; perhaps then, after a certain unpleasantness, the Filipinos would have accepted the inevitable and would have given him credit for strength. Now that Morgan was gone, the whole wretched affair seemed in retrospect inconclusive, particularly because it had ended in deceit. Even so, it was the only alternative to execution.

By the time the launch reached the beach, however, Fertig had brushed his doubts out of his mind. The important thing was that Morgan was gone, and now he could devote his undivided attention to the guerrilla against the Japanese.

BOOK SIX

War

1

COLONEL COURTNEY WHITNEY read Fertig's message to MacArthur, which said:

"Part 2 of your 161, received the night of the 28th, decoded and forwarded to me by runner over trail, requiring five hours, arriving my headquarters at 1600 hours after I had already left for rendezvous, 12 kilometers from my Hqs. Message reached beach after launch left for vessel. More allowance should be made for loss of time in transmission of messages. Due to these circumstances, Morgan is en route."

It was all there: The delay in decoding *Part 2. Part 2* was specifically mentioned to add believable detail. The difficulties of the trail unspecified but left to the vivid imagination. The distances and times all carefully spelled out. Fertig must have worked with a clock in one hand and a map in the other. Then, the blame put on us. It's our fault for not sending the message sooner. Therefore, it's our fault that Morgan is arriving.

Colonel Courtney Whitney read on. Amazingly enough, Fertig was giving General MacArthur orders:

"Morgan is not to return here. I must either send him south or execute him to prevent Moro trouble (Charles M. Smith can get sworn statement if needed) as they intended to use his actions against me as excuse for rising against him and his men who in July and August 42 killed Moros promiscuously. This would have meant massacre of every Christian on north coast Lanao. I can possibly control Moros if they do not start killing but once started only Allah can stop them. . . . In future repatriations, will follow policy exactly."

Faced with a fait accompli, Colonel Whitney merely endorsed Fertig's message and wrote a suggestion for MacArthur's attention:

"Too bad our message disapproving evacuation of Morgan, Henry, and Bonquist arrived too late. Their arrival, particularly that of Morgan, will present a problem, but we will work out its solution in a manner that I trust will eliminate any burden on you. At least we will take a big load off of Fertig's shoulders by having brought these misfits out . . ."

He filed the papers and concentrated on the next problem: that posed by Captain James Lawrence Evans, MD, the difficult young officer in charge of supplies at the base hospital in Brisbane. Captain Evans' trouble was that he had too quick a mind. Ordered to turn over a quantity of cholera serum to an intelligence officer, Evans had refused, on grounds the man was asking for serum enough to inoculate more men than there were in the entire army. When the intelligence operative returned to Evans, armed this time with a handwritten order personally signed by General MacArthur, Evans had stuck to his guns. Worse, Evans' suspicions had been aroused by the fact that an intelligence operative carried such an order. Worse yet, Evans had correctly deduced that the serum was meant to inoculate a population, rather than an army, and had asked the intelligence officer whether this was not so. Worse still, Evans had told the officer that he was tired of being a pill dispenser, that he wished to fight a war, and insisted on being the medical officer assigned to accompany the serum to its mysterious destination.

Obviously, unless something was done quickly about Captain Evans, the cat would be out of the bag. There were plenty of things that could be done, but Colonel Whitney decided to put Evans into the bag with the cat. Indeed, Captain Evans' unique talents made such a course inevitable, for in addition to being a surgeon, desirous of adventure, Captain Evans held a ham radio license. Or so, at least, the Evans 201 file said. Clearly, a chat with the young man was in order.

During the conference that followed, Colonel Whitney sized up the slim doctor's athletic appearance and his quick and fearless replies.

"You understand that everything we have discussed in this room is secret and not to go out of the room? That you are not to discuss, suggest, or imply to anyone anything that you might have learned or guessed from anything I have said?" Colonel Whitney asked.

"Yes, sir," Evans said. "Then it's all set?"

"You will return to your duties," Colonel Whitney said.

Evans' face was stricken with disappointment.

"Is that all?" he asked.

"That is all," Colonel Whitney said.

CAPTAIN EVANS' LIFE resumed its normal, monotonous course among the medical inventories. Weeks passed. And then, one night, in the small hours before dawn, Evans was awakened in his tent by men with hooded lamps who gestured him to be silent. Evans sat up, groping for his clothes. They were gone. His shoes were gone. His uniforms, his footlocker. Gone. He was handed navy work clothing. As he dressed, his visitors silently dismantled his mosquito bar, folded his blankets, folded his cot. It was all done quickly, and Evans' tent mates were not awakened. Within five silent minutes, the personal corner of the tent that had been inhabited by the particular, unique human warmth the world knew as Evans was simply a blank space. Shivering with the morning chill and with apprehension, Evans wondered what his tent mates would think when they woke to find nothing at all in his corner.

His visitors led Evans through camp to a company street where an Army jeep and a Navy truck waited. Evans' effects were put into the jeep. He was loaded in the truck. All the rest of that day, Evans sweated with a Navy work gang, loading supplies into the largest submarine he had ever seen. When the loading was complete,and he was about to leave with the stevedores, someone touched his arm and drew him aside. Another man of Evans' build, in identical, soiled Navy work clothes, took Evans' place in the departing work party, so that, if anyone had been counting the number of stevedores who had gone aboard, he would have seen exactly that number return ashore.

Hours later, the USS *Narwhal,* the largest submarine in the world, was running submerged due north. In the officers' wardroom, Captain Evans was meeting her skipper, Captain Frank Latta, and a stocky, deeply tanned man who wore an air of sleepy charm and endlessly flipped and caught a Chinese silver dollar.

2

"DO YOU THINK they really mean ninety tons on one submarine?"
Hedges asked.

"We checked the message," Fertig said.

"And room for sixty passengers going south?"

"It must be a hell of a submarine."

"I still say we ought to bring it in here."

"Ninety tons of supplies is a lot of supplies," Fertig said. "Twenty
times more than we have had to handle at one time."

"My boys can handle it," Hedges said.

"Sure they can," Fertig said. "But not easily and not safely. It takes
time to get that much stuff out of the sub and into the boats, and out of
the boats and onto the beach. To clear it from the beach in one load, we'd
need 3,500 men to put it on their backs and carry it over the hills. But if
we bring the sub into the river mouth, we can load the stuff right onto
barges and move it up the river into the back country a hell of a lot faster,
farther, and with fewer men."

"Christ, *I* know that," Hedges said. "But I still say it would be safer to
bring it in here. You're going to have women and children going out on
that sub. What if the Japs hit us? McClish's outfit can't give you the protection my boys can."

"That's another reason for moving there," Fertig said. "It's time we
found out just what *is* wrong with that outfit." The two friends studied
the map of Mindanao, which Fertig had divided into six separate areas
that more or less conformed to the provincial boundaries. Each area was
garrisoned by a different guerrilla division, although the word *division* was
more of a military courtesy than a description. Lanao province, home

of Hedges' 108th Division, primarily consisted of wild mountains and a narrow seacoast embraced by headlands garrisoned by Japanese. When a submarine came in on the Lanao coast, it had a Japanese garrison fifteen miles away on one side of it and another Japanese force fifteen miles away on the other.

The Zamboanga Peninsula, including Misamis Occidental, the area of the 105th Division, was too easily divisible from the rest of the island to serve as a center for the distribution of supplies, even if the Japanese had not now been there in force, still hunting for Fertig's headquarters.

Cotabato was an immense province but hardly advantageous, for there were not only plenty of Japanese troops in residence but too many pro-Japanese Moros, and the position of Pendatun, commander of the 106th Division, was by no means clear. Rumor said that Pendatun was trying to sign a truce with the Japanese.

Davao, future home of 107th Division, was out of the question. The province was dominated by Davao City, which, even before the war, had been the largest Japanese city outside the home islands. In Davao before the war, Japanese children had gone to schools that flew the Rising Sun flag rather than the United States or Philippine Commonwealth flags. The people of Davao City were not merely pro-Japanese, they *were* Japanese. Davao province was the site of the Japanese sea and air staging bases for the campaigns of the South Pacific.

One of the troubles with Bukidnon province, home of the 109th Division, was that its seacoast, Macajalar Bay, was firmly Japanese. The Bukidnon seaport, Cagayan, was the second-ranking enemy base on Mindanao, and the Japanese Army Air Force occupied the airfields of Del Monte plantation on the plateau above the city. Moreover, the national road of Mindanao split through the Bukidnon, and this road was in Japanese hands.

This left Agusan province and the 110th Division of Ernest McClish. The area—and indeed the entire island—was dominated by the meandering Agusan River and its dendritic tributaries, a huge complex of waterways. Supplies could be brought up from the sea as far as barges could go, and then barrotos could take barge loads even farther upstream and up the tributaries. Back trails led everywhere from the interior to the barrios on the banks of this natural highway. Supplies could move upriver and then over back trails to the guerrilla commands. Much as Hedges hated the thought of Fertig's moving to Agusan, Hedges could see that the map left no choice. Simple geography made Agusan inevitably the site of a guerrilla headquarters.

"If it hadn't been for Morgan, I'd have gone there when the Japs ran me out of Misamis," Fertig said, looking at the map. "But, as long as we had to worry about him, I wanted to be close enough to handle him but with your outfit as bodyguard."

"What the hell," Hedges said. "I can see it. Particularly about those supplies. That was a hell of a thing, when we lost Knortz and all that ammunition."

"Ball's still broken up about it," Fertig said. "He thinks we're a pretty chickenshit outfit."

The two friends fell silent, remembering the handsome, golden-haired Knortz, who had been everyone's idea of a hero. Absolutely unafraid, glorying in hand-to-hand combat, Knortz had done a marvelous job in bringing rival guerrilla chieftains of Surigao province into line. He had gone among them in what became known as his pacification uniform, which included a Browning automatic rifle, bandoliers of ammunition, a bolo, and crossed gunbelts, stuffed with ammunition, that supported two Colt .45-caliber automatic pistols. Thus armed, and carrying a sheer load of metal that would have foundered a lesser man, Knortz presented a formidable appearance. But his bare hands were dangerous weapons. Persuading when he could and administering physical beatings when he could not, Knortz had singlehandedly cleaned out bandit gangs. He had led attacks on Japanese patrols, and McClish had made him a captain. But a few days ago, Knortz had drowned when a sudden storm at night swamped the overladen motor launch he had been trying to take across Gingoog Bay. In his youth and his pride, Knortz had died trying to swim in a storm while wearing his guns.

To Fertig, however, the point was not Ball's grief nor the poor judgment of Knortz nor even the loss of the supplies on the launch. It was simply that the Japanese, aroused by the arrival of the submarine that had taken Morgan out, had been patrolling the coast so diligently that Knortz had been forced to dare a storm at night. There was as yet no large Japanese installation on the Agusan coast. If unprecedented quantities of material were to arrive and if he was also to send safely out the American refugee families hiding in the back country, Fertig should establish himself on that relatively empty coast as soon as possible.

"I'm going to establish a secondary headquarters and radio station at Misamis," Fertig told Hedges. "I'm going to put Bowler in charge of it. He will take over if anything happens to me."

Then quickly, seeing the hurt in Hedges' face, Fertig said: "By all rights, you should be second in command. I've never met Bowler, and I know you. But, Charley, I need you here in Lanao. Somebody's got to be mother and father and God Almighty to 15,000 Moros, and you're the only one who can be that."

"You know it doesn't make a damn bit of difference to me, Wendell," Hedges said, although it did.

"Well, that's fine," Fertig said, although it wasn't. He was glad that he did not have to tell Hedges why he felt he could not name him as his successor.

The trouble was, Hedges was not called Colonel Goddamn for nothing. Too many Filipinos and Americans hated Charley's guts, complaining that Hedges not only drove men too hard but sometimes drove them with his fists. Hedges' temper might not only lead him into trouble, but Hedges might run the command into trouble by his habit of asking as much of his men as he asked of himself. Besides, although Fertig knew Bowler only by reputation, the reports of mutual friends, and by radio messages, everything he had heard of him was good. Moreover, Bowler was a trained Army officer, a lieutenant colonel, and Hedges was not.

"I'll meet Bowler on my way to Agusan," Fertig said. "I'll brief him on the deal, and send him here to spend some time with you on his way to Misamis."

Before Fertig could leave Lanao, however, there were a number of things that had to be done, apart from deciding upon a second in command. He found that the work went rapidly, now that Morgan's former followers were either resigned to his leadership or were actively supporting it. Indeed, Morgan had so occupied his thoughts for so long that Fertig found it a positive relief to be able to concentrate exclusively on minor matters that had been festering away without attention. One of them was the problem posed in Cotabato province by the Moro Sultan sa Ramain, head of the Alonto family. The Sultan was under the spell of his seventh, and youngest, wife, who was pro-Japanese. The Sultan protested that it was his wish to remain neutral but, to please his wife, he found it necessary at least to sell rice to the Japanese rather than to the guerrilla.

"You tell that old liar," Fertig instructed an agent, "that he can sell rice to the Hapons, providing he tells us when and where the rice is to be delivered, so that we can arrange the ambush."

"You tell the General," the Sultan told Fertig's agent, "that he is a man of much understanding. The Hapons will be happy, for I sell them rice and my people make no trouble. I am happy, for I am paid for my rice in advance, and therefore I am not concerned who eats the rice when I have my money. Also, I am glad that you will be happy to know that the Hapons will send trucks here for the rice early on Wednesday morning. It is a good thing to be able to please everyone."

The practical result of the arrangement was that the Sultan's men harvested the rice, the Japanese paid for it, and the guerrilleros ate it.

Another, more worrisome problem of Cotabato was the erratic leadership of Pendatun. Like Morgan, Pendatun was headstrong, brave, and glittering, overly preoccupied by the pleasures of women and too much bemused by the fascination of the powers of command. And like Morgan, Pendatun was given to stating more than he could accomplish, and, after he had allowed himself to be persuaded to put his force under Fertig's nominal control, his power slipped mysteriously away from him, even as Morgan's had. At about the time Fertig was arranging for his move to Agusan province, a delegation of prominent citizens of Cotabato called on Fertig, asking him to replace Salipada Pendatun as commander of the 106th Division.

"And who would you have?" Fertig asked.

"Colonel McGee," they said.

Nothing could have pleased Fertig more. He knew McGee by reputation. The Colonel had won the Distinguished Service Cross for bravery in the First World War and had lived in the Islands ever since, the master of a plantation. He had been retired for total disability due to wounds and carried a large silver plate in his skull. During peacetime, he had returned to Walter Reed Hospital every two years for an operation on this plate, to relieve the pressure on his brain. Now, unable to receive medical care and in constant and increasing pain, Colonel McGee was nonetheless willing to serve under Fertig and to take over Pendatun's division. For his part, Pendatun surprised Fertig by readily accepting the demotion. Wiser than Morgan, Pendatun saw that his main chance lay in cooperation with the Americans, rather than in opposition. He saved face by acknowledging that Colonel McGee had been "recalled to active duty" and that the rank of United States Regular Army colonel was higher than his own. In return for stepping aside, Pendatun was named McGee's second in command and was given one of the two regiments of the 106th Division.

With the sudden caving-in of Pendatun, Fertig could consider the fact that he now had an American officer commanding each of his six divisions. There was Hedges of the 108th, McClish of the 110th, Grinstead of the 109th, Childress of the 107th, McGee of the 106th, and Bowler to be sent to the 105th. Each of these officers had two or more regiments, usually commanded by Filipino officers. At this time, Fertig had not yet met Grinstead, McGee, or Bowler, and Childress was almost a stranger.

He knew that Clyde Childress was an Army officer who had started a guerrilla with McClish in the early days; that James Grinstead, like McGee, was
a former officer long ago turned planter; that Robert Bowler and Grinstead had taken charge of the resistance in Bukidnon. It was a political
weakness of his command that all the senior officers should be Americans; this was not always the case on other islands, where Filipino leaders
commanded the resistance and American officers served under them. But
on Mindanao, the Americans either had been asked to command, as in
Fertig's case and that of McGee, or had founded guerrillas of their own,
as in the case of Grinstead, Childress, and McClish. Not for the last time,
Fertig found himself wondering about Morgan, wondering where he had
failed, if, indeed, he had.

Before leaving for Agusan, Fertig issued instructions clearly defining the
organization and missions of the Tenth Military District The primary mission was to collect and transmit intelligence to MacArthur's headquarters.

The district's second mission, on which everything was based, was
to defeat the Japanese military forces on Mindanao by means of guerrilla
warfare. To attempt this was flat disobedience of orders from MacArthur,
but there was no doubt in Fertig's mind that, if the guerrillas did not
remain constantly on the offensive, the guerrilla would receive no public support, would quickly be destroyed, and there would shortly be no
more Tenth Military District to send information to anyone.

His immediate problems solved, his organization established, and its
path charted, Fertig was looking around for a means of disguising his
intention to move to Agusan when Hedges sent word that his men had
captured that rarest of all game, a Japanese Army intelligence officer.
Shortly thereafter, Hedges appeared, grinning and strutting, leading an
entourage that included a small, brown man in a gray uniform blotched
with rusty bloodstains. He moved as mechanically as a zombie, and his
black eyes were dead.

"What did you do to him? Can he still talk?" Fertig demanded.

"We never touched him," Hedges said. "We didn't have to. He's a goddamn songbird."

Fertig questioned the prisoner through a Chinese merchant who
spoke Japanese. Hedges was absolutely right: There was nothing the Japanese would not say.

The captured officer told Fertig everything he knew of Japanese troop
strength, locations, movements, and intentions. He explained the reason
the Japanese had failed to attack Misamis Occidental for so many months
was that Japanese intelligence believed Fertig's forces to number more

than 20,000 well-armed men. General Morimoto had gone to the attack fatalistically, expecting disaster. He said the Japanese still believed Fertig to be in Misamis, and their report of Fertig's death had been propaganda to mislead the Filipinos.

All the while he spoke, the Japanese officer's voice was low, steady, and without hope. If his eyes were mirrors of his soul, his soul was gone. For the first time, Fertig was meeting a man who had surrendered.

At that time in the war, it was difficult to capture a Japanese because the Japanese believed they were fighting for God. Japanese schoolchildren were taught that the Sun Goddess had ordered them to conquer the world for Her. They were taught, and believed, that God said She would glorify those who died in battle but that those who refused to obey Her would bring endless disgrace upon themselves, their ancestors, and on their relatives and children as well. Like most religions, Hers was a fine one, an all-or-nothing affair. The surprising thing was that so many Japanese were equal to it. Moreover, being a practical and efficient people in many ways, the Japanese methodically prepared for their fate by printing dollars for their troops to spend in California, pounds to be used in London, and rupees to be squandered in India.

When wounded, a divinely inspired Japanese might be captured, but this did not mean that he was defeated or that he would surrender. Wounded Japanese had to be approached with caution, for they commonly would secrete hand grenades in their clothing, in order to blow themselves and their captors to bits. But, in rare instances, Japanese would surrender. The idea was unthinkable, for there was no phrase for surrender in their language, but now and again one did. This was one of them.

The Japanese officer was beyond hope, having betrayed God. He could not return to Japan, which was the residence of God on earth. There would be no place for him on earth after the war, nor for his family, because Japan would conquer the world and it would all then belong to God and She would give his clan no corner of it. Nor was there any place for him in the afterworld. He had done something for which there was no name. He was worse than dead. It did not matter what questions he answered. Nothing mattered. Nothing at all.

"Ask him who will win the war," Fertig said, fascinated.

"Nippon," the Japanese said in a voice that came from some world beyond death.

"My God," Fertig said to Hedges after the Japanese was led away. "How can you reason with people like that? It's not only that we don't have the same words. When we do, they don't mean the same things."

"Who wants to reason with them?" Hedges said.

"Nobody," Fertig said, returning to the practical from the metaphysical. "But maybe we can get them to believe something."

Accordingly, Fertig ordered the guerrilla counterintelligence activity increased. Moro peddlers, carefully selected for their outstanding abilities as liars, were sent into Japanese garrisons to spread the word that Fertig had moved his headquarters. He was no longer in Misamis Occidental, the peddlers said, but in Bukidnon province. Each named a different town as Fertig's new residence, but their stories agreed that he had escaped from Misamis and was now in Bukidnon. By this means, Fertig hoped first to keep the Japanese attention away from Lanao, where he really was, and to conceal his intention to move to Agusan. Second, to reduce the pressure on Misamis, to make it simpler to insert Bowler there, to establish a subordinate headquarters.

Very sensibly, the Moros helped to establish their credibility among the Japanese by demanding gold for their information. Days later, the pressure eased on Misamis, and Japanese activity increased in the Bukidnon. As soon as this took place, Fertig slipped down his mountainside to the sea, filled with a curious elation. Despite all that had happened to him since the war began, he felt that nothing really had occurred, compared with what was about to begin. He also had the curious feeling that, while time had once been his enemy because there was too much of it, time was now his enemy because there was too little.

3

SUDDEN, DRIVING RAIN SQUALLS that roared down the forested mountainsides and hissed across the sea indicated the northeast monsoon would come early that year, and Fertig and his men were thoroughly wet by the time they reached the beach at Lianga. It was pitch-dark and raining hard, and they could not use lights to help them blunder along the wet sand in the rain because of the Japanese garrison at Iligan close by. The cargadores who carried the heavy radio equipment were exhausted, and Fertig wondered why it always rained during wars.

There were voices ahead. The blacker bulk in the blackness of the night was the *Athena*, a large, twin-masted sailing ship of a type common to the coast. She would have been altogether unremarkable except that, by local standards, she was clean, and for the further fact that she mounted a muzzle-loader, fashioned from a length of four-inch pipe, reinforced by iron bands. It fired more-or-less-round lead balls cast from melted fishing weights. Their trajectories would be interesting, Fertig thought. It seemed to him the gun crew would be in more danger from their weapon than their targets. But no such doubts disturbed the Filipino who positively danced with excitement by Fertig's side.

"Sir, that is the bow-chaser," the Filipino exulted. "For the broadside, I have twenty soldiers with automatic rifles."

Fertig found himself meeting the legendary Zapanta; formerly the bus driver Zapanta; then Zapanta the owner of the small bus line and of the small fleet of Agusan River launches; now Zapanta of The River or, more properly, Major Zapanta, admiral of the Suicide Navy of Mindanao and commander of its flagship *Athena*.

"Sir, I name her after the goddess of war," Zapanta proudly explained, leading Fertig across the *Athena's* rain-wet decks. "We carry 150, all of them unmarried, sir. They are the Special Marines of the Suicide Navy. And that is the goat pen, for the fresh milk and the living emergency rations."

Another enclosure, labeled "Prison," was built of bamboo on the decks amidships, and Zapanta explained that, when one carried young unmarried Special Marines, there were sometimes troubles resulting from those who came aboard from the shore where they had drunk too much tuba. Too bad, but, yes, on these regrettable occasions, he, the major and the admiral of this craft, would of necessity grasp by their necks the drunken marines and throw them into the prison. Sometimes, Zapanta said, when the number of drunks was too many for the prison, the overflow must be confined in the deck-house, aft.

Fertig studied the volatile Filipino with amused respect. He remembered the story of how Zapanta had become a guerrillero. Zapanta's formidable wife had come home one evening to find her husband sitting in their living room drinking tuba.

"The Japanese are landing, and what do you intend to do?" she asked.

"It is my intention to remain here like a sensible man and drink tuba," Zapanta had said.

"Never will I permit such a disgrace," Mrs. Zapanta said. "I would see you dead before you commit such a disgrace."

Zapanta drained his glass of tuba and sighed.

"Very well, my love," he said, "let us get our guns and kill Japanese."

They had gone out into the night together, and Fertig understood that it was Mrs. Zapanta who had encouraged her husband to devise his famous cannons. One had blown apart at the assault on a schoolhouse at Butu'un, but this had not shaken Zapanta's belief in heavy weapons.

For his part, Zapanta seemed clearly delighted to be carrying the Commanding General and his staff; he was impressed by the radio equipment that Fertig was bringing with him, but he was ecstatic when he saw Fertig's men carry aboard a .50-caliber machine gun.

"Sir, with my cannon and with this gun, and with my men who are trained as boarders, we can capture any launch of the Japanese we will meet on the way!" he said.

"Indeed, we are a battleship," Fertig said. "We are very terrible. But with the help of God and your skillful navigation, we will meet no Japanese."

Zapanta shrugged indifferently and stepped aside as Sam Wilson and Hedges came to say goodbye to Fertig. Fertig gave Wilson a series of last-minute instructions, which he was sure Sam would not remember, and he told Hedges to cheer up, which Hedges refused to do. Hedges shook his head at the idea of Fertig being safe without Hedges' army to protect him, and he regarded the idea of going to Agusan by sea as unnecessarily dangerous. For that matter, Fertig felt a tension he had not known since the night he had flown down through the archipelago from Corregidor, sitting in the gunblister and looking everywhere into the night sky for Japanese aircraft, wondering when and where the virtually indefensible and lumbering flying boat would be intercepted. He was aware that everyone felt this tension, even Zapanta. Everyone seemed to need a good omen, and one came. The rain squall fled hissing across the night; the moon, nearly full, emerged from behind a ragged skirt of clouds. The wind fell abruptly, and the sea calmed.

Later, as the *Athena* inched across the calm to the *plump plump plump* of her rickety one-cylinder diesel auxiliary, belching black coconut smoke across the face of the moon, Fertig began to wonder just how good an omen the clearing weather was.

The distance from Lianga to the mouth of the Agusan River was more than 200 sea miles, which, unless the wind came again, would mean four days on the water at the one-cylinder diesel's top speed. By road, the distance was only 100 statute miles, but the road was Japanese between Iligan and Bugo. To take the long route inland behind the road, over the mountains, would be a matter of weeks, and weeks did not remain before the arrival of the submarine *Narwhal.* There was nothing to do but go by sea, sailing principally at night. And the route lay directly across Macajalar Bay, which was a busy Japanese harbor. Worse, the already active Japanese sea patrols could be expected to be even more active now that the moon was filling. For a filling moon seemed to send the Japanese into a frenzy for reasons that had nothing to do with increased visibility. There was something deeper, more mysterious. Escaped prisoners reported that they had lived in fear of full-moon nights, for then the Japanese would come yelling into the compound to seize prisoners to torture.

Fertig felt particularly helpless, sitting on a sailboat that was moving so slowly it seemed to be drifting. The *Athena* moved to sea to give Iligan plenty of room, but the diesel choked, and died. The *Athena* drifted back toward shore while the Filipino engineer, working by the light of a flickering kinkie, tore the engine apart, cleaned it, fiddled with it, and coaxed it back to reluctant life.

Under way once more, Fertig tried to concentrate upon enjoying the sea-smell and the glitter of the moon path and the freshness of the tropical night after rain. He was succeeding fairly well until the lookout cried, "There-oh! What is?"

That was some hell of a lookout, Fertig cursed. Maybe this was the way lookouts hailed the bridge in the Suicide Navy of Major Zapanta. There was a rush of bare feet pounding decks, and the *Athena* nearly lay on her beam as everyone crowded to port to stare in the direction the lookout was pointing.

A dark object on the horizon was clearly not a sailboat. If it was a launch, she was lying to with her motors off.

Major Zapanta climbed the deckhouse roof for a better view, yelling to the engineer to kill the engine. Fertig climbed after him and stood beside Zapanta while the Filipino stared through a pair of antique binoculars.

"What is it?" Fertig asked.

Zapanta looked at him curiously. Then, to the crew, Zapanta bellowed, "It is nothing. A coconut tree only. Start the engine!"

"Give me the glasses," Fertig said.

He could see nothing through them, not even the moon. Thick fungus had completely ruined the prisms inside the lenses. Looking around to make sure they were alone, Fertig said angrily, "Why do you carry these things?"

"To make brave the crew," Zapanta whispered. "The men do not know I cannot see through them, sir. But since I always pretend to see good things, they are content and do not question."

"Hombre," Fertig said, "from the next submarine that comes, I will get you a pair of Navy watch glasses, so that you can at least see danger should it approach."

"Yes, sir," Zapanta said. "That would be very fine, but it would be not good. For if I could see the danger, I would be coward and run away."

The darkness on the horizon made no move; perhaps, as Zapanta said, it was a tree. The *Athena* thumped on through the moonlight, edging toward shore once Iligan was astern, skirting the reefs when she could not run inside them to hug the land shadows, then inside the reefs and into the shadows smelling of dead fish, mud, and rotting leaves, leaving the glittering moon path and the sea-smell; into the shadows and softly aground in an inlet near Alubijid, to be quickly covered with new-cut fronds.

Bowler was anxiously waiting at Alubijid: a calm, somewhat grave officer whose troops were deployed east of Iligan and west of Cagayan, to cut off from the rest of the coast Japanese in those towns. Bowler had mountains at his back, and the trails over them constituted his link to Fertig's guerrilla. His army was in good spirits, but civil government was nonexistent. Bowler and his men were the government. As Bowler talked, confident and tolerant, Fertig felt he had been right in naming this man his successor. To Fertig's mind, the most impressive thing about Bowler was that he was not boastful—a refreshing change from other guerrilla commanders. Bowler's men had destroyed the Cagayan waterworks and the bridge over the Cagayan River. These actions called for considerable skill and daring, yet Bowler had neglected to mention them until Fertig suggested them—only to find that they had already been carried out. Bowler gave every promise of being the kind of man who would never let Hedges' temper annoy him, which made him an unusual man indeed. Yet Fertig was plagued by an indefinable feeling that something about Bowler did not quite add up, and, while he gave Bowler a letter of authority, naming him second in command, the letter limited Bowler's combat control to the eastern half of Mindanao. Hedges, while subordinate to Bowler, was assigned combat control of the western half, for Fertig doubted that Bowler, or any one other than Hedges, could control the semi-independent Moros of the vital province of Lanao.

Fertig's party slept through the day and sailed that night, with Zapanta inching back along the coast, working the unpainted *Athena* under bare poles close by mangrove swamps in the shadows of the steep-to mountains when Japanese patrol launches chugged past, then running well out to sea and under the horizon before daring to make sail—for the loom of the *Athena*'s sails in the moonlight would have quickly exposed her—to cross Macajalar Bay, putting in for provisions late the next afternoon on the far side of the bay in the beautiful, landlocked tiny anchorage at Salay.

The commissary department of the United States Forces in the Philippines was waiting at Salay. Bowler had arranged for it to be there. The commissary department consisted of an old man, a young boy, and a cow. The boy drove the cow to the edge of the sea cliff overlooking the anchorage. The man slashed the cow's throat with a bolo. Together, he and the boy rolled the carcass over the cliff. The cow was floated out to the *Athena,* wallowing awash, staining a brown path across the air-clear water, the hoofs washed clean and turning wetly polished up into the sun as the carcass rolled, and the sharks came steering in, driving fast and accurately, rising and falling across the sea with first the dorsal fins showing, then the scimitar-shaped tails. Hurriedly, Zapanta's men passed a line around the cow and hoisted it over the side with a boom, and everyone watched the sharks speeding around and beneath the anchored ship while the cooks butchered the cow.

4

"**SAIR, BEFORE THE WAR,** we could fat the hog today, so we could die it tomorrow," the teniente told Fertig. "But now we cannot fat the hog, for there is no hog. If there is vianda, the Hapons come and take it. And so the farmer say, 'Why do I plant for the Hapons? If I do not plant, perhaps he will grow hungry and go away.'

"So," the teniente explained, "the farmer goes up the river to become the kainginero, planting for himself and his family only. And here, the fields are empty, and too bad, but yes, many eat the seed corn, for there is no corn. If there is no corn, the people say, 'We must eat the seed corn or starve. When that is gone, it will be up to God.'"

"Then what have you for vianda?" Fertig asked, looking around and past the teniente at the riverside barrio that stood at the edge of fields where no rice grew.

"Sair, for vianda, there are doves; not plenty, but very few only. There are shrimp. Sometimes, a crocodile. There are mud fish. Sair, you have eaten mud fish?"

Fertig had not. Nor did he know of anyone who had, although he had been told these front-legged, scaleless lungfish—survivors from the archaeological past—were muddy-tasting and full of cartilage. The shrimp, he knew, were crawfish.

"As you see," the teniente said, gesturing with his chin to include the world around him, "there are papayas, coconuts, bananas. Also camotes, not plenty, but many. Also," he said with a wry smile, "plenty tuba."

"And palay," Fertig said.

"And palay," the teniente said. "But, yes, there is not much. It is what the people could save from the Hapons. Not much."

"Then you do not starve, but you do not grow fat," Fertig concluded.

"Yes, sair, we do not starve yet," the teniente said. "But, oh, sair, we are spitting blood, for our work is so many and our chow is so few."

And the teniente would be starving as well as spitting blood if the rainy season proves long this year, Fertig thought. For then the crops would not go in the ground early enough to be harvested before the monsoon would return to rot them.

He felt confounded by the unparalleled advantages and disadvantages of the Agusan river country he was now seeing. Nowhere did there seem to be a happy medium. The river was free of Japanese but only because there was nothing to eat.

Leaving the teniente and the people of the barrio—the teniente and the people all happy to see Fertig and his party depart (for, if they had stayed, courtesy would have demanded feeding them)—Fertig continued upriver in his launch. Fertig was searching for the site of a future headquarters, although he told this to no one. Also, he wanted to familiarize himself with the river country, because he could learn it no other way. Even the riverside Filipinos were no great travelers and lived their entire lives within five kilometers of the barrios of their birth. The world that lay beyond was as unknown to them as Mars.

By the time Fertig returned downstream to McClish's headquarters at Buenavista, a pretty little town on the river plain four miles inland, Fertig had the Agusan and its problems well fixed in his head. The river rose in the mountains east of Davao City and flowed almost due north through the broadest part of Mindanao. For more than fifty miles, the Agusan twisted thick and fast through mountains in a bed that was white-water rapids during the dry season. It swung in a great bend of limestone cliffs near the Agusan-Davao provincial frontier, and a road led from this bend sixteen miles to the Pacific Ocean.

Below the sitio of Waloe, in a country populated by Magahat spearmen, the river flooded a vast basin that, above the barrio of Talacogon, was several miles across. The basin was swamp, hummock, and marsh, and, except for the lack of flocks of birds, resembled the Florida Everglades. It was completely inundated during the five months of the rainy season, and here the inhabitants built their houses on rafts. When high water came, raft, house and all simply floated until the runoff subsided and land reappeared. Wherever the house settled was the family's farming area for the ensuing dry season. This was a matter of local law, and everyone abided by the river's decision. It was not a productive swamp, at any rate, and the people seemed to live on a fermented brew made from palms, and from corn that they dried, cracked, and stewed. When there was too much rain, there was too little corn.

Rocky narrows below Talacogon impounded the runoff from the great basin, resulting in the river's being at high stage for five months and at extreme low water for three and a half. Thus, for most of the year, there was either too much water or too little, with each condition creating a different problem in navigation and transportation; but Fertig knew these problems were minor, compared with that of packing hundreds of tons of supplies in backbreaking loads on the shoulders of cargadores.

Past the narrows, the river meandered across a heavily forested plain leading to the sea. Here, the river was a swift, dark green, with orchid-smelling jungle growing flush to the banks. It was a liana-hung forest of giant hardwoods; of apitong, luan, narra, dao, and toog that towered over thick brush at the water's edge. Occasional graceful banaba trees, hung with lilac-like clusters of purple flowers, leaned over the emerald water. Behind sandbars where crocodiles lay as if in open-mouthed death, Fertig could see palms growing; first the thick nipa, then the taller sago, and then the traveler's palm, the betel, and the double-curved coconut. Sometimes villages stood behind the sandbars under the palms, and here were scarlet flame trees in the clearings and bright bursts of bougainvillea climbing the sides of houses half hidden in the light that fell through tattered palm and banana leaves.

Closer to the sea the forest gave way to cleared lands, dominated by the heavily damaged city of Butu'un, once the trading center of the province and home port of the river launches and barges that had brought goods up from the deep-water port of Nasipit at the river's mouth. Some of the barges were of three hundred tons burden. A road connected Butu'un to Nasipit as well, and the road, the plain, the city, and the river had all been fought for by McClish. Everyone counted it a victory that the Japanese had been driven out, but Fertig thought the barrio teniente had the truth of it: After eating all they could find, the Japanese had left. To grow another crop would invite the Japanese to return.

Returning from his inspection trip, Fertig found a backlog of messages. New fighting had broken out in Misamis Occidental, where Japanese reinforcements had inexplicably landed. Colonel Kangleon, leader of the Leyte Island guerrilla, and Major Inginiero of the Bohol Island guerrilla had arrived in Lanao to receive their shares of the *Narwhal*'s supplies. American civilian refugee families had begun to arrive at McClish's headquarters, waiting to be sent out on the expected submarine.

Fertig directed Kangleon and Inginiero to come to Agusan; ordered

Bowler to stay with Hedges in Lanao, rather than try to go to Misamis at this time. The refugees were a problem. News of an unusual concentration of American civilians in one place could not fail to find its way to the Japanese. Moreover, the Americans were seriously taxing the headquarters food supply. Fertig sent them upriver, where a small barrio was converted into an isolation camp. He wondered why McClish had not already done this.

McClish's command had the quality of unfinished business about it. There was the matter of the trucks. As in all other provinces of Mindanao, Filipinos had hidden a few trucks and automobiles from the invading Japanese. Months ago, Fertig had told McClish to distill alcohol from tuba to use as fuel in automobile engines. But little or no tuba alcohol had been produced, and McClish's vehicles were chiefly idle. Angrily, Fertig ordered distillation to begin at once.

Nor had anyone thought to inspect the bunkers of the interisland steamer *Mayon*, now a rusting, bomb-torn hulk in Nasipit harbor. Yet the *Mayon*'s bunkers proved to be filled with 160 tons of fuel oil—more oil than Fertig had known to exist on the island. It could be used in the motors of diesel trucks. Fertig ordered it salvaged immediately. He felt there was something indefinably lacking everywhere in the 110th Division; yet he could not put his finger on the problem. Nothing was seriously wrong, but orders went astray, little things were not done, and, somehow, no one seemed to be at fault. In some odd fashion, McClish's Americans seemed to be a team that, if it did not lack teamwork, did not entirely understand the game.

"The trouble is simple enough," Walter told Fertig. "McClish doesn't know it's time to quit playing soldier and grow up. He doesn't know how to run an outfit or get work out of Filipinos. He just rides around on his horse and imagines he's the Seventh Cavalry. Sooner or later, he's going to get his kids killed or stuck in a Jap prison camp."

Walter's remarks were overheard, and McClish's Americans in turn resented Walter and his friend Fred Varney. Varney was a small, weather-beaten man with a wolfish smile that did not exactly fit his character, although he was as tough and dour as any wolf. Like Walter, Varney was well in his fifties. He had been a civilian mine operator on Mindanao before the war and commanded a guerrilla with Walter in the hills around Anakan. In his faded khakis and high-laced boots, with a gun at his hip and an old campaign hat worn rakishly on one side of his head, Varney looked the picture of an adventurer in the South Seas. But it was a picture some of the young Americans derided. Some felt that the civilian old Phil-

ippine hands—Fertig, Hedges, Varney, Walter, Grinstead, Wilson, et al.—
were running the guerrilla as a kind of Old-Timers' Club for their own
benefit at the expense of Regular service personnel like themselves. Others complained that the Old Filipinos, as the former civilians called themselves, treated Filipinos inhumanly. And none of them, all of whom had
faced death and endured hardship and disease in a strange land for two
years, fighting for their country and for themselves rather than surrendering, appreciated an elderly civilian's accusing them of playing at soldiering.

For his part, Fertig thought there was some truth in what Walter said.
McClish had never impressed him as a tactician, although the young officer was as brave as any man alive, and eager for combat. But the very
location of McClish's headquarters was impossible. It was on a flat plain
that was indefensible against a mobile enemy armed with heavier weapons. The buildings were located in a coconut grove. McClish had not yet
learned that not only did the trees fail to offer adequate concealment but
that Japanese bombs, fused to burst on striking treetops, did more damage
than those which burst in craters on the ground. No one had adequately
prepared against the attack the Japanese would surely mount once they
learned that the area was to serve as a supply depot for all the guerrilla
forces in the southern Philippines. There had been plenty of time for
McClish to have prepared at least preliminary defenses. Fertig thought
it inexcusable for McClish to be absent at this time, for the *Narwhal*'s
scheduled arrival was only days away, and Fertig needed to know what
arrangements, if any, McClish had made for handling her cargo. For to
move a hundred tons from a submarine to a dock and then to clear this
cargo for the interior, all in a matter of hours, meant detailed planning of
arrivals and departures of labor gangs, trucks, barges, and launches and the
preparation of storage areas upriver and provision for guarding those areas.

Fertig began the defensive preparations McClish should have fore-
seen. He reasoned that, while the Japanese could drive the guerrilleros
off the lowland plain, the guerrilleros might well be able to hold the river.
Riflemen, stationed at the bends of the meandering stream, could stop
anything short of armored barges. While no trails paralleled the river,
plenty of trails crossed the jungle to riverside barrios, but Fertig felt
that guerrilleros could block the trails at least long enough to permit a
progressive escape of guerrilla forces up the Agusan. He sent Nick Capistrano to prepare secret headquarters areas at the riverside barrios of
Esperanza and Talacogon into which he could retreat at need. Aware of
the danger that the Japanese could also come downriver, Fertig ordered
Childress to place a guerrilla force near the Agusan-Davao provincial

border to prevent Japanese attacking from Davao from coming upon guerrilla rear areas. Another force under Tony Haratik was sent to shut the side door—the road that led from the Pacific to the great riverbend of the limestone canyons.

At the same time he was busy with these preparations, Fertig was also supervising the radio net, evaluating intelligence reports for transmission to Australia, passing on one American soldier's application for allotments of his accrued pay in Australia to be sent to his family, advising Judge Saguin's civil government of the need for importing potash from the island of Negros, ordering the arrest of a provincial treasurer suspected of stealing guerrilla funds, arranging codes and issuing instructions for the operation of a new intelligence net in southern Luzon, and listening to the endless requests of Filipinos who had problems they wished The One to solve.

Stretched in a hundred different directions at once, Fertig wished he had competent staff officers to handle routine matters while he concentrated on the major problems. Yet, who was to say that all problems were not equally important? The Filipino who complained that the guerrilleros had stolen his barroto was important indeed. For, if Fertig did not solve the matter quickly and equitably, the guerrilleros would shortly discover that all the barrotos in the area had mysteriously disappeared, that their money was no longer acceptable, that food was no longer forthcoming, that sources of information were running dry. Moreover, if Fertig found it almost impossible to delegate such simple matters to subordinates, he was also finding it undesirable to entrust subordinates with purely military affairs. The bamboo telegraph was only too effective, and the less anyone knew of Fertig's manifold affairs, the less information they would be able to spread through idle gossip; the less they could tell under torture.

It was also necessary that Fertig give Kangleon and Inginiero the attention due fellow commanders. Only one day remained before the *Narwhal*'s scheduled arrival, and, while failure was unthinkable—particularly in the presence of witnesses—there were so many things that could so easily go wrong. Inwardly, he seethed with anxiety as he presented a face of untroubled competence to Kangleon and Inginiero. But, quickly as he could, Fertig left his visitors to plunge again into his sea of details. It was exasperating to learn, at this late date, that illuminating gas remained in the tanks of the lighthouse at Nasipit harbor.

Why hadn't someone said this before? Where was the lighthouse keeper? Find him at once. The lighthouse would be used to help guide the *Narwhal* into the harbor. Advise Australia accordingly, in order to pass word to the submarine.

He dispatched a runner to the isolation camp to start the American refugees moving toward the rendezvous. He drove out of his mind any notion that, if contact should be missed, the effect on Kangleon and Inginiero would be disastrous. Their control over their rivals on their own islands was none too secure, and they and Fertig would lose face if the first substantial effort of America to support the guerrilla proved a failure.

Try as he might to refuse to think of failure, Fertig could not believe in the probability of success. He went to bed early on the night before the *Narwhal* was due, only to wake repeatedly. Each time he woke, he was aware that McClish had not returned from wherever he was and from whatever he had been doing. Lying awake in the night, Fertig saw in memory the American women in the refugee camp and heard again the questions they had asked: "Where can we change our pesos? Will anyone meet us in Australia? Will the Army take checks on a Manila bank because all our money was in Manila? Where will we live in Australia? Will we be sent back to the States?"

The civilians certainly had their problems. Fertig wished his own were as simple, but their problems were as real to them as his were to him, and they had suffered more than he, for he had always had the luxury of action, while they had experienced the deadly emptiness of waiting for something—for whatever it was to be—to happen to them.

Where the devil was McClish, and what had he done about the transportation? Fertig tossed in his bed and comforted himself that at least Walter and Varney had come from Anakan for this rendezvous. They were old hands at organizing Filipino labor gangs, and, among the three of them, Fertig felt sure they'd work something out, whether McClish showed up or not.

Toward dawn, Fertig was torn from sleep by a wild swaying of his bed. The nipa house was shaking, and men were shouting in the night, and the earth rippled, muttering and rumbling. Outside the house, Filipinos were fumbling for one another's hands in the darkness, trying to form a line, holding hands, so that, if a fissure opened beneath a man's feet, he would be safely held by a living chain.

The shocks were violent, and Fertig gripped his bed and decided he was as safe there as he could ever hope to be. There were always earthquakes in the Philippines, and there was obviously nothing anyone could do about them but try to fight down the terror of being so insignificantly in the hand of God.

It was not until the earth stopped turning within itself that Fertig wondered what had happened to the concrete pier at Nasipit, on which all his plans were based, and what effect an earthquake would have beneath the dark sea, in which the *Narwhal* was now presumably swimming blindly toward land.

5

THE WORDS *South Sea Islands* filled Evans with an almost unbearable delight, and he thrilled, too, to phrases like *war zone, clangor of arms,* and *savage enemy.* To Evans, a jungle was always a *forbidding jungle,* invariably to be found covering *mysterious hills.* He therefore peered with tense joy at the scene in the periscope—the scene he had come 10,000 miles to see and which now promised to fulfill his dreams exactly. In fact, he had dreamed of it so long that it looked familiar: the blue mountains rising out of the sea, the dense vegetation growing to the waterline, the coconut palms standing sentinel along the narrow beach, the clouds forming out of the rain forests on the flanks of volcanic hills. He was looking at his own South Sea island, populated by an enemy savage enough to satisfy any adventurer's demands, and soon he was to live the drama of a guerrilla soldier in a tropical paradise. Regretfully, he surrendered the periscope to Captain Latta, who had allowed him this one brief view. Evans resigned himself once more to the pale world of oil-smelling machinery, stale air, and dim yellow light that was the *Narwhal's* belly. The submarine's tanks filled, and she settled to the sea floor to await the dusk. Twelve hours later, the *Narwhal* slid up out of the water in a welter of roiling bubbles, hatches clanged open, and Evans climbed the metal ladder to breathe the warm fresh land-smell of flowers and earth after rain. He stood on the wet gratings, looking around in wonder. The *Narwhal* was knifing smoothly across moonlit water, and, all around the submarine, Evans could see the slender dark shapes of outrigger canoes and the wet glint of paddles lifting and falling. He heard the sailors shouting to one another—"Hey, lookit, they have a goddamn lighthouse!"—and he heard the glad calls of the slim brown men in canoes. He saw an outrigger glide alongside the *Narwhal* and watched a tall, thin man in tropical helmet and suntans swing aboard. The tall man wore a .45 pistol on his hip and Evans saw the flash of his teeth as his bearded face split in a smile as he shook hands with Captain Latta. Evans heard someone say, "Fertig."

Was that the Fertig about whom Chick Parsons had talked so much? Evans had only a glimpse of him as the tall man went below, but that single glimpse sent Evans' pulse pounding at the realization that he, Evans, was at last really and truly more than a thousand sea miles behind enemy lines, engaged on a mission that the Army had assured him was so hazardous that he could not expect to return.

The *Narwhal*, surrounded by milling canoes, moved slowly through a tortuous channel, cut by a great river working through coral, toward a village of stilted grass houses that emerged from beneath trees to meet the sea. Evans breathed the rich, fecal odor of Asia mingling with the land-smell and was completely happy. The houses were really made of grass, and the canoes were really made of hollowed logs, and it would be really rough. He was prepared for it to be really rough—*rugged* was the Army word. He was prepared for everything but what greeted him as the *Narwhal* edged slowly past the oil-stained hulk of a bombed ship to berth at a concrete dock.

There were dockworkers to grab the *Narwhal*'s flung messenger lines and haul the heavy Manila cables over bollards; seven trucks waited on the dock apron; launches with lighter barges waited in the river; excited Filipinos laughed and waved to the men on the *Narwhal*; girls in filmy dresses waved and then covered their faces with their hands to conceal the embarrassment they were expected to feel for having been so forward; and a band burst into "Aloha."

The band, all dressed in white trousers and white shirts, was the military band of the 110th Division of the United States Forces in the Philippines, Colonel McClish commanding, and, as the *Narwhal*'s lines were secured, the bittersweet languor of "Aloha" filled the tropical night, and, in the light of moon and flickering torches, Evans could see tears streaming down faces brown and white, and he heard one of the *Narwhal*'s sailors shout huskily, "Jesus Christ, where the hell are we? Hollywood?"

The *Narwhal*'s cargo hatches opened, and the band blared "The Stars and Stripes Forever" with a fervor probably never matched before or since, and sailors in blue denim and bare-chested brown men in shorts worked together to unload the huge submarine. Supplies poured out of her: cases of carbine and rifle ammunition, cases of submachine guns, carbines, rocket launchers called bazookas, D-ration chocolate bars, Spam, cheese, magazines, books, MacArthur's newspaper the *Free Philippines,* medicines, jungle boots, suntan uniforms, jungle camouflage suits, .50-caliber machine guns on tripod mounts, 20-millimeter cannons, millions of pesos in counterfeit Japanese invasion currency, cases of atabrine pills, the new anti-malarial. There were printing plates and paper for manufacture of legal guerrilla currency, jungle hammocks, cigarettes, flashlights, officers' insignia, and spare parts for generators and radios; tools and spark plugs. All this, and more, came pouring out of the *Narwhal* as the band played songs that had been popular in 1941, which were the most recent songs the bandsmen had heard, and one of the sailors called out to the dock, "Hey, where are the Japs?"

"What's the matter? You getting nervous in the service?" a voice answered in good American, and Evans saw a thin, grinning figure in faded, patched khakis push through the dockside crowd.

"It's no sweat," the guerrillero told the sailor. "The Japs are a mile away."

"Mile away? Which way?"

"Oh, a mile that way," the guerrillero said, gesturing. "And a mile or maybe two miles over that way."

"Jesus!" the sailor said, and the people on the dock laughed.

Evans looked at the guerrillero and wondered how long it would be before he, too, had long hair and a straw hat and a uniform as ragged; before his skin, too, was sun-bronzed and he went about barefoot with a gun on his hip and a rifle slung over his shoulder and was nonchalant about the Japanese being a mile away.

"How long you been here?" the sailor asked, and Evans heard, as though in a dream, the guerrillero say, "What do you think we do? Go home for weekends? We been here since it started. Where have you guys been?"

Meanwhile, as Evans stared about as if to fix the scene forever in his memory, Captain Latta sat in the gray steel wardroom below, touched and drawn to the red-bearded man who sat opposite him devouring Spam sandwiches and drinking cups of black coffee as if never had food more delicious been placed before a man more hungry.

As he ate, Fertig listened intently to Latta's news of the outside world. From time to time, he would interrupt to ask questions, and Latta found himself talking with a man whose thirst for exact, detailed information was as thorough as the thirst of a sponge. The range and depth of Fertig's interest was astounding; he seemed to be interested in *everything,* and Latta had the eerie feeling that whatever he said Fertig would remember. Fertig's gray eyes were bright; his bearded face was flushed; his movements were quick and accurate, and Latta thought his guest unusually high-strung—no doubt understandably excited by the safe arrival of a small mountain of supplies. He saw Fertig's hand hovering near the packet of letters from home that Latta had brought him, and Latta wanted to tell the guerrillero to go ahead and read his wife's letters. Latta would have been astonished to know that Fertig's animation and flushed cheeks were due not to excitement but to the beginning of a malarial fever which Fertig intended to cure by stuffing himself with food and immersing himself in work; he would have been even more astonished to know that Fertig had already decided to ration those letters. He would read one each day, in order to make the pleasure last as long as possible. Then he would reread them, one each day, sitting alone in a bamboo house to a solitary supper.

Two other guests—Filipino officers—were drinking coffee in the *Narwhal*'s wardroom, and the elder, a slightly built, frail-seeming aristocrat, was speaking to Chick Parsons in tones of intense passion.

"We need shotgun shells," Kangleon was saying. "In the jungles, the range is not far but very small, and the shotgun shells are the best."

"If you want them, we'll send them," Parsons said. "But a case of shells takes up the same space as 12,000 rounds of carbine ammunition. You can have whichever you want."

"Twelve *thousand* rounds?" Kangleon asked, leaning forward. "But the weight is very much?"

Parsons explained that, in a submarine, weight was not important. It was space that was important. Kangleon thought of this for a long moment.

"I will take whichever is most," the Filipino said.

"And I also," the other Filipino, Major Inginiero, said. "We will use whatever you bring, for we have little. But bring what is most."

Fertig noted that the Filipinos were visibly impressed, as he had intended they should be. He had brought them to the rendezvous with his heart in his mouth, fearing that the earthquake had destroyed the dock, that the trucks and barges would not be there, that the *Narwhal* would not appear, that the promise of American aid would prove a public mockery. But everything had gone well. Despite McClish's absence—it seemed he had gone on a combat patrol—the trucks and barges had appeared, and Varney and Walter had the labor gangs well in hand. When, at the appointed time, the *Narwhal* rose endlessly out of the sea, Fertig felt a thrill of pride in his country, represented there on the dark water in the potent beauty of a man-of-war, and, seeing the look of utter stupefaction that passed between the Filipinos as this incredible submarine drew near, Fertig knew that, if the *Narwhal* looked like a battleship to him, it looked like an entire fleet to Kangleon and Inginiero. He wanted to pound them on the back and shout, as other men were shouting, and it was with some difficulty that he turned gravely to the Filipino officers and asked instead if they would like to go aboard to meet the submarine's commander.

For his part, Captain Latta was impressed, too. In fact, it was the only instance in United States naval history where a United States warship had moored to a pier to discharge cargo in enemy territory, and knowing this, Fertig had carefully set the scene.

Ninety-two tons of cargo were hand-carried from the *Narwhal* in four hours. Each hour was an exquisite mental agony to Fertig, beset by fever, feeling wave on wave of homesickness as he thought of the letters waiting to be read, forcing himself to concentrate on the information Latta was giving him, and fearing that, at any moment, Japanese aircraft would raid this only-too-well-lighted, too-public rendezvous. He had no personal fears. It was simply that he feared that if the *Narwhal* should be lost at this stage of the game, the Navy might well decide not to spend another submarine upon so quixotic an adventure as smuggling supplies to guerrilleros on islands the War Department had already written off as lost.

The same hours were an endless delight to Evans, standing on the *Narwhal's* deck and watching Filipino working parties carrying a store of fresh fruits and vegetables into the submarine. Evans had no idea how much of a sacrifice this was for the people of Agusan province, nor how much the open pleasure of the sailors meant to the Filipinos. He listened to the sailors talking with American guerrilleros, the sailors frankly admitting they lacked the courage to stay a minute on an island full of Japs, and the guerrilleros saying this was nothing but they'd be damned if they would risk their lives in a deathtrap like a submarine, and the sailors saying it was no sweat, and everyone finally deciding you can only die once, anyway, with the guerrilleros preferring to do this on land and the sailors at sea. The guerrilleros wanted to know everything the sailors could tell them of what it was like in the States and how the war was going, and when MacArthur would Return, and where the sailors came from, and when a man would say, "Oklahoma," someone would ask, "Do you know Joe Scott? He comes from Oklahoma, too."

No one ever did know Joe Scott from Oklahoma City or Bill Kowalski from Pittsburgh, Pennsylvania, but no one really expected that anyone would. It was simply good for everyone to hear the once-familiar names of states and cities again, and the sailors wanted to know what the guerrilleros had found out about the Filipino girls and everyone talked about women.

A truck pulled onto the dock apron. Its tailgate banged down, and Evans saw men and women climb out of the truck. A child was handed down to a woman, who carried it in her arms toward the *Narwhal*. The crowd parted to let them pass. Evans was shocked by their ragged clothes, by their pinched faces and the dark blotches of hunger, anxiety, and sleeplessness beneath their eyes. He did not know that the guerrilleros thought the civilians looked well, fit, and happy. As a medical officer, Evans automatically noted the symptoms of malnutrition and the fact that one of the women was very quietly and completely hysterical, moving in a trance toward the miraculous, improbable means of her salvation, while the band played "God Bless America."

There were thirty-two civilians to be evacuated, including Mrs. Stanley Briggs, whose husband had been killed by Moros and who herself had escaped from the Japanese with the aid of nuns who had dressed her as one of themselves; G. E. C. Mears, a British lumberman who had married United States Army Nurse Lieutenant Robertson; Donald and Mrs. McKay and their daughter Mary; Captain John Martin and his wife; Mrs. Welbon and Mrs. Varney, whose husbands would stay behind to serve Fertig's guerrilla; and Mrs. Cryster and two-year-old Steven Cryster, born in a jungle in a war.

Belowdecks, Fertig said good-bye to them, giving Nell Varney money with which to buy Christmas presents for him for Mary and the girls, she promising it would be the first thing she would do on reaching Australia, and, when it seemed that nothing more could be said, Steven Cryster called out, "Cake, Mommy!"

They all saw him excitedly holding up a piece of white bread.

"Cake!" Steven shouted, offering to share this unimaginable delight with his mother, and the sailor who had given the child bread turned quickly away.

The band played "Anchors Aweigh" as the *Narwhal* moved from the dock, the sailors waving and the people calling out to them and the band playing and the people waving and a priest blessing the ship until the submarine disappeared down the tricky river channel into the night.

Left ashore, medical bag in one hand and carbine in the other, Evans saw two men approaching.

"Wendell, this is Doc Evans," Parsons said. "Doc, this is Colonel Fertig—General Fertig, hereabouts."

Evans shook hands with a man who seemed to look through and past him.

"Chick tells me you're a radioman as well as a medical officer," Fertig said.

"Yes, sir," Evans said.

"If you're either one, I can sure use you," Fertig said briefly. He called to a Filipino.

"You will conduct the Captain," Fertig told the Filipino, indicating Evans.

"I will see you later," Fertig promised the doctor.

With that, Fertig nodded and left, and Evans, somewhat startled by his welcome to the irregular service, was led away. Carrying his bag and gun, he climbed aboard an unpainted, derelict-looking river launch that seemed as brutally appropriate as Fertig's words.

Sitting with Parsons in the cab of a truck, bumping along the scraped road to Buenavista, Fertig was near exhaustion from fever and the mental strain that the rendezvous had put on him. He had arrived early to find only one truck at the dock and no alcohol for that truck. Only two of the four launches and lighters had appeared, and there had been no word of the civilians, who should have arrived at the same time he had. Yet, everything had fallen into place at the last minute, and, by the time the *Narwhal* surfaced, Fertig had relearned the lesson it was always so hard to learn: that you could tell Filipinos what to do but not how to do it. They would always do it their way, and you had to trust that it would be done. Somehow, it always was. If the order was to proceed by truck and if it turned out that the Filipino driver had forgot to fill the fuel tank, so that the engine died en route, the move was nevertheless made by truck, with gangs of men pulling with vine ropes and swarms of men pushing behind, while runners went out to find fuel. Meanwhile, it seemed to Fertig that the American Army worked in equally laborious ways, and he spoke of this to Parsons.

"Why the devil did they send printing plates and paper?" Fertig complained. "Why couldn't they print the money in Australia and send it here?"

"Damned if I know," Parsons said. "MacArthur doesn't tell me everything, Wendell."

"If they let me judge what I need, and did what I asked, things would be a lot simpler," Fertig said. "If they printed it there, it would relieve us of a bookkeeping problem, for one thing. Do they think we have an office full of accountants and clerks with typewriters? All we have is Sam Wilson and a pencil."

Parsons said nothing.

"Another thing, Chick," Fertig said. "About those twenty-millimeter guns. When I saw them, damn it, I felt about ten feet tall—until I found out that nobody had sent any shells. Who was the genius who thought we could fire cannons without ammunition?"

"Those are Navy guns, and you're on Army requisitions," Parsons said. "Look at it this way, Wendell: Yesterday, you didn't have any guns or any ammunition. Now you have the guns. Didn't Latta say he's going to get you some shells from Navy stores?"

"Yes," Fertig said. "But it would be nice if those people down there got together on what they're doing."

"All right," Parsons said. "They're doing the best they can. You're not the only worry they have, Wendell."

"Oh, hell, Chick, I know it. It's just that I'm so damned tired."

"Why don't you go to sleep?"

"I can't. It's that coffee."

Fertig had the sour, empty, metallic feeling of a man up too late, operating on the basis of black coffee.

"You'll get the shells next trip," Parsons said. "Latta's coming back in sixteen days with another full load for you."

"Another hundred tons?"

"Another hundred tons."

The truck bumped along in the night.

At the same time, Evans stood in the bow of a river launch, listening to the chunking of a one-cylinder engine and breathing the muddy smell of the Agusan, which came winding out of the deeps of time through a primeval forest like some vast, slow beast. He had learned that the guerrilleros had been teasing the sailors, that there were no Japanese within thirty miles. Evans found this somewhat disappointing, but it by no means entirely dispelled his enchantment. He was now listening for the sound of drums talking in the hills. It seemed to him that, when one went upriver through a tropical jungle, drums should be talking. Instead, there were only the calls of night birds and the liquid voices of the Filipinos and the sound of the one-cylinder diesel.

But then, the river turned, and a huge, dark tree came toward Evans in the night. As if by magic, the tree blossomed with tiny fires; with an immense mass of shimmering, dancing lights that glimmered everywhere on leaf and twig. It became a tree of golden flame in the night.

Never had Evans seen anything more lonely nor more beautiful. He was seeing for the first time the loveliness that a swarm of tropical fireflies can create. He watched the tree come alongside and then slide past him, down the river into the darkness, as he stood in the bow of a puffing launch that carried him toward his unimaginable destination, feeling that he had at last come home to a land he had never seen but had always known.

6

SPUTTERING LAUNCHES meandered up the Agusan, drawing snugly under the high, steep-cut bank at Esperanza to unload crates of limpet mines, booby traps, 20-millimeter cannon shells, shaped charges, rockets, and small-arms ammunition. Fertig watched the sweating cargadores with mixed feelings. The cargo, from the *Narwhal*'s second visit, doubled his armament, and there was promise of more to come, but General MacArthur's personal letter warned Fertig not to use it.

"I have included ordnance supplies in increased quantity and of a much heavier type than you will probably require for your normal operations, and I plan to implement delivery of such materiel to you as transport facility and security will in the future permit me to do so," MacArthur's letter said.

"You should carefully guard against any unwarranted display of increased fire power that would provoke reinforcement of enemy garrisons, increased retaliation upon the people, and a tightening of the enemy blockade against future deliveries and, as soon as possible, cache such materiel as is not required for current operations in secure dispersal areas to serve future requirements.

"As your areas may provide the most secure available points of discharge, it will probably be necessary to deliver thereto supplies destined for distribution to other areas. In such event, I desire that you cooperate fully with other commanders concerned, to the end that the ultimate destination thereof may be reached without undue risk or delay.

"Successful accomplishment of the first movement of accelerated supplies discloses careful planning and coordination of movement which I view with satisfaction and for which I commend both you and the officers and men contributing to the task. Intensified enemy opposition must be expected to each successive future supply movement, to counter which will require the exercise of vigilance and continued careful planning. In this I have confidence in your ability to successfully outmatch the enemy's moves."

Fertig reflected sourly upon these regal sentences as a Filipino work crew piled crates on the rickety wharf below the river bluff. The Filipinos simply piled them one atop the other in single stacks, not in cross-tied staggered courses, until a stack began to waver. At the last possible instant, someone would dash up to remove the last, too-heavy addition, while others frantically held the rest of the crates. Then they would start another single stack. One of the workmen held a clipboard in one hand, while trying to lift crates with the other. He held onto the clipboard because he was the tallyman and it was his badge of office, separating him from common men, but he was helping because of the universal need for speed. If he put his clipboard down and used two hands and tallied the crates after they had been stacked, the work would go much faster, but Fertig could not suggest this. To do so might cost the tallyman so much face that he would return to his barrio. For the same reason, Fertig could not tell cargadores how to stack crates. In their own way, they were doing their best, and Fertig could only watch them and wish that General MacArthur could enjoy this exhibition of careful planning and co-ordination of movement. He also wished that Hedges could share his enjoyment of MacArthur's letter. He knew just what Charley would say. Charley would read it unbelievingly and explode in redfaced profanity, for everything about MacArthur's message seemed almost as distant from reality as Louis XIV—particularly the opening paragraph that said, "By this shipment, I have inaugurated a greatly accelerated supply movement to the Philippine area which I can only sustain if the utmost vigilance is exercised by you and other District Commanders in the preservation of security."

Fertig's lips pursed with distaste. The officer who had written that bilge for MacArthur's signature had obviously never been shot at; had never stared with distended eyes for the black stalk of a periscope on the night sea, straining for the sound of Japanese launch motors and hearing nothing but the slap of slow-rippling water against the wood of the barroto and seeing nothing but the sea glittering like obsidian and feeling nothing but the cold sweat trickling down his sides and the sour emptiness twisting in his stomach.

What the devil did Headquarters expect? That he would tell the Japanese when a submarine would come? That he would tell even his own men? When Fertig moved troops to the beach to guard the trails leading to a rendezvous site, pains were taken to get them there by a roundabout way, concealing the real nature of their mission from the soldiers.

As for the rest of it, security—the Army word for secrecy—was out of the question. The cargadores were unloading cases of D-ration tropical chocolate bars and boxes of MacArthur's *Free Philippines*. MacArthur wanted these distributed throughout the island for propaganda purposes and, at the same time, wanted the submarine arrivals kept secret! Everywhere on Mindanao, everyone, including the Japanese, eagerly looked forward to reading the newspapers and learning whether the new rocket launchers worked. The bamboo telegraph talked of nothing else.

Fertig rubbed his sun-chapped lips with coconut oil, watching the sweating cargadores wrestling with the crates and not looking up when there was the thin, uneven sound of a Japanese aircraft engine. It was the daily courier, flying high on a compass course from Davao to Cagayan. But then Fertig, the cargadores, and everyone looked up when a growing racket burst over the treetops and the shape of a twin-engined bomber hurtled overhead, racing low down the Agusan to the sea.

"Jesus, those damn things scare me," a voice said. It was Evans. His fear of aircraft showed whitely under his tan.

Fertig stared after the dwindling dot of the bomber, rubbing oil on his lips.

"If your name is on that bomb, that's all there is to it," Fertig said. "You'll never know it when it hits you. So you don't have to worry about that one. And if it doesn't have your name on it, it won't hit you, so you don't have to worry about *that* one."

"I'm not worried about the one with my name on it. That one's all right. I'm worried about the one addressed 'to whom it may concern.'"

Evans was perfectly serious, and Fertig did not smile.

"Johnny said you wanted to see me?" Evans said. Johnny was Fertig's cook.

Fertig frowned.

"I didn't tell him that," he said. "Johnny just guessed it. But he's right. I was going to ask if you've been seeing a lot of people in purple clothes."

"There's one over there," Evans said, looking at a line of cargadores, in which a pair of bright violet shorts stood out against the drab faded tan of the rest.

"They're something, aren't they?" Evans said. "The new winter fashion. You're nobody if you don't have purple pants."

"I asked Johnny about it," Fertig said. "He said, 'The people buy the dye from the Medical Corps, but they don't like too much, for it fades very fast when it is washed.' You're the Medical Corps. What's the answer?"

Evans looked at Fertig in a kind of horror.

"By God, it's gentian violet!" he said. "Listen, I'll check it right away. If somebody's been stealing that stuff . . ."

"Now, just a minute," Fertig said. "Johnny said, 'You didn't ask me, or I would have told you about this.' Now how important is that stuff?"

"Medically?"

"Yes."

"I've been using it for tropical ulcers."

"Does it do any good?"

"Some. But not much. The best thing is to wash the sore with hydrogen peroxide, pack the wound with sulfa powder, and wrap it in an airtight bandage."

"Then you haven't lost much, but the people have a nice new dye."

"But we can't have stealing," Evans said.

"Of course not. Johnny tells me the stuff is selling for ten pesos for the amount that just covers the end of a bolo. I figure at that price, gentian violet is worth at least a thousand dollars a pound. I was thinking that, if it isn't much good for ulcers, maybe we ought to sell it as dye, to help raise money for the Army."

The idealist in Evans looked at the pragmatist in Fertig with horrified admiration. But then the idealist in him said, "Wait till I find the son of a bitch who's been stealing it."

"Sure. Check into it and bring him to me," Fertig said calmly. "Don't tell him anything. Just say, 'We will go to the General.'"

Fertig did not trust Evans to handle it, because he thought that Evans made the common American mistake of thinking the Filipinos were wonderful people. He had seen too many new Americans turn sour when they discovered the Filipinos were no more wonderful than anyone else and go on to back a Filipino into a corner from which the Filipino could not escape without losing face. Evans had that look of new Americans who were disappointed to find that the Filipinos were human.

But, idealist or not, Fertig thought, watching Evans walking rapidly away through the heat toward the Medical Corps compound, Evans was the best thing the submarines had brought so far. Evans had cured the eye disease of the wife of a local headman—not because he was asked to but because he saw her and knew his help was needed. News of this miracle raced through the river valley; the people were coming in such droves that the American doctor had already won a nickname: the Mindanao Mender.

In a few days, Evans had done more than anything Fertig had ever done to win the support of the Agusan people to the guerrilla. The people had never got over the feeling that the Americans had cheated them by surrendering. They never had complete faith that McClish and Fertig would not surrender, too, until Evans had arrived with his medical kit. Now they believed. Was this because Evans so obviously believed in them?

Fertig turned back to the river to watch the impractical stacking of the crates. Evans was more than a medical idealist. In his first day, Evans had proved to be the fastest radio operator Fertig had ever seen. He sent so rapidly that Australia's receivers had to ask him to slow down. Moreover, Evans had shown the radio section how to build radios out of the most unlikely materials. The result was that Fertig was now ordering parts, rather than radios. The parts took up less space on the submarine than finished sets, and the space thus saved could be devoted to other necessities.

Purple clothing! Yet money might be raised that way.

It was grotesque to think that he had to be concerned with purple clothing. The very ridiculousness of it reminded Fertig of something equally ridiculous: MacArthur's letter of instruction. Angrily, Fertig had a mental image of an air-conditioned office filled with smooth-shaven officers who blithely wrote him letters of advice about "normal operations."

Normal operations in the Tenth Military District were exactly as far removed from military normality as a full field uniform was distant from a pair of purple pants.

Fertig strolled absently along the high grasses at the riverbank, wondering how best to interpret MacArthur's instruction to act as supply officer for guerrilleros on other islands and to cache the new weapons "in secure dispersal areas to serve future needs."

In the first instance, MacArthur was asking him to do something that MacArthur confessed his own inability to do, and in any case, the creation of supply dumps meant the preparation of defensive positions to safeguard the dumps. But to prepare a defensive area meant troops, and troops ate food. There was no food available. It was difficult enough to find food for the number of men required to transport the supplies upriver from Nasipit. More than two hundred tons had arrived in Esperanza, and Fertig's men had been working for a week merely to sort it out and to repack it in consignments for Fertig's six divisional commands and for guerrilleros on other islands. It would take another week to complete the task. Simple receipt of materiel had thus immobilized his headquarters for a fortnight, and every day in one place not only reduced the food supply in that place but invited Japanese attack.

Returning to the headquarters compound, Fertig spent the rest of the morning trying to speed dispersal of his new riches.

Jealousies must be considered. Already, some Filipino officers were saying that Fertig gave the Americans complete new uniforms, shoes, insignia, and pistols while giving them none. The fact that this was demonstrably untrue did nothing to halt the rumor.

Such an insect matter demanded Fertig's attention as much as weightier affairs. It was not that any of the problems were particularly difficult; it was simply that their resolution took time to arrange. It was simple enough to give the order, 'Ten tons of carbine ammunition is to go to Talakag." But at this point, the complications began.

There were no roads from Esperanza to Talakag. Only trails led across the jungle, through swamps to the rising ground of the Bukidnon plateau. The ammunition must be broken down into back loads for cargadores, and here was a load for four hundred men. Manpower was the cheapest and most plentiful resource in the Islands, but the men would be on the march for a week—one way. Assuming they ate twice a day, provision must be made for the 11,200 meals to be consumed over the round trip. No such amount of food was available at any one time in Esperanza, much less any further provisions for the soldiers who would have to accompany the cargadores. There were, however, many alternatives to consider.

The cargadores could come from Talakag, each man carrying his own food for the two-week march. Or orders could be sent to the barrios on the line of march to assemble foodstuffs according to the estimated times of arrival of the cargadores and their guards in those barrios. Or transportation of this ten tons could be stretched over a longer period of time, with smaller parties taking lesser quantities at each time. Each of these, and all other alternatives, were investigated, and, while Fertig leaned heavily on Nick Capistrano and Rex Reyes to do this sort of staff work for him, Fertig nevertheless had to review the alternatives and give the orders, keeping in mind the mission and needs of the guerrilleros at Talakag with respect to the needs and missions of all other guerrilla forces in his command. It was the kind of work for which neither Fertig nor anyone else in his command had special training. He had admitted as much in a private letter sent to his old commander, Major General Hugh J. Casey, MacArthur's engineer officer.

"To learn soldiering from the top down has been a problem," Fertig said. "No tech manual or other help, no former organization upon which to lean. Just backbiting and jealousy, cowardly officers with too much rank and no guts. I've reverted them to inactive status. Our problem is the same old story of organize, disintegrate under an enemy sustained offensive, then reorganize. Month after month. The strain begins to tell, for I have practically no Filipino officers who were of field grade at the time of surrender. Those who were are old and soft. This is an army of third lieutenants. Yet it is a great thing to see men who in peacetime were farmers or shoeshine boys given a chance in war to take responsibility and show what they can do."

Learning soldiering from the top down was certainly the phrase for it, Fertig thought, envying the former shoeshine boys. When he had joined the guerrilla, it had not occurred to him that soldiering would mean studying reports of the water level at barrios along the Agusan or investigating the rapidity with which trees could be cut. But, when the river rose, the banks were undermined, and huge trees fell across the channel. Many Philippine hardwoods contain so much silicon that a gang of men working with axes frequently needed four days to chop through a single tree two feet thick. Therefore, high water and timber cutting was one military problem; extreme low water presented another: How heavily could a log canoe be loaded? In order to make reasonable plans, Fertig had to study villagers' reports of past rainy seasons in order to make some estimate of the probabilities. If it rains hard next week, how many logs can we expect in the river below Talacogon? If it is dry, how many more barrotos will we need to assemble at Waloe?

The third lieutenants in the ambushes did not have to concern themselves with these affairs, nor with calculations, based on intelligence reports and plain gossip, of Japanese capabilities and probable movements, nor with the printing and accounting of the money that paid them and purchased their food and clothing, nor with the keeping of central rosters, nor with the over-all supervision of the civil government that functioned where and how and as it could, despite the internecine jealousies of politicians and the difficulties of reaching through distances controlled by primitive tribesmen, semi-independent Moro datus, and Japanese garrisons. Yet all these matters had to be understood at once by the Commanding General if the ambushes were to succeed, or even take place. Soldiering from the top down meant having to know everything in order to know something.

Working through the morning, the decisions forming themselves out of the vast store of remembered facts, Fertig was aware that, the more successful he was, the more paperwork there would be. In a sense, MacArthur's phrase about caching arms "to serve future requirements" was ominous.

For the only possible inference was that the guerrilla forces were to be built into a new Philippine army that could take the field against regular Japanese forces. Hence the rockets, the heavy machine guns, the cannons. The strategy was perfectly clear. MacArthur was to land a United States army in Mindanao in a frontal assault. Guerrilla forces, armed with the weapons of heavy infantry, would attack the Japanese rear. Colonel Fertig, United States Infantry, would execute these attacks at times and places ordered by MacArthur's headquarters. Instead of fighting an informal war, for which he had no training but in which he was training himself, Fertig would then be fighting a formal battle for which he had no training at all. Fertig had discussed the falsity of the major premise—on which this strategy depended—in his letter to General Casey.

"We admit that we cannot meet the Nips in open combat, for the Filipino does not stand well in an open attack," Fertig wrote. "A small group with an exceptional officer may, but in general, they won't."

Another false premise was that Fertig would be able to move troops. Even assuming that he could move troops physically, nothing guaranteed they would fight, once moved. For, if the Filipino was an ambush fighter, he was also a fighter for his barrio only.

There was also the false presumption that the guerrilleros *could* be fully armed by submarine contacts prior to MacArthur's return. MacArthur's letter pointed the danger: The Japanese would tighten their blockade the instant the guerrilleros disclosed more serious armament. That bomber that had flown overhead was no accident. The Japanese must already know of Fertig's presence on the Agusan; must even now be planning to seal the coast, take Nasipit, and drive up the Agusan.

A final false presumption was that MacArthur's return could possibly be a surprise. The whole world knew that MacArthur lived only for the day it would take place, and anyone could tell by looking at the map that the first blow would logically fall on Mindanao, largest of the southern Philippines and the key to control of the Sulu and South China seas. The moment it appeared that MacArthur was in any way able to make good his promise, the whole world knew that the Japanese would pour divisions into Mindanao to clean out the guerrilleros and to eliminate any menace to their rear areas. When the Japanese began seriously to prepare for MacArthur, would the guerrilleros simply have to disintegrate and hide until someone won the war?

With a gesture of irritation, Fertig turned to present realities. There was no future in war. There was only today, in which to do what could be done with what there was. Today, he had 20-millimeter automatic cannon and .50-caliber machine guns, and there seemed no point in hiding them.

Armed with heavy weapons, Zapanta's *Athena* and Waldo Neveling's *So What* would be more than a match for any Japanese launches, including armored ones. They could convoy supplies to guerrilla bands along the coasts, raid Japanese interisland commerce, cover guerrilla hit-and-run operations against the coastal highway, protect the mouth of the Agusan River. Fifty-foot sailing ships armed with cannon were nonetheless deadly for being eighteenth-century weapons. They would dominate their seas until taken under fire by twentieth-century destroyers and aircraft. With good luck, it would take the twentieth century a long time to find them.

Fertig smiled thinly to himself, thinking what a pair his admirals made: Zapanta, grandiose and theatrical but just as fearless and enterprising in his swashbuckling way as Neveling was in his methodical, thorough, hard-fisted German way. Not that the German lacked a touch of humor; it was simply that Neveling's was a kind of Teutonic gallows humor. The name he had given to his fifty-six–foot racing banca was an exact description of Neveling's view of life. And mordant but practical wit had led Neveling to mount hard steel circular saws, taken from the sawmills, along the *So What*'s gunwales. "Chust like the shields uff Viking ships," Neveling had said with his derisive blond grin, but, for all that, the saws *were* proof against small-arms fire, and the *So What* was the armored vessel of the Mindanao Navy.

How would Headquarters solve the Neveling problem? After all, the man was an enemy alien, still technically a prisoner of the United States. But Fertig had given the soldier of fortune a commission in the United States Army, which, according to law, made the enemy alien a United States citizen. Headquarters lawyers should have a lot of fun deciding what to do.

The thought reminded Fertig of something even more important: recognition of the commissions he had granted his American enlisted men. He understood their worry about confirmation of their assumed ranks, for he shared it himself. He wondered who at Headquarters could be dragging his feet over such a simple matter of honoring battlefield promotions. Fertig stared moodily at the autographed picture of General MacArthur that the *Narwhal* had brought him. General MacArthur looked haughtily back.

"Just send them a load of bullshit," Charlie Smith's voice said in Fertig's memory. "They eat it up. They love it; they live on it. Just tell them how great they are and how grateful you are, and remember to do it often."

There was much in what Smith said. Having seen MacArthur's staff in action himself, Fertig knew there were only two permissible views of the Supreme Commander: adulation or nothing. Fertig did not know whether MacArthur was deliberately responsible for the groveling, almost Oriental atmosphere of his court or whether MacArthur's personality was so overwhelming that only sycophants seemed able to survive its radiance. Fertig was by no means ready to crawl, but he was prepared to flatter to gain his ends.

"Your autographed picture is worth a million pesos to the effort in convincing the few remaining skeptics," Fertig wrote to the General. "Could you send my wife a duplicate of the picture you sent me? Mine will never reach home, for everyone insists on seeing it and touching it. The Tenth Military District and staff thanks you for the quantity of supplies. God grant that they continue to arrive in ever-increasing amounts."

Getting to the heart of the matter, Fertig continued: "Will you issue commissions to American former enlisted men commissioned by me and actually functioning as officers? These men will remain with me and certainly deserve recognition of services rendered. Should this be granted, many of my problems will be solved. Recall that these men volunteered to remain when offered chance for repatriation. Issue of serial numbers and assurance of pay of officers will enable them to buy war bonds and support family . . ." Fertig read what he had written and dropped it into his Out basket, wondering whom MacArthur had to flatter in order to enjoy the illusion of Supreme Command. No man was less independent than the commander, who was the prisoner not only of himself but of everyone else.

He worked on through the heat of the late morning, ordering compensation paid to fishermen whose barrotos had been commandeered, reading intelligence estimates of political maneuvering within the Filipino puppet government in Manila, querying his Chemical Section as to its progress in converting cinchona bark into quinine, reading documents prepared for his signature. He studied reports that the new carbines were fairly accurate in open country at short ranges but tended to jam and that their bullets were not heavy enough to smash undeflected through twigs and brush. The guerrilleros' preference was the .45-caliber Thompson submachine gun or the .30-caliber Browning automatic rifle. Fertig fitted this information, as nearly as he could, into plans for supplying his units—seeking some approximate balance to an equation compounded of terrain, targets, rate of fire, reliability of troops, propaganda value, and the difficulty of transport.

He worked alone through the morning until it was time to eat the solitary lunch that helped cloak him in the mystery of command. He sipped from a cup of hot, faintly stained water that represented the last of the drip-ground coffee the *Narwhal* had brought and watched Johnny arrange the jungle hammock on the porch. Throughout the Islands, everyone, including the Japanese, took siesta, sleeping, sweating through the impossible midday heat. Fertig wondered whether it occurred to the fresh-shaven officers in the air-conditioned headquarters in Australia that siesta was a major part of the normal operations of the Tenth Military District and that the new jungle hammocks that the *Narwhal* delivered were exclusively devoted to the successful accomplishment of this important military maneuver.

Hammocks, for God's sake. When the same space on the submarine could have been used for medicines, for bullets. Tented hammocks with mosquito netting zippered to them, hammocks that were death traps for soldiers caught in them in surprise night attacks, hammocks that were good only for siestas in safe rear areas. They might as well have sent jockstraps.

We could have made slingshots out of jockstraps.

Fertig wondered if something more than 1,500 miles separated one supreme commander from another.

7

PERHAPS IT WAS in Japan that the Japanese bathed, but here, on Mindanao, was an army that defecated about its own cookfires and slept in the litter of its garbage and excrement. It was a horde of ninth-century Asiatics who made no provision against venereal or other deadly diseases and who had so far suffered more casualties for medical reasons than from enemy action. On a morning of late December 1943, they were busy everywhere along the Lanao coast from Cagayan to the foot of Panguil Bay—a swarm of filthy little men in sloppy uniforms with straw in their helmet nettings and dirty towels tucked into their belts, following flags bearing the color of arterial blood. Wherever the Japanese moved, their stench literally preceded them and lingered after them, and, as they came, fear also drifted ahead of them like a reek winding down a summer air.

On this morning, they came scrambling out of launches grounded in the shallows near Maigo, racing across the narrow beach in the luminous dawn, steel helmets bobbling and equipment flapping, their split-toed sandals churning the gray sand as they sprinted for the trees. They poured across the beach and into the coconuts, and no one shot at them. The shooting was four miles away, and they could hear the air bursts like tree limbs cracking and the dull whump of shells exploding in mud. The shells that burrowed into the earth were Japanese mistakes. Air bursts, showering shrapnel over the defenses, were wanted to keep the guerrilleros pinned in their holes.

Japanese flowed ashore north and south of the shelling, turning toward the sound of it once they gained the coconut groves, spreading out through the trees and hunting quickly toward the battle, the tight hysteria rising in them, their eyes like wet flecks of black glass, and the bayonets locked on the rifles, the officers with their long swords drawn, wearing the white bandage of death about their brows. They filtered rapidly through the gray double-curved stems of the coconuts with the land crabs scuttering away before them.

They came trotting through a hot morning that smelled of mud and fish rotting on the beach and burned powder and oil smoke. They came close enough to feel the battering concussions of their air bursts before the timed barrage lifted. They were very near before a guerrillero smelled them. Then he saw them and fired a *bump-bump-bump* of automatic-rifle bullets.

There was no time for Hedges to save his radio or the supplies Zapanta had brought from Agusan. The cursing lumberman barely got Bowler and their men out of the fast-moving double envelopment, off the beach and through the coconuts, across the road and into the low hills behind the coast. Banana plants grew thickly over the first hills, heavy-fronded and swarming with insects, the ground beneath them a trash heap of rotting stalks. Once among the bananas, flight and pursuit slowed. Setting up ambushes but falling back, losing ground to the attack that had come out of the sea to crumple his flanks, Hedges was pushed yard by yard deeper into the hills, through the bananas toward the mountain jungle where no food grew, farther from the road and the beach, his supplies gone, his supply lines cut, and his communications lost.

"The bastards got my new pants," he kept telling Bowler. Hedges was furious at the loss of the first new clothing he had seen in two years.

ON THIS PARTICULAR morning, as the slow year turned, Fertig glanced at Hedges' message, under attack. Irritably, Fertig put it aside. He thought, if Hedges had considered the attack serious, Hedges would have said so. Therefore, the attack was not serious, and therefore Fertig would once again have to warn guerrilleros against transmission of superfluous messages. The radio net had enough to do without handling trivia. It never crossed Fertig's mind that perhaps those two words were all Hedges had time to send before the attack swept him off the beach, into the bananas, and toward the jungle. Nor was Fertig impressed by news that the Japanese seemed to be stirring everywhere in Mindanao that morning. The Japanese went through cycles of activity. More interesting was a coast-watcher's report of Japanese launches nearing Camiguin Island. If the Japanese landed there, they could command the submarine rendezvous sites all along the northwestern coast. Fertig studied reports from Manila that a Major General Harada had been appointed to clean out guerrilla resistance once and for all and was shortly to embark for Mindanao with an entire division specially trained in anti-guerrilla tactics. Since there was nothing Fertig could do to prevent the arrival of the General Harada, he merely passed the news to Australia. From Davao City, spies sent word of Japanese troopships arriving in the harbor. Japanese reinforcements were always landing at Davao. It was their staging base for the developing battles of the South Pacific. Fertig prepared his morning report for transmission to MacArthur's headquarters and returned to more-immediate worries: a study of the number of barrotos available, and the number under construction along the river, and the number of bags of palay available at Talacogon. For him, it was a morning much like any other.

It also seemed to be a morning like any other of the war to the people of a fishing village on Mindanao's northern coast. The young men had gone to sea before dawn, as usual. True, the times were very hard, and the village was not prosperous. But the village had never been particularly prosperous. It was enough to know the sea held fish and that the Japanese had once again permitted the men to go fishing.

On this morning, the naked children played as usual in the warm shallows beneath the houses that stood on stilts in the sea, and the people watched the customary Japanese patrol launch appear offshore at its accustomed hour. But, on this day, the launch suddenly turned to come speeding toward the village, throwing hissing sheets of spray that traced rainbows in the hot light. The women excitedly called the children out of the water, running across the bamboo catwalks from the houses to the beach, darting inland with their children. The old men remained behind.

That morning, the grass houses burned and the charred bits of them fell hissing into the shallows, the ashes drifting over the bodies of the old men lying on the sand in the clear water with the little fish beginning to inspect them, while the Japanese methodically hunted out the women who tried to hide in the brush behind the beach.

FARTHER SOUTH, in a town long garrisoned by Japanese, the storekeeper Augustin Picar and his wife, Juanita, ate their breakfast of cold rice as usual, unaware of what was going on in the street below. Japanese Thought Police had surrounded their little shop, armed with orders to arrest Filipinos at random. During the night, someone had torn down the posters offering a reward for information leading to the capture of General Fertig, dead or alive, and the Japanese town commander was curious to know who had done it. Wherefore, the terrified shopkeeper and his wife were plucked from their breakfast table, hurried through the early morning streets and into a room at Japanese headquarters.

Picar was bound and thrust to his knees on sharp splinters of bamboo. The Japanese wrestled his wife close in front of him, and one of the soldiers held Picar's head up by the hair so that he could watch the others strip her. They spread-eagled Juanita out in front of him, shackling her to the dirt floor. They showed Picar a length of metal. They pushed it into Juanita's vagina. They attached a wire to this. They clipped another wire to her left breast. They connected the wires to a machine. The watching soldiers giggled. They cranked the machine. Juanita screamed, and her body flopped in its shackles against the hard-packed earth. Picar fainted.

When Picar had been revived, the interpreter asked: "Who take down the signs?"

"Sir, sir, I do not know!" Picar sobbed with utter truth. "Oh, sir, she does not know either. Sir, we do not know one thing. Oh, sir, you have made a great mistake. Oh, sir, on my knees before God . . ."

The interpreter made a sign. The soldiers laughed. Picar surged in the arms of the men who held him jammed down on the bloodied bamboo splinters, his ears filled with the sound of his own shouts and the soldiers' laughter and the shrieks of Juanita, unable to tear his eyes from the wire leading into his wife's jumping body.

The translator explained that, each time Picar failed to give a satisfactory answer, Juanita would experience the raptures of Ineffable Love. Picar wildly searched in the disorder of his mind, only to come against the horrid reality of his ignorance. He sobbed that he knew nothing, nothing, whereupon Juanita screamed and flopped and slapped against the floor exactly like a fish. Desperately, Picar shouted the name of a man whom he believed to be safe in the hills.

"Ah, so," the interpreter said.

ON THIS MORNING, while Hedges' men fell wearily back through the bananas, their nostrils filled with the sweetness of rotting fruit and the fecal odor of the advancing Japanese; while Fertig busied himself with the primitive logistics of the guerrilla, and while a fishing village burned and Augustin Picar answered questions, the war was also fought in Australia, where Colonel Courtney Whitney prepared the daily Philippine reports for General MacArthur's personal attention. He acted on Wendell Fertig's request for an additional photograph.

"Fertig's evaluation of the C-in-C's photograph is as expected—it was undoubtedly the strongest weapon the *Narwhal* delivered—will prove of incalculable value in garnering united Moro support," Colonel Whitney wrote.

He dilated on Fertig's request that a duplicate photograph be sent to Mary Fertig in Colorado.

"This is a very human request that I recommend be approved," he wrote. ". . . His desire that his wife share in this tangible recognition of his service is but a natural reaction of the human spirit on which the survival of the guerrilla movement so largely depends."

It apparently did not occur to Colonel Whitney that the human spirit in question might have regarded confirmation in rank as an even more tangible recognition of services than receipt of an autographed picture of its supreme commander, for, when he read Fertig's iterated plea for commissions for the American guerrilleros, he suggested this be disapproved.

"Should these men be repatriated," he wrote, "after such action, we would have a much greater problem on our hands than we now have with repatriates with an enlisted status.

"Word has gone back to Fertig that his men, upon repatriation, revert to enlisted status upon arrival here. The return to enlisted routine is not to their liking, and consequently, such knowledge has done much to bolster morale in Fertig's area, and create a desire to remain there for the duration. This would not have been the case if these men could have returned in a commissioned status."

Having thus disposed of a trivial matter, Colonel Whitney gave deeper thought to the rest of Fertig's message. Japanese activity was increasing in Zamboanga, Misamis Occidental, Misamis Oriental, Cotabato, and Lanao provinces and everywhere along the coast. Japanese had landed at Maigo, and Colonel Hedges' radio had gone off the air. Further, Japanese landings had been made at Camiguin Island, which commanded the approaches to Macajalar, Gingoog, and Butu'un bays and the Agusan estuary. Fertig feared that Camiguin would be used as the springboard for a Japanese attack up the river but that, with increased supplies, he could hold out in the Agusan country until relief arrived. Fertig suggested the Navy net-control station and the guerrilla mint, both of which Sam Wilson operated in Lanao province, be moved to Agusan province. Because the Japanese were intensifying their patrols against guerrilla sailing craft, Fertig suggested that the *Narwhal* be used to bring Wilson, his Navy radio, and his mint to Agusan.

All this was most disturbing to Colonel Whitney, for it indicated that Fertig was out of touch with reality.

"Fertig may be departing from his highly mobile defense to concentrate too much on one headquarters area," Colonel Whitney wrote. "We should warn him not to expect early relief."

Colonel Whitney suggested Fertig be disabused of the notion that the Navy had more than one submarine to put at his disposal. Nor could the *Narwhal* be risked for the sake of moving radios around an island. The answer, Colonel Whitney wrote, was simply to send Fertig a duplicate Navy transmitter and a supply of printed money on the *Narwhal's* next supply mission, together with a warning that Fertig's use of supplies must be confined to normal operations—"to help him continue as he has been."

Having thus analyzed the problems of promotion, morale, strategy, and supply on Mindanao for the benefit of all concerned, Colonel Whitney set the wheels in motion for procurement of a photograph of the Supreme Commander, suitable for inscription and framing, to be sent (with covering letter) to Mrs. Wendell Fertig of Golden, Colorado. But he also set in train the collection of much larger supplies of munitions for the guerrilleros, for Colonel Whitney not only conceived the resistance movement to be a source of military information but to have potential combat value. Willoughby disagreed, but Colonel Whitney had his way.

WHILE COLONEL Whitney was thus engaged, the normal life of Mindanao continued under the hot violence of the tropical sun. Two additional Japanese troopships arrived in Davao harbor, the soldiers sweating on the burning iron decks and regarding the dilapidated shores of their new home without enthusiasm. Irish priests, inured to hardship after two years of nothing else, made their way through back trails to bring the mysteries of the mass into the rude huts of refugees, at the same time carrying to guerrilla bands military information gleaned from spies, orders from Fertig's remote headquarters, regulations promulgated by the fugitive Free Philippines Government, D-ration chocolate bars whose wrappers promised *I Shall Return,* gossip, medicines, and ammunition.

IN THE HILLS behind Maigo, the dead stalks beneath the bananas were burning with a thick yellow-gray smoke, with the flames beginning to tug at the clothing of bodies lying beneath the ripe fruit, while the hunt persisted in the farther hills. On the northern coast, a Japanese launch returned to sea carrying seven young women who had been judged the more promising of the women discovered hiding in the brush. In the headquarters of the Thought Police, the interpreter fanned himself as he listened patiently to the noises being made by the man Augustin Picar had believed to be safe in the hills. In the Agusan country, the day's early sunlight had given way to hard rain, and Fertig watched the compound become brimming puddles of muck, saw the Agusan filling yellow with mud and with half-sunken logs that drifted slowly, turning end for end. The rains were coming early this year and earlier each day, and the river was rising before its time, undercutting its banks, flooding its valley, drowning fields where food might have been planted.

As the days passed, the rain fell earlier, harder, and longer in the Agusan country, and the people could not remember a worse flood, or a season of less food. The trickle of Japanese reinforcements landing at Davao City became a spate. The harbor filled with troopships, and, as still more Japanese arrived, the war that had smoldered and flickered on the island, like the red heart of a stubborn fire burning under wet leaves, began to flare up in earnest, as when a dampened fire begins to lick on leaves it has dried. With new troops, the Japanese pushed outward from the areas they already held. They spread along the northwestern coast and down the Sayre Highway that splits the island in two. From strong points along the coast, they patrolled the inshore waters, watching for submarines, for bancas carrying guerrilla supplies, raiding the fishing fleets and the villages. Every move of the Japanese drew the increased fire of the better-armed guerrilleros, with result that what had happened in the town of the Picars was only the beginning.

It seemed that the Japanese had learned at last the truth of the Chinese saying that a guerrilla army is a fish and that the people are the water. Now, as the year turned, the Japanese sought at once to kill the fish and to poison the water. No longer did their patrols pass through barrios within Japanese lines for routine inspections or simple pillage. Purely for demonstrative purposes, the Japanese would torture a man in the street of his village to suggest the fate of the enemies of Divine Nippon. Japanese torture became increasingly marked by a sick sexuality, and it was visited indiscriminately upon men, women, and children, sometimes for no reason other than idle whim. They also tortured with a purpose, having confidence that, if torment drove a victim insane without enlarging the Japanese knowledge, it would make no difference. For another Filipino—man or woman, anyone would do—would next be put to the question, and, sooner or later, the Japanese would learn what they wished to know.

The answers were forthcoming soon enough—not because the Filipinos were an uncommonly weak race but because the Thought Police were uncommonly patient, industrious, and unthinkably imaginative. The Japanese listened to a welter of screams, piecing together bits of information until they knew enough to draw a circle on a map. The center of it was within fifteen miles of Fertig's exact location, although the Filipinos from whom the information had been extracted lived in another province and had as little personal knowledge of the Agusan country as they had of Africa. The Thought Police regarded the map with satisfaction. They had been right: Rumor was all-pervasive and accurate. Any Filipino would do, for purposes of interrogation. The terror spread.

IN THE HALF-DROWNED Agusan country, Fertig listened to the news of increasing Japanese atrocities with grim satisfaction.

"Well, that's fine," he told a horrified Evans. "If the Japs put a philanthropist in charge, where would we be? It's tough on the people, but it puts it up to them: They are either for us and against the Japanese, or they are against us and for the Japanese. If they help us, the Japs will get them. If they help the Japs, we'll kill them or plant the word that they've really been helping us, so that the Japs will kill them for us."

Neither Fertig nor the Japanese were concerned with the truth that terror, in the long run, always fails. For there was no future in Mindanao. There was only the present that grew imperceptibly worse, moving from violence to a deeper violence, meeting terror with terror, deepening in intensity as the slow year died. As the year turned, a quality of desperation was added to the war, as if civilians, guerrilleros, and Japanese alike had long been running on a treadmill but now somehow sensed that none could run much longer and so began to sprint in a frenetic effort to escape, which made the treadmill fly the faster beneath their feet, whereupon they began to run more wildly still. There was no hope, except at night, that incredible relief from the unendurable heat of the day. At night, the tropical world becomes beautiful, and the brilliance of a billion stars silvers what by day is merely squalid, and the shadows soften into velvet, and the land draws breath from the battering of the sun. On these nights at the end of the year, when it was increasingly necessary to find relief from the hot violence of the day, Filipino men, women, and children gathered at every house where there was still a radio that worked and wherever it seemed momentarily safe enough to listen. The punishment for listening to the radio was death, but greater than the Filipinos' fear was their need to hear words that promised life.

In tense silence, they listened to a friendly voice that spoke to them first in English, then in Tagalog—which most Filipinos did not understand. On one star-strewn night as the year died, the voice spoke with the boyish confidence of the American soul, which views all of life's more massive experiences from the perspective of a football game. It spoke of the great victory won that day in Russia.

The miles gained, the guns destroyed, the men killed, the prisoners taken, the men missing—all these facts, concepts, and lives were described as numbers, and the numbers were favorable that day in Russia. Things were also going well in the skies over France, where hundreds of American aircraft had apparently dropped thousands of tons of bombs, with never a miss, on specific targets. All the American aircraft had happily returned to their bases, after destroying not only the targets but also the scores of German aircraft that tried to intercept them. In Italy, the numbers were not quite so favorable, but the radio said (aware of no incongruity) the fighting was going according to plan. And, in the South Pacific, MacArthur's forces had gained new miles in the Solomons and in New Guinea. Eight medium bombers had attacked the Japanese stronghold in Rabaul, where twenty-three Japanese ships had been sunk.

To most of the Filipinos who listened for some word of hope, the radio voice of America might as well have been describing some incomprehensible game. To the relatively few Filipinos who knew where Russia, France, Italy, and New Guinea were, the news was disastrous.

"No one fights Germans in Germany," one told another fearfully. "They are fighting Germans in Russia and in Italy. It is good that our friend Macario is attacking in New Guinea, but look: The Japanese are so close to Australia. Yes, the Americanos send hundreds of airplanes to bomb France but not to Germany, and to bomb Rabaul, there are eight airplanes only. Tchk, the war will be very long, and, for us, maybe The Aid will not come."

All this was bad enough, but the radio next in a firm, manly way promised the Filipinos that the heroic sacrifices of the guerrilleros would be remembered as long as the love of liberty burned in human hearts and that the United States faithfully guaranteed to grant independence . . .

No one heard the rest of it. This was something all understood, and the word *independence* was enough.

"They wash their hands of us!" a Filipino cried. "They say they cannot help! They abandon us to our cruel fates!"

"Independence, horseshit!" a Filipino swore. "We want our friend Macario to return back and chase these sonsabits out of here!"

8

AS THE FIRST LONG shadows edged across the valleys of Mindanao, the muezzin's wailing call to prayer drifted through the still air. Dutifully, Busran Kalaw bent toward Mecca, repeating the centuries-old words to himself and to Allah. This done, he returned to his interrupted reading. It was his favorite author, the Japanese propaganda officer Major Hiramatsu, who this time wanted Busran to know that "even the United States mainland was bombed several times by Imperial Nipponese airplanes, and the Yankee, at present, are living in melancholy life.

"We are following the sublime wishes of God," Major Hiramatsu's letter assured Busran, "to build up Lanao and uplift the people here, who also desire to establish happy and contented homes. So we must shake hands and work together for the betterment of the province of Lanao. Come and visit us in Dansalan."

The Moro Datu sighed happily. Whenever the Japanese sent such a letter, Busran always replied. It seemed only decent, for the Japanese never wrote him offering peace unless they intended to attack him, and Busran was always appreciative of early warnings. Therefore, in the soft light of the still, short evening, Busran drafted his formal acceptance of the Japanese invitation.

"Who does not know the fates of Korea, Manchuria, etc., who were being made as subject people?" Busran wrote to Major Hiramatsu. "We do not want nor expect you to perform your slavery mission in our provinces, nor do we give you complete rest while here, to make you pay for the killings of our innocent men, women, and children, your looting and burning of looted homes with your army. You Japs have killed so many people in cool blood and have burned several hundred homes after it is looted. For all your plundering, we are trying also our best to score more from you once and again until peacetime, and by peacetime I mean when you are badly defeated. We are as daring a killer as you Nips, but we do it properly. Our ambushes will at least teach you lessons that killing is bad. It will make you respect the Moros, and you will behave better if we will go on with our fight. You can't shake hands with me, nor any alive Nip, now and forever, unless you and all your men around Lanao surrender formally. I have sworn on our sacred book, Koran, that I'll not surrender nor stop fighting until after I am dead and my forces gone so that I don't want to see or meet any alive Jap without killing him in any way possible. If I am as tricky and treacherous as you and your kind, I may have accepted your request and other Japanese officials, to come and meet somewhere without arms, so that I can kill or hang my enemy in cool blood. You have so many attacks to the American people which are all false. We know them more than you fellows. Their stay in the Philippines have been a blessing to the Filipinos and the Moros in particular, which we may not be able to reciprocate. This is not the time to narrate, but our status before this war were the convincing proofs of America's benevolent attitude toward the upliftment of the Filipino race in the same level with the other nations.

"I'll advise you and other Japanese officials to stop writing so many letters so we'll go on with our historical drama—until General MacArthur and his forces will come to liberate us, or even if they never come, still I'll always give the best I could to entertain the Japs with blades and gun salutes to make your short stay in Lanao more lively and interesting as you probably have not expected. My dear friend, this is the era of the supreme test to decide the fates of the Great and Mightiest Japanese Imperial Forces, samurai, versus the Fighting Bolo Battalion Unit, Maranao warriors, in this particular spot of the Philippines. In other words, it's a struggle between the kris with a few rusty guns, and the modern rifles, artillery pieces, mortars, armored trucks, tanks, and planes. I am a tough Maranao warrior by birthright, so with my men, and you are the samurai. We are ready to fight and die against an overwhelming odds, whether America will or will not compensate us, our widows, and children if they ever come. So stop writing and try hiking to attack us so that we will have some more war trophies. Your friend and enemy, Busran Kalaw, Commanding General, Fighting Bolo Battalion Unit, Maranao Militia Force."

The Moro's turbaned head nodded contentedly as he reread what he had written. It occurred to him that there was still something else to say, but the light was fading rapidly, and he decided against a postscript. He would include his further thoughts in the next letter. The Moro lord looked upon his darkening valley, watching the first fruit bats flitting among the trees. Someone in the Moro camp was playing a nose flute, and, beneath the sound of this and the voices of men talking, there was a steady scraping. As men talked together around the light of cookfires, they methodically sharpened their krises on footstones, joking and laughing quietly among themselves. To the Moros, the war was entirely satisfactory.

THE GUERRILLEROS who guarded the river mouth knew it was hopeless. The sound grew heavily in the darkness, and then the men who watched could see the black shadows of the four armored launches feeling their way among the blacknesses of the night river. The guerrilleros fired, and the launches replied. The flashes were orange in the night. The launches moved steadily into the shadows, but the sound of motors grew louder, and the guerrilleros watched the first of the troopships bulk hugely into the night. Already, the countryside was emptying. The people who lived on the north bank of the Agusan were moving toward Surigao, and those who lived on the south bank made for the hills beyond the river plain, taking with them those who lived on the plain, the whole countryside emptying and stumbling away from the river in the blackness before dawn.

Two troopships followed the launches. By first light, the flotilla was winding around the meandering bends below Butu'un. Troops were put ashore, pushing rapidly through the thin beach defenses. By noon, Japanese patrols were moving through the deserted city, and the troopships were unloading at Butu'un's docks. The next morning, the Japanese were moving rapidly and somewhat carelessly across the dusty plain above Butu'un when McClish said, "Fire!"

The Army's 37-millimeter cannon was not, properly speaking, a fieldpiece. It was designed to stop the tank of World War I, and, despite its abject failure in the Spanish Civil War, when all of the future Western combatants of World War II tested their weapons upon Spaniards, the 37-millimeter gun was still the standard antitank rifle of the United States Army. To the guerrilleros, however, the slender cannons were enormous, and, to the Japanese, they were a complete surprise. They were the first United States artillery to speak in the Philippines since the fall of Corregidor, and, with them, a jubilant McClish, who had won and lost and won this country before, blew the Japanese back into Butu'un. At that point, the Japanese called for air support.

Meanwhile, entirely unaware of these events, an armored warship steered for the Agusan river mouth.

Waldo Neveling seemed a barefoot Viking in tattered modern dress, standing by the wheel, the sea wind tugging at his open shirt and ash-blond hair. He leaned easily to meet the motion of the banca as it flew over the slow sea hills like a low-hunting bird, the two big sails goose-winged and the outriggers dipping and rising, stitching streaks of white bubbles across the clean seas.

Filipino riflemen sprawled on the narrow deck, content in the sun, laughing when flung spray came pattering over them to dry almost at once, listening to the rush of water beneath the shallow keel and to the sound of wool and cordage working. In the galley, the Chinese cook was pulling a chicken to tiny pieces and talking to Elmer, who thought he was a human being. Elmer swam with the crew and slept under blankets at night, and, when he met other pigs, he had nothing to do with them. Forward, in the shade of the canvas that shrouded the 20-millimeter antiaircraft cannon, the first officer Domingo Alvarez and the mestizo mechanic Luiz watched the twin masts sweep back and forth across the trade-wind clouds and decided that, of all the ways to go to war, this was by far the best. This did not mean they preferred cruising in a racing banca to fighting Japanese. Rather, they hoped to fight, to catch a Japanese launch, to sweep its decks with automatic rifles and the .50-caliber machine gun, to sink it with the cannon and drown the survivors. The *So What* went looking for trouble, but, when there was no trouble, there was the clean sea wind and the hiss of the banca over the swells. It was better than hacking through muddy jungles or beneath banana leaves or wading nipa swamps, and, after the fighting at sea, there was just as much tuba and as many girls for the sailors as for those who fought on land. The sailors brought the coastal people arms and supplies from Fertig's headquarters and went hunting launches, and, in return, the people gave the sailors fiesta, and the girls gave themselves.

The only man not completely at ease was Tony, the pilot. He was a middle-aged brown man who now stood beside the blond German captain, nervously studying the gliding-by dense green hills of Mindanao as if making his first landfall, although he had been a government pilot for twenty years.

"Sair, we must turn now," he pleaded.

Neveling regarded him with sardonic amusement, understanding and enjoying Tony's anxiety. When the Japanese first came, Tony had served *them* as pilot. They made him do it, Tony said, but the guerrilleros who had captured Tony had not believed this. In token of their suspicions, they had buried him standing, up to his chin in sand, and left him to experience the sun, the thirst, the land crabs, and the insects until he died. Luckily, one of Fertig's Americans, Robert Spielman, had shortly afterwards come across the still-alive head in the sand and talked to it, with the result that Tony had been dug up and recruited as pilot for the guerrilla navy. His experience had made Tony very serious about his pilotage, for he believed that, if he made one mistake, he would be replanted and that no one would again interrupt the land crabs and the insects.

"Now now, huh?" Neveling teased. "Not need to turn now, yes?"

"Oh, sair, even now," Tony said passionately. "There is the point; if we go too far, there is plenty coral."

Neveling shouted; the sailors sprang to life; the port sail was brought over, and Neveling laid the banca on a broad reach for land. The ship cut through the shallowing water to fetch the Agusan river mouth, tacking up the channel under sail until the current quickened and the wind fell, then entering the river under power. The puffing diesel, like the circular saw shields and the heavy guns, was another of the banca's surprises.

After the thrum of wind in the shrouds and the burst and hiss of the sea, there was now only the hot, empty silence of the noonday jungle, broken by the rhythmic pumping of the diesel. The *So What* shouldered up against the current flying the United States and the Philippine flags, past the rising banks at Maugahay and the wreck of an interisland steamer, but no one waved from the shore. The docks and the riverbanks were empty.

"Vhwere iss effrybotty?" Neveling muttered to himself, thinking the country had too much the look and feel of other countries he had known. Since the early twenties, Neveling had fought all the way across the face of Asia, and, in the Asian countries when war came, the morale of the people disintegrated, and the people fled, and the country had the look and feel of something used and wasted. But, in the Philippines, the morale of the people had gone up, rather than down; the Filipino farmers had voluntarily shared their food with the guerrilleros; the people gave the guerrilleros welcome everywhere and crowded around them whenever they appeared, and, to a soldier of fortune like Neveling, this relationship of soldier and civilian was as unique as it was inexplicable. It was the strangest thing he had ever seen, and he had told Fertig as much. But now as the *So What* moved past Nasipit, her sails hanging slack and the diesel belching blackly into the stifling air, no barrotos glided out to meet her. No woman beat laundry with sticks on the sandbars. The town was deserted, and the lower Agusan country had that wasted look, and the Filipinos aboard the *So What* gripped their rifles and peered into the tangle of muddy vegetation that steamed in the sun. As Maugahay fell astern, Domingo and Luiz removed the canvas covers from the cannon and the machine gun. Domingo came aft to speak with Neveling.

"Sair," Domingo said, "there should be plenty people here. But there is not one. You have seen no one, yes?"

"Ja, a funny business," Neveling said. He rubbed his blond-stubbled jaw. Fertig's radio message had ordered the *So What* to Butu'un to pick up munitions for guerrilleros in Surigao. That had been three days ago, and, in all that time, the *So What* had been at sea. Neveling looked dourly at a silent marsh.

"In Butu'un, ve will find oudt vhat happens," he said.

But they never reached Butu'un. They came upriver only as far as the bend below the town, when two ragged boys burst from cover to race out on a sandbar, calling, "Hi! Hindi! Oh, sair! Plenty, plenty Hapons!"

Instantly, Neveling swung the wheel over. The slack sails flapped emptily as their booms creaked across deck with the motion. The boys dived back into the brush, but Neveling did not see them disappear. He gave the wheel to Domingo and shouted at Luiz to open up the diesel and ran to the 20-millimeter cannon. The automatic riflemen knelt behind their shields, and the *So What* dropped quickly down the current with the diesel racing. Where the river widens above Nasipit, there was a Japanese steamer loaded with troops, coming up the channel. The Japanese saw the *So What's* flags, and no one on either ship waited for an order to fire.

A completely happy man, Neveling took the Japanese ship's bridge in the cannon's ring sights. The shot slammed home; Neveling could see the bright wink as the shell burst, and he cheered himself when the Japanese radio mast came crashing down. The *So What's* heavy machine gun was battering away, a steady, heavy hammer sound amid the racket of rifle fire and the ring of bullets striking the steel saw blades and the sharp cracks of bullets hitting wood. Neveling could see the Japanese soldiers scurrying for cover behind the steamer's gunwales, and he concentrated on the bridge and pumped shells into it, cursing when they failed to explode, cheering when they did. The automatic cannon was a sheer delight to Neveling, who was a remarkable marksman with it, but, at such a range, no one could miss. He threw shell after shell into the bridge, wanting to make sure of the radio and hoping to disable the Japanese ship's controls and kill her officers. Bullets slit through the air around him, and Neveling ignored them. He felt the cannon's base was some protection, and meanwhile he was lost in the trance of exultation his ancestors had known ten centuries earlier.

The Chinese cook opened the galley door, took one look at the

Japanese steamer looming hugely out of the river, and slammed the door. In that instant, Elmer scrabbled squealing across the deck and nestled alongside a rifleman crouched behind a shield. The pilot, Tony, was huddled against a rail, aft, and Domingo was lying on the deck, steering with his feet. It was necessary for the *So What* to leave the channel for the shallows to get past the steamer, and, from time to time, Domingo would raise his head to see where he was going.

The *So What* slid along the river edge, past the steamer, and downstream, but the steamer swung slowly around to give chase. At the same time, the Japanese opened fire with a deck cannon, and a geyser of mud erupted off the *So What*'s starboard bow at the same instant Neveling heard the splitting crack of the cannon. The range widened beyond the limits of rifle fire as the *So What* hugged the edges of the river mouth, clinging to the shallows where the Japanese could not follow. There was no wind. The wind would not come again until late afternoon. With a wind, the banca could outrace the steamer into the open sea. She could not outrun the steamer under power, for the Japanese ship, in deep water in the center of the estuary, was in the position of the hub of a wheel. The Japanese needed to move only slightly to keep the *So What* under fire as the banca tried to flee around the rim of the semicircular bay toward the sea.

"Take her ashore!" Neveling shouted to Domingo.

To the mechanic Luiz, Neveling said, "Vun lucky shot, and ve are finish. There iss no need to kill also the sailors und the cook. Get those people off. Tell them to walk to the point, and, if ve are still alife by five o'clock, ve pick them up at the point. Chust you, Domingo und the soldiers vill stay aboardt."

During the slow afternoon, the two ships traded slow shot for shot, the Japanese cannoneers overshooting and Neveling concentrating on the steamer's bridge and cabin. Neveling felt an icy hand close around his heart when the aircraft came. The Japanese radio must still be working, he thought, seeing the fighters come boring in low across the bay, arrowing toward the *So What*. But the planes shot on through the heavy air, steering toward Butu'un, oblivious of the ships below.

At five o'clock, the *So What* had worked around the bay to the point, the Japanese following slowly on their interior lines, and at the stroke of five, as if by magic, the *So What*'s bullet-torn sails filled with a gathering wind. The Japanese held back, expecting the *So What* to turn once more toward the river mouth, but, with the freshening breeze, the banca headed into the open sea.

On the cabin roof, a Filipino was waving his rifle and a clenched fist, shouting into the wind.

"Come on and fight, you sonsabits!" he shouted at the steamer, now falling well astern and undershooting the darting, veering banca. "You come on, we kill you!"

"Hey, Amado!" Neveling called. "The fact iss, ve are the vuns who are runnink avay!"

The soldier saw Neveling's powder-blackened face laughing at him, and he grinned shyly and then laughed at himself. But then, very seriously, he said: "Yes, sair, that is true, but, if they could catch us, we would kill them."

THE AIRCRAFT NEVELING had seen flashed low across the thick green treetops of the Agusan country, skimmed the rice fields, and dove, shooting, at the guerrillero defense line in which McClish had entrenched his cannons. Another flight, this one of twin-engined bombers, swept in higher overhead. One by one, single bombers left the formation to slant down upon the barrios strung like beads along the winding river. The distant thudding of their bombs could be felt in Talacogon, where Fertig worked in his new headquarters.

Talacogon consisted of a wooden church with a tin roof, a straggle of bamboo houses hidden among palms and bananas, and a two-room frame schoolhouse next to a weed-choked cemetery of cement crypts. The schoolhouse was Fertig's office, and now, as he read McClish's radio reports and listened to the mutter of the bombing downriver, he congratulated himself.

Despite flood waters, a scarcity of launches, barrotos, and cargadores, Fred Varney and Cecil Walter had managed to clear all supplies from the lower river before the Japanese appeared. McClish was holding the line at Vitos. There was nothing left for the Japanese to find in Butu'un or in Esperanza, and they would not yet have learned of his presence in Talacogon. Fertig felt his luck was running well, although it was the sort of good fortune a man experiences when he breaks a leg instead of his neck. It was unfortunate that there had been no way to warn Neveling. Port Lamon said Neveling had already sailed. Fertig guessed the German would be entering the Agusan now. He put the matter out of his mind. Neveling would have to look out for himself. The important thing was, the munitions Neveling was to have picked up in Butu'un had been safely brought out of the city before the Japanese arrived.

A delicious scent of roasting pig hung in the still air of the school-house compound. The pig was part of the good luck. Indeed, it seemed a miracle when the villagers came to him that morning, bringing a spindly, dejected young boar, with the priest and the barrio teniente leading the procession.

"Sair, it is for you and the U.S.A. who help us Filipinos," the teniente had said.

The teniente spoke seriously of the overflowful hearts, of anguished tears, and of the mixed-up bloods of the brave fallen, while the pig grunted disconsolately. It must have been the last animal left in Tala-cogon, saved for some unimaginable day of happiness, but the villages gave it to Fertig as though consecrating a sacrifice. And also, Fertig suspected, to establish the basis for a claim on his future services.

It was just after midday when Fertig sat down to dine at a work-bench set up as a table in his office. Because of the nature of the gift and because the pig constituted the first fresh meat Fertig's men had seen in days, he broke a rule and invited his staff to dine. Pedro, the houseboy, set the smoking, golden-brown pig before Fertig when the noise burst upon them all.

The bomber came over at tree level, the backwash of its propellers tossing the leaves and buffeting the flimsy schoolhouse, coming low and fast and unheard until it was on them, and the first stick of bombs walked across the schoolhouse compound. One instant there was a group of officers laughing and joking as they sat down to a feast, and, in the next, there was the rushing racket of the plane that was all a part of the ground shaking and spurting and the whole wall of the schoolhouse strangely dissolving and men shouting.

Evans ran crazily around a smoking crater and into the weedgrown cemetery. He dived for a slit trench dug beside one of the cement sar-cophagi in which Filipinos are laid above ground. He fell with a breath-bursting jar on the body of Pedro, who had preceded him, and, before Evans caught his breath, a body hurtled onto his back. It was the new officer, Lieutenant Commander Wheeler, who had no idea how he had got out of the schoolhouse but who soon realized that the slit trench was so badly overpopulated that his back was exposed.

Wheeler scrambled off of Evans and wedged himself beside a cement crypt that seemed to promise some protection. Evans, who hastily looked up to see who or what had fallen on him, saw Wheeler nestling beside the sarcophagus, patting it, and distinctly heard Wheeler say, "Move over, old fellow, I'm sure there is room for two of us in there."

The bomber turned on a wing and came sliding back, and the earth shook as the second stick of bombs walked across the barrio of Talacogon. Then, quickly as it had come, the aircraft vanished. Evans pressed against the trembling body of Pedro beneath him and lay there long after the noise passed, until he heard Wheeler say, "My God. Look at that."

Evans was shaking badly, but he got his head up.

"What?" he whispered.

"The Old Man," Wheeler said emptily, staring at what was left of the schoolhouse.

The side wall of the building was torn off and lay in a jumble with blown papers scattered through it, and Evans could look into Fertig's office as if it were a stage set.

There, incredibly still sitting at the table, was Fertig. He was picking splinters and dirt from the still-smoking carcass of the pig.

Wheeler and Evans saw him sitting there, picking the dirt away, burning his fingers on the hot pig and blowing on them, wiping his hands on his trousers, and then picking away at the pig.

He's crazy, Evans decided. He's as crazy as any of them.

"Are you all right?" Wheeler asked.

Fertig looked up from the pig.

"They made a goddamned mess," he said. "But we can still eat it."

"You weren't hurt?" Evans asked.

"Larry," Fertig said, "I told you before that, if it doesn't have your name on it, it can't hurt you."

In utter silence, the two officers climbed into the ruin of the schoolhouse and sat down at the table as in a dream, watching Fertig carve the pig. Without a word, Pedro reappeared to serve the plates that Fertig filled.

9

EVERY DAY, JAPANESE aircraft came boring up the Agusan, hitting all the river towns one after the other. The only surprising thing about the Japanese was the stolidity of their tactics. Their aircraft always came at the same time, and they always started with the downriver towns and worked their way up. It was Misamis all over again, with everyone leaving the towns for the bombing and returning immediately thereafter. The only difference was, the Japanese came twice a day. But the Japanese infantry attack upriver from Butu'un barely moved.

Fertig had always suspected McClish's merits as a commander, yet here was McClish, holding the Japanese before Vitos for days on end, skillfully containing the advance, disputing every yard. Whatever Mc-Clish's shortcomings may have been—and Fertig was never able to learn what they were—there was clearly nothing wrong with McClish as a combat leader.

For nearly a month, the war seemed to hang still for Fertig, despite the daily bombings and the inchworm Japanese advance upriver, and there was good news from every other province of Mindanao.

Japanese activity had slacked off in Misamis Occidental, where Bowler was now ensconced, able to assume command at need. Bowler reported work progressing on the Farm Projects. The Japanese did not seem to understand these projects. Apparently, they thought the clearings in the forest were actually intended to be farms and looked forward to collecting the harvests. In fact, they were landing strips that Fertig was preparing for United States aircraft against MacArthur's return.

For the first time in three months, there was direct word from Hedges in Lanao. The lumberman had lost his radio and all his supplies in the

Japanese attack that thrust him off the beach, but Zapanta had somehow got through with new equipment for him, and Hedges—though penned in the hills—was as virulently alive as ever.

There was good news, too, of Neveling. Rounding the Surigao Straits, the soldier of fortune fought off two Japanese launches, badly damaging one and killing seventeen of her crew, and driving the other away. The following day, Neveling was attacked by two more launches as he neared Port Lamon, and this time he set one afire while the other fled. On making port, the *So What* was attacked by an airplane. Incredibly, the German shot it down with his 20-millimeter cannon. As far as Fertig knew, it was the only instance in history when a sailing ship destroyed an aircraft, but, more important, Neveling had salvaged the newest Japanese bombsight from the wreck. Fertig planned to send the instrument out on the next submarine.

In every unoccupied area, the civil government continued to hold court. Despite increased shortages of every commodity and the virtual ruin of interisland trade, the price line was maintained on Mindanao. Fertig suspected the fact that black marketeers were shot out of hand had much to do with this, but it was good to believe that the people's faith in themselves played at least some part. Meanwhile, letters, stamped with the blue stamps of the Free Philippines Government, were carried by post office couriers. Fanners sold palay to the Government at Fertig's pegged price, and the Government rationed it to guerrilleros and civilians. Villagers wove nipa roofing, and the Government bought it to disguise the galvanized iron of the schools and churches that, winking in the sun, would otherwise guide Japanese aircraft In all the unoccupied areas, Josefa Capistrano's Women's Auxiliary Service made cloth, bullets, and bandages and shared the labor of the men.

By mid April, the news seemed even better. The Japanese attack upriver had finally reached a landing opposite Amparo, but, instead of crossing the Agusan, they withdrew downstream to Butu'un. This was indeed fortunate, for, if the Japanese had taken Amparo, they would have captured the guerrilleros' vital store of fuel oil, salvaged from the bunkers of the *Mayon*. Fertig realized he should long ago have sent someone to the Pacific coast to develop additional supplies of coconut oil against the possible loss of the bunker fuel. He cursed himself for not remembering there is no such thing in war as having too much of anything, particularly of oil. That was the simplest thing to have remembered, for, without oil, the diesel generators would not run. Without them, no electricity; without electricity, no radio contact with Australia. Without communications, no hope. But amazingly enough, the Japanese had once again turned back from the brink of victory, and Fertig felt his luck running strong. He was lucky, and the news good.

And then the news abruptly turned bad.

"He did *what?*" Fertig nearly shouted, interrupting a courier's report.

"Yes, sair, the Hapons were bery near; he had much fright. Besides, it was for the ship, only."

"It is no more? It is all finish?" Fertig demanded.

"Yes, sair," the courier said. "It is no more. It is all use up."

For a terrible moment, Fertig digested the enormous fact that one of his Americans had dumped all sixty tons of the *Mayon's* bunker fuel into the Agusan as the Japanese came near. The American had not known that the radio section had been using bunker fuel for months in their diesels, although the engineering handbooks said it could not be done. Believing it useless, the American officer had therefore not tried to carry it away, but, obeying orders to leave nothing behind, he had dumped it into the river. Since stupidity is never a crime in any army, it is never punished. Fertig merely swore to himself never to give that man another position of the slightest responsibility. But, before Fertig could recover from the shock of this disaster, worse news came crowding in.

The last Japanese attack toward Amparo had so badly frightened some of McClish's officers that they had fled into the mountains, meanwhile re-porting that all was lost on the river. While the truth was eventually estab-lished—and indeed reached Fertig first—the result had been a preliminary flood of field orders from McClish, all based on erroneous information furnished by these officers, many of whom had fled from empty rumors without having actually seen the Japanese whose presence they reported to McClish. The tiredness that Evans had feared had given way at last to panic, and McClish's command was in a snarl.

New reports now made clear why Bowler had been able to begin work in Misamis Occidental and why Hedges was alive. General Harada had arrived to supervise the systematic destruction of Fertig's guerrilla. Taking first things first, the Japanese commander had begun by pulling troops out of Zamboanga, Misamis Occidental, and Lanao provinces, and these troops had been all this time at sea, sailing completely around the island, and were now coming ashore on the eastern coast of Surigao province. Another Japanese force was steaming up the east coast of Davao province, shelling the coastal towns as it came, occasionally sending troops ashore to loot and burn, and was even now entering Port Lamon. A third Japa-nese force, commanded by General Harada, had come up the Agusan to join the troops that had returned to Butu'un. The thrust toward Amparo had been a reconnaissance in force, made by second-class troops. General Harada was bringing warriors specially trained in jungle war, whose mission was twofold: to destroy the guerrilla and prepare defenses against the possible attempt of the United States Army to return to the Philippines.

With the Agusan blocked downstream to the west and Japanese landing along the east coast from Davao to Surigao and coming ashore at Port Lamon, Fertig was caught in a vast version of that painfully standard Japanese maneuver, the double envelopment. His position on the river was now totally pointless, since there was no possibility of arranging submarine rendezvous on either coast to make use of river transport. Future rendezvous would have to be held off the southern coast of Mindanao, with the goods painfully dragged over mountain trails. When news of Japanese landings came from Port Lamon, Fertig frantically canceled a rendezvous scheduled off that port. This not only meant no additional supplies for Fertig in the foreseeable future but also that his radio section now had to send, as messages, a flood of low-priority information that would have otherwise gone out as mail on the submarine. It meant that the diesel generators would drink fuel faster than it could be replaced by the manufacture of coconut oil. The last news from Port Lamon added that Waldo Neveling's *So What* had been captured ashore, that the German was believed to have escaped into the hills, but that no one knew for sure.

Worse, Fertig's guerrilleros were no longer taking chances. Where once they had ambushed, they now waited for the Japanese to come to find them. The report of one guerrillero regiment was typical.

In this, as in all cases, the word *regiment* was a military courtesy used to describe an armed band. This one was based near the Sayre Highway. Its mission was to harass Japanese movement on the highway. In the past nine months, the regiment had made sixteen attacks on Japanese garrisons, had arranged eighteen ambushes along the road—most of these during the first of those nine months—and their patrols had collided with Japanese patrols on eleven occasions. The balance sheet was good: 270 Japanese killed, 219 wounded. Only twenty guerrilleros had been hurt, seventeen killed, four captured, and one missing. The one that was missing was probably the coward. But the important fact was that this regiment had *accepted forty-one Japanese attacks on its positions,* and that was not guerrilla. Guerrilleros never received attacks in Fertig's book. They always either attacked or ran, but never defended. That regiment was losing its will to attack and was allowing itself to be surprised.

Together with this story of disaster, the real bombing began. No longer did lone, light bombers strike the river towns. A squadron of six heavy bombers began methodically to obliterate them, beginning with Esperanza. Days later, Esperanza was a pile of smoking sticks. Then the bombers struck the next village. Thanking God for the Japanese lack of imagination, Fertig sent Nick Capistrano farther up the Agusan to prepare a new headquarters at Waloe. By the time the bombers reached Talacogon, where they dropped seventy bombs among the flimsy houses at the first strike, Fertig's headquarters was in motion, with most of its equipment moved. Nearly everything had been cleared from Talacogon by the time the bombers returned, but, this time, the destruction was complete. Few things among the jumbled debris were recognizable for what they might once have been. One was a torn and charred scrap of cloth, fluttering among the ruins of the schoolhouse. It was the remnant of a cutwork tablecloth that had once graced the principal table on the saint's day of the barrio fiesta; it had been the gift of love of the ladies of Talacogon to the American general who had come to protect them from the terror of the Japanese.

10

IT WAS AT WALOE that Fertig's guerrilla began to fall apart. Waloe was a clearing on high ground in a jungle surrounded by a swamp. It was the center of an area of Magahats, a collection of pagan bandits and Christian outlaws who had been fighting against the prewar Philippine Constabulary for a decade and who would gladly spear anyone for the sake of the clothes he wore. While the Magahats were not a serious military problem to the heavily armed guerrilleros, Fertig nevertheless had to patrol against them, and, for the first time since he came to Mindanao, Fertig found himself in an area where he could expect nothing from the populace.

Not that there was much to expect. There was even less to eat than there had been at Talacogon, where the diet had run heavily to bamboo shoots. At Waloe, the diet consisted of edible ferns, a few muddy fish, coconuts, bamboo, whatever kind of meat could be found flying, hopping, or wriggling, and a few camotes and a ration of rice or corn. The rice and most of the camotes and coconuts was packed in. Cargadores, starting in Misamis Oriental, crept through 120 miles of Japanese-infested country, then labored over 200 miles of mountainous jungle to bring a few sacks of palay to Waloe. The journey took a month.

Finally, despite the adjacent jungle, Waloe offered no real concealment, for the heavy volume of radio traffic that Fertig's headquarters handled made Japanese triangulation a simple matter, even with their primitive radio-detection equipment. Moreover, as Fertig moved deeper into the island, radio transmission to Australia became more difficult, requiring the precise placement, on high, exposed ground, of heavy V-beam antennas. Japanese bombers, flying to the pinpoint determined by triangulation, had only to look for the branching arms of the antennas.

Meanwhile, Japanese reinforcements continued to pour into Cagayan and Davao harbors, and the map of Mindanao began increasingly to resemble the body of a child coming down with a severe case of measles. When the first rash appears, the child is said to have red spots. But as the rash continues to spread, the child may be said to be red, with occasional white blotches—and this could be said for large areas of the map of Mindanao. On the body of Mindanao, however, the red and the white areas were in seething movement. What turned red for a few hours would turn white again when the Japanese moved on. Only the large Japanese bases were permanently red, while the complexion of the surrounding country constantly changed as Japanese patrols filtered ceaselessly through it.

Governed by Fertig's radio command station, the guerrilla persisted in and around the moving Japanese. But couriers who once walked confidently along back-country trails now stepped with furtive care. Supply parties were forced to long, hazardous detours. Guerrilla organizations were being hit by surprise attacks. The shadow civil government was functioning, but its hand-printed cash was running short. Far worse, and infinitely ominous, was the report that the Chinese merchants, those accurate weathervanes of Asia, were refusing credit to the guerrilla.

A solitary man, divorced by his position from the lonely perils his coastwatchers knew and from the venomous, sudden short-range combats on the trails; a friendless man because of the necessity to command, Fertig felt weariness sweeping over him. Increasingly, his diary entries said, "I am so tired." He hoped his weariness did not show, but it was becoming more difficult for him to appear newly starched, crisp, and competent while his world was quite obviously collapsing.

And, at this time, MacArthur's headquarters made things no easier. The quick radio operators in Australia who had been handling Fertig's traffic were replaced by new personnel who could not receive at the guerrilleros' sending rate of thirty coded groups per minute.

"Don't they know what they're doing to us?" Evans demanded. "Can't you get them to put a couple of good operators on our traffic?"

Evans' complaint was not trivial. Fertig's organization was responsible for collecting and transmitting all military intelligence coming out of the Philippine Islands. Since the new operators in Australia could receive only at a rate of ten coded groups per minute, this meant that Fertig's radiomen now had to remain three times longer on the air at any one time than they had before—thus wasting precious fuel, thus giving the Japanese so much longer to obtain fixes on their positions. It also meant that messages began to pile up, to move days late and then a week late.

When Fertig angrily passed Evans' demand to MacArthur, Australia replied that Fertig's complaint was groundless, for each of the new operators in Australia had successfully passed the army course in field communications, which demanded a reception speed of ten groups per minute.

Fertig shook his head. Supreme Headquarters apparently lived in a world of its own. For that matter, what could they have been thinking of when they sent him the four radio operators who had come on the last submarine? They were first of all too slow. Worse, they were American-born Filipinos. They were exactly as much at home in the Philippines as an American of English ancestry would be at home if suddenly put down in a Celtic-speaking corner of Wales. Fertig took one look at them and realized they were a disaster, but he did not know how much of a disaster they were until the day Captain Lagman came bursting into his office, saying, "Sair! You must let me shoot him!"

There was no trace of Lagman's usual droll humor in the Filipino's face. He was plainly a brave, intelligent, angry man who very badly needed to kill one of the new American-Filipinos, and Fertig wondered why.

"Because, sair, that brown American called me a *native* and he is more black than I am!"

It was a mark of the tension that grew at Waloe that Fertig was not easily able to restore Lagman's normal cheerfulness, that the incident was deadly serious. And Evans was quite serious, too, when the Japanese bombers found their way to Waloe.

"I can't help it," Evans said. "Look, I'll take my chances on combat patrol. I just can't take it any more. Don't tell me again how safe I am in a foxhole. I won't believe you. I'm scared of those things, and I can't help it."

The answer Fertig found was to relieve Evans of his duties and send him to Cabadbaran, one of the more-or-less–constant white blotches on the shifting map. It was a municipality north of Butu'un, where Sam Wilson was supervising Navy communications and acting as finance officer. Wilson's area was under attack, and his radios were malfunctioning. Fertig reasoned that Evans could repair the radios and put new heart into the Manila millionaire, whom Fertig always regarded as an invaluable but reluctant dragon of the guerrilla. Further, Evans would be freed from the terror of the air raids, and the trip would give Evans ample opportunity to satisfy his thirst for adventure. Sending a man into combat seemed an odd way of giving him a furlough but, if that was what Evans wanted, there was nothing easier to grant.

With Evans gone, Fertig felt more lonely than ever. Cut off from supplies with Japanese forces closing on him, penned in an inhospitable area on starvation rations, commanding no headquarters garrison of his own but dependent for his protection on guerrilla units that were retreating, his overland communications tenuous and his radio communications seriously threatened by a diminishing stock of oil and a shortage of magnet wire, Fertig found little reason to hope.

The sole remaining source of coconut oil was the municipality of Bislig, on the east coast. The Japanese had occupied every other east coast municipality, and Fertig knew it was only a matter of time until they moved into Bislig. Then there would be no more oil. Then, silence.

Before that time, it might be possible to transfer command of the guerrilla to Bowler at Misamis Occidental, where the Japanese pressure was less intense. Indeed, Fertig knew it would be wise to do so at once, but he could not bring himself to let go of the organization he had created. He had grown so used to command that he did not believe anyone was as capable as himself. He took what hope he could in the fact that the Filipinos of Mindanao were bending, rather than breaking, under pressure. Unless the Japanese succeeded in killing every Filipino who held death preferable to surrender, the guerrilla would continue whether The Aid came or not.

Somehow, the guerrilla would go on until the end, but Fertig could not hope to see the end of it. Increasingly, he withdrew into himself, pushing more and more of the routine administration onto his new staff officer, Wheeler. He devoted the empty time he thus created to rereading the two books he had carried with him through everything: the life of Richelieu and *Gone With the Wind.*

Fertig felt he had largely succeeded in playing Gray Eminence to a banana republic, subtly arranging the appointment and dismissal of officials, suggesting when it was obvious he was really commanding, allowing others to appear as instigators of his policies, controlling the politics and economy of a nation, while waging war. If his world was crumbling, at least he could say he had built it, and he was not going to let go of it until there was nothing left of it to grasp. Until the end, he would be like Scarlett O'Hara. It was the last section of *Gone With the Wind* that he read most carefully. He agreed with Scarlett that what did not bear thinking about today, he would think about tomorrow.

Fertig also read over and again the letters from Mary that the submarines had brought. Now there would be no more submarines, no more letters.

At the end of each worsening day, Fertig turned to prayer. His prayer was always the same each night: "God, give us time."

THROUGHOUT THE ISLANDS, this prayer was echoed in a thousand ways by equally lonely men of Fertig's command, including one whom Fertig had never seen but knew only as an indication on the southern tip of the map of Luzon Island.

Gerald Chapman was a coastwatcher who lived alone on a hill. He was an old man of 23 who, weak from malnutrition, picked his way carefully each morning to a sea cliff overlooking the San Bernardino Straits. He was also weak from malaria, weak from beri-beri, weak from the constant drain of a tropical ulcer that would not heal, and, on a morning in June, he was sick from the news that had come. The Japanese had killed the messenger who had carried letters from Chapman's radio shack in the mountains to a girl who lived in Irosin. Chapman had no idea what had happened to the girl. The people who brought the news had talked only of the Japanese appearing in their barrio and of the way in which the Japanese had killed the messenger.

"It was very terrible," they said, and Chapman believed them.

He made his barefoot way now to the cliff, a little dizzy from fever and empty from a vague nausea. He was taking a concoction of herbs the local doctor recommended. The Filipino doctor was a quack, which in the Islands means an unlicensed physician but not necessarily an incompetent one nor a cheat. Chapman suspected that *his* quack was incompetent, and knew he was a cheat. The quack had a store of ether and specialized in operations. He would tell the patients who complained of bellyache that it was appendicitis, take them into a locked room, etherize them, bandage their bellies, and, when they regained consciousness, he would show them a bloody knife and tell them an operation had been performed and not to remove the bandage for seven days. On the seventh day, he would take off the bandage and proudly point out that the operations he performed left no scars. Since, in most cases, the abdominal pains had disappeared during the week, the quack enjoyed a great reputation. If the pains had not gone, the quack assured his patients they were merely feeling the aftereffects of the operation, and thus his reputation did not suffer. If the patients died, it was because God had sent for them, and, since this was a matter over which the quack of course had no control, he could never be blamed for the deaths. Therefore, the quack had a thriving practice. Chapman was well aware of the basis of the quack's popularity, but he felt the herbs he was taking were nevertheless doing him some good.

Wearily, Gerald Chapman sank into his lookout post, staring down on the blue emptiness of the San Bernardino Straits, looking across to the green mass of the islands beyond. Staring at nothing, Chapman became aware of shapes appearing on the sea to the west. He swung around, searching the western horizon with his binoculars, adjusting the focus.

They were ships!

Ships! Warships! But whose?

Chapman's heart pounded as he strained, as if, by an effort of will, to increase the power of his binoculars. More ships appeared as dots over the rim of the world.

An hour later, Chapman was looking down on their decks. He kept searching them with his eyes, looking at them and then at the Navy book of silhouettes that had been sent to him, matching the drawings with the ships passing close beneath his sea cliff, sweating as he marked them down in the schoolboy notebook that lay on his lap.

He had never seen such a fleet, not even when he had come through Pearl Harbor on his way to the Islands before the war. There were slim gray destroyers, knifing easily through the currents that lump in the straits. Behind them, the sleek, deadly shapes of cruisers. Chapman thrilled at the sight of the huge battleships that sent a wash crashing among the rocks below his perch on the cliff. Coming behind the battleships were the flat, boxlike aircraft carriers—more carriers than Chapman knew existed. It was all as clear and radiant as a dream; the ships beautiful and potent in the bright sun, moving into the morning across the blue sea. There was no need for binoculars. As the carriers passed below, Chapman could see the sailors laughing and talking as they sunned themselves on the wide decks forward of the neatly packed ranks of aircraft. One sailor pointed, and the others looked, and Chapman thought they were looking at him. He wondered if he should wave, as he stared down on the endless parade passing slowly beneath him, seeing the sailors lining the rails looking at the islands going by, and seeing the huge battle flags streaming in the sun, hearing the roar of wash roiling among the stones at the base of the cliff.

"God." Chapman said, looking down upon the battle line, *"help* our boys."

The skies split with the uneven, racketing grind of Japanese aircraft engines, and the shadows of aircraft swept over the cliff and the sea, and then he saw the glinting shapes of them, sweeping ahead of the fleet into the morning.

When the last of the ships had passed, Chapman ran to his radio shack, pelting barefoot up the trail down which he had hobbled. Feverishly, he composed and encoded a message. This was an emergency for the flash line that engirdled the Islands, leaping along the coasts to Fertig's headquarters on Mindanao, jumping across the oceans to Australia; out across the Pacific to Commander-in-Chief, Pacific at Pearl Harbor and thence to Washington. Chapman broke into normal radio traffic, sending a three-part message with no more than momentary breaks between the parts. He did not care whether, in sending for so long continuously, he was giving the Japanese a chance to pinpoint his secret station. This was no time to send in squirts or to think of himself at all.

"BALLS PD," he rapped out, sending the first word of a code phrase. The message would be found within the opening and closing words of the phrase.

JAP NAVAL FLEET CONSISTING OF TWO SMALL PATROL BOATS CMA ELEVEN DESTROYERS CMA TEN CRUISERS CMA THREE BATTLESHIPS CMA NINE AIRCRAFT CARRIERS PD NR THREE FIVE PD FROM WEST CMA LAST SHIP PASSED LONG ONE TWO FOUR DEGREES NINE MIN LAT ONE TWO DE-GREES THREE FOUR MIN AT SIXTEEN TWO NINE HOW PD FIRST SHIP AT FIFTEEN NIL FIVE PD DETAILS NEXT MSG PD OF FIRE

Next, he sent:

GO PD LAST SEEN GOING EAST NORTHEAST IN THIS ORDER COLON TWO PATROL BOATS CMA TWO DESTROY-ERS CMA TWO ATAGO CRUISERS CMA TWO MOGAMI CRUIS-ERS CMA TWO TONE CRUISERS CMA TWO DESTROYERS CMA TWO KONGO CLASS BATTLESHIPS CMA THREE CARRIERS REPEAT CARRIERS ONE AGANO CMA TWO NACHI CLASS CRUISERS TWO DESTROYERS

And he sent:

GET PD THREE CARRIERS CMA TWO DESTROYERS CMA THREE CARRIERS CMA ONE DESTROYER CMA ONE BATTLE-SHIP NAGATO CLASS CMA ONE CRUISER TONE CLASS PD PROCEEDING EAST WITH AERIAL ESCORT PD AFTER PASS-ING SAN BERNARDINO THE SHIPS SPREAD OUT PD THEM

Go get them!
But with what?
With Waldo Neveling's banca? With the cargo-carrying submarine

Narwhal? With Zapanta's *Athena* and its homemade cannon? These were the only Allied ships Chapman had seen for years.

Chapman repeated his message, throwing it into the vastness of the Pacific skies, until a thin, angry chirping in his headset told him it had been received and understood.

What Chapman had seen was the Imperial Japanese Fleet making its sortie into the Philippine Sea on its way toward the Mariana Islands. But Chapman had no knowledge of what was taking place in the Marianas, nor that a United States flag lieutenant would hand Chapman's message to an admiral who, having read it with deep satisfaction, would say, "Acknowledge. And, oh yes, Send Well Done."

All Chapman knew was that, after more than two years of war, the strength of Japan had barely been touched. He kept thinking of the sailors laughing and talking together, forward of the confidently packed new aircraft on the glistening decks; of the battle flags flying free in the sun. And he knew, too, that he would have to find a new hiding place among the coastal hills, for surely a Japanese patrol would have started by now toward the sound of his sending.

As in a nightmare, he saw the ships again as he mounted a climbing forest track and wondered how long the war would last. He could not hope to see the end of it, although the jungle offered some protection, and the Filipinos, despite the suffering his presence caused them, seemed still loyal.

That night, he ate a supper of cold rice, sitting alone in a grass hut the Filipinos hastily made for him. He drank a bit of the herb medicine and told himself that it was doing him some good. Then he began to shake with the first chills of recurring malaria.

11

ON JUNE 17, 1944, General Douglas MacArthur's headquarters found itself confronted by a rumor so utterly fantastic that it clamored for belief. The rumor was that the Joint Chiefs of Staff had just asked General MacArthur to tell them what he thought of plans, already approved, to defeat Japan by means that did not call for invasion of the Philippines.

To ask General MacArthur what he thought of breaking his word was obscene.

But the rumor was true. In the hushed atmosphere of his office, General MacArthur coldly spelled out exactly why he thought invasion of the Islands was a military imperative. And he concluded:

"Even if this were not the case, and unless military factors demanded another line of action, it would, in my opinion, be necessary to reoccupy the Philippines. It is American territory, where our unsupported forces were destroyed by the enemy. Practically all of the 17,000,000 Filipinos remain loyal to the United States and are undergoing the greatest privation and suffering because we have not been able to support or succor them. We have a great national obligation to discharge. I feel also that a decision to eliminate the campaign for the relief of the Philippines, even under appreciable military considerations, would cause extremely adverse reactions among the citizens of the United States. I request that I be accorded the opportunity of personally proceeding to Washington to present fully my views."

"With regard to the reconquest of the Philippines," General George C. Marshall, Chief of the Joint Chiefs of Staff, radioed in reply, "we must be careful not to allow our personal feeling and Philippine political considerations to overrule our great objective."

But, General Marshall said, "as to your expressed desire to be accorded the opportunity of personally proceeding to Washington to present fully your views, I see no difficulty about that. If the issue arises, I will speak to the President . . ."

The phrase "if the issue arises" was by no means lost upon Douglas MacArthur. It was clear to him what the Joint Chiefs thought. If he was to redeem his word and honor, he would have to sway the mind of President Roosevelt, who had George Marshall constantly at his side.

The result of this correspondence was MacArthur's mid-Pacific conference with the President at Pearl Harbor, where MacArthur called up from the depths of his soul all of his talents of logic and oratory to convince the President that all of the Joint Chiefs were wrong and that he alone was right. He dealt as best he could with the considerable military reasons that suggested—if they did not prove—that reinvasion of the Philippines was a waste of American time, money, and lives. Finally, he put matters squarely to the President as a political expedient. Politics was something the aging President understood.

"Mr. President," General MacArthur argued, "if your decision be to bypass the Philippines and leave its millions of wards of the United States and thousands of American internees and prisoners of war to continue to languish in their agony and despair, I dare to say that the American people would be so aroused that they would register most complete resentment against you at the polls this fall."

It was not a particularly edifying argument, and it spoke volumes of General MacArthur's opinion of President Roosevelt, but the General was willing to use any weapon that came to hand. He argued, too, on grounds of international diplomacy. After the war, he said, Americans would have no face in East Asia, no matter how completely they destroyed the Japanese, if the United States refused to rescue the tortured Filipinos when it held the power to do so; if it did not redeem, on Philippine soil, the most calamitous defeat of American arms. General MacArthur spoke of the loyalty of the Filipinos, of the bitter guerrilla they, together with unsurrendered American patriots, were waging. Indeed, he said, returning to military considerations, the existence of the guerrilla was a dagger held to the back of the Japanese while an avenging army thrust at the Japanese breast.

WHILE MACARTHUR spoke in the clean, potent world of gold braid, air-conditioning, protocol, and Class-A uniforms, one of the daggers, Captain J. Lawrence Evans, jumped stark naked out of a stream and smashed into the bushes where he had left his clothes.

Evans hadn't seen them coming. No one had.

One moment Evans was washing in the stream in the sleepy sunlight that filtered through the forest, scrubbing away the filth of the trail and joking, and the next he was running with the sound of muffled firecrackers popping around him.

Evans started to pull on his shirt, then tore it off and feverishly dried himself with a towel as the little firecracker sound of the rifles was joined by the *tuk-tuk-tuk* of the Japanese machine gun the guerrilleros called the woodpecker.

What the hell am I drying myself for? Evans shouted silently to himself.

He threw his clothes on anyhow and ran, the heavy Colt automatic pistol flopping against his hip.

He drew the pistol from its holster as he hurtled through the brush to the trail. What good was a .45 against machine guns?

Evans skidded beneath the stilts of a grass house in a tiny clearing. There, Hanson, a mestizo, was sitting in the shadow, looking down the trail over the sights of an air-cooled .30-caliber machine gun.

The Japanese came running, more than twenty of them, not a platoon but an armed mob, haring after naked men who jumped out of streams.

The expressionless Hanson opened up with the machine gun, the muzzle blasts kicking dust and Japanese falling on the trail.

Evans heard the Japanese scream and saw them stagger around to go pelting back, throwing away their rifles and helmets as they went, while Hanson calmly swung the blasting muzzle as the trail curved.

When the machine gun stopped, Evans heard the heavy burst of a Springfield in the forest.

One of the bathers, his khakis wet from his not having dried himself, came carefully into the clearing, carrying his rifle before him. He studied the three bodies on the trail. He watched the bodies as he edged to the house, where Hanson had gathered the spent cartridge cases and was folding the machine gun's tripod.

"Let's get out," the rifleman said.

No one bothered with the bodies or with the discarded rifles and helmets. The Japanese panic would not last long, and, when the Japanese returned, this time hunting in military order, there would be even more of them—many, many more of them than there were guerrilleros.

A week later, Evans was still trying to work around the Japanese units that seemed to be everywhere. He never reached Cabadbaran. Instead, what was left of Cabadbaran came walking in Evans' bivouac early one morning.

First came a tired man carrying a huge mattress on his head. Then four more, carrying a wooden crate suspended from bamboo poles that ate into their shoulders, and, bringing up the rear of this bizarre expedition, wearing the manner of a worried Oriental potentate, was Sam Wilson.

"Oh, gee, Larry, they ran me out," Wilson said, stopping to lean against a tree as his men dropped their burdens to squat around them.

"We just did get out," Wilson said. "Gee, Larry, they cleaned me out. We had to leave. They ran right over us. We lost the radios, all the stuff, everything."

"Does the Old Man know?" Evans asked.

"What did you say?" Wilson said in the loud voice of the partially deaf.

"Did you tell the Old Man?"

"They got my radio," Wilson said.

"Let's tell him now," Evans said.

He unpacked the Australian portable transceiver he carried, and called McClish's headquarters to relay the news of Cabadbaran to Fertig, while Wilson slumped wearily against a tree, impatient in his weariness.

During the days that followed, the Japanese were never more than half a day's march behind as Wilson and Evans worked their way back toward Waloe. The pace was held to that of Wilson's cargadores, who struggled with the heavy crate, and, what with Wilson's nervousness, Evans was jumping at shadows.

"Look, Sam," Evans pleaded. "Let's leave that stuff and get moving."

"Oh, I can't, Larry," Sam said. "I can't leave it."

"You don't need that damned mattress."

"It isn't heavy, Larry. The boy can carry the mattress."

"Sam, we have food for today and tomorrow. We have to go light. For God's sake, let's hide that junk and get moving."

"I have to keep it," Wilson said.

"What is in that mattress—money?"

"It's just a mattress," Wilson said. He had kept the mattress and the crate all through his wanderings, and they were his luck.

"Well, what's in the crate?"

"Secrets."

"Well, let's burn the damned secrets. It's carrying that thing that slows us."

"They won't burn. You can't burn them."

"The hell they won't burn," Evans promised.

Wilson caught at Evans' sleeve. He looked warily around. "You won't tell?"

"Of course not," Evans said.

"Nobody knows," Wilson said.

"That's all right."

"It's canned peaches," Wilson said.

"It's *what*?"

"A whole crate of canned peaches," Wilson said happily. "I'm saving them for an emergency."

"Good luck, Sam," Evans said, rising. "I'll see you at Waloe."

But he never did. Neither of them would ever see Waloe.

AT THIS SAME TIME, in a northern corner of Mindanao, Waldo Neveling was also solving a transportation problem. Herr Neveling's problem was that he was trying to move 9,800 pounds of guns and ammunition on the backs of fewer than a hundred men, and to move them faster than a pursuing battalion of Japanese could follow. Compounding the problem was the fact that Neveling's party could not use the trails but had to cut their own through a precipitous jungle. They were guiding on compass up the eastern mountains, trying to reach Fertig's area, with Neveling's soldiers serving as rear guard, at once trying to delay the Japanese advance and to guard against any attempts of the cargadores to throw their loads into the jungle and disappear. Neveling's column had been hungry for three days and had marched the last day without any food at all, and now, as the column stopped to rest, the problem presented itself in terms of a cargadore who told Neveling it was no use. "Sair, I am finish," the cargadore said. "I cannot do." The man's voice was weak and his face was haggard. Painfully, he removed a bloody patch of leaves to bare one shoulder. The pack straps had cut the flesh nearly to he bone. Blood welled from the already festering wound, and the other shoulder was as badly hurt.

"Dot iss too bad," Neveling said, glancing at the shoulders. "The other men, they haff scratches like dot, too."

"Sair, I am suffering," the cargadore said. "I can do no more."

"I vill do vhat I can," Neveling said, drawing his pistol. "I don't vant you to suffer, und for dot reason, I vill shoot you so your suffering vill end." Neveling held the pistol to the man's head.

"Oh, sair!" the cargadore shouted. "I suffer no more!"

"Gut," Neveling said. "I am glad you haff recoveret."

Turning to the others, who had breathlessly followed every detail of the scene, Neveling asked, "How iss efferybotty? Anyvun suffer?"

The squatting cargadores lowered their eyes.

"Gut," Neveling said, putting his pistol back in its holster. "Now dot ve had a nice rest, let's go."

Listlessly, the cargadores got to their feet, stuffed leaves beneath the pack straps, shouldered their unbearable loads, and the column toiled again up the mountainside behind men who swung bolos to clear the way.

12

THE SOUND OF ENGINES was faint in the noonday stillness, and Chapman, drowsing in the hot shade of a traveler's palm, automatically rose and moved sleepily into the clearing. It was his duty to report all movements of Japanese aircraft as well as ships.

He shaded his eyes, searching the sky in the direction of the Manila airfields. The sound became a deep, sonorous song of controlled power that was not at all familiar. A fretful memory stirred in him.

They're not coffee grinders! They're not Japs!

Chapman shouted and waved his straw hat as four white-bellied, gray-blue aircraft swept precisely overhead, the sun glinting from their plastic canopies. They bore markings Chapman had never seen before—white stars that lacked the red-center ball of the prewar military aircraft—but there was no chance of mistaking the shape of the thick-cambered cargo wing, any more than there was of mistaking that full, round drone of power, so unlike the Japanese engines.

A Filipino came running into the clearing, twisting his head around to look at the steadily vanishing formation, and, for a long time afterwards, neither he nor Chapman could trust themselves to speak. They looked at each other, laughing, with brimming eyes, embraced, and stared into the now empty sky, listening to the diminishing sound.

WHILE CHAPMAN RAN to his radio shack to send, AT TWELVE FIVE EIGHT SAW FOUR US RPT US DOUGLAS DIVE BOMBERS GOING SOUTHEAST PD NR ONE THREE X WHOOPEE, a blond young Navy ensign frantically tore back the canopy of his

Grumman fighter, choking in the oil smoke, unhooked his safety belt, and went rolling headfirst out of the burning aircraft.

Minutes later, he was wriggling free of his parachute harness as the sea came rising toward his feet. He dropped clear into the warm water, pulling the cord that inflated his rubber life jacket as the sea closed over his head. He came up, shaking the salt water out of his eyes, as his parachute drifted on to crumple like a blown scarf on the waves. He turned himself toward the green mass of the mountainous island, thinking that, all things considered, he was still a lucky son of a bitch. A few miles the other way, and he would have been hanging up in a tree on the side of a mountain . . .

He struck out for the distant shore, swimming slowly to conserve his strength, so intent on his work that he did not see the barroto speeding toward him until he heard someone shout, "Halloa, Joe! You are OK!"

The swimming pilot tread water as the paddlers swept up to him.

THE FOLLOWING MORNING, Chapman was excitedly reporting THE AID PD BETWEEN SIX ONE FOUR HOW AND SIX THREE FIVE HOW TIME ONE TWO SEVEN US RPT US PLANES PASSED OVERHEAD GOING WEST PD TWO PLANES DIVED AND FIRED AT UNSEEN OBJECT NEAR BULUSAN ABOUT SIX FOUR FIVE HOW PD IS HERE, and the rescued pilot was back aboard his aircraft carrier, dressed in new khakis, drinking black coffee, and telling his air intelligence officer how it was.

"Those guys got themselves a real outfit," he said. "They picked me up five minutes after I hit the water. I noticed the time because, when I got in the canoe, I looked at my watch to see if it was still going. I gave one of the guys my watch, and I gave the other one my gun, and, Jesus, they couldn't do enough for me. They kept saying how sorry they were they didn't have anything better to give me to eat when, Christ, all they'd done for me was save my life. They took me to this American who had this radio in this dinky grass shack . . ."

The air intelligence officer nodded. Arrangements had been made through the guerrilla flash line for a black, night-flying seaplane to pick up the rescued pilot and return him to the carrier. The officer patiently allowed the pilot to tell of his surprise on finding a flourishing resistance movement functioning on an island the Japanese had held for nearly three years, and then he pressed him for details of the strike.

"We clobbered them," the pilot said. "Didn't the guys tell you? I know I got hits on at least six Zekes on the field. I hauled back, and, when I came around again, everything was burning. It was another turkey shoot, like the Marianas. We clobbered them on the ground, and what they got up in the air, we splashed. It was just my luck to get flak on the way out . . ."

Admiral Halsey listened intently to the reports of his intelligence officers. The carrier raid striking Luzon Island was the result of the destruction of the Japanese fleet that Chapman had reported steaming east. Alerted by the guerrilla radio, the United States Navy trapped the Japanese off the Marianas, and, following up the victory, Halsey was now conducting a reconnaissance in force over Luzon. As impressed by the guerrilleros' rescue of his downed airmen as he was by the weakness of Japanese air opposition, Halsey lost no time communicating his views to Pearl Harbor. The Navy had always opposed reinvasion of the Philippines, and its view of MacArthur was best expressed in the song the marines sang:

We asked for the Army at Guadalcanal,
But General MacArthur said "No."
He gave as his reason "'Tis now the hot season;
Besides, there is no USO."

But Halsey's opinion of MacArthur was more generous. If Mac wanted to go back, there seemed no reason to Halsey why he didn't go at once. To Halsey, the Philippines were obviously full of weak Japs and strong guerrilleros.

THE AID. . . IS HERE, Chapman had sent, and, in the jungle at Waloe, excited men crowded around the radio shack, grinning and jubilant, telling themselves over and again every shred of fact and rumor, the Americans shouting to each other what they would do when they got home.

". . . and *then,* I'm going to take my shoes off!"

For a moment, even Fertig believed it was The Aid. From the instant the first message came, Fertig haunted the radio shack. But, when it became clear that the Navy raid was nothing more than a raid and that MacArthur was still more than 900 sea miles away from the nearest Philippine island, Fertig's hope sank to something near despair. Yet, if the Navy could come so close . . .

If they can hit Luzon, they can drop us supplies, Fertig reasoned.

The matter seemed perfectly simple. All they had to do was rig bundles with parachutes and drop them instead of bombs. No doubt the Navy would be glad to divert a few planes for the purpose. Surely everyone would understand that supplies dropped to an army in the field would be worth relatively more than a few bombs that might very well miss their targets.

"There's no reason why we have to stay here," Fertig told Wheeler.

"No," the Navy officer agreed. "If they can send an airplane to this island, they can send it anywhere on the island."

"Exactly," Fertig said. "If they can get air in here, we won't have to hand-carry stuff over the mountains. We can lay on air drops so that the stuff goes directly to each of the outfits. We won't have to worry about meeting subs or using the river and the trails. All we have to do is dodge Japs and take drops wherever we go."

It seemed an extraordinarily simple plan, and Fertig felt his spirits rise. The Navy strike had seemed like a tantalizing mirage of The Aid, but the possibility of air drops was no mirage. To Fertig's mind, anything that was possible was practical. If each of the guerrilla units on Mindanao was under pressure, each was nevertheless still intact. All were joined together by the thin song of the radio to the central brain of Fertig's headquarters. But, since the radio's song could reach everywhere, it did not matter where, in particular, Fertig's headquarters was, as long as food and armament could be dropped to it. And each of the guerrilla units could radio its needs to Fertig, who could arrange for air drops to each unit. This would not only eliminate the desperate problem of supply by means of cargadores, but it would also ease the pressure on civilians everywhere, who shared what food they had with the guerrilleros. Further, the sight of United States aircraft dropping supplies to the resistance would put new heart in civilians and guerrilleros alike and dismay the Japanese. Indeed, what with the Japanese controlling the coasts, the air drop was the only means to survival, and to Fertig's survival in particular, for the Japanese had interdicted all the trails that led from Waloe but one—the one leading into the inhospitable mountains of Bukidnon province where there was nearly no food at all. With air drops, Fertig could exist in the mountains, and the Japanese Army, which lived off the land, would be unable to follow.

"Just be sure to ask for more than we need," Wheeler cautioned. "That headquarters is just like a government agency. If you ask for five dollars, they'll laugh at you, but, if you ask for fifty billion, they'll give you a check."

IN SUPREME HEADQUARTERS, South West Pacific Area, Major General Stephen J. Chamberlain read Fertig's message.

"If we continue present method of dodging the Jap, we must expect constant and serious interruption of our radio net," the message said. "This applies equally to both this station and alternate (now alternate cannot take over net due enemy pressure in Misamis Occidental). The only way to assure steady, efficient, continuous operation, without interruption and very probably loss of power and radio equipment, is to move so far back into Bukidnon that any chance of enemy penetration is reduced to minimum. This is now being done, but we must have supplies by air if we are to survive, since Bukidnon areas are without sufficient food to maintain minimum station personnel. Minimum supplies needed monthly basis (delivery to start within sixty days). Food: 2,000 pounds dehydrated fruits, vegetables, and processed meats; salt, sugar, condiments, coffee, tea, rice, and canned fish. Equal poundage of supplies: batteries, additional equipment, replacement and maintenance parts, morale items. Gasoline or fuel oil. Location near clearing at 08 degrees 02 minutes north, 125 degrees 30 minutes east sufficiently large to be used for drops. Radio supplies can be distributed by trails to Davao, Agusan, Surigao, and Bukidnon provinces and even to western Mindanao if required."

All this struck General Chamberlain as most unbusinesslike. He had recently arrived in the Pacific from Washington to serve as General MacArthur's planning officer, and, as he read Fertig's message, he saw fallacies everywhere.

"Colonel Fertig's message does not disclose realistic prior planning," General Chamberlain wrote, preparing his recommendation for MacArthur's attention. "Else he would have had a series of such prepared positions as he now intends to occupy in the Bukidnon, widely dispersed, equipped, and provisioned for an indefinite period against any emergency. . . . Action recommended: None."

"NONE?" FERTIG ECHOED unbelievingly, staring at the message Wheeler passed him. "No air drops? With a whole fleet standing offshore, they can't send one bomber over with a ton of food?"

Wheeler was speechless in the presence of Fertig's wrath. Lieutenant Commander Montgomery Wheeler was a naval intelligence officer sent in by submarine to take charge of transmission of information of the Navy flash line, and Fertig, glad of a trained staff officer, had kept Wheeler by his side as chief of staff. Since his arrival, Wheeler thought he had come as close as any man to making friends with the distant, somewhat didactic guerrilla chieftain, but he had never seen such a look of naked brutality on Fertig's bearded face.

"Why goddamn it, who is this? . . . Hellfire, don't they know, have they forgotten down there that, all during Corregidor, we were flying *civilian* aircraft off and on the Rock, through bombs, shells, and Jap fighters?"

"There's new blood in Plans and Operations," Wheeler said.

Fertig put the message back on Wheeler's desk with utter disgust. The answer to his plea was first of all a statement that air supply was impossible. There followed three instructions: Fertig was to keep his messages to a minimum in order to conserve generator fuel, he was to avoid destruction of his headquarters by not allowing the Japanese to capture him, and he was to furnish Supreme Headquarters with his intranetwork codes in order that Headquarters could, in event of his capture, take over control of the guerrilla and command it from Australia.

"That's just plain dumb," Fertig said. "That's just as stupid as their telling me we have no complaint their operators can't handle thirty groups a minute, because they've taken the fast operators off and put slow ones on. How anybody can be so plain stupid . . .

The only recent good that had come out of Australia was news that General MacArthur had personally seen to it that Fertig's Americans received their commissions. MacArthur never forgot any of the officers who had served him on Bataan and Corregidor, and the General had overruled Colonel Whitney's suggestion that the commissions be denied. But, apart from that, Fertig wondered, what did Headquarters truly know of conditions on Mindanao?

Could they understand, or believe, what was meant by the news that Japanese reinforcements were continuing to flood into Mindanao—24,000 in April, 50,000 in June?

Bowler was again in trouble in Misamis Occidental; Childress was retreating from Davao. Neveling had saved a cache of arms from Port Lamon but was hiding somewhere in the hills. Wilson had arrived alone, without baggage, at McClish's fugitive headquarters near Talacogon, his health precarious and in no condition to continue. Evans had disappeared. Japanese patrols were inexorably pressing closer to Waloe, despite daily losses to unseen guerrilleros who struck from ambush, but the guerrilleros were yielding ground without exacting the toll they might have taken, and there was little country left to yield. What Fertig did not entirely understand was that news of the Navy strike, the mirage of The Aid, had reduced the guerrilleros' efficiency; that others, like himself, were now thinking purely in terms of survival until The Aid arrived. He knew with utmost clarity that his coconut-oil stock was dropping faster than it could be replaced and that there was less than ten days' supply of food at Waloe. And that, every day, the Japanese patrols edged closer along the trails while their aircraft bombed the clearings ahead of them. Eleven thousand Japanese were converging on Waloe, and the fact that the jungle and less than three hundred guerrilleros were successfully slowing that advance to glacial speed was a victory that could only end in death. For slowly as a glacier moves, it nonetheless moves.

That afternoon, there was a message from Bowler. Two weeks earlier, Bowler said, an unannounced submarine had surfaced off the malarial Cotabato coast in southern Mindanao. Five men had paddled a rubber boat ashore. Fortunately, they had run into guerrilleros on the coast, who had sent them on to Bowler. Four of them were Army Air Force enlisted men—weather observers—and they came ashore with automatic weapons, pistols, daggers, a small heap of emergency rations, and the special thermometers of their trade. The fifth was a Major Harold Rosenquist, who refused to say anything other than he was an intelligence officer on a mission. He would not say what his mission was, and Bowler wanted to know what to do with his unlooked-for visitors.

"Did you know anybody named Rosenquist in Australia?" Fertig asked Wheeler.

"No, I didn't," the intelligence officer said.

"You send a message to Bowler," Fertig said. "Tell him to disarm those weather people and turn their stuff over to people who can use it. They're carrying enough guns to outfit a platoon. Make clear that we won't interfere with their basic mission of wetting their fingers to find out which way the wind's blowing. But tell Bowler that those people must understand that all personnel reporting to Mindanao come under my direct command and that their activities will be directed by me. Bowler is to tell Rosenquist that, as far as we're concerned, Rosenquist is just a visiting staff officer without authority. Until I find out what his mission is, and approve it, he is not to issue orders to any of our men. Tell Bowler to keep Rosenquist where he is, until we have talked with Headquarters.

"And then," Fertig concluded, "send a message to Headquarters asking them what in hell is going on. Tell them all activities in the island of Mindanao must, and will be, controlled by me. You'd think those thickheads would know by this time that we can't have a bunch of people running around here at cross-purposes."

With that, Fertig dismissed Wheeler and sat back to consider the fact that he was doing little for himself at Headquarters except storing up ill will.

The hell with them. Their problem is, they have too many staff sections each working independently to plan the Great Man's Return.

The weathermen, for example. Just what could four weather observers add to Supreme Headquarters' knowledge of Mindanao that a simple study of the island's climatology would not show? The weathermen would report that tropical air was warm and wet—which any fool knew. In the rainy season, they could report rain. The mean temperatures, relative humidities, average rainfall, wind speeds and directions, and the predictable number of clear days in any given month were all matters of government record. The weather observers could add nothing, on any given day, that Fertig's coastwatchers could not report. And there were coastwatchers all up and down the length of the archipelago—a hell of a lot more of them than four people—and instead of sending in four more men to feed and guard, Headquarters could simply have sent Fertig instructions to have the coastwatchers report cloud types, altitudes, and directions. On the other hand, the arrival of weather personnel obviously presaged an early increase in United States air activity, and Fertig's men could certainly use the guns the weathermen had brought.

The arrival of an intelligence officer was something else again. Special missions were all very well, unless it turned out that their performance would jeopardize the guerrilla itself.

"Headquarters," Wheeler said, returning to Fertig's office, "says we are to furnish Rosenquist with any aid and assistance he may require."

"What is his mission?"

"They won't say," Wheeler said. "Just that it's of 'greatest importance' and that all we have to do is follow orders."

"I haven't stayed alive here for more than two years by allowing a crowd of dreamers 15,000 miles away to tell me what *I* have to do," Fertig said. "And, by God, I'm not going to start now. I'm not going to have them sending special missions in here that could get my tail in a crack without my knowing what's happened until it's too late. Therefore, you will tell Bowler to send that Rosenquist to me, and *I'll* decide whether we'll help him or not."

When Wheeler had gone, Fertig stared at the walls of his bamboo prison.

The Japanese were twenty miles away. If he moved, he would starve. If he stayed where he was, he would be killed.

There was an alternative. He could chuck the whole bloody business.

Since Bowler was presently unable to take over the net, Fertig could surrender control of the guerrilla to Supreme Headquarters, cache his radios, and tell his men to scatter into the hills. A few men, traveling alone, could always find something to eat. He could wander across the mountains, searching for food, until The Aid came.

Why not? Hadn't he done enough? After the Regular Army surrendered, his makeshift army had killed 7,000 Japanese. He had re-established a government. He had denied the Japanese any practical benefit of their conquest of Mindanao. Instead, Mindanao had been a constant drain on Japanese resources. They had had to divert 150,000 men to Mindanao in an unsuccessful effort to crush resistance. From an arithmetical standpoint, it was already an enormous victory. Forty thousand guerrilleros had killed 7,000 of the enemy and, in effect, had taken 150,000 prisoners. There were also the incalculable benefits accruing from guerrilla intelligence. Supreme Headquarters had never specified whether any particular sightings had led to any particular sinkings, but the Navy had sent the coastwatchers its highest compliment: Well Done. More important, the guerrilla had done much to restore the face America had lost by its abject surrender. The Filipinos would never again allow Americans to call them "little brown brothers." After all, the resistance was almost entirely a Filipino operation: Fertig was an invited guest. But Americans who refused to surrender, and instead accepted the invitation, had done much to salvage the essential image of an America that was the friend of the Filipino people.

Now, with the end so near, why not simply withdraw into the hills to remain alive until The Aid arrived? Hadn't he done enough for a headquarters that, except for sending a few tons of supplies by submarine, had sent him little else but impractical if not vapid directives, a catalogue of misunderstandings, and an autographed picture of General MacArthur? When before, in all United States military history, had a colonel been asked to lead a military district in two years of combat? Without promotion? Few non-combatant colonels in rear areas could escape promotion during two years of war. And a military district was not properly a colonel's command even in peacetime but was a major general's.

Fertig felt the weight of the Moro silversmith's stars on his collar. He was Colonel Fertig to Australia, but here, on his island, he wore his stars. On Mindanao, he was and would remain The General.

We'll move to Bukidnon, Fertig decided.

He would take his radio section and all its equipment, and he would remain in command as long as his fuel oil and food and the Japanese allowed. He would see it out to the end before he reverted to what he had been in the beginning, after the surrender: a lonely wanderer, searching for food, seeking only to stay alive.

13

THE PLACE THEY CALLED Bukidnon was a camp of bamboo and grass bahis that Nick Capistrano's working party had built on a forested hill. A stream came down the hill past the camp. It was difficult to see the bahis from the air, because of the trees. Immense durians, heavy with their melonlike fruit, soared more than a hundred feet above the houses, the leaves and shadows creating a pleasant green and dappled light.

Wheeler liked everything about the camp except its stench, which was exactly that of an open, untended latrine.

"That is durian," Fertig said, breathing the odor of the ripening fruit. "We'll have some for breakfast; it'll make a new man of you."

He told Wheeler how, in peacetime, when the durians were ripe, Chinese would come from distant islands to the trees that grew in the more accessible areas of the north Mindanao coast.

"The Chinese say there's nothing like it to rejuvenate the aging male," Fertig said. "They believe that anything that smells that bad must be good for you."

He told Wheeler what a sight it was to see an old Chinaman, one of the parchment-skinned patriarchs with a wispy white beard, sitting under a gigantic tree with his concubines, some of the girls no more than pubescent children, waiting for the fruit to drop; of the sight of the Chinaman gobbling the creamy, evil-smelling flesh of the durian with evident enjoyment, his beard waggling; the Chinaman eating with one hand and feeling hopefully under his robes with the other; the Chinaman looking hungrily at his concubines while he stuffed himself; the girls shyly watching their master out of the corners of their eyes and giggling to one another.

"Does it really work?" Wheeler asked, half in jest.

"The Chinese and the Filipinos think so," Fertig said.

The two officers followed their baggage to a new, fresh-smelling house of bamboo and thatch. Here Fertig and Wheeler would live together, Fertig having rationalized his need for companionship by convincing himself that this was no show of favoritism but an acknowledgment of Army-Navy joint command. With Wheeler at his side, Fertig hoped to enlist Navy support of the guerrilla if Army support was not forthcoming. Or so he told himself.

In the morning, the houseboy placed a durian on the table, and, when Fertig cut into it, the fecal odor was magnified into a stench that turned Wheeler quite pale beneath the golden tan that atabrine and the tropical sun had given him.

"It tastes as good as it smells bad," Fertig said comfortably, spooning out the creamy meat. "Once you taste it, you're not conscious of the smell."

This was something Fertig had been told, for he had never eaten durian before. He found it absolutely true. The fruit was incredibly delicious.

"*I'm* conscious of the smell," Wheeler said, blanching and rising.

"Aren't you going to try it?"

"No."

"Aren't you going to eat breakfast?"

"You can have it," Wheeler said, leaving the bamboo porch and climbing down the bahi's ladder. "Save it. Do what you want with it. I don't care what you do. I couldn't eat a thing. That smell made me sick."

"You've given me a good idea," Fertig called after him. "We'll serve durian every meal. You'll get so sick you won't want your chow. Then our chow will last twice as long."

Wheeler smiled wanly and walked rapidly away to the new radio shack Capistrano had built in the forest.

It might not be such a bad idea at that, Fertig thought as he finished his durian and began to wolf down his portion of roughcracked corn that had been boiled like rice. Anything that would inhibit the appetite was welcome, for there was no more than a ten-day supply of food on hand. The cracked corn came from that supply. A sack of it had been found hidden in a village on the east coast and brought over the mountains to Waloe and thence to Bukidnon. There would be no more grain from that coast. In order to maintain the food supply at a ten-day level, Capistrano and Walter were leading daily search parties into the hills, to see what might yet be growing wild in deserted kaingins. There was sufficient fuel for sixty days, and when that was gone . . .

Fertig did not want to think of the day the last of the coconut oil was poured into the thirsty diesel generators. He was cut off from the coconut coast to the east, but perhaps the coastal villagers could secretly make the oil and cache it in bamboo tubes; perhaps guerrilla patrols could filter through the Japanese perimeter, pick up the tubes, and work or fight their way out with them . . .

By such means, the radios were kept on the air throughout July, although the oil stocks were never augmented but, rather, shrank less rapidly. Meanwhile, the backlog of messages grew. It was a sardonic paradox of the time that, while Fertig himself was penned into the hungry hills with his immediate headquarters limited to a few key men, the demands on his leadership fantastically increased: Messages poured into the camp beneath the durian trees.

The Navy strike, signaling the imminence of The Aid, had stirred the Japanese throughout the Islands: The coastwatchers had more to report. The coastwatchers' reports demanded instant transmission. To send all of them was impossible, even had there been sufficient fuel for the generators, for they would have to be sent at a faster rate than Australia's new operators could receive. Equally insistent messages came crowding in, concerning intraisland affairs. If the Navy raid had a subtle effect on the tiring guerrilleros, making them less willing to dare, it had an opposite effect on Filipinos who had neither fought nor helped the guerrilla. Those who had not fought now clamored to join the resistance, in order to be counted among the deserving patriots when MacArthur returned. The guerrilleros wanted nothing to do with the newcomers. Instead, they wanted to kill many they suspected as traitors. What were the General's commands?

Fertig fell under increasing pressure to choose among his duties as his fuel stocks dwindled. Even after all the decisions were ruthlessly pared to the absolute essential, the lack of fuel prohibited transmission of *all* the decisions it was necessary to make. Daily, Fertig was asked to choose between how much oil should be spent on MacArthur and how much should be devoted to the people of the barrios, who stood face to face with their enemy.

During this time, the food supply likewise was not augmented but merely shrank less rapidly than Fertig feared. Each day, Nick Capistrano and Cecil Walter managed to return with something to eat, but it was plain that their men used more calories searching for food than the food they found would replace. The only benefit of Fertig's camp was that the Japanese seemed content to leave him in it. They had located the camp by triangulation, and, each day, their bombers came looking for it, but the nearest Japanese patrols were miles away, moving more slowly than ever. It was as if the Japanese, having won control of the Agusan from source to mouth and of the coasts and main trails, were content to have driven Fertig into the hills to starve, and to destroy his radios by air. Yet, their patrols *were* moving, however slowly, and Capistrano was sent even farther into Bukidnon to prepare yet another hiding place.

When the time came that there was less than four days' supply of food in reserve, Fertig suffered an exquisite torture on hearing that single Navy long-range, land-based aircraft had begun to bomb Davao harbor.

"*Land*-based planes!" Fertig exclaimed. "Not carrier planes. We can reach the Islands from *land.* For God's sake, Monty! You're the Navy. If those people can hit Davao from some damned island, why the hell can't they lay on a food drop for us?"

"If I were the Admiral, I'd do it right away, sir," Wheeler said. "All you have to do is ask me for anything you want."

Fertig accepted the rebuke in silence. He repeated his question, almost as violently, in a message to MacArthur. The answer was, Fertig's request was impossible; he should have prepared food caches in the hills long ago. But, Headquarters said, they would try to send a submarine to the south coast of Mindanao in late September.

Late September was nearly two months away, and Fertig ordered the already slender food ration cut again. Perhaps it could be stretched until the cargadores from Misamis Oriental arrived. They had started weeks ago, with what cracked corn Grinstead had been able to spare, but nothing had been heard from the cargadores since they left Grinstead's area.

It was at this point that still another mouth arrived to help consume the sack of cracked corn, the sixteen coconuts, the edible ferns, and the unappetizing durian fruits that constituted the four-day reserve of the sixty men who lived at Bukidnon. It belonged to a cheerful blond man, travel-worn but alert and curious. He came walking in alone, save for a guide, and said his name was Rosenquist.

Harold Rosenquist, or M15-X as he was known in the lugubrious nomenclature of secret services, was so pleased by what he had seen since his surreptitious arrival in Mindanao, that he had already encoded a preliminary report to send to Australia when he reached Fertig's radio control station:

"Guard and outposts covering trails, roads and rivers everywhere; one rifle, fifteen rounds ammunition per two men of front-line units, which are familiar with respective sectors. Plans formulated for road-blocks, bridge construction, trail coverage, and delaying enemy action. Food a definite problem many sectors especially Agusan province;

clothing meager everywhere. Troop and civilian morale high. Our trip untold value that respect. All expect early landing."

"It won't be long, now," he promised, as soon as he was introduced to Fertig. "I don't know when it's going to be, but it's an open secret that it will be soon. The rear-area bases are closing down, and everything is moving up. And, Colonel, I want you to know that everyone thinks you've done one hell of a fine job."

Rosenquist beamed with genuine admiration upon the bearded officer whose faded khakis hung loosely about him. Fertig regarded his optimistic visitor without enthusiasm.

"My instructions are to give you any assistance I can," Fertig said, in the tone of a man immune to compliments or curses. "But whether I can depends on whether your mission is practical. I want to make that clear."

Rosenquist said it was. He had great confidence in his mission, and it had been confirmed by everything he had seen as the guerrilla units passed him smoothly across the island. But he had seen only those areas the guerrilleros firmly controlled.

"If I decide not to help you," Fertig continued flatly, "you have two alternatives. You can remain in this area as a staff officer on visit, without command authority, subject to a letter of instruction that will be furnished you. Or you are welcome to serve with this command in such capacity as I see fit.

"I don't mean to be abrupt, Major," Fertig said. "I just want you to understand that I will be the judge of any operations within my area. Now, just what do you intend to do?"

Armed with the credentials of a staff officer from Supreme Headquarters on secret duty, Rosenquist had imagined all he need do was ask Fertig to put men under his command and that no questions would be asked. To surrender information violated everything that an intelligence officer held dear, but Rosenquist realized there was no way out.

"We intend to free the American prisoners from Davao before they can be moved," he said.

"I have no information that they are about to be moved," Fertig told him. "When are they going, and where are they going?"

Rosenquist sought to parry the question with a question.

"Do you think it is impossible to get them out of there?" he suggested.

"Certainly not," Fertig said. "The prison camp is not heavily guarded. Twelve of my men escaped from it. They were working on a road gang, under one Japanese guard. One day, they rushed the guard, beat him to death with their shovels, and walked away."

Rosenquist felt his enthusiasm return. When he first heard of his mission, he had been caught up in the excitement of the idea of freeing 2,000 Americans who had been systematically beaten, tortured, and starved for more than two years.

"How many men do you think I'll need?" Rosenquist eagerly wanted to know.

"Tell me this," Fertig continued in his flat way. "Is Headquarters going to provide a hospital ship to pick up the prisoners as soon as they are released? A hospital ship and a task force to protect it?"

The look on Rosenquist's face told Fertig the answer. The planning in MacArthur's headquarters had gone no farther than the idea of releasing the prisoners. The problem of moving the sick who could not walk, the problems of providing food, medicine, and clothing had not even been discussed, let alone solved.

"I know what's going on in that camp," Fertig said. "Some of those men are friends of mine. I know damned well what kind of hell they've been going through. But I have enough trouble already, without adding 2,000 stir-crazy Americans to my burdens. The men who escape from that place are wild or sick. They come out wanting to lead a suicide attack or to get their hands on a Jap alone. Or they come out half dead, unable to walk another yard.

"Now let me ask you this," Fertig went on. "Can you imagine anybody stupid enough to think of releasing 2,000 men who can't take care of themselves on an overburdened local economy that is absolutely incapable of sustaining or protecting them? On an economy that can barely sustain or protect itself?"

Rosenquist had nothing to say.

"We can't even arm those prisoners," Fertig said. "We have only half enough weapons for our own command as it is. Now let me tell you something else: When the twelve men killed that guard, the Japs retaliated by taking twenty-five prisoners to the chopping block and publicly beheading them.

"The Jap can't stand to lose face," Fertig continued. "If we rescued those men, I can tell you exactly what would happen. The Japs would lose so much face that they wouldn't rest until they'd ruthlessly hunted down every single American and butchered them together with the entire local population of every area in which one of those Americans was found.

"Therefore," Fertig concluded, "you will attempt no such rescue. Headquarters can call my refusal to cooperate with you any damn thing it likes. On the other hand, if you want to remain here as one of my intelligence officers, to organize and prepare reports that will be valuable to an invasion force, I will be glad to have you."

Seeing the unbelieving disappointment on Rosenquist's round face, Fertig added, "I don't ask you to accept my word for the situation. I want you to go to Davao and see for yourself. But, until you can show me that I'm wrong, you are to make no attempt to get those men out of there."

What neither Fertig nor Rosenquist knew at this time was that MacArthur's headquarters had learned from separate intelligence sources that the Japanese were about to remove the Americans to Formosa as part of their preparations against the threatened invasion of the Islands. It was not until after Rosenquist had gone to Davao to determine conditions for himself that the news came to the camp in the durian trees, where men now lived from day to day, with no food in reserve.

The news was this: The Japanese packed their American prisoners into the holds of freighters. Only too efficient, Fertig's coastwatchers reported ships leaving Davao harbor. American submarines, alerted by the report, intercepted the convoy off the Zamboanga coast. One torpedo blew a huge hole in the hold of one of the freighters, and, when the Americans who survived the explosion threw themselves out of this hole and into the sea, Japanese guards on other ships machine-gunned them as the Americans tried to swim ashore. The tale was told by the few survivors whom guerrilla units picked up, half drowned, on the beach. Thus perished the bulk of those who had surrendered with Generals Fort and Sharp, men who had survived war, disease, starvation, and two years of Japanese brutality, sustained only by their prayers that The Aid would come.

When he heard this news, Fertig sought out Wheeler.

"Come with me, Monty," he said. "Let's take a walk." Fertig's face was ashen beneath the sunburn that would never tan, and the words came with great difficulty. Wheeler jumped up and followed Fertig without a word. All during the time the two officers had shared quarters together, the darkly handsome Wheeler had found their relationship baffling. Fertig would call him "Monty" and joke with him. Fertig had the Westerner's enjoyment of rough, practical humor, but he was far from appreciative of jokes aimed at himself. There was no great difference between their ages, but there was something about Fertig that prevented Wheeler from calling him "Wendell." Since Wheeler, a Westerner himself, was not the kind of man who could live with anyone who must be called "sir," or "General," the naval officer had compromised by avoiding all use of names and honorifics. He neither worshiped nor loathed Fertig. He respected the mining engineer's profound knowledge of Mindanao and the Philippines and the man's fantastic memory. Fertig's politics and aesthetic tastes impressed Wheeler as almost primitive, except for the fact that they were so ingeniously practical. Wheeler felt that he knew Fertig as well as anyone ever had, and yet he could not call his knowledge of the man either intimate or accurate.

The two men walked in silence from the camp and into the wet green depths of the forest. When they came to a fallen log, Fertig said, "Let's sit down."

They sat down.

Fertig said nothing, and Wheeler, worried by Fertig's stricken look, waited for Fertig to say whatever it was that Fertig could not seem to say.

If they had only told me those men were going to be moved that soon, we could have done something, Fertig accused himself. He saw in memory the faces of officers he had known: the faces of men who had fought with Wainwright in Bataan and had surrendered. He saw again the faces in that long-ago Fourth of July parade down the road to Iligan.

If they had only told me, we could have got some of them out. We could have fixed up something.

He had refused to obey an order from Headquarters, thinking it stupid, and his friends had died, killed by friends.

Fertig sat on the fallen log in the forest, his head in his hands, tired past coherent thought.

Wheeler listened to the sounds of the million small lives among the leaves and did not look at the man beside him.

"Am I ever going to see Mary again, Monty? Will I ever see my girls? Will I ever see the aspens change again?"

Fertig was sitting straight. To Wheeler's horror, Fertig's eyes filled with tears. Fertig made no attempt to check them. He simply leaned forward once more, his head in his hands, and sobbed, his thin shoulders shaking as he sobbed. He was seeing the clean light of the Colorado hills when the aspens turn to clouds of moving golden hearts, the hearts slipping one by one from the trembling branches, fluttering away on the wind. He saw this clearly, and he cried.

Wheeler wished there was something he could say. He wished that he could put his arm across Fertig's shoulders. But he could no more do this than he could clap Fertig on the back and tell him to buck up.

He's had it, Wheeler realized. *How are we going to get him out of here? Who is going to take over?*

Wheeler thought it would be better if Fertig would cry out loud. Nothing was more horrible than that silent, gasping grief that could not be borne but which defied being shared.

Wheeler turned so that Fertig might not find him watching him. He followed, with his eyes, the slow, long loop of a liana that swung near the ground to disappear among branches that grew nearly a hundred feet above. Fertig's hand fell heavily on Wheeler's shoulder.

"All right, Monty, let's get back to camp," Fertig's usual voice commanded, as if it had been Wheeler, and not Fertig, who had needed to be indulged but who now must be sent back to work.

Fertig led the way to camp, and, when they came near the durians, Fertig was reminded of the Chinamen, sitting hopefully under the huge trees with their giggling concubines. It made him think of a good name for one of those Chinamen: *Fat Chance*. The fact was, durian didn't do a thing for you.

14

EVANS WOKE TO the sound of distant thunder. The sun was well up, and the skies were clear, and yet there was the sound of thunder. The Islands were full of curious things, and no one was more keenly aware of this than Evans. He was growing stronger every day, and, as soon as he was entirely well, he would no doubt come upon more curiosities when he resumed his travels.

One of the odd facts was that neither Evans nor his hosts knew where he was. He had come to this mountain weeks before. The night after he had left Wilson, Evans had lost his radio. He had been traveling alone but for a guide, and, during the night, he woke, raised the shutter of the deserted bahi he had commandeered, and saw them coming into the clearing. Leaving his equipment behind, Evans plunged into the night jungle and, in the morning, began to follow a stream that would, he hoped, lead him to the headwaters of the Agusan.

Days later, emaciated and hobbling because of a painfully split big toe, accompanied by a terrified Manobo who would not leave him because the Manobo, too, was lost, Evans was struggling up the mountain, following a dim game trail, when he met the naked spearmen.

The spearmen were infinitely more startled than Evans, for they belonged to a tribe that had lost its racial memory. They were literally unaware of the existence of other men. Once, early in the war, a Japanese aircraft had swept over their mountain, and the men and women of the tribe ran and hid. Then, their better sense coming to their rescue, the elders of the tribe decided that, since the aircraft's wings had not moved, the thing seemed dead. But, since it flew about, it was not dead. Therefore, it was a made thing, like a spear. But, since there were no other men on earth, it was not made by man. It had been made by their mountain spirit; it was the form the mountain spirit had taken to look at his mountain.

But now, incredibly—as incredible as it would seem if a visitor appeared from space—a bearded man with white skin appeared on the mountainside, together with another man, not too different from themselves, who spoke a language vaguely like their own. The Manobo spearmen of the mountains were as natives of a time before Chaucer confronted by a man who spoke modern English.

It was there, on a mountainside among a forgotten tribe, that Evans slowly regained his health and practiced a little simple medicine. Conversing by means of signs and the roots of words common to his Manobo guide and to his primitive hosts, Evans learned of the mountain spirit who flew about. He tried to tell the people about the war but soon gave up. Instead, he invented the wheel. He whittled a disc of wood, formed an axle, and demonstrated that wheels can carry weight. But, since there was nothing the tribe had to carry and since the terrain was too precipitous and overgrown for the use of wheels even had there been something to carry, Evans' wheel became a toy for children to roll back and forth along a fallen tree.

The wildest of Evans' most romantic dreams had come true: He was living as a god among a wild tribe on a South Sea island. If the reality of this dream was somewhat unsatisfactory, there was nevertheless nothing he could do about it until he could travel again.

The sound of thunder continued, and the naked mountain people called excitedly. Evans peered out of his tree house to see what it was.

THE SOUND THAT woke Evans was heard in Bukidnon.

Everyone except the radio operators poured out of the houses beneath the durians.

A vast, bumbling drone slowly swelled above the sporadic, muffled kettledrumming of the distant thunder.

"Sair! Sair! There they are!" Crisanto said urgently, lifting his chin toward the southeastern sky.

Moving splinters of light flickered high near the sun. As Fertig followed Crisanto's gaze, the kettledrums muttered again.

"They're hitting Davao!" Wheeler called.

Fertig plunged toward the radio shack. The aircraft were too far away to be seen clearly. The coastwatchers and guerrilla units encircling Davao could tell him more.

A grinning radioman tore off his headset as Fertig strode into the room. He held one earpiece to his head, and Fertig leaned over him to take the other.

"Roger, Red Leader," the earpiece said tinnily across a rasp of static. "Wilco, over."

"We're knocking the piss out of them," the radioman whispered happily. "Sir."

"You're clear, Blue Five," the earpiece said. "Go in Blue Five, over."

Fertig surrendered the earpiece and gripped the operator's shoulder. He moved to sit beside the radioman who monitored the guerrilla net.

A coastwatcher was shouting in clear English into the Mindanao air.

"There are so many I can't count them!" the voice exulted.

"Ask him what kind they are," Fertig told the operator.

"How the hell do I know?" the coastwatcher babbled. "I never seen them before! It's the goddamnedest Air Corps you ever saw!"

The bumbling drone became a gathering, pulsating booming, and Fertig darted out into the sunlight to see new squadrons coming in, steering over the mountains toward Davao.

There were three flights of them, stacked into staggered boxes that climbed toward the sun. They were four-engined bombers with fat bellies, thin wings, and twin rudders. The coastwatcher was quite right: No one had seen aircraft like this before. They were glistening silver instead of the olive drab that Fertig remembered, and, as he watched, still stranger, smaller shapes overtook the bombers, flashing beneath and ahead of their formations. The new aircraft seemed to be made of two fuselages joined to a common wing and tail boom. They were fighters, and they slid across the sky in a long stream, flying two by two, veering on a slant to the south while still another swarm of them appeared high over the stately bombers.

Fertig swallowed as the sound boomed around him. He watched the strange aircraft and swallowed as he thought of the Philippine Air Corps of 1941, of that handful of Martin bombers and Boeing P-26s. They had been United States first-line military aircraft in 1933, and the Filipino pilots were sent up in them against the Japanese Zeros and Betties of 1941, and that was the end of the Philippine Air Corps.

He remembered the United States Army Air Corps of 1941. He remembered the new B-17s burning in orderly rows on Clark Field two days after the war began, and everyone wondering why. He remembered P-40s being hastily uncrated while Japanese bombs fell on Manila, and the P-40 that had been assembled in a side street, using the boulevard to take off. He remembered the P-40 pilots, newly graduated from Randolph Field, arriving before the war wearing cavalry campaign hats and leather jackets, and fighting as infantry in Bataan because there were no aircraft for them.

The squadrons diminished into the south, and again the distant kettle-drums muttered.

It was not until late that day, September 1, 1944, that Fertig learned the new aircraft were Liberators and Lightnings of the newly created Army Air Force and that 130 tons of bombs had fallen on Davao. It was no great tonnage compared with the sickening weight then falling on German cities, but the bombs that struck Davao had great effect. The aircraft had aimed at targets outlined in meticulous detail by Fertig's spies in the Japanese-held city. Fertig's agents had not only reported the precise houses and bodegas in which Japanese aviation fuel and munitions were stored but also the number and kind of antiaircraft guns and their locations. They had gone so far as to make pencil-and-paper rubbings of the serial numbers of those guns, by way of proving the accuracy of their information.

"Sir, two of the bombers were shot down," a radioman told Fertig. "But the boys got everybody that jumped. By the time the parachutes hit the ground, our guys were waiting for them. They want to know, what to do with the fly boys?"

"Keep them safe until we can get them back to their units," Fertig said. "Those people are not to go on patrol."

Fertig had no desire to spend the lives of trained airmen, who, with new aircraft, would be far more valuable as a fighting unit than they would ever be as guerrillero infantry. The following day, the Lightnings and Liberators returned to Davao, surprising forty Japanese aircraft on the ground and breaking the back of Japanese air defenses in that city. Whereupon the drone of long-range Liberators filled the air of southern Mindanao day and night. Gleeful guerrilleros reported nine Japanese ships sunk in Davao harbor. As the Army Air Force struck in even greater strength on September 9, flight after flight of strange aircraft began to cross eastward over Fertig's camp, steering for the Japanese airfields at Del Monte plantation.

"They're Japs!" someone said.

"They don't sound like Japs," someone said.

"They're Grummans!" one of Fertig's former navy radiomen shouted. "They're some new kind of Grummans; they got that Grumman wing!"

An argument as to whether the Japanese had produced a new aircraft modeled after the early Grummans was abruptly silenced when the air began to shake to the reverberation of heavy bombing. The airfields at Del Monte were more than sixty airline miles away, over mountains, but the new Navy fighters came over in unending streams, and the guerrilleros beneath the durian trees could feel the air shake and the ground tremble as the Japanese airfields at Del Monte burst apart. The Grummans streamed over all day long.

Caught as they were in the drama of this tremendous raid, it seemed almost anticlimactic to the guerrilleros when the cargadores came walking in from Grinstead's area, bringing sacks of corn.

"The way were bery hard, and our chow were so few, but we are here," their lieutenant said. "Oh, sair, the Nip are having tough time, you bet! You have seen the aero-flanes? We are too many! We are many, many! Keep 'em flying, sair!"

Fertig immediately put the desperately needed food under armed guard. Although everyone at his headquarters was dizzy from hunger, the sacks of corn must be strictly rationed. It was too few, as the lieutenant said. With careful use, it would keep the headquarters alive for a week. Perhaps it would last until a food drop could be arranged. Surely, Fertig thought, with land-based bombers and fighters coming in strength, someone would answer his frantic pleas for food. But, busy with more-instant affairs, no one did. Nor could the men who commanded the Navy Grummans be bothered.

In the afternoon, while the Grummans poured overhead, an excited coastwatcher began to describe, as though he were broadcasting a sports event, something that was taking place off the eastern coast.

"They missed it again!" he shouted. "They missed . . . no, they've got it! They've got it! They hit it again! That's one sunk so far, and this one burning!"

The coastwatcher was witnessing the ordeal of forty-nine Japanese merchant ships and light escort vessels. For some reason known only to the Japanese—and most probably due to their decisive ineptitude at communications and to their inability to react quickly to unplanned-for circumstance—the convoy was steaming close ashore down the coast toward Davao in broad daylight, straight into the American air attacks.

The Grummans saw the ships and called the fleet, and Admiral Halsey's surface units dashed in to pin the convoy against the shore. Ships that tried to flee were ground against the widespread coral reefs that are the curse of that coast, where they burned as shells poured into them. Others ran aground in shallow bays. The Japanese fighting ships turned toward Halsey's fleet and sank.

"Everybody's going down to the beach!" the coastwatcher radioed. "They're killing them as they come ashore!"

The coastwatcher could see the beach clearly below his hidden shelter. He could see the people gathering, in that mysterious way Filipinos seem to materialize from an empty landscape. He saw them wading waist-deep into the soft surf, patiently waiting for the tired swimmers. He saw the sun glinting on the bolos as the Filipinos hacked at the swimmers.

Not until the following day did Fertig learn of the magnitude of this victory. When the air strikes began, the Japanese ordered their troops in Surigao withdrawn from the coast and sent to Davao. They had gone aboard the convoy and perished with their troopships. There were no survivors from the troopships. Those who escaped, from the thirty-two vessels that ran aground in the bays, had been quite literally butchered, as the coastwatcher reported. The people stripped the bodies and shoved them out to sea on the outgoing tide. Then the work of salvage began. Guerrilleros, rematerializing out of the inshore hills in which they had long been penned, recovered sufficient Japanese materiel from the beached ships to arm and uniform a complete regiment.

"I know it's probably against whatever rules there are," Fertig told Wheeler. "But we're going to do it anyway. I'd rather have our people wearing Jap uniforms than going around half naked in rags."

There were not only the Japanese uniforms and weapons but a store of Japanese army rations. The east coast was cleared of Japanese in this single naval victory; once more, Fertig had ready access to the coconut oil he badly needed; once more, he could look east for food. Even with the Japanese rations, food was scarce along that shore, but it is the virtue of a coconut coast that it always produces something to eat, if not enough.

And still the air strikes continued. After Mindanao, the bombs fell on Cebu, Negros, Leyte, and Panay islands and once more upon Luzon. Wheeler and Fertig, carefully tabulating reports flooding into the guerrilla radio net, concluded that 700 Japanese aircraft had been destroyed and 176 ships sunk or crippled in the first ten days of the bombing.

"When are we landing?" everyone wanted to know.

Bound up in the mounting excitement, none of the Filipinos and Americans at Fertig's headquarters wanted to sleep. Everyone invented reasons to gather around the radio shack, but the word they waited for did not come. When Evans came wandering out of the forest, with a story of having lived like a god and inventing the wheel, Fertig barely heard him.

"Larry, we thought you were dead," Fertig greeted him. "By God, it's good to have you back. We can certainly use you."

And with that, Evans, with his adventure yet to be told to an appreciative audience, found himself ushered into the excitement of the radio shack.

"You might think I was gone for the weekend," Evans complained, but no one heard his complaint. Hourly, everyone waited for word to come from MacArthur's headquarters, telling them when and where a landing would be made. Fertig had no doubt that MacArthur would come ashore first on Mindanao, largest and most southerly of the major islands. But no word came, nor did the coastwatchers report an invasion fleet offshore.

Instead, news poured in from guerrilla units that the Japanese were withdrawing everywhere. The slow-moving patrols closest to Fertig's headquarters abruptly moved back to the Agusan River. Japanese were pouring down the Agusan to Butu'un, where they took ship for Cagayan. In Davao province, they fled so hurriedly from the flat plains that they abandoned trucks, fuel, and food to the pursuing guerrilleros. They pulled their troops in from the country in Misamis Occidental, leaving only a strong garrison in the Spanish cota at Misamis City. They deserted Iligan and fled toward Zamboanga. They ran as quickly as they could toward defensive positions their engineers were feverishly building in the Cagayan-Cotabato-Davao triangle, the triangle that the Americans had been unable to defend when the war began.

Unbelievable changes have followed the air raids, Fertig told his diary as the reports came in. The Agusan River was open; the coasts were everywhere again in guerrillero hands. As the Japanese retreated, the guerrilleros who had once bent beneath their pressure now sprang forward with a vicious effectiveness they had never demonstrated before. In their headlong retreat, ten of every hundred Japanese died in ambushes, and the Japanese did not pause to burn their dead.

In Lanao province, a grimly content Busran Kalaw handed strings of ears to a never-quite-satisfied Hedges, who said, as he counted out bullets and silver twenty-centavo pieces, "Is this the best your bunch of old women can do?" And from Misamis Occidental, Bowler reported his ability now to take over control of the net. He said Sam Wilson had arrived and was once more printing money on the old, worn, wooden plates and that the Chinese were once more granting credit.

Looking at his map, Fertig realized that more than 90 percent of Mindanao had suddenly become guerrilla country as the Japanese withdrew into their defenses. There was no longer a reason for him to remain in the hills.

He could return to the Casa Ozamis; he could rejoin Hedges and his Moros on the cool, malaria-free beach. He could go wherever he wished on the island he ruled.

But, even as he considered moving, reason appeared to prevent it.

Radio messages said two submarines had arrived; one with eight tons of food for him had surfaced off Misamis Oriental, and cargadores were already carrying the crates across the spine of the island. The second had more logically appeared off the east coast, bringing in thirty tons of radio equipment.

"Now there's a fine thing," Fertig said. "Now that we can land anywhere we want, they drop the food off on the other side of the island. With the whole damned Air Force overhead, we're limited to the pace of a porter carrying a piano uphill."

Thus Fertig grumbled as he waited for the cargadores. But his fretfulness vanished under the continual accounts of guerrilla victories and Japanese retreats. Events were obviously moving to a climax, as coastwatchers reported submarine sinkings before their eyes; as they reported Japanese ships under surface gunfire; as the drone of American aircraft engines grew heavier each day. Fertig listened soberly to a story of horror: 5,000 Japanese, with women and children, were marched the entire distance from Surigao to Cagayan. Fertig could well imagine the pace the Japanese set; the brutality which they visited on their American prisoners was nothing they did not visit on themselves. And all during this cruel march, guerrilleros ambushed that procession, and less than 3,400 Japanese and very few of the women and children reached Cagayan.

The Japanese retreats and the air raids that struck Japanese concentrations at Davao and the airfields on the plateau above Cagayan were not, however, The Aid. They were merely indications that The Aid was close at hand. Fertig's fretfulness returned as the aircraft swept ceaselessly overhead and as no word came naming a place and day.

"It can come at any time to any coast," he said one night as he and Wheeler sat beneath a kinkie lamp, playing casino with a deck of cards a submarine had brought.

"A logical place would be Macajalar Bay," Wheeler said, shuffling the cards.

"Charley Hedges and I saw the Japs come in there," Fertig said. "That was a long time ago."

Wheeler dealt the cards.

"By God," Fertig said, "when MacArthur comes ashore, I want to be on the beach to meet him. We'll have an honor guard for him . . ."

"And when he steps out of the boat," Wheeler said, "you'll say, 'General MacArthur, I presume? Where have you been keeping yourself?'"

"We don't have to stay here," Fertig said shortly. "We'll move this oufit to the west coast. We want to be where we can get to the landing area in a day's march, if possible. We'll have at least that much notice."

But that evening, as the two men sat at cards in a grass house beneath a durian tree, a message came from the radio code section building. It was quite simple:

YOU WILL RELINQUISH CONTROL OF ALL RADIO STA-TIONS IN THE LEYTE-SAMAR AREA TO INTELLIGENCE OF-FICERS OF THE SIXTH ARMY, NOW ASHORE. ADDRESS TRAF-FIC TO COMMANDING GENERAL, SIXTH ARMY, AND KEEP HIM INFORMED OF ANY CHANGES. OUR ABILITY TO SUP-PLY YOU BY SURFACE CRAFT BASED AT TACLOBAN AFTER 15 NOVEMBER.

"WELL," FERTIG SAID at last, "MacArthur has returned." He handed the note to Wheeler.

"Now ashore!" Wheeler burst out. "We're landing on Leyte!"

"Yes," Fertig said emptily. "After all this time."

Fertig had the look of a man who, having climbed a mountain, was contemplating the descent.

ENVOI

THE SKIES ABOVE MINDANAO filled with the constant muttering thunder of aircraft. Silvery high overhead, the bombers stacked in precise arrangements threw patterned shadows over the cogon lands and jungled mountains. Hunting low, wind shrieking in their gun barrels, darting fighters swarmed over the island like swallows veering for insects rising from a lake at dusk. The aircraft were the storm crows of MacArthur's triumphant Return.

In the thud and shriek and bursting noise of that Return, Wendell Fertig's adventure died, and the war was finally lost.

The Aid, the long-prayed-for Aid, arrived in the whistling shapes of fighter-bombers that threw rockets, bombs, flaming gasoline, and machine-gun fire into guerrilla positions as well as into those of the Japanese. The Aid came in the form of shells that tore Japanese defenses apart and flattened towns where there were no Japanese, towns that waited in fiesta finery to sing Te Deum when the Americans marched in.

Frantically, Fertig radioed Headquarters to stop sending The Aid to towns and areas he controlled. He called attention to the fact that he had already supplied Headquarters with precise information as to where The Aid was wanted. In its own impersonal way, The Aid continued to arrive. It wrought far greater devastation in the Philippines than the years of Japanese occupation, and by no means all of the devastation was physical.

The regrettable accidents were understood to be accidents at the time. It was easier for the Americans at the Supreme Commander's headquarters to understand this than it was for the people of Mindanao. Still, the Filipinos made the effort to understand as they stared at a smoking ruin, sticky-sweet with the smell of burned corpses, and contemplated the torn banner, fluttering from what was left of the town hall, which said, "Welcome Our Liberators."

With the Japanese withdrawing into isolated areas of Mindanao, Fertig took the earliest opportunity to report to MacArthur's new headquarters on Leyte Island. An aircraft was sent for him, and he was welcomed as a returning hero for whom nothing was too good, as long as he did not unduly interfere with people who were trying to win the war. What did he want at the Post Exchange? He had only to name it, and he could buy it. The Post Exchange was one of the first places Fertig was taken.

He looked in a daze at the profusion of cigars, cigarettes, candy bars, shaving lotions, cigarette lighters, toothbrushes, shoes, garrison caps, insignia, shoe polish, Blitz cloths, wrist watches, and fountain pens.

What did he want?

Perhaps it was an unfair question to put to a man who for three years had been trying to answer questions that fell into other categories. Fertig looked at the goods in the Post Exchange and decided that there was nothing there that he did want. He bought a bottle of hair tonic as a gift for Hedges.

The important thing was to arrange proper liaison between the guerrilla units and the air forces that brought the impersonal Aid to Mindanao, and, in the days that followed, Fertig tried to arrange that. At Headquarters, he also learned the nature of his future mission. Mindanao would not be reinvaded at this time. The strategy called for MacArthur's men to lance straight up the island chain to Manila, while Fertig held the flank. That is, he was to keep pressure on the Japanese on Mindanao, to confine them to their fortified areas until the rest of the Philippines was conquered. Then an American task force would be sent to clean up Mindanao. This was a personal compliment, and recognition of the fact that Fertig's guerrilleros already controlled 90 percent of their island, but the practical effect of the order was that Fertig would not be relieved. He had fought a lonely war for three years, and his specific reward would be permission to continue to fight it. A number of small ships, some aircraft, and a few reinforcements would be put under his command. He was given an assignment few general officers could hope to receive, but nothing was said of promoting Colonel Fertig to a rank commensurate with his responsibility as military governor and commander of land, sea, and air forces of the second largest island in the Philippine Archipelago. He was not promoted then, or ever.

It would serve no useful purpose here to detail the rest of Fertig's experience on Mindanao. The guerrilla was his adventure. What ensued, after The Aid arrived, was a standard military operation, not remarkably distinguished from any since the time of Darius. There were, of course, the usual number of contretemps to be expected between an independent commander and a remote headquarters. Once, when Headquarters disbelieved Fertig's estimate of Japanese casualties, Fertig sent them two demijohns filled with matched pairs of ears that the Moros had collected. Headquarters never publicly doubted Fertig's estimates of enemy casualties thereafter. Eventually, after all other Philippine islands were reconquered, American forces landed on Mindanao, and guerrilla forces supported them in frontal attacks on Japanese positions, and Filipinos and Americans died, and the Japanese were exterminated.

It was during the extirpation of the Japanese and in the months that followed the victory that the war was lost in the Philippines. It was lost with the best of intentions, inadvertently, through pity. It began to be lost on the first day that an American soldier—one of the New Americans as men of the Liberation Army were called—looked up from the letter he was writing home, to see a ragged, barefoot woman smiling on him like a shy angel.

"Good noon, sair," she said. "Do you have laundry? I will be The One to wash for you."

The soldier was startled and pleased to be called sir and to find someone willing to do his wash. For two years in the jungles to the south, he had boiled his khakis in an ashcan, stirring them with a stick, and the only thing anyone ever called him in the Army was Mac.

"Laundry? Hell, yes . . . I mean, sure, lady, sure. How much you want?"

The woman bit her lip. The soldier did not understand that she was not a professional lavandera and that she was offering a gift of love.

"Nothing, sair," she said. "Please, enough soap to wash your clothes and mine, only."

She had not intended to ask for soap, for she was willing to beat the clothes clean on stones in the riverbed, but perhaps the soldier felt he should pay something, and, if that was the case, she would make him feel less obligated by suggesting the soap.

"Jesus," the soldier muttered to himself.

He rummaged in his barracks bag and handed the woman a bar of thick, yellow army soap. The woman's eyes widened in utter disbelief. She groped for words to tell the soldier that this was far, far too much, but he, guiltily feeling that he was getting his laundry done far too cheaply, pressed the soap into her hands. He gave her his soiled uniforms, socks, and underwear and asked when she would bring them back.

"This day, sair," the woman said, close to tears. "This day I will return back to you."

The soldier watched her leave, wondering if he would ever see his clothes again. He shrugged, and returned to his letter-writing. The woman, who hid the miracle of an entire bar of new soap in among the clothes, walked quickly from the army bivouac with her heart going like a hammer. One tiny sliver of soap would have been enough. With the rest of it, she could buy . . .

Why, with that much soap, there was almost nothing she could not buy from the hidden stores of the Chinese merchant. Everything she had heard about the Americanos was true. They were indeed the unselfish benefactors of the Filipinos. She thanked God for the Americanos. The destruction of the barrio of her cousin had been an accident, and she had said so at the time.

But when the woman arrived at the riverbank to wash the clothes of her Americano, her view of the Americanos was subtly changed. From another woman, she learned that one Americano had paid five pesos for his laundry to be done. Five pesos! It was as much as a man might earn in a week!

While individual soldiers overpaid the Filipinos out of ignorance and out of pity, the official pity arrived. The philosophy of the official pity was that the Filipinos were the Americans' little brown brothers who needed to be governed by their big white brothers for their own good. Wherefore the military government experts appeared, and then it was no longer possible for Fertig to shoot black marketeers out of hand. The experts had never seen the Philippines prior to their arrival in the rearguard of the Liberation Army, and they knew nothing of the languages or the people of Mindanao, but they felt competent to tell Fertig how the island should be administered, and the black market spread. Within weeks, a new expression entered the Filipino language: "Before the war, very cheap; now, very dear."

And thus the process of losing the war was begun. Within a few months, the Philippine Islands' economy was destroyed. The black market mushroomed. An army mess sergeant could earn $500 by handing a Filipino a bag of army rice. He could also buy cigarettes at $1 a carton from the Army Post Exchange and sell them for $10, and with the $10 he could buy a chicken dinner and a bottle of whisky. The chicken was the loser of a cockfight, and the whisky was raw nipa alcohol that came in a pop bottle and was labeled "Guaranteed not poison, 100% Satisfaction."

The military government experts also came with lists of names of those who should be appointed to office, lists made on the basis of pre-war information. Thus, many ilustrados who had either collaborated with the Japanese or who had done nothing for the guerrilla found their way back to wealth and power, and there was little Fertig could do about that outside of Mindanao. A feeling grew in the Islands that the Americanos were either fools to be taken in by such ilustrados or that the Americanos were in league with them.

The experts also decided that Fertig's guerrilla currency should not be redeemed at face value. Sam Wilson had kept meticulous records, and each pitiful piece of hand-inked kraft paper bore the pledge of the United States to a stricken people, but it appeared that promises were to be broken. In Manila, Philippine Army officers were busily altering Fertig's troop rosters to delete the names of guerrilleros in order to write in the names of relatives, so that, when there came time to pay the guerrilleros, the officers and their relatives received the money instead. There were many scandals, many broken promises. But whether or not the Americans were always at fault in whatever went wrong, the Americans were blamed.

Meanwhile, the Filipinos were meeting Americans in large numbers for the first time. Before the war, there had been relatively few Americans in the Islands. The military personnel had stayed fairly close to its bases, and the Americanos that most Filipinos met were schoolteachers, civil servants singularly dedicated to the loftier ideals of their profession, and fair-dealing businessmen. In those days, any other kind of American businessman was sent home. Now, however, there were many, many Americanos, and the Americanos and Filipinos stared at one another curiously.

Five lavanderas, for example, watched with interest as three American soldiers soaped themselves beneath a shower. The soldiers had punched holes in the bottom of an ash can, and, when water was poured into the can, it came sprinkling down on them, and the women were fascinated. One of the soldiers, who had been embarrassed at the presence of women in the camp, heard a woman say "tubig."

Tubig is the Tagalog word for water, but the soldier took it as a personal compliment.

"Too big, huh?" he called, grinning.

The women smiled back, amused by the impromptu lesson in language. The soldier grasped his penis and pointed it at them.

"You want to make it bigger?" he asked.

The women fled, and the soldiers laughed.

"I hear these Flips don't have hair on their snatch," one said.

"Well, why the hell don't we find out?" the first soldier said.

That was one of the innocent ways in which *that* began. The incidence of rape was negligible. There is always some raping in the neighborhood of any army; even in the neighborhood of an army in its own country. The Filipinos understood that. But what was not so understandable to a people who take as natural a view of sex as the Filipinos was the Army's predilection for whores. In one camp, there was always a line waiting to enter the big mess tent that served as a brothel, where the women lay on rows of cots, and a shorter line moved more rapidly into the back of the tent. Soldiers standing in the shorter line paid twice as much because that line moved twice as fast, but the men who stood in it had to pass the heap of used condoms that grew higher and higher beside the rear exit of the tent. The Filipinos shook their heads in wonder. The Americanos' need for whores seemed identical with the needs of the Japanese.

Then there was the drunkenness. There was also the blindness and the death caused by poisonous alcohol sold to Americanos by the bootleggers, and the bamboo telegraph magnified all the rumors of the isolated whorehouses and the occasional lurid drunkenness into a characterization of Americans. And the latrine rumors of the Army characterized the Filipinos as black-marketing sons of bitches who'd as soon slit your throat as sell you poisoned rotgut and there's not a damned one of them that isn't as crooked as a corkscrew and most of the women have clap. Thus it was, that, within months of the victory, the New Americans were calling the Filipinos slopeheads and Flips. The Old Army had called them gooks, and the New Americans called them Flips. And thus it was, that an elderly Filipino lawyer who had at first looked upon the advancing tanks and trucks of the Liberation Army with tears in his eyes, now told his sons, "I have seen four peoples come to our Islands. The Spaniards were very bad. The Americanos were worse. Worse than the Americanos were the Hapons. But worst of all, worse than the Hapons, are the New Americanos."

As the Liberation became an occupation, many Filipinos remembered the mistakes of The Aid and found them more difficult to understand. Steadily, a devastated nation plunged deeper into economic disaster and goods disappeared into the black market. All through the war, Fertig had been able to peg prices and ration commodities on the island of Mindanao, but, with return of the exiled national government and the return of self-serving ilustrados to places of vantage and with the mistakes of the experts of military government, the horrors of national recovery swept over the Philippines. Meanwhile, there were the New Americans, far too many of them, possessed of all the wealth of the world, paying too much for everything, driving the prices up, serving as the black market's principal source of supply, making the rich richer and the poor poorer, clamoring for drink and whores, the soldiers propositioning married women on the streets. It became increasingly difficult for a Filipino to look upon the New Americans and on what was happening to his country and to remember the Americans with whom he had served in the jungles and to recall the idealistic America of his schoolboy textbooks.

Fertig watched the process of demoralization corrode what might have been the victory. He did what he could to protect the people of his own island, to whom he owed his life. He warned the experts that this Filipino was a collaborator, argued that that Filipino should be made governor of the province, suggested controls for the economy, and urged the fundamental necessity of honoring his currency at face value. But he was one man, and there were many experts, and, in the end, he was tired and glad enough to be relieved and sent home to Colorado to receive the well-deserved rest due a man who has fought with honor for his country. Mary was waiting for him, of course. The dark mass of her hair was now gray, and the little daughters were grown quite tall and did not altogether remember him.

VIEWED IN PERSPECTIVE, it is difficult to say whether Fertig's operations on Mindanao had military significance beyond the transmission of intelligence data. It was Fertig's passionate belief that guerrilla operations are always victorious, given certain conditions. The conditions are: a terrain favorable to ambush, a plentiful food supply, a sadistic enemy, the overwhelming support of the people, some reason to hope for victory and material support from a powerful outside nation that is also waging external war upon the guerrilleros' enemy. Not all of these conditions were always met on the island of Mindanao, and the purely military issue was never resolved, except for the ultimate arrival of The Aid. For Fertig was never at any time able to prevent the Japanese from moving wherever they wished whenever they really made the effort, and, in those last days in the swamps at Waloe, he faced utter defeat. On the other hand, it could be argued that his operations were of military value in that they drew the attention of a division of Japanese and confined other Japanese forces to circumscribed areas on the island and therefore, in effect, kept that many Japanese from fighting against the United States Army and from exploiting the island they had seized. But this accomplishment falls somewhat short of complete military victory. If Fertig won a victory, it was in other realms.

The real measure of his accomplishment is that he created a nation out of chaos on the island of Mindanao. Whether another man could have done it is moot. If another man could have done it, another would have, for the times demanded the thing be done. Fertig happened to be the man who brought the Moros, pagans, Christian Filipinos, and white men of Mindanao together in a common cause. This was a feat that four centuries of Spanish, and forty years of prior American, rule had failed to accomplish. If much of the credit must be put to the sadistic qualities of the Japanese, the rest belongs to Fertig. For, while it was true that the inimical populations of Mindanao were united in a loathing of the Japanese, it was also true that they did not love one another. Indeed, when Fertig first began to build, he had to wipe out internecine warfare among guer-rilla bands, to put down two mutinies within his own command, and to arrange a truce with the Moros that was as tenuous as it was expeditious.

Fertig was able to do this not only because he understood the subtle-ties of patience and face-saving in the Orient but also because he was more of a catalyst than a leader. He was a catalyst in that he was a symbol. He personally embodied the qualities of utter honesty, practicality, cour-age, patriotism, and an absolute faith in his nation and in eventual victory. He was the living image of a man who refused to accept any part of the concept of surrender; of a man who, in Hemingway's phrase, could be killed but not defeated. At a time when many surrendered and others hid, he stood straight among the storm wrack and patiently said, "This is what we can do; therefore, this is what we will do." Then he set to work, build-ing a nation out of junk and hope.

When Fertig arrived on the stage of Mindanao, most Filipinos had an image of America that the textbooks describe. To a great extent, the Japanese victory destroyed that image, but it was never wholly lost, and Fertig rebuilt it by personal example. Apart from his insistence on honesty and justice and the idea that the guerrilla army be a process of a respon-sible civil government, his fundamental contribution to Mindanao was his concern that the reward for performance should always be increased responsibility. In his command, demonstrated competence was the sole means to promotion, and no man was denied an opportunity to prove himself. This concept built a nation in North America, and it built another on Mindanao. It was a concept that heretofore had existed only as a text-book ideal on an island that, for four centuries, had known little other than the repression, nepotism, and fatalism that so unfortunately distinguish the Spanish culture. Fertig put the ideal to practical use; rather, he gave the Filipinos an opportunity to employ it.

In all this, Fertig was fortunate in his Filipinos. For, if Mindanao suffered from the influence of the Spanish tradition, it was also more of a pioneer island than those that lie to the north. The land that the Christians held on Mindanao had to be wrung from Moro and pagan warriors. It was, and still is, a missionary island, and no place for the fainthearted. If Fertig built with what he had, what he chiefly had was a populace of warriors. Without them, there would have been no guerrilla, and no Fertig. Too much cannot be said to the point that every American who served on Mindanao owed his life to the charity, courage, and protection given him by Filipinos. It is tempting to say the Filipinos were loyal to the Americans, but this is wishful thinking. Rather, the Filipinos were loyal to the idea that *they* could not be defeated, and, if they protected Americans, it was because they knew very well that the Americans were on their side. They also believed in an eventual American victory from the moment the first submarine arrived, but their belief in this was secondary to their discovered belief in themselves. It was Fertig, more than any other man, who gave the Filipinos of Mindanao increasing reason to believe in themselves. This, rather than a military victory, was Fertig's triumph.

THROUGHOUT THIS BOOK, characters have appeared, only to drop out of sight. In a novel, characters never just disappear. But novels have an artificial order, and life has none. In life, and particularly in war, people appear, join us for a while, and then slowly or quickly vanish, as each of us walks on toward his lonely death. Any book that tries to deal with reality must reflect this. But, for the benefit of readers who wish to know the end of the story, if indeed there is an end to reality, I will say that Fertig's Filipino officers are largely the elected officeholders in Mindanao today. They are very much responsible for the island's relatively rapid recovery from the economic disasters of the Liberation and from those of a national independence granted at the very worst of times. The island's progress, in turn, is chiefly due to Mindanao's relative political freedom from Manila, and the reason for that freedom is chiefly that Fertig's men learned their lessons well.

Salvador Lluch, who disappeared first and without a trace from this book, survived the war to resume his place as one of the first citizens of Lanao. Salipada Pendatun became a senator of the Philippine Republic. Nick Capistrano and his lovely wife, Josefa, are the millionaire owners of a lumber concession and other business enterprises. Chick Parsons is back in Manila, having become a citizen of the Philippine Republic. Cecil Walter is still in Mindanao, near the scene of his battles, married to a strikingly beautiful young Filipina. In his seventies, Walter is still as alert and as hard and tough as he was during the war.

Morgan died in an aircraft accident after the war, but Sinang is alive, as is Bill Tait. The Casa Ozamis is as well-appointed and as well-run as it ever was, and dona Carmen and her sisters returned to it from their refuge in the hills following the victory. They live there still. Sam Wilson entered Manila with the First Cavalry Division to find his wife and sons thin as rakes but still alive, and he handed his son a flag given him by General MacArthur to be raised over the liberated prison camp of Santo Tomas University. Sam, who had been a millionaire in the Philippines, is now a millionaire in California. Chief Elwood Offret was retired from the United States Navy as a lieutenant commander. Charley Hedges is very much alive in Oregon, and it is impossible to imagine that he will not always be very much alive. In fact, almost all of the guerrilleros survived the war, for it is the nature of guerrilla that the fighting men suffer negligible casualties. It was the civilians that the Japanese killed. Almost without exception, the guerrilleros who emerged alive have done exceptionally—indeed, remarkably—well in civil life, and many of them attribute their success to Fertig. They say he was the first man to give them a chance to demonstrate what they could do and that their first taste of responsibility led to a thirst for more.

And Fertig?

Today, Wendell Fertig lives with his wife Mary in Colorado. The daughters are grown and married, and Fertig is a grandfather. He is well-known to a small number of men in the Department of Defense, to which he is still summoned as a consultant on guerrilla operations. He is well-known as a mining engineer, and the people in Colorado remember that he had some sort of unusual experience during the war, that he was on one of those islands out there, and that there was something about it in the papers when he came home. He is more widely and more accurately known in the Philippines.

ONE DAY IN JUNE, close to the fourteenth anniversary of the day that Fertig and Hedges sat together on a hill watching the Japanese land at Cagayan, the interisland motor vessel *Cagayan de Oro* came nosing into Macajalar Bay. The ship was small and trim, built in Japan as part of the war reparations owed to the Philippine Republic. There were carabaos on her foredeck, their heavy horns swaying, and, as the ship slowed coming into the harbor, the smell of the carabaos and the crates of chickens grew more stifling and the morning's heat more perceptible.

The ship's captain approached a tall man dressed in wash-and-wear tropical clothes and said, "Sair, I think friends wait for you."

The tall man, who dabbed at his sun-chapped lips with a Chapstick, did not hear the captain's soft voice but stood on the ship's bridge watching barrotos arrowing out from the harbor to meet the *Cagayan de Oro*. One of them raced ahead under the power of an outboard motor, with the men in it waving and holding up a sign.

"Welcome and Mabuhay!" the sign said, and the men who held it laughed as their barroto swirled close alongside the motor vessel, and then one of the men pointed excitedly at the tall man standing on the bridge with the captain and, standing up, nearly overturned the log canoe.

"Sair," the captain hopefully suggested, "I think maybe you go ashore first, for, until you do, we cannot unload the ship, for there are many on the dock who wait for you."

There were many, indeed. There were thousands of Filipinos waiting at the waterfront at Cagayan that hot June morning. They had come from every corner of Mindanao, where the bamboo telegraph still works very well. There were masses of women in the white uniforms of Josefa Capistrano's Women's Auxiliary Service and men wearing caps of the Philippine Veterans Legion, and the red fezzes of Moros in malongs, and standing proudly aloof, and watchful, was the burly, dark-visaged, bareheaded figure of Crisanto.

The men in the circling barrotos were shouting, and the women were singing as the *Cagayan de Oro* eased up to the dock, and the crowd surged forward, and the man in tropical clothes waved his Panama hat, and the crowd cheered. Then Mary Fertig, who was standing on the bridge beside her husband and the captain, saw the huge banner for the first time. She had been too busy looking at the barrotos and at the cheering people to see it before, but she saw it plainly now and something turned inside her as she read:

WELCOME THE INDOMITABLE PATRIOT WHO HAVE LESSENED HUMAN SUFFERING ON MINDANAO

The crowd eddied around him as Fertig stepped ashore on Mindanao. He had returned to the Islands on a business trip, but the populace clearly had other plans for him. Crisanto unobtrusively resumed his duties, falling into place one step to the left rear, his formidable presence automatically clearing a place around the man who would always be his Tai Tai.

Then there was the drive through the dusty streets in the hot morning with the flags of the United States and the Philippine Republic fluttering and the crowd following, to the cathedral, where they sang Te Deum, and afterwards, although it was still early morning, to a feast at an open pavilion where women stood behind the chairs, whisking flies from the rice.

There was fiesta at every city that Fertig visited in Mindanao during what he had imagined would be a business trip. There were banners stretched across the dirt highway at the edge of barrios along the way. At every barrio, there were people waiting to see The One. At some barrios, the people had been waiting beneath the banners for days, both because the bamboo telegraph is not absolutely infallible and because they dared not miss the car that would return back the General. At each barrio, Fertig would climb out of the car to shake hands with men who had fought for these towns of grass houses fourteen years ago, and he would say something to the crowds, and then the people would capture him and lead him to a table where food waited. Always there would be food, and long speeches that were translated into Visayan. Often men who spoke in English would then give their speeches in Visayan, which made the occasion twice as enjoyable for them and for the people who had waited patiently in the sun under the welcoming banners. Then there would be singing. At Iligan, where the Japanese had paraded their American prisoners on the Fourth of July 1942, the people sang "God Bless the Philippines," and then, the singing swelling to an even greater strength, everyone sang "God Bless America" and many wept as they sang.

John Keats
Mindanao, Philadelphia, Ontario
1958–1962

APPENDIX

THE AUTHOR REGRETS that it was technically impossible to include a detailed account of the adventures and contributions of each of the American guerrilleros of Mindanao. His selection of a few to portray in no way implies that he thinks their contribution was greater than all others. Rather, the selection was quite arbitrary and was dictated by the author's conception of literary need.

Each man who served on Mindanao lived an adventure well worth the telling, and the nation owes each of them a debt it cannot repay.

Some were killed in action. No distinction is made here as to the immediate cause of death of those who are buried on Mindanao, since the general, underlying reason for all the deaths was refusal to surrender.

There follows a list of American guerrilleros of Mindanao, as set forth in the *Historical Record Mindanao Guerrilla Resistance Movement, 10th Military District, from 16 September 1942, to 30 June 1945, Col. Wendell W. Fertig Commanding*. This volume was prepared in the field by the historical section of Colonel Fertig's staff. The *Historical Record* identifies the following as "American Guerrilleros on Mindanao":

Clyde M. Abbott
Michael J. Amrich
Robert Andrews

Robert B. Ball
Edward Bates, died July 10, 1942
Thomas R. Baxter
Kenneth L. Bayley

Julian Benac
Leo A. Boelens, died January 22, 1944
Alexander R. Bonner
Robert V. Bowler
Durward L. Brooks
Oscar G. Brown
Edward W. Browning
Andrew T. Buckoviensky
Anthony Bujnowski

John F. Cain
Marvin H. Campbell
Lucian V. Campeau
Timothy C. Casey
Reid C. Chamberlain
Bruce Chapman, died April 14, 1943
Gerald G. Chapman
Clyde C. Childress
Noel R. Chiota, died April 14, 1943
Edward O. Chmeilewski
Michael Chuckray
Jack R. Clarke
Joseph P. Coe
Earl A. Cook
Richard L. Cook
Robert M. Crump

Bill E. Dallenback
Lincoln H. DaPron
George D. Davis
Marvin H. DeVries
Frank Divino
Michael Dobervich
Vincent K. Douglass
Frank W. Duff
William E. Dyess

Bruce G. Elliot
James L. Evans, Jr.

Beverly P. Farrens
Fred S. Faust
Frederich A. Feigel, died July 26, 1944
Alfred Fernandez
Wendell W. Fertig
George Finnegan
Paul R. Flowers, died July 27, 1942

Glenn E. Gamber
James L. Garland
Robert E. Gentry
Paul A. Gill
Dewitt Glover
John W. Grant, died November 1, 1943
Samuel Grashio
James R. Grinstead
Cyril A. Grosh

James D. Habume
Arthur R. Hage, Jr.
James E. Halkyard
George O. Hall
Charles Hansen
Anton J. Haratik
Frank Harayda
Jack Hawkins
Elmer R. Hayes
Charles W. Hedges
Truman Heminway
Earl G. Hilliard
Jack W. Hofeman
McE. Hoke
Lowell G. Holder
Earle C. Homan, Jr.
John L. Houlihan
Forrest A. Howard

William H. Johnson
Erling H. Jonassen
Thomas W. Jurika

Albert R. Kirby, Jr.
William A. Knortz, died September 11, 1943
John Kolodie
William F. Konko
John Korysinski

Richard B. Lang
Donald J. LeCouvre
Leonard LeCouvre
John L. Lewis
William W. Lowry, died June 19, 1943
Ray J. Lozano

Ernest E. McClish
James McClure
Melvyn H. McCoy
Warren L. McFadden, died May 10, 1942
Frank D. McGee, died August 7, 1945
Charles E. McGrath
Weyman L. McGuire
James E. McIntyre
William L. F. McLaughlin
James McNeil
Aldo F. Maccagli
William Madison
Andrew Mancuso
Clayton A. Manners, Jr.
Paul H. Marshall
Harold D. Martin
Stephen Mellnick
Leonard L. Merchant
Walter R. Mester
Alma B. Mills
Leonard Minter
Glyn W. Mitchell
Thomas Mitsos
Willard L. Money

Francis Napolillo, Jr.

Bernard S. Nemzura, died February 26, 1943
William L. Newman, died November 1942 (no date)

Frank O. Noel
Leo O'Connor
Elwood H. Offret
Reece A. Oliver
Paul A. Owen

Herbert Page
Charles Parsons
Frank Y. Patten
Robert L. Pease
Dalcua A. Phillips
Nicholas D. Poliluyko
Michael Pritz, Jr., died September 3, 1943

Lee C. Ragsdale, died August 15, 1943
Iliff Richardson
Louis Robertson
Charles E. Robinson
Harold A. Rosenquist
Lewis C. Roybal
Elwood A. Royer
Henry C. Rook
Lee R. Rutherford
John E. Ruziechki

Joseph St. John
Jack L. Samples
Walter W. Sanders
James E. Schoen
Peter Schur
Austin C. Shofner
John D. Simmons
Thomas L. Sinclair
Charles Smith
James S. Smith
Oscar F. Smith
Russell H. Smith

Robert B. Spielman
John E. Spruill
Robert E. Stahl
John W. Starky
Adolph E. Sternberg, Jr.
Tommy Stewart
Oscar E. Swanson
Robert Q. Synde

Frederick M. Taylor
Chandler B. Thomas
Richard L. Thommes
Carlyle G. Townswick
Franklin J. Trammel
Tracy S. Tucker
John L. Tuggle
Glenn Turner

Fred W. Varney

Cecil E. Walter
Loyd Waters
Hadley C. Watson
Howard R. Watson
Roy E. Weebon, died January 24, 1944
Royce F. Wendover
Major M. Wheeler
Perry T. Whitley
William W. Williams
Donald H. Wills
Owen P. Wilson
Sam J. Wilson
George W. Winget
Mark M. Wohlfield
Frederic L. Worcester
John F. Wood, Jr.
Halbert Woodruff
Sidney T. Wright